Roger Caras'

Treasury of
Great Fishing
Stories

Roger Caras'

Treasury of
Great Fishing
Stories

GALAHAD BOOKS
NEW YORK

PUBLISHER'S NOTE

This collection of classic tales contains certain old-fashioned styles of spelling and punctuation, as well as words expressing the sentiments of earlier, less-objective times. The original texts have been reproduced exactly as written to maintain the integrity of the stories; we hope the modern reader will view these works within the context of their time period. The opinions expressed are not those of the publisher.

First Galahad Books edition published in 1999.

Galahad Books
A division of BBS Publishing Corporation
386 Park Avenue South
New York, NY 10016

Galahad Books is a registered trademark of
BBS Publishing Corporation.

Library of Congress Catalog Card Number: 98-75462

ISBN: 1-57866-052-1

Text design by Hannah Lerner.
Cover design by Steve Diggs & Friends, Nashville.

Printed in the United States of America.

Contents

Acknowledgments

Foreword

MY SON, CLAY, has always been good with his hands. He is building a canoe now (for use in bass fishing, of course) and it is going to be a museum piece from the looks of it. He paints, does wonderful stained glass work, lamps, boxes, panels, all manner of treasures. And he is a fly fisherman. He does not distinguish between these enterprises, not when aesthetics is the criteria. They are all art forms he has selected to help fulfill himself as a person.

The number of times fishing, the recreational kind not the brutish commercial enterprise, has been likened to both art and religion is beyond counting. To some people time alone on a stream is truly a kind of religious pursuit. The fly fisherman is alone with his thoughts in a cathedral of His making. This mere man or woman is interacting with miraculous creatures of His design. In what he does he comes to know his own place, his worth, his purpose and something of His plan. Surely that must be religion. And as for art, try it yourself. Sit up late studying the lives of insects, think like a fish, then with the hands of a surgeon and the eye of an eagle tie a fly, and a small bit of perfection it must be. Then, at dawn, journey to that special stream you know, that magical place where surely He dwells. Whip your gossamer thread around and around in loops and turns that form a ballet of your intent against the sky and drop that fly this side of the log tangle, that side of the riffle, between those rocks and beyond the channel. Your target will be the size of a tea saucer on a good day, a dinner plate when you are not really up to form. Now go back to the stage of thinking like a fish. Set the hook upon the strike and play the game, pit your genius against that of the brook the brownie or the rainbow. Oh, yes, it is art. And back to religion, at such times you know His true work as few people can, unless they master this art as well. People who think fishing is just about frying fish don't understand it at all. I have known Clay to take a dozen bass in a few hours of fishing but he always comes home empty handed. The fish are back in their world doing their own work. For people who want to eat fish they invented the fish store. For people who want to know Him they invented fishing.

Then there is the other kind that many people prefer. Ride the heavy chop and the swell of the shelf, get beyond it to where the water is black with its depth and play out the line in your wake. Be it a giant tuna, a mako shark or the sculptured reality of a great bill fish, wait for the strike, it will come in time like an express train at speed. With all of your muscle and will engaged set the giant hook and wait for your reel to smoke as the monster seeks the bottom of the sea. Your arms will ache, your back will seem about to break, your throat will be parched, your mouth will taste like sand. But you will stay the course until at last the monstrous animal in the raw majesty of power will breech and flop against the sky before plunging back with a great splash into the sea to play again below and torture your muscles and your bones anew. Where fly fishing for a salmon, a bass or a trout is a dance and a poem, this is war and in the end brute strength and fierce determination will win. Here, too, many fisherman today cut their adversary loose should the line not part and it loses the fight. Some pose with their victim held high by rope and winch for a victim is what it becomes when removed from the sea. One supposes the gladiator needs that moment of posing. It is better, though, more in keeping with the spirit of the fisherman, not to judge. The time one spends fishing is like time alone with a companion dog, it is non-judgmental.

Recent finds by archaeologists in the southern third of Africa reveal the startling scenario that man was fishing there with specialized equipment between 80 and 90,000 years ago. That is a full 50,000 years earlier than that was supposed to have been done by early Neolithic hunters and gatherers in Europe. Fishing and man go back a long way together. It is difficult, impossible really, to know when a survival enterprise became art, when aesthetics rose above hunger on the agenda. But it happened and ever since man has had literature at hand to sculpt his ideas into words he has been writing about fishing with humor, grace, instruction, contemplation and awe. And that is what this sampling is about. Herein a touch of the wit and the wisdom of people who will pit their wit against that of a fish and in that contest see Him.

Roger Caras

Big Two-Hearted River

Ernest Hemingway

PART ONE

THE TRAIN WENT on up the track out of sight, around one of the hills of burnt timber. Nick sat down on the bundle of canvas and bedding the baggage man had pitched out of the door of the baggage car. There was no town, nothing but the rails and the burned-over country. The thirteen saloons that had lined the one street of Seney had not left a trace. The foundations of the Mansion House hotel stuck up above the ground. The stone was chipped and split by the fire. It was all that was left of the town of Seney. Even the surface had been burned off the ground.

Nick looked at the burned-over stretch of hillside, where he had expected to find the scattered houses of the town and then walked down the railroad track to the bridge over the river. The river was there. It swirled against the log spiles of the bridge. Nick looked down into the clear, brown water, colored from the pebbly bottom, and watched the trout keeping themselves steady in the current with wavering fins. As he watched them they changed their positions by quick angles, only to hold steady in the fast water again. Nick watched them a long time.

He watched them holding themselves with their noses into the current, many trout in deep, fast moving water, slightly distorted as he watched far down through the glassy convex surface of the pool, its surface pushing and swelling smooth against the resistance of the log-driven piles of the bridge. At the bottom of the pool were the big trout. Nick did not see them at first. Then he saw them at the bottom of the pool, big trout looking to hold themselves on the gravel bottom in a varying mist of gravel and sand, raised in spurts by the current.

Nick looked down into the pool from the bridge. It was a hot day. A kingfisher flew up the stream. It was a long time since Nick had looked into a stream and seen trout. They were very satisfactory. As the shadow of the kingfisher moved up the stream, a big trout shot upstream in a long angle, only his shadow marking the angle, then lost his shadow as he came through the surface of the water, caught the sun, and then, as he went back into the stream under the surface, his shadow seemed to float down the stream with the current, unresisting, to his post under the bridge where he tightened facing up into the current.

Nick's heart tightened as the trout moved. He felt all the old feeling.

He turned and looked down the stream. It stretched away, pebbly-bottomed with shallows and big boulders and a deep pool as it curved away around the foot of a bluff.

Nick walked back up the ties to where his pack lay in the cinders beside the railway track. He was happy. He adjusted the pack harness around the bundle, pulling straps tight, slung the pack on his back, got his arms through the shoulder straps and took some of the pull off his shoulders by leaning his forehead against the wide band of the tumpline. Still, it was too heavy. It was much too heavy. He had his leather rod-case in his hand and leaning forward to keep the weight of the pack high on his shoulders he walked along the road that paralleled the railway track, leaving the burned town behind in the heat, and then turned off around a hill with a high, fire-scarred hill on either side onto a road that went back into the country. He walked along the road feeling the ache from the pull of the heavy pack. The road climbed steadily. It was hard work walking up-hill. His muscles ached and the day was hot, but Nick felt happy. He felt he had left everything behind, the need for thinking, the need to write, other needs. It was all back of him.

From the time he had gotten down off the train and the baggage man had thrown his pack out of the open car door things had been different. Seney was burned, the country was burned over and changed, but it did not matter. It could not all be burned. He knew that. He hiked along the road, sweating in the sun, climbing to cross the range of hills that separated the railway from the pine plains.

The road ran on, dipping occasionally, but always climbing. Nick went on up. Finally the road after going parallel to the burnt hillside reached the top. Nick leaned back against a stump and slipped out of the pack harness. Ahead of him, as far as he could see, was the pine plain. The burned country stopped off at the left with the range of hills. On ahead islands of dark pine trees rose out of the plain. Far off to the left was the line of the river. Nick followed it with his eye and caught glints of the water in the sun.

There was nothing but the pine plain ahead of him, until the far blue hills that marked the Lake Superior height of land. He could hardly see them, faint and far away in the heat-light over the plain. If he looked too steadily they were gone. But if he only half-looked they were there, the far-off hills of the height of land.

Nick sat down against the charred stump and smoked a cigarette. His pack balanced on the top of the stump, harness holding ready, a hollow molded in it from his back. Nick sat smoking, looking out over the country. He did not need to get his map out. He knew where he was from the position of the river.

As he smoked, his legs stretched out in front of him, he noticed a grasshopper walk along the ground and up onto his woolen sock. The grasshopper was black. As he had walked along the road, climbing, he had started many grasshoppers from the dust. They were all black. They were not the big grasshoppers with yellow and black or red and black wings whirring out from their black wing sheathing as they fly up. These were just ordinary hoppers, but all a sooty black in color. Nick had wondered about them as he walked, without really thinking about them. Now, as he watched the black hopper that was nibbling at the wool of his sock with its fourway lip, he realized that they had all turned black from living in the burned-over land. He realized that the fire must have come the year before, but the grasshoppers were all black now. He wondered how long they would stay that way.

Carefully he reached his hand down and took hold of the hopper by the wings. He turned him up, all his legs walking in the air, and looked at his jointed belly. Yes, it was black too, iridescent where the back and head were dusty.

"Go on, hopper," Nick said, speaking out loud for the first time. "Fly away somewhere."

He tossed the grasshopper up into the air and watched him sail away to a charcoal stump across the road.

Nick stood up. He leaned his back against the weight of his pack where it rested upright on the stump and got his arms through the shoulder straps. He stood with the pack on his back on the brow of the hill looking out across the country, toward the distant river and then struck down the hillside away from the road. Underfoot the ground was good walking. Two hundred yards down the hillside the fire line stopped. Then it was sweet fern, growing ankle high, to walk through, and clumps of jack pines; a long undulating country with frequent rises and descents, sandy underfoot and the country alive again.

Nick kept his direction by the sun. He knew where he wanted to strike the river and he kept on through the pine plain, mounting small rises to see other rises ahead of him and sometimes from the top of a rise a great solid island of pines off to his right or his left. He broke off some sprigs of the heathery sweet fern, and put them under his pack straps. The chafing crushed it and he smelled it as he walked.

He was tired and very hot, walking across the uneven, shadeless pine plain. At any time he knew he could strike the river by turning off to his left. It could not be more than a mile away. But he kept on toward the north to hit the river as far upstream as he could go in one day's walking.

For some time as he walked Nick had been in sight of one of the big islands of pine standing out above the rolling high ground he was crossing. He dipped down and then as he came slowly up to the crest of the ridge he turned and made toward the pine trees.

There was no underbrush in the island of pine trees. The trunks of the trees went straight up or slanted toward each other. The trunks were straight and brown without branches. The branches were high above. Some interlocked to make a solid shadow on the brown forest floor. Around the grove of trees was a bare space. It was brown and soft underfoot as Nick walked on it. This was the over-lapping of the pine needle floor, extending out beyond the width of the high branches. The trees had grown tall and the branches moved high, leaving in the sun this bare space they had once covered with shadow. Sharp at the edge of this extension of the forest floor commenced the sweet fern.

Nick slipped off his pack and lay down in the shade. He lay on his back and looked up into the pine trees. His neck and back and the small of his back rested as he stretched. The earth felt good against his back. He looked up at the sky, through the branches, and then shut his eyes. He opened them and looked up again. There was a wind high up in the branches. He shut his eyes again and went to sleep.

Nick woke stiff and cramped. The sun was nearly down. His pack was heavy and the straps painful as he lifted it on. He leaned over with the pack on and picked up the leather rod-case and started out from the pine trees across the sweet fern swale, toward the river. He knew it could not be more than a mile.

He came down a hillside covered with stumps into a meadow. At the edge of the meadow flowed the river. Nick was glad to get to the river. He walked upstream through the meadow. His trousers were soaked with the dew as he walked. After the hot day, the dew had come quickly and heavily. The river made no sound. It was too fast and smooth. At the edge of the meadow, before he mounted to a piece of high ground to make camp, Nick looked down the river at the trout rising. They were rising to insects come from the swamp on the other side of the stream when the sun went down. The trout jumped out of water to take them. While Nick walked through the little stretch of meadow alongside the stream, trout had jumped high out of water. Now as he looked down the river, the insects must be settling on the surface, for the trout were feeding steadily all down the stream. As far down the long stretch as he could see, the trout were rising, making circles all down the surface of the water, as though it were starting to rain.

The ground rose, wooded and sandy, to overlook the meadow, the stretch of river and the swamp. Nick dropped his pack and rod-case and looked for a level piece of ground. He was very hungry and he wanted to make his camp before he cooked. Between two jack pines, the ground was quite level. He took the ax out of the pack and chopped out two projecting roots. That leveled a piece of ground large enough to sleep on. He smoothed out the sandy soil with his hand and pulled all the sweet fern bushes by their roots. His hands smelled good from the sweet fern. He smoothed the uprooted earth. He did not want anything making lumps under the blankets. When he had the ground smooth, he spread his three blankets. One he folded double, next to the ground. The other two he spread on top.

With the ax he slit off a bright slab of pine from one of the stumps and split it into pegs for the tent. He wanted them long and solid to hold in the ground. With the tent unpacked and spread on the ground, the pack, leaning against a jackpine, looked much smaller. Nick tied the rope that served the tent for a ridge-pole to the trunk of one of the pine trees and pulled the tent up off the ground with the other end of the rope and tied it to the other pine. The tent hung on the rope like a canvas blanket on a clothesline. Nick poked a pole he had cut up under the back peak of the canvas and then made it a tent by pegging out the sides. He pegged the sides out taut and drove the pegs deep, hitting them down into the ground with the flat of the ax until the rope loops were buried and the canvas was drum tight.

Across the open mouth of the tent Nick fixed cheesecloth to keep out mosquitoes. He crawled inside under the mosquito bar with various things from the pack to put at the head of the bed under the slant of the canvas. Inside the tent the light came through the brown canvas. It smelled pleasantly of canvas. Already there was something mysterious and homelike. Nick was happy as he crawled inside the tent. He had not been unhappy all day. This was different though. Now things were done. There had been this to do. Now it was done. It had been a hard trip. He was very tired. That was done. He had made his camp. He was settled. Nothing could touch him. It was a good place to camp. He was there, in the good place. He was in his home where he had made it. Now he was hungry.

He came out, crawling under the cheesecloth. It was quite dark outside. It was lighter in the tent.

Nick went over to the pack and found, with his fingers, a long nail in a paper sack of nails, in the bottom of the pack. He drove it into the pine tree, holding it close and hitting it gently with the flat of the ax. He hung the pack up on the nail. All his supplies were in the pack. They were off the ground and sheltered now.

Nick was hungry. He did not believe he had ever been hungrier. He opened and emptied a can of pork and beans and a can of spaghetti into the frying pan.

"I've got a right to eat this kind of stuff, if I'm willing to carry it," Nick said. His voice sounded strange in the darkening woods. He did not speak again.

He started a fire with some chunks of pine he got with the ax from a stump. Over the fire he stuck a wire grill, pushing the four legs down into the ground with his boot. Nick put the frying pan on the grill over the flames. He was hungrier. The beans and spaghetti warmed. Nick stirred them and mixed them together. They began to bubble, making little bubbles that rose with difficulty to the surface. There was a good smell. Nick got out a bottle of tomato catchup and cut four slices of bread. The little bubbles were coming faster now. Nick sat down beside the fire and lifted the frying pan off. He poured about half the contents out into the tin plate. It spread slowly on the plate. Nick knew it was too hot. He poured on some tomato catchup. He knew the beans and spaghetti were still too hot. He looked at the fire, then at the tent, he was not going to spoil it all by burning his tongue. For years he had never enjoyed fried bananas because he had never been able to wait for them to cool. His tongue was very sensitive. He was very hungry. Across the river in the swamp, in the almost dark, he saw a mist rising. He looked at the tent once more. All right. He took a full spoonful from the plate.

"Chrise," Nick said, "Geezus Chrise," he said happily.

He ate the whole plateful before he remembered the bread. Nick finished the second plateful with the bread, mopping the plate shiny. He had not eaten since a cup of coffee and a ham sandwich in the station restaurant at St. Ignace. It had been a very fine experience. He had been that hungry before, but had not been able to satisfy it. He could have made camp hours before if he had wanted to. There were plenty of good places to camp on the river. But this was good.

Nick tucked two big chips of pine under the grill. The fire flared up. He had forgotten to get water for the coffee. Out of the pack he got a folding canvas bucket and walked down the hill, across the edge of the meadow, to the stream. The other bank was in the white mist. The grass was wet and cold as he knelt on the bank and dipped the canvas bucket into the stream. It bellied and pulled hard in the current. The water was ice cold. Nick rinsed the bucket and carried it full up to the camp. Up away from the stream it was not so cold.

Nick drove another big nail and hung up the bucket full of water. He dipped the coffee pot half full, put some more chips under the grill onto the fire and put the pot on. He could not remember which way he made coffee. He could remember an argument about it with Hopkins, but not which side he had taken. He decided to bring it to a boil. He remembered now that was Hopkins's way. He had once argued about everything with Hopkins. While he waited for the coffee to boil, he opened a small can of apricots. He liked to open cans. He emptied the can of apricots out into a tin cup. While he watched the coffee on the fire, he drank the juice syrup of the apricots, carefully at first to keep from spilling, then meditatively, sucking the apricots down. They were better than fresh apricots.

The coffee boiled as he watched. The lid came up and coffee and grounds ran down the side of the pot. Nick took it off the grill. It was a triumph for Hopkins. He put sugar in the empty apricot cup and poured some of the coffee out to cool. It was too hot to pour and he used his hat to hold the handle of the coffee pot. He would not let it steep in the pot at all. Not the first cup. It should be straight Hopkins all the way. Hop deserved that. He was a very serious coffee drinker. He was the most serious man

Nick had ever known. Not heavy, serious. That was a long time ago. Hopkins spoke without moving his lips. He had played polo. He made millions of dollars in Texas. He had borrowed carfare to go to Chicago, when the wire came that his first big well had come in. He could have wired for money. That would have been too slow. They called Hop's girl the Blonde Venus. Hop did not mind because she was not his real girl. Hopkins said very confidently that none of them would make fun of his real girl. He was right. Hopkins went away when the telegram came. That was on the Black River. It took eight days for the telegram to reach him. Hopkins gave away his .22 caliber Colt automatic pistol to Nick. He gave his camera to Bill. It was to remember him always by. They were all going fishing again next summer. The Hop Head was rich. He would get a yacht and they would all cruise along the north shore of Lake Superior. He was excited but serious. They said good-bye and all felt bad. It broke up the trip. They never saw Hopkins again. That was a long time ago on the Black River.

Nick drank the coffee, the coffee according to Hopkins. The coffee was bitter. Nick laughed. It made a good ending to the story. His mind was starting to work. He knew he could choke it because he was tired enough. He spilled the coffee out of the pot and shook the grounds loose into the fire. He lit a cigarette and went inside the tent. He took off his shoes and trousers, sitting on the blankets, rolled the shoes up inside the trousers for a pillow and got in between the blankets.

Out through the front of the tent he watched the glow of the fire, when the night wind blew on it. It was a quiet night. The swamp was perfectly quiet. Nick stretched under the blanket comfortably. A mosquito hummed close to his ear. Nick sat up and lit a match. The mosquito was on the canvas, over his head. Nick moved the match quickly up to it. The mosquito made a satisfactory hiss in the flame. The match went out. Nick lay down again under the blanket. He turned on his side and shut his eyes. He was sleepy. He felt sleep coming. He curled up under the blanket and went to sleep.

PART TWO

In the morning the sun was up and the tent was starting to get hot. Nick crawled out under the mosquito netting stretched across the mouth of the tent, to look at the morning. The grass was wet on his hands as he came out. He held his trousers and his shoes in his hands. The sun was just up over the hill. There was the meadow, the river and the swamp. There were birch trees in the green of the swamp on the other side of the river.

The river was clear and smoothly fast in the early morning. Down about two hundred yards were three logs all the way across the stream. They made the water smooth and deep above them. As Nick watched, a mink crossed the river on the logs and went into the swamp. Nick was excited. He was excited by the early morning and the river. He was really too hurried to eat breakfast, but he knew he must. He built a little fire and put on the coffee pot.

While the water was heating in the pot he took an empty bottle and went down over the edge of the high ground to the meadow. The meadow was wet with dew and Nick wanted to catch grasshoppers for bait before the sun dried the grass. He found plenty of good grasshoppers. They were at the base of the grass stems. Sometimes they clung to a grass stem. They were cold and wet with the dew, and could not jump until the sun warmed them. Nick picked them up, taking only the medium-sized brown ones, and put them into the bottle. He turned over a log and just under the shelter of the edge were several hundred hoppers. It was a grasshopper lodging house. Nick put about fifty of the medium browns into the bottle. While he was picking up the hoppers the others warmed in the sun and commenced to hop away. They flew when they hopped. At first they made one flight and stayed stiff when they landed, as though they were dead.

Nick knew by the time he was through with breakfast they would be as lively as ever. Without dew in the grass it would take him all day to catch a bottle full of good grasshoppers and he would have to crush many of them, slamming at them with his hat. He washed his hands at the stream. He was excited to be near it. Then he walked up to the tent. The hoppers were already jumping stiffly in the grass. In the bottle, warmed by the sun, they were jumping in a mass. Nick put in a pine stick as a cork. It plugged the mouth of the bottle enough, so the hoppers could not get out and left plenty of air passage.

He had rolled the log back and knew he could get grasshoppers there every morning.

Nick laid the bottle full of jumping grasshoppers against a pine trunk. Rapidly he mixed some buckwheat flour with water and stirred it smooth, one cup of flour, one cup of water. He put a handful of coffee in the pot and dipped a lump of grease out of a can and slid it sputtering across the hot skillet. On the smoking skillet he poured smoothly the buckwheat batter. It spread like lava, the grease spitting sharply. Around the edges the buck-wheat cake began to firm, then brown, then crisp. The surface was bubbling slowly to porousness. Nick pushed under the browned under surface with a fresh pine chip. He shook the skillet sideways and the cake was loose on the surface. I won't try and flop it, he thought. He slid the chip of clean wood all the way under the cake, and flopped it over onto its face. It sputtered in the pan.

When it was cooked Nick regreased the skillet. He used all the batter. It made another big flapjack and one smaller one.

Nick ate a big flapjack and a smaller one, covered with apple butter. He put apple butter on the third cake, folded it over twice, wrapped it in oiled paper and put it in his shirt pocket. He put the apple butter jar back in the pack and cut bread for two sandwiches.

In the pack he found a big onion. He sliced it in two and peeled the silky outer skin. Then he cut one half into slices and made onion sandwiches. He wrapped them in oiled paper and buttoned them in the other pocket of his khaki shirt. He turned the skillet upside down on the grill, drank the coffee, sweetened and yellow brown with the condensed milk in it, and tidied up the camp. It was a good camp.

Nick took his fly rod out of the leather rod-case, jointed it, and shoved the rod-case back into the tent. He put on the reel and threaded the line through the guides. He had to hold it from hand to hand, as he threaded it, or it would slip back through its own weight. It was a heavy, double tapered fly line. Nick had paid eight dollars for it a long time ago. It was made heavy to lift back in the air and come forward flat and heavy and straight to make it possible to cast a fly which has no weight. Nick opened the aluminum leader box. The leaders were coiled between the damp flannel pads. Nick had wet the pads at the water cooler on the train up to St. Ignace. In the damp pads the gut leaders had softened and Nick unrolled one and tied it by a loop at the end of the heavy fly line. He fastened a hook on the end of the leader. It was a small hook; very thin and springy.

Nick took it from his hook book, sitting with the rod across his lap. He tested the knot and the spring of the rod by pulling the line taut. It was a good feeling. He was careful not to let the hook bite into his finger.

He started down to the stream, holding his rod, the bottle of grasshoppers hung from his neck by a thong tied in half hitches around the neck of the bottle. His landing net hung by a hook from his belt. Over his shoulder was a long flour sack tied at each corner into an ear. The cord went over his shoulder. The sack flapped against his legs.

Nick felt awkward and professionally happy with all his

equipment hanging from him. The grasshopper bottle swung against his chest. In his shirt the breast pockets bulged against him with the lunch and his fly book.

He stepped into the stream. It was a shock. His trousers clung tight to his legs. His shoes felt the gravel. The water was a rising cold shock.

Rushing, the current sucked against his legs. Where he stepped in, the water was over his knees. He waded with the current. The gravel slid under his shoes. He looked down at the swirl of water below each leg and tipped up the bottle to get a grasshopper.

The first grasshopper gave a jump in the neck of the bottle and went out into the water. He was sucked under in the whirl by Nick's right leg and came to the surface a little way down stream. He floated rapidly, kicking. In a quick circle, breaking the smooth surface of the water, he disappeared. A trout had taken him.

Another hopper poked his face out of the bottle. His antennae wavered. He was getting his front legs out of the bottle to jump. Nick took him by the head and held him while he threaded the slim hook under his chin, down through his thorax and into the last segments of his abdomen. The grasshopper took hold of the hook with his front feet, spitting tobacco juice on it. Nick dropped him into the water.

Holding the rod in his right hand he let out line against the pull of the grasshopper in the current. He stripped off line from the reel with his left hand and let it run free. He could see the hopper in the little waves of the current. It went out of sight.

There was a tug on the line. Nick pulled against the taut line. It was his first strike. Holding the now living rod across the current, he brought in the line with his left hand. The rod bent in jerks, the trout pumping against the current. Nick knew it was a small one. He lifted the rod straight up in the air. It bowed with the pull.

He saw the trout in the water jerking with his head and body against the shifting tangent of the line in the stream.

Nick took the line in his left hand and pulled the trout, thumping tiredly against the current, to the surface. His back was mottled the clear, water-over-gravel color, his side flashing in the sun. The rod under his right arm, Nick stooped, dipping his right hand into the current. He held the trout, never still, with his moist right hand, while he unhooked the barb from his mouth, then dropped him back into the stream.

He hung unsteadily in the current, then settled to the bottom beside a stone. Nick reached down his hand to touch him, his arm to the elbow under water. The trout was steady in the moving stream, resting on the gravel, beside a stone. As Nick's fingers touched him, touched his smooth, cool, underwater feeling he was gone, gone in a shadow across the bottom of the stream.

He's all right, Nick thought. He was only tired.

He had wet his hand before he touched the trout, so he would not disturb the delicate mucus that covered him. If a trout was touched with a dry hand, a white fungus attacked the unprotected spot. Years before when he had fished crowded streams, with fly fishermen ahead of him and behind him, Nick had again and again come on dead trout, furry with white fungus, drifted against a rock, or floating belly up in some pool. Nick did not like to fish with other men on the river. Unless they were of your party, they spoiled it.

He wallowed down the stream, above his knees in the current, through the fifty yards of shallow water above the pile of logs that crossed the stream. He did not rebait his hook and held it in his hand as he waded. He was certain he could catch small trout in the shallows, but he did not want them. There would be no big trout in the shallows this time of day.

Now the water deepened up his thighs sharply and coldly. Ahead was the smooth dammed-back flood of water above the logs. The water was smooth and dark; on the left, the lower edge of the meadow; on the right the swamp.

Nick leaned back against the current and took a hopper from the bottle. He threaded the hopper on the hook and spat on him for good luck. Then he pulled several yards of line from the reel and tossed the hopper out ahead onto the fast, dark water. It floated down towards the logs, then the weight of the line pulled the bait under the surface. Nick held the rod in his right hand, letting the line run out through his fingers.

There was a long tug. Nick struck and the rod came alive and dangerous, bent double, the line tightening, coming out of water, tightening, all in a heavy, dangerous, steady pull. Nick felt the moment when the leader would break if the strain increased and let the line go.

The reel ratcheted into a mechanical shriek as the line went out in a rush. Too fast. Nick could not check it, the line rushing out, the reel note rising as the line ran out.

With the core of the reel showing, his heart feeling stopped with the excitement, leaning back against the current that mounted icily his thighs, Nick thumbed the reel hard with his left hand. It was awkward getting his thumb inside the fly reel frame.

As he put on pressure the line tightened into sudden hardness and beyond the logs a huge trout went high out of water. As he jumped, Nick lowered the tip of the rod. But he felt, as he dropped the tip to ease the strain, the moment when the strain was too great; the hardness too tight. Of course, the leader had broken. There was no mistaking the feeling when all spring left the line and it became dry and hard. Then it went slack.

His mouth dry, his heart down, Nick reeled in. He had never seen so big a trout. There was a heaviness, a power not to be held, and then the bulk of him, as he jumped. He looked as broad as a salmon.

Nick's hand was shaky. He reeled in slowly. The thrill had been too much. He felt, vaguely, a little sick, as though it would be better to sit down.

The leader had broken where the hook was tied to it. Nick took it in his hand. He thought of the trout somewhere on the bottom, holding himself steady over the gravel, far down below the light, under the logs, with the hook in his jaw. Nick knew the trout's teeth would cut through the snell of the hook. The hook would imbed itself in his jaw. He'd bet the trout was angry. Anything that size would be angry. That was a trout. He had been solidly hooked. Solid as a rock. He felt like a rock, too, before he started off. By God, he was a big one. By God, he was the biggest one I ever heard of.

Nick climbed out onto the meadow and stood, water running down his trousers and out of his shoes, his shoes squelchy. He went over and sat on the logs. He did not want to rush his sensations any.

He wriggled his toes in the water, in his shoes, and got out a cigarette from his breast pocket. He lit it and tossed the match into the fast water below the logs. A tiny trout rose at the match, as it swung around in the fast current. Nick laughed. He would finish the cigarette.

He sat on the logs, smoking, drying in the sun, the sun warm on his back, the river shallow ahead entering the woods, curving into the woods, shallows, light glittering, big water-smooth rocks, cedars along the bank and white birches, the logs warm in the sun, smooth to sit on, without bark, gray to the touch; slowly the feeling of disappointment left him. It went away slowly, the feeling of disappointment that came sharply after the thrill that made his shoulders ache. It was all right now. His rod lying out on the logs, Nick tied a new hook on the leader, pulling the gut tight until it grimped into itself in a hard knot.

He baited up, then picked up the rod and walked to the far end of the logs to get into the water, where it was not too deep. Under and beyond the logs was a deep pool. Nick walked around the shallow shelf near the swamp shore until he came out on the shallow bed of the stream.

On the left, where the meadow ended and the woods began, a great elm tree was uprooted. Gone over in a storm, it lay back into the woods, its roots clotted with dirt, grass growing in them, rising a solid bank beside the stream. The river cut to the edge of the uprooted tree. From where Nick stood he could see deep channels, like ruts, cut in the shallow bed of the stream by the flow of the current. Pebbly where he stood and pebbly and full of boulders beyond; where it curved near the tree roots, the bed of the stream was marly and between the ruts of deep water green weed fronds swung in the current.

Nick swung the rod back over his shoulder and forward, and the line, curving forward, laid the grasshopper down on one of the deep channels in the weeds. A trout struck and Nick hooked him.

Holding the rod far out toward the uprooted tree and sloshing backward in the current, Nick worked the trout, plunging, the rod bending alive, out of the danger of the weeds into the open river. Holding the rod; pumping alive against the current, Nick brought the trout in. He rushed, but always came, the spring of the rod yielding to the rushes, sometimes jerking under water, but always bringing him in. Nick eased downstream with the rushes. The rod above his head he led the trout over the net, then lifted.

The trout hung heavy in the net, mottled trout back and silver sides at the meshes. Nick unhooked him; heavy sides, good to hold, big undershot jaw, and slipped him, heaving and big sliding, into the long sack that hung from his shoulders in the water.

Nick spread the mouth of the sack against the current and it filled, heavy with water. He held it up, the bottom in the stream, and the water poured out through the sides. Inside at the bottom was the big trout, alive in the water.

Nick moved downstream. The sack out ahead of him sunk heavy in the water, pulling from his shoulders.

It was getting hot, the sun hot on the back of his neck.

Nick had one good trout. He did not care about getting many trout. Now the stream was shallow and wide. There were trees along both banks. The trees of the left bank made short shadows on the current in the forenoon sun. Nick knew there were trout in each shadow. In the afternoon, after the sun had crossed toward the hills, the trout would be in the cool shadows on the other side of the stream.

The very biggest ones would lie up close to the bank. You could always pick them up there on the Black. When the sun was down they all moved out into the current. Just when the sun made the water blinding in the glare before it went down, you were liable to strike a big trout anywhere in the current. It was almost impossible to fish then, the surface of the water was blinding as a mirror in the sun. Of course, you could fish upstream, but in a stream like the Black, or this, you had to wallow against the current and in a deep place, the water piled up on you. It was no fun to fish upstream with this much current.

Nick moved along through the shallow stretch watching the banks for deep holes. A beech tree grew close beside the river, so that the branches hung down into the water. The stream went back in under the leaves. There were always trout in a place like that.

Nick did not care about fishing that hole. He was sure he would get hooked in the branches.

It looked deep though. He dropped the grasshopper so the current took it under water, back in under the overhanging branch. The line pulled hard and Nick struck. The trout threshed heavily, half out of water in the leaves and branches. The line was caught. Nick pulled hard and the trout was off. He reeled in and holding the hook in his hand, walked down the stream.

Ahead, close to the left bank, was a big log. Nick saw it was hollow; pointing up river the current entered it smoothly, only a little ripple spread each side of the log. The water was deepening. The top of the hollow log was gray and dry. It was partly in the shadow.

Nick took the cork out of the grasshopper bottle and a hopper clung to it. He picked him off, hooked him and tossed him out. He held the rod far out so that the hopper on the water moved into the current flowing into the hollow log. Nick lowered the rod and the hopper floated in. There was a heavy strike. Nick swung the rod against the pull. It felt as though he were hooked into the log itself, except for the live feeling.

He tried to force the fish out into the current. It came, heavily.

The line went slack and Nick thought the trout was gone. Then he saw him, very near, in the current, shaking his head, trying to get the hook out. His mouth was clamped shut. He was fighting the hook in the clear flowing current.

Looping in the line with his left hand, Nick swung the rod to make the line taut and tried to lead the trout toward the net, but he was gone, out of sight, the line pumping. Nick fought him against the current, letting him thump in the water against the spring of the rod. He shifted the rod to his left hand, worked the trout upstream, holding his weight, fighting on the rod, and then let him down into the net. He lifted him clear of the water, a heavy half circle in the net, the net dripping, unhooked him and slid him into the sack.

He spread the mouth of the sack and looked down in at the two big trout alive in the water.

Through the deepening water, Nick waded over to the hollow log. He took the sack off, over his head, the trout flopping as it came out of water, and hung it so the trout were deep in the water. Then he pulled himself up on the log and sat, the water from his trousers and boots running down into the stream. He laid his rod down, moved along to the shady end of the log and took the sandwiches out of his pocket. He dipped the sandwiches in the cold water. The current carried away the crumbs. He ate the sandwiches and dipped his hat full of water to drink the water running out through his hat just ahead of his drinking.

It was cool in the shade, sitting on the log. He took a cigarette out and struck a match to light it. The match sunk into the gray wood, making a tiny furrow. Nick leaned over the side of the log, found a hard place and lit the match. He sat smoking and watching the river.

Ahead the river narrowed and went into a swamp. The river became smooth and deep and the swamp looked solid with cedar trees, their trunks close together, their branches solid. It would not be possible to walk through a swamp like that. The branches grew so low. You would have to keep almost level with the ground to move at all. You could not crash through the branches. That must be why the animals that lived in swamps were built the way they were, Nick thought.

He wished he had brought something to read. He felt like reading. He did not feel like going on into the swamp. He looked down the river. A big cedar slanted all the way across the stream. Beyond that the river went into the swamp.

Nick did not want to go in there now. He felt a reaction against deep wading with the water deepening up under his armpits, to hook big trout in places impossible to land them. In the swamp the banks were bare, the big cedars came together overhead, the sun did not come through, except in patches; in the fast deep water, in the half light, the fishing would be tragic. In the swamp fishing was a tragic adventure. Nick did not want it. He did not want to go down the stream any further today.

He took out his knife, opened it and stuck it in the log. Then he pulled up the sack, reached into it and brought out one of the trout. Holding him near the tail, hard to hold, alive, in his hand, he whacked him against the log. The trout quivered, rigid. Nick laid him on the log in the shade and broke the neck of the other fish the same way. He laid them side by side on the log. They were fine trout.

Nick cleaned them, slitting them from the vent to the tip of the jaw. All the insides and the gills and tongue came out in one piece. They were both males; long gray-white strips of milt, smooth and clean. All the insides clean and compact, coming out all together. Nick tossed the offal ashore for the minks to find.

He washed the trout in the stream. When he held them back up in the water they looked like live fish. Their color was not gone yet. He washed his hands and dried them on the log. Then he laid the trout on the sack spread out on the log, rolled them up in it, tied the bundle and put it in the landing net. His knife was still standing, blade stuck in the log. He cleaned it on the wood and put it in his pocket.

Nick stood up on the log, holding his rod, the landing net hanging heavy, then stepped into the water and splashed ashore. He climbed the bank and cut up into the woods, toward the high ground. He was going back to camp. He looked back. The river just showed through the trees. There were plenty of days coming when he could fish the swamp.

Daniel Webster and the Sea Serpent

Stephen Vincent Benét

IT HAPPENED, ONE summer's day, that Dan'l Webster and some of his friends were out fishing. That was in the high days of his power and his fame, when the question wasn't if he was going to be President but when he was going to be President, and everybody at Kingston depot stood up when Dan'l Webster arrived to take the cars. But in spite of being Secretary of State and the biggest man in New England, he was just the same Dan'l Webster. He bought his Jamaica personal and in the jug at Colonel Sever's store in Kingston, right under a sign saying ENGLISH AND WEST INDIA GOODS, and he never was too busy to do a hand's turn for a friend. And, as for his big farm at Marshfield, that was just the apple of his eye. He buried his favorite horses with their shoes on, standing up in a private graveyard, and wrote Latin epitaphs for them, and he often was heard to say that his big Hungarian bull, St. Stephen, had more sense in his rear off-hoof than most politicians. But, if there was one thing he loved better than Marshfield itself, it was the sea and the waters around it, for he was a fisherman born.

23

This time, he was salt-water fishing in the *Comet*, well out of sight of land. It was a good day for fishing, not too hazy, but not too clear, and Dan'l Webster enjoyed it, as he enjoyed everything in life, except maybe listening to the speeches of Henry Clay. He'd stolen a half-dozen days to come up to Marshfield, and well he needed the rest, for we'd nearly gone to war with England the year before, and now he was trying to fix up a real copper-riveted treaty that would iron out all the old differences that still kept the two countries unfriendly. And that was a job, even for Dan'l Webster. But as soon as he stepped aboard the *Comet*, he was carefree and heartwhole. He had his real friends around him and he wouldn't allow a word of politics talked on the boat—though that rule got broken this time, and for a good reason, as you'll see. And when he struck his first cod, and felt the fish take the hook, a kind of big slow smile went over his features, and he said, "Gentlemen, this is solid comfort." That was the kind of man he was.

I don't know how many there were of them aboard—half a dozen or so—just enough for good company. We'll say there were George Blake and Rufus Choate and young Peter Harvey and a boy named Jim Billings. And, of course, there was Seth Peterson, Dan'l's boat captain, in his red flannel shirt, New England as cod and beach plums, and Dan'l Webster's fast friend. Dan'l happened to be Secretary of State, and Seth Peterson happened to be a boat captain, but that didn't make any difference between them. And, once the *Comet* left dock, Seth Peterson ran the show, as it's right that a captain should.

Well, they'd fished all morning and knocked off for a bite of lunch, and some had had segars and snoozes afterward, and some hadn't, but in any case, it was around midafternoon, and everybody was kind of comfortable and contented. They still fished, and they fished well, but they knew in an hour or so they'd be heading back for home with a fine catch on board. So maybe there was more conversation than Seth Peterson would have approved of earlier, and maybe some jokes were passed and some stories told. I don't know, but you know how it is when men get together at the end of a good day. All the same, they were still paying attention to their business—and I guess it was George Blake that noticed it first.

"Dan'l," he said, breathing hard, "I've got something on my line that pulls like a Morgan horse."

"Well, yank him in!" sang out Dan'l, and then his face changed as his own line began to stiffen and twang. "George," he said, "I beat you! I got something on my line that pulls like a pair of steers!"

"Give 'em more line, Mr. Webster!" yells Seth Peterson, and Dan'l did. But at that, the line ran out so fast it smoked when it hit the water, and any hands but Dan'l Webster's would have been cut to the bone. Nor you couldn't see where it went to, except Something deep in the waters must be pulling it out as a cat pulls yarn from a ball. The veins in Dan'l Webster's arm stood out like cords. He played the fish and played the fish; he fought it with every trick he knew. And still the little waves danced and the other men gaped at the fight—and still he couldn't bring the Something to time.

"By the big elm at Marshfield!" he said at last, with his dark face glowing and a fisherman's pride in his eyes. "Have I hooked on to a frigate with all sails set? I've played out a mile of my own particular line, and she still pulls like ten wild horses. Gentlemen, what's this?"

And even as he said it, the tough line broke in two with a crack like a musket shot, and out of the deep of ocean, a mile away, the creature rose, majestic. Neighbors, that was a sight! Shaking the hook from its jaw, it rose, the sea serpent of the Scriptures, exact and to specifications as laid down in the Good Book, with its hairy face and its furlong on furlong of body, wallowing and thrashing in the troubled sea. As it rose, it gave a long low melancholy hoot, like a kind of forsaken steamboat;

and when it gave out that hoot, young Jim Billings, the boy, fainted dead away on the deck. But nobody even noticed him—they were all staring at the sea serpent with bulging eyes.

Even Dan'l Webster was shaken. He passed his hand for a moment across his brow and gave a sort of inquiring look at the jug of Jamaica by the hatch.

"Gentlemen," he said in a low voice, "the evidence—the ocular evidence would seem to be conclusive. And yet, speaking as a lawyer—"

"Thar she blows! I never thought to see her again!" yells Seth Peterson, half-driven out of his mind by the sight, as the sea serpent roiled the waters. "Thar she blows, by the Book of Genesis! Oh, why ain't I got a harpoon?"

"Quiet, Seth," said Dan'l Webster. "Let us rather give thanks for being permitted to witness this glorious and unbelievable sight."And then you could see the real majesty of the man, for no sooner were the words out of his mouth than the sea serpent started swimming straight toward the *Comet*. She came like a railway train and her wake boiled out behind her for an acre. And yet, there was something kind of skittish about her, too— you might say that she came kind of shaking her skirts and bridling. I don't know what there was about her that made you sure she was a female, but they were all sure.

She came, direct as a bullet, till you could count the white teeth shining in her jaws. I don't know what the rest of them did—though doubtless some prayers were put up in a hasty way—but Dan'l Webster stood there and faced her, with his brow dark and his eyes like a sleepy lion's, giving her glance for glance. Yes, there was a minute, there, when she lifted her head high out of water and they looked at each other eye to eye. They say hers were reddish but handsome. And then, just as it seemed she'd crash plumb through the *Comet*, she made a wide wheel and turned. Three times she circled the boat, hooting lone-somely, while the *Comet* danced up and down like a cork on the waves. But Dan'l Webster kept his footing, one hand gripping the mast, and whenever he got a chance, he fixed her with his eye. Till finally, on the third circuit, she gave one last long hoot—like twenty foghorns at once, it was, and nearly deafened them all—and plunged back whence she'd come, to the bottomless depths of the sea.

But even after the waters were calm again, they didn't say anything for quite a while. Till, finally, Seth Peterson spoke.

"Well, Mr. Webster," he said, "that one got away"—and he grinned a dry grin.

"Leviathan of the Scriptures! Give me paper and pen," said Dan'l Webster. "We must write this down and attest it." And then they all began to talk.

Well, he wrote an account of just what they'd seen, very plain and honest. And everybody there signed his name to it. Then he read it over to them again aloud. And then there was another silence, while they looked at one another.

Finally, Seth Peterson shook his head, slow and thoughtful.

"It won't do, Dan'l," he said, in a deep voice.

"Won't do?" said Dan'l Webster, with his eyes blazing. "What do you mean, Seth?"

"I mean it just won't do, Dan'l," said Seth Peterson, perfectly respectful, but perfectly firm. "I put it up to you, gentlemen," he said, turning to the others. "I can go home and say I've seen the sea serpent. And everybody'll say, 'Oh, that's just that old liar, Seth Peterson.' But if it's Dan'l Webster says so—can't you see the difference?"

He paused for a minute, but nobody said a word.

"Well, I can," he said. He drawled out the words very slow. "Dan'l Webster—Secretary of State—sees and talks to a sea serpent—off Plymouth Bay. Why, it would plumb ruin him! And I don't mind being ruint, but it's different with Dan'l Webster. Would you vote for a man for President who claimed he'd saw the sea serpent? Well, would you? Would anybody?"

There was another little silence, and then George Blake spoke.

"He's right, Dan'l," he said, while the others nodded. "Give me that paper." He took it from Dan'l Webster's hand and threw it in the sea.

"And now," he said in a firm voice, "I saw cod. Nothing but cod. Except maybe a couple of halibut. Did any gentleman here see anything else?"

Well, at that, it turned out, of course, that nobody aboard had seen anything but cod all day. And with that, they put back for shore. All the same, they all looked over their shoulders a good deal till they got back to harbor.

And yet Dan'l Webster wasn't too contented that evening, in spite of his fine catch. For, after all, he had seen the sea serpent, and not only seen her but played her on the line for twenty-seven minutes by his gold repeater, and, being a fisherman, he'd like to have said so. And yet, if he did—Seth was right—folks would think him crazy or worse. It took his mind off Lord Ashburton and the treaty with England—till, finally, he pushed aside the papers on his desk.

"Oh, a plague on the beast!" he said, kind of crossly. "I'll leave it alone and hope it leaves me alone." So he took his candle and went up to bed. But just as he was dropping off to sleep, he thought he heard a long low hoot from the mouth of Green Harbor River, two miles away.

The next night the hooting continued, and the third day there was a piece in the Kingston paper about the new government foghorn at Rocky Ledge. Well, the thing began to get on Dan'l Webster's nerves, and when his temper was roused he wasn't a patient man. Moreover, the noises seemed to disturb the stock—at least his overseer said so—and the third night his favorite gray kicked half the door out of her stall. "That sea serpent's getting to be an infernal nuisance," thought Dan'l Webster. "I've got to protect my property." So, the fourth night he put on his old duck-shooting clothes and took his favorite shotgun, Learned

Selden, and went down to a blind at the mouth of Green Harbor River, to see what he could see. He didn't tell anybody else about his intentions, because he still felt kind of sensitive about the whole affair.

Well, there was a fine moon that night, and sure enough, about eleven o'clock, the sea serpent showed up, steaming in from ocean, all one continuous wave length, like a giant garden hose. She was quite a handsome sight, all speckled with the moonlight, but Dan'l Webster couldn't rightly appreciate it. And just as she came to the blind, she lifted her head and looked sorrowfully in the direction of Marshfield and let out a long low soulful hoot like a homesick train.

Dan'l Webster hated to do it. But he couldn't have a sea serpent living in Green Harbor River and scaring the stock—not to speak of the universal consternation and panic there'd be in the countryside when such a thing was known. So he lifted Learned Selden and gave her both barrels for a starter, just a trifle over her head. And as soon as the gun exploded, the sea serpent let out a screech you could hear a mile and headed back for open sea. If she'd traveled fast before, she traveled like lightning now, and it wasn't anytime before she was just a black streak on the waters.

Dan'l Webster stepped out of the blind and wiped his brow. He felt sorry, but he felt relieved. He didn't think she'd be back, after that sort of scare, and he wanted to leave everything shipshape before he went down to Washington, next morning. But next day, when he told Seth Peterson what he'd done, he didn't feel so chipper. For, "You shouldn't have done that, Mr. Webster," said Seth Peterson, shaking his head, and that was all he would say except a kind of mutter that sounded like "Samanthy was always particular set in her likes." But Dan'l didn't pay any attention to that, though he remembered it later, and he was quite short with Seth for the first time in their long relationship.

So Seth shut up like a quahog, and Dan'l took the cars for Washington.

When he got there he was busy enough, for the British treaty was on the boil, and within twenty-four hours he'd forgot all about the sea serpent. Or thought he had. But three days later, as he was walking home to his house on Lafayette Square, with a senator friend of his, in the cool of the evening, they heard a curious noise. It seemed to come from the direction of the Potomac River.

"Must have got a new whistle for the Baltimore night boat," said the senator. "Noisy too."

"Oh, that's just the bullfrogs on the banks," said Dan'l Webster steadily. But he knew what it was, just the same, and his heart sank within him. But nobody ever called Dan'l Webster a coward. So, as soon as he'd got rid of the senator, he went down to the banks of the Potomac. Well, it was the sea serpent, all right.

She looked a little tired, as well she might, having swum from Plymouth Bay. But as soon as she saw Dan'l Webster, she stretched out her neck and gave a long low loving hoot. Then Dan'l knew what the trouble was and, for once in his life, he didn't know what to do. But he'd brought along a couple of roe herring, in a paper, just in case; so he fed them to her and she hooted, affectionate and grateful. Then he walked back to his house with his head bowed. And that very night he sent a special express letter to Seth Peterson at Marshfield, for, it seemed to him, Seth must know more about the business than he let on.

Well, Seth got to Washington as fast as the cars would bring him, and the very evening he arrived Dan'l sent him over to interview the serpent. But when Seth came back, Dan'l could see by his face that he hadn't made much progress.

"Could you talk to her, Seth?" he said, and his voice was eager. "Can she understand United States?"

"Oh, she can understand it all right," said Seth. "She's even picking up a few words. They was always a smart family, those Rocky Ledge serpents, and she's the old maid of the lot, and the best educated. The only trouble with 'em is they're so terrible sot in their ways."

"You might have warned me, Seth," said Dan'l Webster, kind of reproachful, and Seth looked uncomfortable.

"Well, to tell you the truth," he said, "I thought all of 'em was dead. Nor I never thought she'd act up like this—her father was as respectable a serpent as you'd see in a long summer's day. Her father—"

"Bother her father!" said Dan'l Webster and set his jaw. "Tell me what she says."

"Well, Mr. Webster," said Seth, and stared at his boots, "she says you're quite a handsome man. She says she never did see anybody quite like you," he went on. "I hate to tell you this, Mr. Webster, and I feel kind of responsible, but I think you ought to know. And I told you that you oughtn't to have shot at her—she's pretty proud of that. She says she knows just how you meant it. Well, I'm no great hand at being embarrassed, Mr. Webster, but, I tell you, she embarrassed me. You see, she's been an old maid for about a hundred and fifty years, I guess, and that's the worst of it. And being the last of her folks in those particular waters, there's just no way to restrain her—her father and mother was as sensible, hardworking serpents as ever gave a feller a tow through a fog, but you know how it is with those old families. Well, she says wherever you go, she'll follow you, and she claims she wants to hear you speak before the Supreme Court—"

"Did you tell her I'm a married man?" said Dan'l. "Did you tell her that?"

"Yes, I told her," said Seth, and you could see the perspiration on his forehead. "But she says that doesn't signify—her being a serpent and different—and she's fixing to move right in. She says Washington's got a lovely climate and she's heard all about the balls and the diplomatic receptions. I don't know how she's heard about them, but she has." He swallowed. "I got her to promise she'd kind of lie low for two weeks and not come up the Potomac by daylight—she was fixing to do that because she wants to meet the President. Well, I got her to promise that much. But she says, even so, if you don't come to see her once an evening, she'll hoot till you do, and she told me to tell you that you haven't heard hooting yet. And as soon as the fish market's open, I better run down and buy a barrel of flaked cod, Mr. Webster—she's partial to flaked cod and she usually takes it in the barrel. Well, I don't want to worry you, Mr. Webster, but I'm afraid that we're in a fix."

"A fix!" said Dan'l Webster. "It's the biggest fix I ever was in in my life!"

"Well, it's kind of complimentary, in a way, I guess," said Seth Peterson, "but—"

"Does she say anything else?" said Dan'l Webster, drawing a long breath.

"Yes, Mr. Webster," said Seth Peterson, his eyes on his boots. "She says you're a little shy. But she says she likes that in a man."

Dan'l Webster went to bed that night, but he didn't sleep. He worked and worked those great brains of his till he nearly wore out the wheels, but he still couldn't think of a way to get rid of the sea serpent. And just about the time dawn broke, he heard one long low hoot, faithful and reminiscent, from the direction of the Potomac.

Well, the next two weeks were certainly bad ones for him. For, as the days wore on, the sea serpent got more and more restive. She wanted him to call her Samanthy, which he wouldn't, and she kept asking him when he was going to introduce her into society, till he had to feed her Italian sardines in olive oil to keep her quiet. And that ran up a bill at the fish market that he hated to think of—besides her continually threatening to come up the Potomac by day. Moreover, and to put the cap on things, the great Webster-Ashburton treaty that was to make his name as Secretary of State had struck a snag and England didn't seem at all partial to admitting the American claims. Oh, it was a weary fortnight and a troublesome one!

The last afternoon of the fortnight, he sat in his office and he didn't know where to turn. For Lord Ashburton was coming to see him for a secret conference that night at nine, and he had to see the sea serpent at ten, and how to satisfy either of them he didn't know. His eyes stared wearily at the papers on his desk. He rang the bell for his secretary.

"The corvette *Benjamin Franklin* reports—" he said. "This should have gone to the Navy Department, Mr. Jones." Then he glanced at the naval report again and his eyes began to glow like furnaces. "By the bones of Leviathan! I've got it!" he said, with a shout. "Where's my hat, Mr. Jones. I must see the President at once!"

There was a different feeling about the house on Lafayette Square that evening, for Dan'l Webster was himself again. He cracked a joke with Seth Peterson and took a glass of Madeira and turned it to the light. And when Lord Ashburton was announced—a nice, white-haired old gentleman, though a little stiff in his joints—he received him with all the courtesy of a king.

"I am glad to see you so much restored, Mr. Webster," said Lord Ashburton, when the greetings had been exchanged. "And yet I fear I bring you bad news. Concerning clauses six and seven of the proposed treaty between Her Majesty's Government and the United States of America, it is my duty to state—"

"My lord, let us drop the clauses for a moment and take the wider view," said Dan'l Webster, smiling. "This is a matter concerning the future welfare and peace of two great nations. Your government claims the right to search our ships; that right we deny. And our attitude seems to you preposterous. Is that not so?"

"I would hesitate to use the word 'preposterous,'" said Lord Ashburton cautiously. "Yet—"

"And yet," said Dan'l Webster, leaning forward, "there are things which may seem preposterous, and yet are not. Let me put a case. Let us say that Great Britain has the strongest navy afloat."

"Britannia rules the waves," said Lord Ashburton, with a noble smile.

"There were a couple she didn't rule in 1812," said Dan'l Webster, "but let that pass. Let me ask you, Lord Ashburton, and let me ask you solemnly, what could even the power and might of Britain's navy avail against Leviathan?"

"Leviathan?" said Lord Ashburton, rather coldly. "Naturally, I understand the Biblical allusion. Yet—"

"The sea serpent," said Dan'l Webster, kind of impatient. "What could all Britain's navy do against the sea serpent out of the Scriptures?"

Lord Ashburton stared at him as if he had gone mad. "God bless my soul, Mr. Secretary!" he said. "But I fail to see the point of your question. The sea serpent doesn't exist!"

"Doesn't he—I mean she?" said Dan'l, calmly. "And suppose I should prove to you that it does exist?"

"Well, 'pon my word! God bless my soul!" said Lord Ashburton, kind of taken aback. "Naturally—in that case—however—but even so—"

Dan'l Webster touched a bell on his desk. "Lord Ashburton," he said, kind of solemn, "I am putting my life, and what is dearer to me, my honor and reputation in your hands. Nevertheless, I feel it necessary, for a better understanding between our two countries."

Seth Peterson came into the room and Dan'l nodded at him.

"Seth," he said, "Lord Ashburton is coming with us to see Samanthy."

"It's all right if you say so, Mr. Webster," said Seth Peterson, "but he'll have to help carry the sardines."

"Well, 'pon my word! Bless my soul! A very strange proceeding!" said Lord Ashburton, but he followed along.

Well, they got to the banks of the Potomac, the three of them, and when they were there, Seth whistled. Samanthy was lying mostly under water, behind a little brushy island, but when she heard the whistle, she began to heave up and uncoil, all shining in the moonlight. It was what you might call a kind of impressive sight. Dan'l Webster looked at Lord Ashburton, but Lord Ashburton's words seemed sort of stuck in his throat.

Finally he got them out. "Bless my soul!" he said. "You Americans are very extraordinary! Is it alive?"

But then all he could do was goggle, for Samanthy had lifted her head, and giving a low friendly hoot, she commenced to swim around the island.

"Now, is that a sea serpent or isn't it?" said Dan'l Webster, with a kind of quiet pride.

"Indubitably," said Lord Ashburton, staring through his eyeglass. "Indubitably," and he kind of cleared his throat. "It is, indeed and in fact, a serpent of the sea. And I am asleep and in bed, in my room at the British Embassy." He pinched himself. "Ouch!" he said. "No, I am not."

"Would you call it sizable, for a sea serpent?" persisted Dan'l Webster.

Lord Ashburton stared again through his eyeglass. "Quite," he said. "Oh, yes, quite, quite!"

"And powerful?" asked Dan'l.

"I should judge so," said Lord Ashburton, faintly, as the sea serpent swam around and around the island and the waves of its wake broke crashing on the bank. "Yes, indeed, a very powerful engine of destruction. May I ask what it feeds upon?"

"Italian sardines, for preference," said Dan'l. "But that's beside the point." He drew a long breath. "Well, my lord," he said, "we're intending to commission that sea serpent as a regular and acknowledged war vessel in the United States Navy. And then, where's your wooden walls?"

Lord Ashburton, he was a diplomat, and his face didn't change expression as he stared first at the sea serpent and then at the face of Dan'l Webster. But after a while, he nodded. "You need not labor the point, Mr. Secretary," he said. "My government, I am sure, will be glad to reconsider its position on the last two clauses and on the right of search."

"Then I'm sure we can reach an agreement," said Dan'l Webster, and wiped the sweat from his brow. "And now, let's feed Samanthy."

He whistled to her himself, a long musical whistle, and she came bounding and looping in toward shore. It took all three of them to heave her the barrel of sardines, and she swallowed it down in one gulp. After that, she gave a hoot of thanks and gratitude, and Lord Ashburton sat down on the bank for a minute and took snuff. He said that he needed something to clear his mind.

"Naturally," he said, after a while, "Her Majesty's Government must have adequate assurances as to the good conduct of this— this lady." He'd meant to say "creature" at first, but Samanthy rolled her eye at him just then, and he changed the word.

"You shall have them," said Dan'l Webster, and whistled Samanthy even closer. She came in kind of skittish, flirting her coils, and Lord Ashburton closed his eyes for a minute. But when Dan'l Webster spoke, it was in the voice that hushed the Senate whenever he rose.

"Samanthy," he said, "I speak to you now as Secretary of State of the United States of America." It was the great voice that had rung in the Supreme Court and replied to Hayne, and even a sea serpent had to listen respectful. For the voice was mellow and deep, and he pictured Samanthy's early years as a carefree young serpent, playing with her fellows, and then her hard life of toil and struggle when she was left lone and lorn, till even Seth Peterson and Lord Ashburton realized the sorrow and tragedy of her lonely lot. And then, in the gentlest and kindest way you could ask, he showed her where her duty lay.

"For, if you keep on hooting in the Potomac, Samanthy," he said, "you'll become a public menace to navigation and get sat upon by the Senate Committee for Rivers and Harbors. They'll drag you up on land, Samanthy, and put you in the Smithsonian Institution; they'll stick you in a stagnant little pool and children will come to throw you peanuts on Sundays, and their nurses will poke you with umbrellas if you don't act lively enough. The U.S. Navy will shoot at you for target practice, Samanthy, and the scientists will examine you, and the ladies of the Pure Conduct League will knit you a bathing suit, and you'll be bothered every minute by congressmen and professors and visitors and foreign celebrities till you won't be able to call your scales your own. Oh, yes, it'll be fame, Samanthy, but it won't be good enough. Believe me, I know something about fame and it's begging letters from strangers and calls from people you don't know and don't want to know, and the burden and wear and tear of being a public character till it's enough to break your heart. It isn't good enough, Samanthy; it won't give you back your free waters and your sporting in the deep. Yes, Samanthy, it'd be a remarkable thing to have you here in Washington, but it isn't the life you were meant for and I can't take advantage of your trust. And now," he said to Seth Peterson, "just what does she say?"

Seth Peterson listened, attentive, to the hootings.

"She says the Washington climate isn't what she thought it was," he said. "And the Potomac River's too warm; it's bad for her sciatica. And she's plumb tired of sardines."

"Does she say anything about me?" asked Dan'l Webster, anxiously.

"Well," said Seth Peterson, listening, "she says—if you'll excuse me, Mr. Webster—that you may be a great man, but you wouldn't make much of a sea serpent. She says you haven't got enough coils. She says—well, she says no hard feelings, but she guesses it was a mistake on both sides."

He listened again. "But she says one thing," he said. "She says she's got to have recognition and a husband, if she has to take this Lord Ashburton. She says he doesn't look like much, but he might get her introduced at Court."

A great light broke over Dan'l's face and his voice rang out like thunder. "She shall have them both," he said. "Come here, Samanthy. By virtue of the authority vested in me as Secretary of State, and by special order of the President of the United States and the Secretary of Navy, as witness the attached commission in blank which I now fill in with your name, I hereby attach you to the United States Navy, to rank as a forty-four-gun frigate on special duty, rating a rear admiral's flag and a salute of the appropriate number of guns, wherever encountered in American waters. And, by virtue of the following special order, I hereby order you to the South Seas, there to cruise until further orders for the purpose of seeking a suitable and proper husband, with all the rights, privileges, duties, and appurtenances pertaining to said search and said American citizenship, as aforesaid and Hail Columbia. Signed John Tyler, President. With which is subjoined a passport signed by Daniel Webster, Secretary of State, bidding all foreign nations let pass without hindrance the American citizen, Samanthy Doe, on her lawful journeys and errands." He dropped his voice for a moment and added reflectively, "The American corvette, *Benjamin Franklin*, reports sighting a handsome young male sea serpent on February third of the present year, just off the coast of the Sandwich

Islands. Said serpent had forty-two coils by actual count, and when last sighted was swimming SSW at full speed."

But hardly had he spoken when Samanthy, for the last time, lifted her head and gave out a last long hoot. She looked upon Dan'l Webster as she did so, and there was regret in her eye. But the regret was tinctured with eagerness and hope.

Then she beat the water to a froth, and, before they really saw her go, she was gone, leaving only her wake on the moonlit Potomac.

"Well," said Dan'l Webster, yawning a little, "there we are. And now, Lord Ashburton, if you'll come home with me, we can draw up that treaty."

"Gladly," said Lord Ashburton, brushing his coat with his handkerchief. "Is it really gone? 'Pon my soul! You know, for a moment, I imagined that I actually saw a sea serpent. You have a very vivid way of putting things, Mr. Webster. But I think I understand the American attitude now, from the—er—analogy you were pleased to draw between such a—er—fabulous animal and the young strength of your growing country."

"I was confident that you would appreciate it, once it was brought to your attention," said Dan'l Webster. But he winked one eye at Seth Peterson, and Seth Peterson winked back.

And I'll say this for Dan'l Webster, too—he kept his promises. All through the time he was Secretary of State, he saw to it that the forty-four-gun frigate, *Samanthy Doe*, was carried on a special account on the books of the Navy. In fact, there's some people say that she's still so carried, and that it was her give Ericsson the idea for building the *Monitor* in the Civil War—if she wasn't the *Monitor* herself. And when the White Fleet went around the world in Teddy Roosevelt's time—well, there was a lookout in the crow's-nest of the flagship, one still calm night, as they passed by the palmy isles of the South Seas. And all of a sudden, the water boiled, tremendous and phosphorescent, and there was a pair of sea serpents and seven young ones, circling, calm and majestic, three times around the fleet. He rubbed his eyes and stared, but there they were. Well, he was the only one that saw it, and they put him in the brig for it next morning. But he swore, till the day he died, they were flying the Stars and Stripes.

Father Mapple's Jonah Sermon

Herman Melville

(from "Moby Dick," 1851)

IN THIS SAME New Bedford there stands a whaleman's Chapel, and few are the moody fishermen, shortly bound for the Indian Ocean or Pacific, who fail to make a Sunday visit to the spot. I am sure that I did not.

Returning from my first morning stroll, I again sallied out upon this special errand. The sky had changed from clear, sunny cold, to driving sleet and mist. Wrapping myself in my shaggy jacket of the cloth called bearskin, I fought my way against the stubborn storm. Entering, I found a small scattered congregation of sailors, and sailors' wives and widows. A muffled silence reigned, only broken at times by the shrieks of the storm. Each silent worshipper seemed purposely sitting apart from the other, as if each silent grief were insular and incommunicable. The chaplain had not yet arrived; and there these silent islands of men and women sat steadfastly eyeing several marble tablets, with black borders, masoned into the wall on either side of the pulpit.

*   *   *

I had not been seated very long ere a man of a certain
venerable robustness entered; immediately as the storm-pelted
door flew back upon admitting him, a quick regardful eyeing of
him by all the congregation, sufficiently attested that this fine
old man was the chaplain. Yes, it was the famous Father Mapple,
so called by the whalemen, among whom he was a very great
favorite. He had been a sailor and a harpooner in his youth, but
for many years past had dedicated his life to the ministry. At the
time I now write of, Father Mapple was in the hardy winter of
a healthy old age; that sort of old age which seems merging into
a second flowering youth, for among all the fissures of his
wrinkles, there shone certain mild gleams of a newly developing
bloom—the spring verdure peeping forth even beneath February's snow. No one having previously heard his history, could
for the first time behold Father Mapple without the utmost
interest, because there were certain engrafted clerical peculiari-
ties about him, imputable to that adventurous maritime life he
had led. When he entered I observed that he carried no
umbrella, and certainly had not come in his carriage, for his
tarpaulin hat ran down with melting sleet, and his great pilot
cloth jacket seemed almost to drag him to the floor with the
weight of the water it had absorbed. However, hat and coat and
overshoes were one by one removed, and hung up in a little
space in an adjacent corner; when, arrayed in a decent suit, he
quietly approached the pulpit.

Like most old fashioned pulpits, it was a very lofty one, and
since a regular stairs to such a height would, by its long angle
with the floor, seriously contract the already small area of the
chapel, the architect, it seemed, had acted upon the hint of
Father Mapple, and finished the pulpit without a stairs, substi-
tuting a perpendicular side ladder, like those used in mounting
a ship from a boat at sea. The wife of a whaling captain had
provided the chapel with a handsome pair of red worsted

man-ropes for this ladder, which, being itself nicely headed, and stained with a mahogany color, the whole contrivance, considering what manner of chapel it was, seemed by no means in bad taste. Halting for an instant at the foot of the ladder, and with both hands grasping the ornamental knobs of the man-ropes, Father Mapple cast a look upwards, and then with a truly sailor-like but still reverential dexterity, hand over hand, mounted the steps as if ascending the main-top of his vessel.

The perpendicular parts of this side ladder, as is usually the case with swinging ones, were of cloth-covered rope, only the rounds were of wood, so that at every step there was a joint. At my first glimpse of the pulpit, it had not escaped me that however convenient for a ship, these joints in the present instance seemed unnecessary. For I was not prepared to see Father Mapple after gaining the height, slowly turn round, and stooping over the pulpit, deliberately drag up the ladder step by step, till the whole was deposited within, leaving him impregnable in his little Quebec.

I pondered some time without fully comprehending the reason for this. Father Mapple enjoyed such a wide reputation for sincerity and sanctity, that I could not suspect him of courting notoriety by any mere tricks of the stage. No, thought I, there must be some sober reason for this thing; furthermore, it must symbolize something unseen. Can it be, then, that by that act of physical isolation, he signifies his spiritual withdrawal for the time, from all outward worldly ties and connexions? Yes, for replenished with the meat and wine of the world, to the faithful man of God, this pulpit, I see, is a self-containing stronghold—a lofty Ehrenbreitstein, with a perennial well of water within the walls.

But the side ladder was not the only strange feature of the place, borrowed from the chaplain's former sea-farings. Between the marble cenotaphs on either hand of the pulpit, the wall which formed its back was adorned with a large painting representing a gallant ship beating against a terrible storm off a lee coast of black rocks and snowy breakers. But high above the flying scud and dark-rolling clouds, there floated a little isle of sunlight, from which beamed forth an angel's face; and this bright face shed a distinct spot of radiance upon the ship's tossed deck, something like that silver plate now inserted into the Victory's plank where Nelson fell. "Ah, noble ship," the angel seemed to say, "beat on, beat on, thou noble ship, and bear a hardy helm; for lo! the sun is breaking through; the clouds are rolling off—serenest azure is at hand."

Nor was the pulpit itself without a trace of the same sea-taste that had achieved the ladder and the picture. Its panelled front was in the likeness of a ship's bluff bows, and the Holy Bible rested on a projecting piece of scroll work, fashioned after a ship's fiddle-headed beak.

What could be more full of meaning?—for the pulpit is ever this earth's foremost part; all the rest comes in its rear; the pulpit leads the world. From thence it is the storm of God's quick wrath is first descried, and the bow must bear the earliest brunt. From thence it is the God of breezes fair or foul is first invoked for favorable winds. Yes, the world's a ship on its passage out, and not a voyage complete; and the pulpit is its prow.

Father Mapple rose, and in a mild voice of unassuming authority ordered the scattered people to condense. "Starboard gangway, there! side away to larboard—larboard gangway, to starboard! Midships! midships!"

There was a low rumbling of heavy sea-boots among the benches, and a still slighter shuffling of women's shoes, and all was quiet again, and every eye on the preacher.

He paused a little; then kneeling in the pulpit's bows, folded his large brown hands across his chest, uplifted his closed eyes, and offered a prayer so deeply devout that he seemed kneeling and praying at the bottom of the sea.

This ended, in prolonged solemn tones, like the continual tolling of a bell in a ship that is foundering at sea in a fog—in such tones he commenced reading the following hymn; but changing his manner towards the concluding stanzas, burst forth with a pealing exultation and joy—

> "The ribs and terrors in the whale,
>   Arched over me a dismal gloom,
> While all God's sun-lit waves rolled by,
>   And lift me deepening down to doom.
>
> "I saw the opening maw of hell,
>   With endless pains and sorrows there;
> Which none but they that feel can tell—
>   Oh, I was plunging to despair.
>
> "In black distress, I called my God,
>   When I could scarce believe him mine,
> He bowed his ear to my complaints—
>   No more the whale did me confine.
>
> "With speed he flew to my relief,
>   As on a radiant dolphin borne;
> Awful, yet bright, as lightning shone
>   The face of my Deliverer God.
>
> "My song for ever shall record
>   That terrible, that joyful hour;
> I give the glory to my God,
>   His all the mercy and the power."

Nearly all joined in singing this hymn, which swelled high above the howling of the storm. A brief pause ensued; the preacher slowly turned over the leaves of the Bible, and at last, folding his hand down upon the proper page, said: "Beloved shipmates, clinch the last verse of the first chapter of Jonah— 'And God had prepared a great fish to swallow up Jonah.'

"Shipmates, this book, containing only four chapters—four yarns—is one of the smallest strands in the mighty cable of the Scriptures. Yet what depths of the soul does Jonah's deep sea-line sound! what a pregnant lesson to us is this prophet! What a noble thing is that canticle in the fish's belly! How billow-like and boisterously grand! We feel the floods surging over us; we sound with him to the kelpy bottom of the waters; sea-weed and all the slime of the sea is about us! But *what* is this lesson that the book of Jonah teaches? Shipmates, it is a two-stranded lesson; a lesson to us all as sinful men, and a lesson to me as a pilot of the living God. As sinful men, it is a lesson to us all, because it is a story of the sin, hard-heartedness, suddenly awakened fears, the swift punishment, repentance, prayers, and finally the deliverance and joy of Jonah. As with all sinners among men, the sin of this son of Amittai was in his wilful disobedience of the command of God—never mind now what that command was, or how conveyed—which he found a hard command. But all the things that God would have us do are hard for us to do—remember that—and hence, he oftener commands us than endeavors to persuade. And if we obey God, we must disobey ourselves; and it is in this disobeying ourselves, wherein the hardness of obeying God consists.

"With this sin of disobedience in him, Jonah still further flouts at God, by seeking to flee from Him. He thinks that a ship made by men, will carry him into countries where God does not reign, but only the Captains of this earth. He skulks about the wharves of Joppa, and seeks a ship that's bound for Tarshish. There lurks, perhaps, a hitherto unheeded meaning here. By all accounts Tarshish could have been no other city than the modern Cadiz. That's the opinion of learned men. And where is Cadiz, shipmates? Cadiz is in Spain; as far by water, from Joppa, as Jonah could possibly have sailed in those ancient days, when the Atlantic was an almost unknown sea. Because Joppa, the modern Jaffa, shipmates, is on the most easterly coast of the Mediterra-

nean, the Syrian; and Tarshish or Cadiz more than two thousand
miles to the westward from that, just outside the Straits of
Gibraltar. See ye not then, shipmates, that Jonah sought to flee
world-wide from God? Miserable man! Oh! most contemptible
and worthy of all scorn; with slouched hat and guilty eye,
skulking from his God; prowling the shipping like a vile burglar
hastening to cross the seas. So disordered, self-condemning is his
look, that had there been policemen in those days, Jonah, on the
mere suspicion of something wrong, had been arrested ere he
touched a deck. How plainly he's a fugitive! no baggage, not a
hat-box, valise, or carpet-bag,—no friends accompany him to
the wharf with their adieux. At last, after much dodging search,
he find the Tarshish ship receiving the last items of her cargo;
and as he steps on board to see its Captain in the cabin, all the
sailors for the moment desist from hoisting in the goods, to mark
the stranger's evil eye. Jonah sees this; but in vain he tries to
look all ease and confidence; in vain essays his wretched smile.
Strong intuitions of the man assure the mariners he can be no
innocent. In their gamesome but still serious way, one whispers
to the other—'Jack, he's robbed a widow;' or, 'Joe, do you mark
him; he's a bigamist;' or, 'Harry lad, I guess he's the adulterer
that broke jail in old Gomorrah, or belike, one of the missing
murderers from Sodom.' Another runs to read the bill that's
stuck against the spile upon the wharf to which the ship is
moored, offering five hundred gold coins for the apprehension
of a parricide, and containing a description of his person. He
reads, and looks from Jonah to the bill; while all his sympathetic
shipmates now crowd round Jonah, prepared to lay their hands
upon him. Frighted Jonah trembles, and summoning all his
boldness to his face, only looks so much the more a coward. He
will not confess himself suspected; but that itself is strong
suspicion. So he makes the best of it; and when the sailors find
him not to be the man that is advertised, they let him pass, and
he descends into the cabin.

"Who's there?" cries the Captain at his busy desk, hurriedly making out his papers for the Customs—'Who's there?' Oh! how that harmless question mangles Jonah! For the instant he almost turns to flee again. But he rallies. 'I seek a passage in this ship to Tarshish; how soon sail ye, sir?' Thus far the busy Captain had not looked up to Jonah, though the man now stands before him; but no sooner does he hear that hollow voice, than he darts a scrutinizing glance. 'We sail with the next coming tide,' at last he slowly answered, still intently eyeing him. 'No sooner, sir?'—'Soon enough for any honest man that goes a passenger.' Ha! Jonah, that's another stab. But he swiftly calls away the Captain from that scent. 'I'll sail with ye,'—he says,—'the passage money, how much is that?—I'll pay now.' For it is particularly written, shipmates, as if it were a thing not to be overlooked in this history, 'that he paid the fare thereof?' ere the craft did sail. And taken with the context, this full of meaning.

"Now Jonah's Captain, shipmates, was one whose discernment detects crime in any, but whose cupidity exposes it only in the penniless. In this world, shipmates, sin that pays its way can travel freely, and without a passport; whereas Virtue, if a pauper, is stopped at all frontiers. So Jonah's Captain prepares to test the length of Jonah's purse, ere he judge him openly. He charges him thrice the usual sum; and it's assented to. Then the Captain knows that Jonah is a fugitive; but at the same time resolves to help a flight that paves its rear with gold. Yet when Jonah fairly takes out his purse, prudent suspicions still molest the Captain. He rings every coin to find a counterfeit. Not a forger, any way, he mutters; and Jonah is put down for his passage. 'Point out my state-room, Sir,' says Jonah now, 'I'm travel-weary; I need sleep.' 'Thou look'st like it,' says the Captain, 'there's thy room.' Jonah enters, and would lock the door, but the lock contains no key. Hearing him foolishly fumbling there, the Captain laughs lowly to himself, and mutters something about the doors of convicts' cells being never allowed to be locked within. All dressed and dusty as he is, Jonah throws himself into his berth, and finds the little state-room ceiling almost resting on his forehead. The air is close, and Jonah gasps. Then, in that contracted hole, sunk, too, beneath the ship's water-line, Jonah feels the heralding presentiment of that stifling hour, when the whale shall hold him in the smallest of his bowel's wards.

"Screwed at its axis against the side, a swinging lamp slightly oscillates in Jonah's room; and the ship, heeling over towards the wharf with the weight of the last bales received, the lamp, flame and all, though in slight motion, still maintains a permanent obliquity with reference to the room; though, in truth, infallibly straight itself, it but made obvious the false, lying levels among which it hung. The lamp alarms and frightens Jonah; as lying in his berth his tormented eyes roll round the place, and this thus far successful fugitive finds no refuse for his restless glance. But that contradiction in the lamp more and more appalls him. The floor, the ceiling, and the side, are all awry. 'Oh! so my conscience hangs in me!' he groans, 'straight upward, so it burns; but the chambers of my soul are all in crookedness!'

"Like one who after a night of drunken revelry hies to his bed, still reeling, but with conscience yet pricking him, as the plungings of the Roman race-horse but so much the more strike his steel tags into him; as one who in that miserable plight still turns and turns in giddy anguish, praying God for annihilation until the fit be passed; and at last amid the whirl of woe he feels, a deep stupor steals over him, as over the man who bleeds to death, for conscience is the wound, and there's naught to staunch it; so, after sore wrestlings in his berth, Jonah's prodigy of ponderous misery drags him drowning down to sleep.

"And now the time of tide has come; the ship casts off her cables; and from the deserted wharf the uncheered ship for Tarshish, all careening, glides to sea. That ship, my friends, was the first of recorded smugglers! the contraband was Jonah. But the sea rebels; he will not bear the wicked burden. A dreadful storm comes on, the ship is like to break. But now when the boatswain calls all hands to lighten her; when boxes, bales, and jars are clattering overboard; when the wind is shrieking, and the men are yelling, and every plank thunders with trampling feet right over Jonah's head; in all this raging tumult, Jonah sleeps his hideous sleep. He sees no black sky and raging sea, feels not the reeling timbers, and little hears he or heeds he the far rush of the mighty whale, which even now with open mouth is cleaving the seas after him. Aye, shipmates, Jonah was gone down into the sides of the ship—a berth in the cabin as I have taken it, and was fast asleep. But the frightened master comes to him, and shrieks in his dead ear, 'What meanest thou, O sleeper! arise!' Startled from his lethargy by that direful cry, Jonah staggers to his feet, and stumbling to the deck, grasps a shroud, to look out upon the sea. But at last moment he is sprung upon by a panther billow leaping over the bulwarks. Wave after wave thus leaps into the ship, and finding no speedy vent runs roaring fore and aft, till the mariners come nigh to drowning while yet afloat. And ever, as the white moon shows her affrighted face from the steep gullies in the blackness overhead, aghast Jonah sees the rearing bowsprit pointing high upward, but soon beat downward again towards the tormented deep.

"Terrors upon terrors run shouting through his soul. In all his cringing attitudes, the God-fugitive is now too plainly known. The sailors mark him; more and more certain grow their suspicions of him, and at last, fully to test the truth, by referring the whole matter to high Heaven, they fall to casting lots, to see for whose cause this great tempest was upon them. The lot is Jonah's; that discovered, then how furiously they mob him with their questions. 'What is thine occupation? Whence comest thou? Thy country? What people?' But mark now, my shipmates, the behavior of poor Jonah. The eager mariners but ask him who he is, and where from; whereas, they not only receive an answer to those questions, but likewise another answer to a question not put by them, but the unsolicited answer is forced from Jonah by the hard hand of God that is upon him.

"'I am a Hebrew,' he cries—and then—'I fear the Lord the God of Heaven who hath made the sea and the dry land!' Fear him, O Jonah? Aye, well mightest thou fear the Lord God *then!* Straightway, he now goes on to make a full confession; whereupon the mariners became more and more appalled, but still are pitiful. For when Jonah, not yet supplicating God for mercy, since he but too well knew the darkness of his deserts,—when wretched Jonah cries out to them to take him and cast him forth into the sea, for he knew that for *his* sake this great tempest was upon them; they mercifully turn from him, and seek by other means to save the ship. But all in vain; the indignant gale howls louder; then, with one hand raised invokingly to God, with the other they not unreluctantly lay hold of Jonah.

"And now behold Jonah taken up as an anchor and dropped into the sea; when instantly an oily calmness floats out from the east, and the sea is still, as Jonah carries down the gale with him, leaving smooth water behind. He goes down in the whirling heart of such a masterless commotion that he scarce heeds the moment when he drops seething into the yawning jaws awaiting him; and the whale shoots-to all his ivory teeth, like so many white bolts, upon his prison. Then Jonah prayed unto the Lord out of the fish's belly. But observe his prayer, and learn a weighty lesson. For sinful as he is, Jonah does not weep and wail for direct deliverance. He feels that his dreadful punishment is just. He leaves all his deliverance to God, contenting himself with this, that spite of all his pains and pangs, he will still look towards His holy temple. And here, shipmates, is true and faithful repentance; not clamorous for pardon, but grateful for punishment. And how pleasing to God was this conduct in Jonah, is shown in the eventual deliverance of him from the sea and the whale. Shipmates, I do not place Jonah before you to be copied for his sin but I do place him before you as a model for repentance. Sin not; but if you do, take heed to repent of it like Jonah."

While he was speaking these words, the howling of the shrieking, slanting storm without seemed to add new power to the preacher, who, when describing Jonah's sea-storm, seemed tossed by a storm himself. His deep chest heaved as with a ground-swell; his tossed arms seemed the warring elements at work; and the thunders that rolled away from off his swarthy brow, and the light leaping from his eye, made all his simple hearers look on him with a quick fear that was strange to them.

There now came a lull in his look, as he silently turned over the leaves of the Book once more; and, at last, standing motionless, with closed eyes, for the moment, seemed communing with God and himself.

But again he leaned over towards the people, and bowing his head lowly, with an aspect of the deepest yet manliest humanity, he spake these words:

"Shipmates, God has laid but one hand upon you; both his hands press upon me. I have read ye by what murky light may be mine the lesson that Jonah teaches to all sinners; and therefore to ye, and still more to me, for I am a greater sinner than ye. And now how gladly would I come down from this mast-head and sit on the hatches there where you sit, and listen as you listen, while some one of you reads *me* that other and more awful lesson which Jonah teaches to *me*, as a pilot of the living God. How being an anointed pilot-prophet, or speaker of true things, and bidden by the Lord to sound those unwelcome truths in the ears of a wicked Nineveh, Jonah appalled at the hostility he should rise, fled from his mission, and sought to escape his duty and his God by taking ship at Joppa. But God is everywhere; Tarshish he never reached. As we have seen, God came upon him in the whale, and swallowed him down to living gulfs of doom, and with swift slantings tore him along 'into the midst of the seas,' where the eddying depths sucked him ten thousand fathoms down, and 'the weeds were wrapped about his head,' and all the watery world of woe bowled over him. Yet even then beyond the reach of any plummet—'out of the belly of hell'—when the whale grounded upon the ocean's utmost bones, even then, God heard the engulfed, repenting prophet when he cried. Then God spake unto the fish; and from the shuddering cold and blackness of the sea, the whale came breeching up towards the warm and pleasant sun, and all the delights of air and earth; and 'vomited out Jonah upon the dry land;' when the word of the Lord came a second time; and Jonah, bruised and beaten—his ears, like two sea-shells, still multitudinously murmuring of the ocean—Jonah did the Almighty's bidding. And what was that, shipmates? To preach the Truth to the face of Falsehood! That was it!

"This, shipmates, this is that other lesson; and woe to that pilot of the living God who slights it. Woe to him whom this world charms from Gospel duty! Woe to him who seeks to pour oil upon the waters when God has brewed them into a gale! Woe to him who seeks to please rather than to appal! Woe to him whose good name is more to him than goodness! Woe to him who, in this world, courts not dishonor! Woe to him who would not be true, even though to be false were salvation! Yea, woe to him who, as the great Pilot Paul has it, while preaching to others is himself a castaway!"

He drooped and fell away from himself for a moment; then lifting his face to them again, showed a deep joy in his eyes, as he cried out with a heavenly enthusiasm—"But oh! shipmates! on the starboard hand of every woe, there is a sure delight; and higher the top of that delight, than the bottom of the woe is deep. Is not the main-truck higher than the kelson is low? Delight is to him—a far, far upward, and inward delight—who against the proud gods and commodores of this earth, ever stand forth his own inexorable self. Delight is to him whose strong arms yet support him, when the ship of this base treacherous world has gone down beneath him. Delight is to him, who gives no quarter in the truth, and kills, burns, and destroys all sin though he pluck it out from under the robes of Senators and Judges. Delight, top-gallant delight is to him, who acknowledges no law or lord, but the Lord his God, and is only a patriot to heaven. Delight is to him, whom all the waves of the billows of the seas of the boisterous mob can never shake from this sure Keel of the Ages. And eternal delight and deliciousness will be his, who coming to lay him down, can say with his final breath—O Father!—chiefly known to me by Thy rod—mortal or immortal, here I die. I have striven to be Thine, more than to be this world's, or mine own. Yet this is nothing; I leave eternity to Thee; for what is man that he should live out the lifetime of his Gods?"

He said no more, but slowly waving a benediction, covered his face with his hands, and so remained kneeling, till all the people had departed, and he was left alone in the place.

Plain Fishing

~~~~~~~~~~~~~~~~~~~

Frank R. Stockton

"WELL, SIR," SAID old Peter, as he came out on the porch with his pipe, "so you come here to go fishin'?"

Peter Gruse was the owner of the farmhouse where I had arrived that day, just before supper-time. He was a short, strong-built old man, with a pair of pretty daughters, and little gold rings in his ears. Two things distinguished him from the farmers in the country round about: one was the rings in his ears, and the other was the large and comfortable house in which he kept his pretty daughters. The other farmers in that region had fine large barns for their cattle and horses, but very poor houses for their daughters. Old Peter's earrings were indirectly connected with his house. He had not always lived among those mountains. He had been on the sea, where his ears were decorated, and he had travelled a good deal on land, where he had ornamented his mind with many ideas which were not in general use in the part of his State in which he was born. This house stood a little back from the highroad, and if a traveller wished to be entertained, Peter was generally willing to take him

55

in, provided he had left his wife and family at home. The old man himself had no objection to wives and children, but his two pretty daughters had.

These two young women had waited on their father and myself at supper-time, one continually bringing hot griddle cakes, and the other giving me every opportunity to test the relative merits of the seven different kinds of preserves, which, in little glass plates, covered the unoccupied spaces on the tablecloth. The latter, when she found that there was no further possible way of serving us, presumed to sit down at the corner of the table and begin her supper. But in spite of this apparent humility, which was only a custom of the country, there was that in the general air of the pretty daughters which left no doubt in the mind of the intelligent observer that they stood at the wheel in that house. There was a son of fourteen, who sat at table with us, but he did not appear to count as a member of the family.

"Yes," I answered, "I understood that there was good fishing hereabouts, and, at any rate, I should like to spend a few days among these hills and mountains."

"Well," said Porter, "there's trout in some of our streams, though not as many as there used to be, and there's hills a plenty, and mountains too, if you choose to walk fur enough. They're a good deal furder off than they look. What did you bring with you to fish with?"

"Nothing at all," I answered. "I was told in the town that you were a great fisherman, and that you could let me have all the tackle I would need."

"Upon my word," said old Peter, resting his pipe-hand on his knee and looking steadfastly at me, "you're the queerest fisherman I've seed yet. Nigh every year, some two or three of 'em stop here in the fishin' season, and there was never a man who didn't bring his jinted pole, and his reels, and his lines, and his hooks, and his dry-good flies, and his whisky-flask with a long strap to it. Now, if you want all these things, I haven't got 'em."

"Whatever you use yourself will suit me," I answered.

"All right, then," said he. "I'll do the best I can for you in the mornin'. But it's plain enough to me that you're not a game fisherman, or you wouldn't come here without your tools."

To this remark I made answer to the effect, that though I was very fond of fishing, my pleasure in it did not depend upon the possession of all the appliances of professional sport.

"Perhaps you think," said the old man, "from the way I spoke, that I don't believe them fellers with the jinted poles can ketch fish, but that ain't so. That old story about the little boy with the pin-hook who ketched all the fish, while the gentleman with the modern improvements, who stood alongside of him, kep' throwin' out his beautiful flies and never got nothin', is a pure lie. The fancy chaps, who must have ev'rythin' jist so, gen'rally gits fish. But for all that, I don't like their way of fishin', and I take no stock in it myself. I've been fishin', on and off, ever since I was a little boy, and I've caught nigh every kind there is, from the big jew-fish and cavalyoes down South, to the trout and minnies round about here. But when I ketch a fish, the first thing I do is to try to git him on the hook, and the next thing is to git him out of the water jist as soon as I kin. I don't put in no time worryin' him. There's only two animals in the world that likes to worry smaller creeturs a good while afore they kill 'em; one is the cat, and the other is what they call the game fisherman. This kind of a feller never goes after no fish that don't mind being ketched. He goes fur them kinds that loves their home in the water and hates most to leave it, and he makes it jist as hard fur 'em as he kin. What the game fisher likes is the smallest kind of a hook, the thinnest line, and a fish that it takes a good while to weaken. The longer the weak'nin' business kin be spun out, the more the sport. The idee is to let the fish think there's a chance fur him to git away. That's jist like the cat with her mouse. She lets the little creetur hop off, but the minnit he gits fur enough down, she jabs on him with her claws, and then, if there's any game left in him, she lets him try agen. Of course, the game fisher could have a strong line and a stout pole and git his fish in a good sight quicker, if he wanted to, but that wouldn't be sport. He couldn't give him the butt and spin him out, and reel him in, and let him jump and run till his pluck is clean worn out. Now, I likes to git my fish ashore with all the pluck in 'em. It makes 'em taste better. And as fur fun, I'll be bound I've had jist as much of that, and more, too, than most of these fellers who are so dreadful anxious to have everythin' jist right, and think they can't go fishin' till they've spent enough money to buy a suit of Sunday clothes. As a gen'ral rule they're a solemn lot, and work pretty hard at their fun. When I work I want to be paid fur it, and when I go in fur fun I want to take it easy and comfortable. Now I wouldn't say so much agen these fellers," said old Peter, as he arose and put his empty pipe on a little shelf under the porch-roof, "if it wasn't for one thing, and that is, that they think that their kind of fishin' is the only kind worth considerin'. The way they look down upon plain Christian fishin' is enough to rile a hitchin'-post. I don't want to say nothin' agen no man's way of attendin' to his own affairs, whether it's kitchen gardenin', or whether it's fishin', if he says nothin' agen my way; but when he looks down on me, and grins me, I want to haul myself up, and grin him, if I kin. And in this case, I kin. I s'pose the house-cat and the cat-fisher (by which I don't mean the man who fishes fer cat-fish) was both made as they is, and they can't help it; but that don't give 'em no right to put on airs before other bein's, who gits their meat with a square kill. Good night. And sence I've talked so much about it, I've a mind to go fishin' with you to-morrow myself."

The next morning found old Peter of the same mind, and after breakfast he proceeded to fit me out for a day of what he called "plain Christian trout-fishin'." He gave me a reed rod, about nine feet long, light, strong, and nicely balanced. The tackle he

produced was not of the fancy order, but his lines were of fine
strong linen, and his hooks were of good shape, clean and sharp,
and snooded to the lines with a neatness that indicated the hand
of a man who had been where he learned to wear little gold
rings in his ears.

"Here are some of these feather insects," he said, "which you
kin take along if you like." And he handed me a paper
containing a few artificial flies. "They're pretty nat'ral," he said,
"and the hooks is good. A man who come here fishin' gave 'em
to me, but I shan't want 'em to-day. At this time of year
grasshoppers is the best bait in the kind of place where we're
goin' to fish. The stream, after it comes down from the mountains, runs through half a mile of medder land before it strikes
into the woods agen. A grasshopper is a little creature that's got
as much conceit as if his jinted legs was fish-poles, and he thinks
he kin jump over this narrer run of water whenever he pleases;
but he don't always do it, and them of him that don't git snapped
up by the trout that lie along the banks in the medder is floated
along into the woods, where there's always fish enough to come
to the second table."

Having got me ready, Peter took his own particular pole,
which he assured me he had used for eleven years, and hooking
on his left arm a good-sized basket, which his elder pretty
daughter had packed with cold meat, bread, butter, and preserves, we started forth for a three-mile walk to the fishing-
ground. The day was a favourable one for our purpose, the sky
being sometimes overclouded, which was good for fishing, and
also for walking on a highroad; and sometimes bright, which
was good for effects of mountain scenery. Not far from the spot
where old Peter proposed to begin our sport, a small frame-
house stood by the roadside, and here the old man halted and
entered the open door without knocking or giving so much as a
premonitory stamp. I followed, imitating my companion in
leaving my pole outside, which appeared to be the only cer-

emony that the etiquette of those parts required of visitors. In the room we entered, a small man in his shirt sleeves sat mending a basket handle. He nodded to Peter, and Peter nodded to him.

"We've come up a-fishin'," said the old man. "Kin your boys give us some grasshoppers?"

"I don't know that they've got any ready ketched," said he, "for I reckon I used what they had this mornin'. But they kin git you some. Here, Dan, you and Sile go and ketch Mister Gruse and this young man some grasshoppers. Take that mustard-box, and see that you git it full."

Peter and I now took seats, and the conversation began about a black cow which Peter had to sell, and which the other was willing to buy if the old man would trade for sheep, which animals, however, the basket-mender did not appear just at that time to have in his possession. As I was not very much interested in this subject, I walked to the back door and watched two small boys in scanty shirts and trousers and ragged straw hats, who were darting about in the grass catching grasshoppers, of which insects, judging by the frequent pounces of the boys, there seemed a plentiful supply.

"Got it full?" said their father when the boys came in.

"Crammed," said Dan.

Old Peter took the little can, pressed the top firmly on, put it in his coat-tail pocket, and rose to go. "You'd better think about that cow, Barney," said he. He said nothing to the boys about the box of bait; but I could not let them catch grasshoppers for us for nothing, and I took a dime from my pocket, and gave it to Dan. Dan grinned, and Sile looked sheepishly happy, and at the sight of the piece of silver an expression of interest came over the face of the father. "Wait a minute," said he, and he went into a little room that seemed to be a kitchen. Returning, he brought with him a small string of trout. "Do you want to buy some fish?" he said. "These is nice fresh ones. I ketched 'em this mornin'."

To offer to sell fish to a man who is just about to go out to catch them for himself might, in other cases, be considered an insult, but it was quite evident that nothing of the kind was intended by Barney. He probably thought that if I bought grasshoppers, I might buy fish. "You kin have 'em for a quarter," he said.

It was derogatory to my pride to buy fish at such a moment, but the man looked very poor, and there was a shade of anxiety on his face which touched me. Old Peter stood by waiting without a word. "It might be well," I said, turning to him, "to buy these fish, for we may not catch enough for supper."

"Such things do happen," said the old man.

"Well," said I, "if we have these we will feel safe in any case." And I took the fish and gave the man a quarter. It was not, perhaps, a professional act, but the trout were well worth the money, and I felt that I was doing a deed of charity.

Old Peter and I now took our rods, and crossed the road into an enclosed lot, and thence into a wide stretch of grassland, bounded by hills in front of us and to the right, while a thick forest lay to the left. We had walked but a short distance, when Peter said: "I'll go down into the woods, and try my luck there, and you'd better go along upstream, about a quarter of a mile, to where it's rocky. P'raps you ain't used to fishin' in the woods, and you might git your line cotched. You'll find the trout'll bite in the rough water."

"Where is the stream?" I asked.

"This is it," he said, pointing to a little brook, which was scarcely too wide for me to step across, "and there's fish right here, but they're hard to ketch, fur they git plenty of good livin', and are mighty sassy about their eatin'. But you kin ketch 'em up there."

Old Peter now went down toward the woods, while I walked up the little stream. I had seen trout-brooks before, but never one so diminutive as this. However, when I came nearer to the

point where the stream issued from between two of the foot-
hills of the mountains, which lifted their forest-covered heights
in the distance, I found it wider and shallower, breaking over its
rocky bottom in sparkling little cascades.

Fishing in such a jolly little stream, surrounded by this
mountain scenery, and with the privileges of the beautiful
situation all to myself, would have been a joy to me if I had had
never a bite. But no such ill-luck befell me. Peter had given me
the can of grasshoppers after putting half of them into his own
bait-box, and these I used with much success. It was grasshopper
season, and the trout were evidently on the lookout for them. I
fished in the ripples under the little waterfalls; and every now
and then I drew out a lively trout. Most of these were of
moderate size, and some of them might have been called small.
The large ones probably fancied the forest shades, where old
Peter went. But all I caught were fit for the table, and I was very
well satisfied with the result of my sport.

About an hour after noon I began to feel hungry, and thought
it time to look up the old man, who had the lunch-basket. I
walked down the bank of the brook, and some time before I
reached the woods I came to a place where it expanded to a
width of about ten feet. The water here was very clear, and the
motion quiet, so that I could easily see to the bottom, which did
not appear to be more than a foot below the surface. Gazing into
this transparent water, as I walked, I saw a large trout glide
across the stream, and disappear under the grassy bank which
overhung the opposite side. I instantly stopped. This was a much
larger fish than any I had caught, and I determined to try for
him.

I stepped back from the bank, so as to be out of sight, and put
a fine grasshopper on my hook; then I lay, face downward, on
the grass, and worked myself slowly forward until I could see the
middle of the stream; then quietly raising my pole, I gave my
grasshopper a good swing, as if he had made a wager to jump

over the stream at its widest part. But as he certainly would have failed in such an ambitious endeavour, especially if he had been caught by a puff of wind, I let him come down upon the surface of the water, a little beyond the middle of the brook. Grasshoppers do not sink when they fall into the water, and so I kept this fellow upon the surface, and gently moved him along, as if, with all the conceit taken out of him by the result of his ill-considered leap, he was ignominiously endeavouring to swim to shore. As I did this, I saw the trout come out from under the bank, move slowly toward the grasshopper, and stop directly under him. Trembling with anxiety and eager expectation, I endeavoured to make the movements of the insect still more natural, and, as far as I was able, I threw into him a sudden perception of his danger, and a frenzied desire to get away. But, either the trout had had all the grasshoppers he wanted, or he was able, from long experience, to perceive the difference between a natural exhibition of emotion and a histrionic imitation of it, for he slowly turned, and, with a few slight movements of his tail, glided back under the bank. In vain did the grasshopper continue his frantic efforts to reach the shore; in vain did he occasionally become exhausted, and sink a short distance below the surface; in vain did he do everything that he knew, to show that he appreciated what a juicy and delicious morsel he was, and how he feared that the trout might yet be tempted to seize him; the fish did not come out again.

Then I withdrew my line, and moved back from the stream. I now determined to try Mr. Trout with a fly, and I took out the paper old Peter Gruse had given me. I did not know exactly what kind of winged insects were in order at this time of the year, but I was sure that yellow butterflies were not particular about just what month it was, so long as the sun shone warmly. I therefore chose that one of Peter's flies which was made of the yellowest feathers, and removing the snood and hook from my line, I hastily attached this fly, which was provided with a hook quite suitable for my desired prize. Crouching on the grass, I again approached the brook. Gaily flitting above the glassy surface of the water, in all the fancied security of tender youth and innocence, came my yellow fly. Backward and forward over the water he gracefully flew, sometimes rising a little into the air, as if to view the varied scenery of the woods and mountains, and then settling for a moment close to the surface, better to inspect his glittering image as it came up from below, and showing in his every movement his intense enjoyment of summertime and life.

Out from his dark retreat now came the trout; and settling quietly at the bottom of the brook, he appeared to regard the venturesome insect with a certain interest. But he must have detected the iron barb of vice beneath the mask of blitheful innocence, for, after a short deliberation, the trout turned and disappeared under the bank. As he slowly moved away, he seemed to be bigger than ever. I must catch that fish! Surely he would bite at something. It was quite evident that his mind was not wholly unsusceptible to emotions emanating from an awakening appetite, and I believed that if he saw exactly what he wanted, he would not neglect an opportunity of availing himself of it. But what did he want? I must certainly find out. Drawing myself back again, I took off the yellow fly, and put on another. This was a white one, with black blotches, like a big miller moth which had fallen into an ink-pot. It was certainly a conspicuous creature, and as I crept forward and sent it swooping over the stream, I could not see how any trout, with a single insectivorous tooth in his head, could fail to rise to such an occasion. But this trout did not rise. He would not even come out from under his bank to look at the swiftly flitting creature. He probably could see it well enough from where he was.

But I was not to be discouraged. I put on another fly; a green one with a red tail. It did not look like any insect that I had ever seen, but I thought that the trout might know more about such things than I. He did not come out to look at it, but probably considering it a product of that modern æstheticism which sacrifices natural beauty to mediæval crudeness of colour and form, he returned without evincing any disposition to countenance this style of art.

It was evident that it would be useless to put on any other flies, for the two I had left were a good deal bedraggled, and not nearly so attractive as those I had used. Just before leaving the house that morning Peter's son had given me a wooden matchbox filled with worms for bait, which, altogether I did not expect to need, I put in my pocket. As a last resort I determined to try the trout with a worm. I selected the plumpest and most comely of the lot; I put a new hook on my line; I looped him about it in graceful coils, and cautiously approached the water, as before. Now a worm never attempts to leap wildly across a flowing brook, nor does he flit in thoughtless innocence through the sunny air, and over the bright transparent stream. If he happens to fall into the water, he sinks to the bottom; and if he be of a kind not subject to drowning, he generally endeavours to secrete himself under a stone, or to burrow in the soft mud. With this knowledge of his nature I gently dropped my worm upon the surface of the stream, and then allowed him to sink slowly. Out sailed the trout from under the bank, but stopped before reaching the sinking worm. There was a certain something in his action which seemed to indicate a disgust at the sight of such plebeian food, and a fear seized me that he might now swim off, and pay no further attention to my varied baits. Suddenly there was a ripple in the water, and I felt a pull on the line. Instantly I struck; and then there was a tug. My blood boiled through every vein and artery, and I sprang to my feet. I did not give him the butt: I did not let him run with yards of line down the brook; nor reel him in, and let him make another mad course upstream: I did not turn him over as he jumped into the air; nor endeavour, in any way, to show him that I understood those tricks, which his depraved nature prompted him to play upon the angler. With an absolute dependence upon the strength of old Peter's tackle, I lifted the fish. Out he came from the water, which held him with a gentle suction as if unwilling to let him go, and then he whirled through the air like a meteor flecked with rosy fire, and landed on the fresh green grass a dozen feet behind me. Down on my knees I dropped before him as he tossed and rolled, his beautiful spots and colours glistening in the sun. He was truly a splendid trout, fully a foot long, round and heavy. Carefully seizing him, I easily removed the hook from the bony roof of his capacious mouth thickly set with sparkling teeth, and then I tenderly killed him, with all his pluck, as old Peter would have said, still in him.

I covered the rest of the fish in my basket with wet plantain leaves, and laid my trout-king on this cool green bed. Then I hurried off to the old man, whom I saw coming out of the woods. When I opened my basket and showed him what I had caught, Peter looked surprised, and, taking up the trout, examined it.

"Why, this is a big fellow," he said. "At first I thought it was Barney Sloat's boss trout, but it isn't long enough for him. Barney showed me his trout, that gen'rally keeps in a deep pool, where a tree has fallen over the stream down there. Barney tells me he often sees him, and he's been tryin' fur two years to ketch him, but he never has, and I say he never will, fur them big trout's got too much sense to fool round any kind of victuals that's got a string to it. They let a little fish eat all he wants, and then they eat him. How did you ketch this one?"

I gave an account of the manner of the capture, to which Peter listened with interest and approval.

"If you'd a stood off and made a cast at that feller, you'd either have caught him at the first flip, which isn't likely, as he didn't seem to want no feather-flies, or else you'd a skeered him away. That's all well enough in the tumblin' water, where you gen'rally go fur trout, but the man that's got the true feelin' fur

fish will try to suit his idees to theyrn, and if he keeps on doin'
that, he's like to learn a thing or two that may do him good.
That's a fine fish, and you ketched him well. I've got a lot of 'em,
but nothin' of that heft."

After luncheon we fished for an hour or two, with no result
worth recording, and then we started for home.

When we reached the farm the old man went into the barn,
and I took the fish into the house. I found the two pretty
daughters in the large room, where the eating and some of the
cooking was done. I opened my basket, and with great pride
showed them the big trout I had caught. They evidently thought
it was a large fish, but they looked at each other, and smiled in
a way that I did not understand. I had expected from them, at
least, as much admiration for my prize and my skill as their
father had shown.

"You don't seem to think much of this fine trout that I took
such trouble to catch," I remarked.

"You mean," said the elder girl, with a laugh, "that you bought
of Barney Sloat."

I looked at her in astonishment.

"Barney was along here to-day," she said, "and he told about
your buying your fish of him."

"Bought of him!" I exclaimed indignantly. "A little string of
fish at the bottom of the basket. I bought of him, but all the
others, and this big one, I caught myself."

"Oh, of course," said the pretty daughter, "bought the little
ones and caught all the big ones."

"Barney Sloat ought to have kept his mouth shut," said the
younger pretty daughter, looking at me with an expression of
pity. "He'd got his money, and he hadn't no business to go telling
on people. Nobody likes that sort of thing. But this big fish is a
real nice one, and you shall have it for your supper."

"Thank you," I said, with dignity, and left the room.

I did not intend to have any further words with these young

women on this subject, but I cannot deny that I was annoyed and mortified. This was the result of a charitable action. I think I was never more proud of anything than of catching that trout; and it was a very considerable downfall suddenly to find myself regarded as a mere city man fishing with a silver hook. But, after all, what did it matter? But the more I said this to myself, the more was I impressed with the fact that it mattered a great deal.

The boy who did not seem to be accounted a member of the family came into the house, and as he passed me he smiled good-humouredly, and said: "Buyed 'em!"

I felt like throwing a chair at him, but refrained out of respect to my host. Before supper the old man came out on to the porch where I was sitting. "It seems," said he, "that my gals has got it inter their heads that you bought that big fish of Barney Sloat, and as I can't say I seed you ketch it, they're not willin' to give in, 'specially as I didn't git no such big one. 'Tain't wise to buy fish when you're goin' fishin' yourself. It's pretty certain to tell agen you."

"You ought to have given me that advice before," I said, somewhat shortly. "You saw me buy the fish."

"You don't s'pose," said old Peter, "that I'm goin' to say anythin' to keep money out of my neighbour's pockets. We don't do that way in these parts. But I've told the gals they're not to speak another word about it, so you needn't give your mind no worry on that score. And now let's go in to supper. If you're as hungry as I am, there won't be many of them fish left fur breakfast."

For two days longer I remained in this neighbourhood, wandering alone over the hills, and up the mountainsides, and by the brooks, which tumbled and gurgled through the lonely forest. Each evening I brought home a goodly supply of trout, but never a great one like the noble fellow for which I angled in the meadow stream.

On the morning of my departure I stood on the porch with old

Peter waiting for the arrival of the mail driver, who was to take me to the nearest railroad town.

"I don't want to say nothin'," remarked the old man, "that would keep them fellers with the jinted poles from stoppin' at my house when they comes to these parts a-fishin'. I ain't got no objections to their poles; 'taint that. And I don't mind nuther their standin' off, and throwin' their flies as fur as they've a mind to; that's not it. And it ain't even the way they have of worryin' their fish. I wouldn't do it myself, but if they like it, that's their business. But what does rile me is the cheeky way in which they stand up and say that there isn't no decent way of fishin' but their way. And that to a man that's ketched more fish, of more different kinds, with more game in 'em, and had more fun at it, with a lot less money and less tom-foolin' than any fishin' feller that ever come here and talked to me like an old cat tryin' to teach a dog to ketch rabbits. No, sir; agen I say that I don't take no money fur entertainin' the only man that ever come out here to go a-fishin' in a plain, Christian way. But if you feel tetchy about not payin' nothin', you kin send me one of them poles in three pieces, a good, strong one, that'll lift Barney Sloat's trout, if ever I hook him."

I sent him the rod; and next summer I am going up to see him use it.

Little Rivers

~~~~~~~~~~~~~~~~~~~~

Henry Van Dyke

A RIVER IS the most human and companionable of all inanimate things. It has a life, a character, a voice of its own, and is as full of good fellowship as a sugar-maple is of sap. It can talk in various tones, loud or low, and of many subjects, grave and gay. Under favourable circumstances it will even make a shift to sing, not in a fashion that can be reduced to notes and set down in black and white on a sheet of paper, but in a vague, refreshing manner, and to a wandering air that goes

"Over the hills and far away."

For real company and friendship, there is nothing outside of the animal kingdom that is comparable to a river.

I will admit that a very good case can be made out in favour of some other objects of natural affection. For example, a fair apology has been offered by those ambitious persons who have fallen in love with the sea. But, after all, that is a formless and disquieting passion. It lacks solid comfort and mutual confi-

dence. The sea is too big for loving, and too uncertain. It will not
fit into our thoughts. It has no personality because it has so
many. It is a salt abstraction. You might as well think of loving a
glittering generality like "the American woman." One would be
more to the purpose.

Mountains are more satisfying because they are more individual. It is possible to feel a very strong attachment for a certain
range whose outline has grown familiar to our eyes, or a clear
peak that has looked down, day after day, upon our joys and
sorrows, moderating our passions with its calm aspect. We come
back from our travels, and the sight of such a well-known
mountain is like meeting an old friend unchanged. But it is a
one-sided affection. The mountain is voiceless and imperturb-
able: and its very loftiness and serenity sometimes make us the
more lonely.

Trees seem to come closer to our life. They are often rooted in
our richest feelings, and our sweetest memories, like birds, build
nests in their branches. I remember, the last time that I saw
James Russell Lowell (only a few weeks before his musical voice
was hushed), he walked out with me into the quiet garden at
Elmwood to say good-bye. There was a great horse-chestnut tree
beside the house, towering above the gable, and covered with
blossoms from base to summit—a pyramid of green supporting
a thousand smaller pyramids of white. The poet looked up at it
with his gray, pain-furrowed face, and laid his trembling hand
upon the trunk. "I planted the nut," said he, "from which this
tree grew. And my father was with me and showed me how to
plant it."

Yes, there is a good deal to be said in behalf of tree-worship;
and when I recline with my friend Tityrus beneath the shade of
his favourite oak, I consent in his devotions. But when I invite
him with me to share my orisons, or wander alone to indulge
the luxury of grateful, unlaborious thought, my feet turn not to
a tree, but to the bank of a river, for there the musings of solitude

find a friendly accompaniment, and human intercourse is puri-
fied and sweetened by the flowing, murmuring water. It is by a
river that I would choose to make love, and to revive old
friendships, and to play with the children, and to confess my
faults, and to escape from vain, selfish desires, and to cleanse my
mind from all the false and foolish things that mar the joy and
peace of living. Like David's hart, I pant for the water-brooks,
and would follow the advice of Seneca, who says, "Where a
spring rises, or a river flows, there should we build altars and
offer sacrifices."

The personality of a river is not to be found in its water, nor in
its shore. Either of these elements, by itself, would be nothing.
Confine the fluid contents of the noblest stream in a walled
channel of stone, and it ceases to be a stream; it becomes what
Charles Lamb calls "a mockery of a river—a liquid artifice—a
wretched conduit." But take away the water from the most
beautiful river-banks, and what is left? An ugly road with none
to travel it; a long, ghastly scar on the bosom of the earth.

The life of a river, like that of a human being, consists in the
union of soul and body, the water and the banks. They belong
together. They act and react upon each other. The stream
moulds and makes the shore; hollowing out a bay here, and
building a long point there; alluring the little bushes close to its
side, and bending the tall slim trees over its current; sweeping a
rocky ledge clean of everything but moss, and sending a still
lagoon full of white arrow-heads and rosy knotweed far back
into the meadow. The shore guides and controls the stream; now
detaining and now advancing it; now bending it in a hundred
sinuous curves, and now speeding it straight as a wild-bee on its
homeward flight; here hiding the water in a deep cleft overhung
with green branches, and there spreading it out, like a mirror
framed in daisies, to reflect the sky and the clouds; sometimes
breaking it with sudden turns and unexpected falls into a form

of musical laughter, sometimes soothing it into a sleepy motion like the flow of a dream.

And is it otherwise with the men and women whom we know and like? Does not the spirit influence the form, and the form affect the spirit? Can we divide and separate them in our affections?

I am no friend to purely psychological attachments. In some unknown future they may be satisfying, but in the present I want your words and your voice with your thoughts, your looks, and your gestures to interpret your feelings. The warm, strong grasp of Greatheart's hand is as dear to me as the steadfast fashion of his friendships; the lively, sparkling eyes of the master of Rudder Grange charm me as much as the nimbleness of his fancy; and the firm poise of the Hoosier Schoolmaster's shaggy head gives me new confidence in the solidity of his views of life. I like the pure tranquillity of Isabel's brow as well as her

> "most silver flow
> Of subtle-paced counsel in distress."

The soft cadences and turns in my lady Katrina's speech draw me into the humour of her gentle judgments of men and things. The touches of quaintness in Angelica's dress, her folded kerchief and smooth-parted hair, seem to partake of herself, and enhance my admiration for the sweet order of her thoughts and her old-fashioned ideals of love and duty. Even so the stream and its channel are one life. I cannot think of the swift, brown flood of the Batiscan without its shadowing primeval forests, or the crystalline current of the Boquet without its beds of pebbles and golden sand and grassy banks embroidered with flowers.

Every country—or at least every country that is fit for habitation—has its own rivers; and every river has its own quality; and it is the part of wisdom to know and love as many as you can, seeing each in the fairest possible light, and receiving

from each the best that it has to give. The torrents of Norway
leap down from their mountain homes with plentiful cataracts,
and run brief but glorious races to the sea. The streams of
England move smoothly through green fields and beside ancient, sleepy towns. The Scotch rivers brawl through the open
moorland and flash along steep Highland glens. The rivers of the
Alps are born in icy caves, from which they issue forth with
furious, turbid waters; but when their anger has been forgotten
in the slumber of some blue lake, they flow down more softly to
see the vineyards of France and Italy, the gray castles of
Germany, and the verdant meadows of Holland. The mighty
rivers of the West roll their yellow floods through broad valleys,
or plunge down dark canons. The rivers of the South creep
under dim arboreal archways heavy with banners of waving
moss. The Delaware and the Hudson and the Connecticut are
the children of the Catskills and the Adirondacks and the White
Mountains, cradled among the forests of spruce and hemlock,
playing through a wild woodland youth, gathering strength
from numberless tributaries to bear their great burdens of
lumber and turn the wheels of many mills, issuing from the hills
to water a thousand farms, and descending at last, beside new
cities, to the ancient sea.

Every river that flows is good, and has something worthy to be
loved. But those that we love most are always the ones that we
have known best,—the stream that ran before our father's door,
the current on which we ventured our first boat or cast our first
fly, the brook on whose banks we first picked the twinflower of
young love. However far we may travel, we come back to
Naaman's state of mind: "Are not Abana and Pharpat, rivers of
Damascus, better than all the waters of Israel?"

It is with rivers as it is with people: the greatest are not always
the most agreeable, nor the best to live with. Diogenes must have
been an uncomfortable bedfellow; Antinoüs was bored to death
in the society of the Emperor Hadrian; and you can imagine

much better company for a walking trip than Napoleon Bonaparte. Semiramis was a lofty queen, but I fancy that Ninus had more than one bad quarter-of-an-hour with her: and in "the spacious times of great Elizabeth" there was many a milkmaid whom the wise man would have chosen for his friend, before the royal red-haired virgin. "I confess," says the poet Cowley, "I love Littleness almost in all things. A little convenient Estate, a little chearful House, a little Company, and a very little Feast, and if I were ever to fall in Love again (which is a great Passion, and therefore, I hope, I have done with it,) it would be, I think, with Prettiness, rather than with Majestical Beauty. I would neither wish that my Mistress, nor my Fortune, should be a *Bona Roba*, as *Homer* uses to describe his Beauties, like a daughter of great *Jupiter* for the stateliness and largeness of her Person, but as *Lucretius* says:

'*Parvula, pumilio,* Χαριτων μια, *tota merum sal.*'"

Now in talking about women it is prudent to disguise a prejudice like this, in the security of a dead language, and to entrench it behind a fortress of reputable authority. But in lowlier and less dangerous matters, such as we are now concerned with, one may dare to speak in plain English. I am all for the little rivers. Let those who will, chant in heroic verse the renown of Amazon and Mississippi and Niagara; but my prose shall flow—or straggle along at such a pace as the prosaic muse may grant me to attain—in praise of Beaver-kill and Neversink and Swiftwater, of Saranac and Raquette and Ausable, of Allegash and Aroostook and Moose River. "Whene'er I take my walks abroad," it shall be to trace the clear Rauma from its rise on the *fjeld* to its rest in the *fjord*; or to follow the Ericht and the Halladale through the heather. The Ziller and the Salzach shall be my guides through the Tyrol; the Rotha and the Dove shall lead me into the heart of England. My sacrificial flames shall be kindled with birchbark along the wooded still-waters of the Penobscot and the Peribonca, and my libations drawn from the pure current of the Ristigouche and the Ampersand, and my altar of remembrance shall rise upon the rocks beside the falls of Seboomok.

I will set my affections upon rivers that are not too great for intimacy. And if by chance any of these little ones have also become famous, like the Tweed and the Thames and the Arno, I at least will praise them, because they are still at heart little rivers.

If an open fire is, as Charles Dudley Warner says, the eye of a room; then surely a little river may be called the mouth, the most expressive feature, of a landscape. It animates and enlivens the whole scene. Even a railway journey becomes tolerable when the track follows the course of a running stream.

What charming glimpses you catch from the window as the train winds along the valley of the French Broad from Asheville, or climbs the southern Catskills beside the Æsopus, or slides down the Pusterthal with the Rienz, or follows the Glommen and the Gula from Christiania to Throndhjem.

Here is a mill with its dripping, lazy wheel, the type of somnolent industry; and there is a white cascade, foaming in silent pantomime as the train clatters by; and here is a long, still pool with the cows standing knee-deep in the water and swinging their tails in calm indifference to the passing world; and there is a lone fisherman sitting upon a rock, rapt in contemplation of the point of his rod. For a moment you become the partner of his tranquil enterprise. You turn around, you crane your neck to get the last sight of his motionless angle. You do not know what kind of fish he expects to catch, nor what species of bait he is using, but none the less do you pray that he may have a bite before the train swings around the next curve. And if perchance your wish is granted, and you see him gravely draw some unknown, reluctant, shining reward of patience from the water, you feel like swinging your hat from the window and crying out, "Good luck!"

Little rivers seem to have the indefinable quality that belongs to certain people in the world,—the power of drawing attention without courting it, the faculty of exciting interest by their very presence and way of doing things.

The most fascinating part of a city or town is that through which the water flows. Idlers always choose a bridge for their place of meditation when they can get it; and, failing that, you will find them sitting on the edge of a quay or embankment, with their feet hanging over the water. What a piquant mingling of indolence and vivacity you can enjoy by the river-side! The best point of view in Rome, to my taste, is the Ponte San Angelo; and in Florence or Pisa I never tire of loafing along the Lung' Arno. You do not know London until you have seen it from the Thames. And you will miss the charm of Cambridge unless you take a little boat and go drifting on the placid Cam, beneath the bending trees, along the backs of the colleges.

But the real way to know a little river is not to glance at it here or there in the course of a hasty journey, nor to become acquainted with it after it has been partly civilized and partly spoiled by too close contact with the works of man. You must go to its native haunts; you must see it in youth and freedom; you must accommodate yourself to its pace, and give yourself to its influence, and follow its meanderings whithersoever they may lead you.

Now, of this pleasant pastime there are three principal forms. You may go as a walker, taking the river-side path, or making a way for yourself through the tangled thickets or across the open meadows. You may go as a sailor, launching your light canoe on the swift current and committing yourself for a day, or a week, or a month, to the delightful uncertainties of a voyage through the forest. You may go as a wader, stepping into the stream and going down with it all day long, through rapids and shallows and deeper pools, until you come to the end of your courage and the daylight. Of these three ways I know not which is best. But in all of them the essential thing is that you must be willing and glad to be led; you must take the little river for your guide, philosopher, and friend.

And what a good guidance it gives you! How cheerfully it lures you on into the secrets of field and wood, and brings you acquainted with the birds and the flowers. The stream can show you, better than any other teacher, how Nature works her enchantments with colour and music.

Go out to the Beaverkill

"In the tassel-time of spring,"

and follow its brimming waters through the budding forests, to that corner which we call the Painter's Camp. See how the banks are all enamelled with the pale hepatica, the painted trillium, and the delicate pink-veined spring beauty. A little later in the year, when the ferns are uncurling their long fronds, the troops of blue and white violets will come dancing down to the edge of the stream, and creep venturously out to the very end of that long, moss-covered log in the water. Before these have vanished, the yellow crowfoot and the cinquefoil will appear, followed by the stargrass and the loose-strife and the golden St.-John's-wort. Then the unseen painter will begin to mix the royal colour on his palette, and the red of the bee-balm will catch your eye. If you are lucky, you may find in midsummer the slender, fragrant spikes of the purple-fringed orchis, and you cannot help finding the somewhat slatternly blue blossoms of the universal self-heal. A little later, yellow returns in the drooping flowers of the jewel-weed, and blue repeats itself in the trembling hare-bells, and scarlet is glorified in the flaming robe of the cardinal-flower. Later still, the summer closes in a splendour of bloom, with gentians and asters and goldenrod.

You never get so close to the birds as when you are wading quietly down a little river, casting your fly deftly under the branches for the wary trout, but ever on the lookout for all the various pleasant things that nature has to bestow upon you. Here you shall come upon the catbird at her morning bath, and hear her sing, in a clump of pussy-willows, that low, tender, confidential song which she keeps for the hours of domestic intimacy. The spotted sandpiper will run along the stones before you, crying, "*Wet-feet, wet-feet!*" and bowing and teetering in the friendliest manner, as if to show you the way to the best pools. In the thick branches of the hemlocks that stretch across the stream, the tiny warblers, dressed in their coats of many colours, chirp and twitter confidingly above your head; and the Maryland yellow-throat, flitting through the bushes like a little gleam of sunlight, calls, "*Witchery, witchery, witchery!*" That plaintive, forsaken, persistent note, never ceasing, even in the noonday silence, comes from the wood-pewee, drooping upon the bough of some high tree, and complaining, like Mariana in the moated grange, "*Weary, weary, wé-a-ry.*"

When the stream runs out into the old clearing, or down through the pasture, you find other and livelier birds,—the robin, with his sharp, saucy call and breathless, merry warble; the bluebird, with his notes of pure gladness, and the oriole, with his wild, flexible whistle; the chewink, bustling about in the thicket, talking to his sweetheart in French, "*Chérie, chérie!*" and the song-sparrow, perched on his favourite limb of a young maple, close beside the water, and singing happily, through sunshine and through rain. This is the true bird of the brook, after all, the winged spirit of cheerfulness and contentment, the patron saint of little rivers, the fisherman's friend. He seems to enter into your sport with his good wishes, and for an hour at a time, while you are trying every fly in your book, from a black gnat to a white miller, to entice the crafty old trout at the foot of the meadow-pool, the song-sparrow, close above you, will be chanting patience and encouragement. And when at last success crowns your endeavour, and the parti-coloured prize is glittering in your net, the bird on the bough breaks out in an ecstasy of congratulation: *"Catch 'im, catch 'im, catch 'im; oh, what a pretty fellow! sweet!"*

There are other birds that seem to have a very different temper. The blue-jay sits high up in the withered pine-tree, bobbing up and down, and calling to his mate in a tone of affected sweetness, *"Salúte-her, salúte-her,"* but when you come in sight he flies away with a harsh cry of *"Thief, thief, thief!"* The kingfisher, ruffling his crest in solitary pride on the end of a dead branch, darts down the stream at your approach, winding up his reel angrily, as if he despised you for interrupting his fishing. And the catbird, that sang so charmingly while she thought herself unobserved, now tries to scare you away by screaming *"Snake, snake!"*

As evening draws near, and the light beneath the trees grows yellower, and the air is full of filmy insects out for their last dance, the voice of the little river becomes louder and more distinct. The true poets have often noticed this apparent increase in the sound of flowing waters at nightfall. Gray, in one of his letters, speaks of "hearing the murmur of many waters not audible in the daytime." Wordsworth repeats the same thought almost in the same words:

> "A soft and lulling sound is heard
> Of streams inaudible by day."

And Tennyson, in the valley of Cauteretz, tells of the river

> "Deepening his voice with deepening of the night."

It is in this mystical hour that you will hear the most celestial and entrancing of all bird-notes, the songs of the thrushes,—the hermit, and the wood-thrush, and the veery. Sometimes, but not often, you will see the singers. I remember once, at the close of a beautiful day's fishing on the Swiftwater, I came out just after sunset into a little open space in an elbow of the stream. It was still early spring, and the leaves were tiny. On the top of a small sumac, not thirty feet away from me, sat a veery. I could see the pointed spots upon his breast, the swelling of his white throat, and the sparkle of his eyes, as he poured his whole heart into a long liquid chant, the clear notes rising and falling, echoing and interlacing in endless curves of sound,

"Orb within orb, intricate, wonderful."

Other bird-songs can be translated into words, but not this. There is no interpretation. It is music,—as Sidney Lanier defines it,—

"Love in search of a word."

But it is not only to the real life of birds and flowers that the little rivers introduce you. They lead you often into familiarity with human nature in undress, rejoicing in the liberty of old clothes, or of none at all. People do not mince along the banks of streams in patent-leather shoes or crepitating silks. Corduroy and homespun and flannel are the stuffs that suit this region; and the frequenters of these paths go their natural gaits, in cow-hide or rubber boots, or bare footed. The girdle of conventionality is laid aside, and the skirts with the spirits.

A stream that flows through a country of upland farms will show you many a pretty bit of *genre* painting. Here is the laundry-pool at the foot of the kitchen garden, and the tubs are set upon a few planks close to the water, and the farmer's daughters, with bare arms and gowns tucked up, are wringing out the clothes. Do you remember what happened to Ralph

Peden, in *The Lilac Sunbonnet*, when he came on a scene like this? He tumbled at once into love with Winsome Charteris,—and far over his head.

And what a pleasant thing it is to see a little country lad riding one of the plough-horses to water, thumping his naked heels against the ribs of his stolid steed, and pulling hard on the halter as if it were the bridle of Bucephalus! Or perhaps it is a riotous company of boys that have come down to the old swimming-hole, and are now splashing and gambolling through the water like a drove of white seals very much sunburned. You had hoped to catch a goodly trout in that hole, but what of that? The sight of a harmless hour of mirth is better than a fish, any day.

Sometimes you overtake another fisherman on the stream. It may be one of those fabulous countrymen, with long cedar poles and bed-cord lines; who are commonly reported to catch such enormous strings of fish, but who rarely, so far as my observation goes, do anything more than fill their pockets with fingerlings. The trained angler, who uses the finest tackle, and drops his fly on the water as accurately as Henry James places a word in a story, is the man who takes the most and the largest fish in the long run. Perhaps the fisherman ahead of you is such an one,—a man whom you have known in town as a lawyer or a doctor, a merchant or a preacher, going about his business in the hideous respectability of a high silk hat and a long black coat. How good it is to see him now in the freedom of a flannel shirt and a broad-brimmed gray felt with flies stuck around the band!

In Professor John Wilson's *Essays Critical and Imaginative*, there is a brilliant description of a bishop fishing, which I am sure is neither imaginative nor critical, but realistic and appreciative. "Thus a bishop, sans wig and petticoat, in a hairy cap, black jacket, corduroy breeches and leathern leggins, creel on back and rod in hand, sallying from his palace, impatient to reach a famous salmon-cast ere the sun leave his cloud, . . . appears not only a pillar of his church, but of his kind, and in such a costume is manifestly on the high road to Canterbury and the Kingdom-Come." I have had the good luck to see quite a number of bishops, parochial and diocesan, in that style, and the vision has always dissolved my doubts in regard to the validity of their claims to the true apostolic succession.

Men's "little ways" are usually more interesting, and often more instructive, than their grand manners. When they are off guard, they frequently show to better advantage than when they are on parade. I get more pleasure out of Boswell's *Johnson* than I do out of *Rasselas* or *The Rambler*. The *Little Flowers of St. Francis* appear to me far more precious than the most learned German and French analyses of his character. There is a passage in Jonathan Edwards's *Personal Narrative*, about a certain walk that he took in the fields near his father's house, and the blossoming of the flowers in the spring, which I would not exchange for the whole of his dissertation *On the Freedom of the Will*. And the very best thing of Charles Darwin's that I know is a bit from a letter to his wife: "At last I fell asleep," says he, "on the grass, and awoke with a chorus of birds singing around me, and squirrels running up the tree, and some woodpeckers laughing; and it was as pleasant and rural a scene as ever I saw; and I did not care one penny how any of the birds or beasts had been formed."

Little rivers have small responsibilities. They are not expected to bear huge navies on their breast or supply a hundred thousand horse-power to the factories of a monstrous town. Neither do you come to them hoping to draw out Leviathan with a hook. It is enough if they run a harmless, amiable course, and keep the groves and fields green and fresh along their banks, and offer a happy alteration of nimble rapids and quiet pools,

> "With here and there a lusty trout,
> And here and there a grayling."

When you set out to explore one of these minor streams in your canoe, you have no intention of epoch-making discoveries, or thrilling and world-famous adventures. You float placidly down the long still-waters, and make your way patiently through the tangle of fallen trees that block the stream, and run the smaller falls, and carry your boat around the larger ones, with no loftier ambition than to reach a good camp-ground before dark and to pass the intervening hours pleasantly, "without offence to God or man." It is an agreeable and advantageous frame of mind for one who has done his fair share of work in the world, and is not inclined to grumble at his wages. There are few moods in which we are more susceptible of gentle instruction; and I suspect there are many tempers and attitudes, often called virtuous, in which the human spirit appears less tolerable in the sight of Heaven.

It is not required of every man and woman to be, or to do, something great; most of us must content ourselves with taking small parts in the chorus, as far as possible without discord. Shall we have no little lyrics because Homer and Dante have written epics? And because we have heard the great organ at Freiburg, shall the sound of Kathi's zither in the alpine hut please us no more? Even those who have greatness thrust upon them will do well to lay the burden down now and then, and congratulate themselves that they are not altogether answerable for the conduct of the universe, or at least not all the time. "I reckon," said a cow-boy to me one day, as we were riding through the Bad Lands of Dakota, "there's some one bigger than me running this outfit. He can 'tend to it well enough, while I smoke my pipe after the round-up."

There is such a thing as taking ourselves and the world too seriously, or at any rate too anxiously. Half of the secular unrest and dismal, profane sadness of modern society comes from the vain idea that every man is bound to be a critic of life, and to let no day pass without finding some fault with the general order of things, or projecting some plan for its improvement. And the other half comes from the greedy notion that a man's life does consist, after all, in the abundance of the things that he possesseth, and that it is somehow or other more respectable and pious to be always at work trying to make a larger living, than it is to lie on your back in the green pastures and beside the still-waters, and thank God that you are alive.

Come, then, my gentle reader (for by this time you see that this chapter is only a preface in disguise,—a declaration of principles or of the want of them, an apology or a defence, as you choose to take it), and if we are agreed, let us walk together; but if not, let us part here without ill will.

You shall not be deceived in this book. It is nothing but a handful of rustic variations on the old tune of "Rest and be thankful," a record of unconventional travel, a pilgrim's script with a few bits of blue-sky philosophy in it. There is, so far as I know, very little useful information and absolutely no criticism of the universe to be found in this volume. So if you are what Izaak Walton calls "a severe, sour-complexioned man," you would better carry it back to the bookseller, and get your money again, if he will give it to you, and go your way rejoicing after your own melancholy fashion.

But if you care for plain pleasures, and informal company, and friendly observations on men and things (and a few true fish-stories), then perhaps you may find something here not unworthy your perusal. And so I wish that your winter fire may burn clear and bright while you read these pages; and that the summer days may be fair, and the fish may rise merrily to your fly, whenever you follow one of these little rivers.

Crocker's Hole

~~~~~~~~~~

R. D. Blackmore

PART I

THE CULM, WHICH rises in Somersetshire, and hastening into a fairer land (as the border waters wisely do) falls into the Exe near Killerton, formerly was a lovely trout stream, such as perverts the Devonshire angler from due respect toward Father Thames and the other canals round London. In the Devonshire valleys it is sweet to see how soon a spring becomes a rill, and a rill runs on into a rivulet, and a rivulet swells into a brook; and before one has time to say, "What are you at?"—before the first tree it ever spoke to is a dummy, or the first hill it ever ran down has turned blue, here we have all the airs and graces, demands and assertions of a full-grown river.

But what is the test of a river? Who shall say? "The power to drown a man," replies the river darkly. But rudeness is not argument. Rather shall we say that the power to work a good undershot wheel, without being dammed up all night in a pond, and leaving a tidy back-stream to spare at the bottom of the orchard, is a fair certificate of riverhood. If so, many Devonshire streams attain that rank within five miles of their spring; aye, and rapidly add to it. At every turn they gather aid, from ash-clad dingle and aldered meadow, mossy rock and ferny wall, hedge-trough roofed with bramble netting, where the baby water lurks, and lanes that coming down to ford bring suicidal tribute. Arrogant, all-engrossing river, now it has claimed a great valley of its own; and whatever falls within the hill scoop, sooner or later belongs to itself. Even the crystal "shutt" that crossed the farmyard by the woodrick, and glides down an aqueduct of last year's bark for Mary to fill the kettle from; and even the tricklets that have no organs for telling or knowing their business, but only get into unwary oozings in and among the water-grass, and there make moss and forget themselves among it—one and all, they come to the same thing at last, and that is the river.

The Culm used to be a good river at Culmstock, tormented already by a factory, but not strangled as yet by a railroad. How it is now the present writer does not know, and is afraid to ask, having heard of a vile "Culm Valley Line." But Culmstock bridge was a very pretty place to stand and contemplate the ways of trout; which is easier work than to catch them. When I was just big enough to peep above the rim, or to lie upon it with one leg inside for fear of tumbling over, what a mighty river it used to seem, for it takes a treat there and spreads itself. Above the bridge the factory stream falls in again, having done its business, and washing its hands in the innocent half that has strayed down the meadows. Then under the arches they both rejoice and come to a slide of about two feet, and make a short, wide pool below, and indulge themselves in perhaps two islands, through which a little river always magnifies itself, and maintains a mysterious middle. But after that, all of it used to come together, and make off in one body for the meadows, intent upon nurturing trout with rapid stickles, and buttercuppy

corners where fat flies may tumble in. And here you may find in
the very first meadow, or at any rate you might have found,
forty years ago, the celebrated "Crocker's Hole."

The story of Crocker is unknown to me, and interesting as it
doubtless was, I do not deal with him, but with his Hole. Tradition
said that he was a baker's boy who, during his basket-rounds,
fell in love with a maiden who received the cottage-loaf, or
perhaps good "Households," for her master's use. No doubt she
was charming, as a girl should be, but whether she encouraged
the youthful baker and then betrayed him with false *rôle*, or
whether she "consisted" throughout,—as our cousins across the
water express it,—is known to their *manes* only. Enough that
she would not have the floury lad; and that he, after giving in his
books and money, sought an untimely grave among the trout.
And this was the first pool below the breadwalk deep enough to
drown a five-foot baker boy. Sad it was; but such things must be,
and bread must still be delivered daily.

A truce to such reflections,—as our foremost writers always
say, when they do not see how to go on with them,—but it is a
serious thing to know what Crocker's Hole was like; because at
a time when (if he had only persevered, and married the maid,
and succeeded to the oven, and reared a large family of
short-weight bakers) he might have been leaning on his crutch
beside the pool, and teaching his grandson to swim by precept
(that beautiful proxy for practice)—at such a time, I say, there
lived a remarkably fine trout in that hole. Anglers are notori-
ously truthful, especially as to what they catch, or even more
frequently have not caught. Though I may have written fiction,
among many other sins,—as a nice old lady told me once,—
now I have to deal with facts; and foul scorn would I count it
ever to make believe that I caught that fish. My length at that
time was not more than the butt of a four-jointed rod, and all I
could catch was a minnow with a pin, which our cook Lydia
would not cook, but used to say, "Oh, what a shame, Master

Richard! they would have been trout in the summer, please God! if you would only a' let 'em grow on." She is living now, and will bear me out in this.

But upon every great occasion there arises a great man; or to put it more accurately, in the present instance, a mighty and distinguished boy. My father, being the parson of the parish, and getting, need it be said, small pay, took sundry pupils, very pleasant fellows, about to adorn the universities. Among them was the original "Bude Light," as he was satirically called at Cambridge, for he came from Bude, and there was no light in him. Among them also was John Pike, a born Zebedee, if ever there was one.

John Pike was a thick-set younker, with a large and bushy head, keen blue eyes that could see through water, and the proper slouch of shoulder into which great anglers ripen; but great still are born with it; and of these was Master John. It mattered little what the weather was, and scarcely more as to the time of year, John Pike must have his fishing every day, and on Sundays he read about it, and made flies. All the rest of the time he was thinking about it.

My father was coaching him in the fourth book of the Æneid and all those wonderful speeches of Dido, where passion disdains construction; but the only line Pike cared for was of horsehair. "I fear, Mr. Pike, that you are not giving me your entire attention," my father used to say in his mild dry way; and once when Pike was more than usually abroad, his tutor begged to share his meditations. "Well, sir," said Pike, who was very truthful, "I can see a green drake by the strawberry tree, the first of the season, and your derivation of 'barbarous' put me in mind of my barberry dye." In those days it was a very nice point to get the right tint for the mallards's feather.

No sooner was lesson done than Pike, whose rod was ready upon the lawn, dashed away always for the river, rushing headlong down the hill, and away to the left through a private yard, where "no thoroughfare" was put up, and a big dog stationed to enforce it. But Cerberus himself could not have stopped John Pike; his conscience backed him up in trespass the most sinful when his heart was inditing of a trout upon the rise.

All this, however, is preliminary, as the boy said when he put his father's coat upon his grandfather's tenterhooks, with felonious intent upon his grandmother's apples; the main point to be understood is this, that nothing—neither brazen tower, hundred-eyed Argus, nor Cretan Minotaur—could stop John Pike from getting at a good stickle. But, even as the world knows nothing of its greatest men, its greatest men know nothing of the world beneath their very nose, till fortune sneezes dexter. For two years John Pike must have been whipping the water as hard as Xerxes, without having ever once dreamed of the glorious trout that lived in Crocker's Hole. But why, when he ought to have been at least on bowing terms with every fish as long as his middle finger, why had he failed to know this champion? The answer is simple—because of his short cuts. Flying as he did like an arrow from a bow, Pike used to hit his beloved river at an elbow, some furlong below Crocker's Hole, where a sweet little stickle sailed away down stream, whereas for the length of a meadow upward the water lay smooth, clear, and shallow; therefore the youth, with so little time to spare, rushed into the downward joy.

And here it may be noted that the leading maxim of the present period, that man can discharge his duty only by going counter to the stream, was scarcely mooted in those days. My grandfather (who was a wonderful man, if he was accustomed to fill a cart in two days of fly-fishing on the Barle) regularly fished down stream; and what more than a cartload need anyone put into his basket?

And surely it is more genial and pleasant to behold our friend the river growing and thriving as we go on, strengthening its voice and enlarging its bosom, and sparkling through each successive meadow with richer plenitude of silver, than to trace it against its own grain and good-will toward weakness, and littleness, and immature conceptions.

However, you will say that if John Pike had fished up stream, he would have found this trout much sooner. And that is true; but still, as it was, the trout had more time to grow into such a prize. And the way in which John found him out was this. For some days he had been tormented with a very painful tooth, which even poisoned all the joys of fishing. Therefore he resolved to have it out, and sturdily entered the shop of John Sweetland, the village blacksmith, and there paid his sixpence. Sweetland extracted the teeth of the village, whenever they required it, in the simplest and most effectual way. A piece of fine wire was fastened round the tooth, and the other end round the anvil's nose, then the sturdy blacksmith shut the lower half of his shop door, which was about breast-high with the patient outside and the anvil within; a strong push of the foot upset the anvil, and the tooth flew out like a well-thrown fly.

When John Pike had suffered this very bravely, "Ah, Master Pike," said the blacksmith, with a grin, "I reckon you won't pull out thic there big vish,"—the smithy commanded a view of the river,—"clever as you be, quite so peart as thiccy."

"What big fish?" asked the boy, with deepest interest, though his mouth was bleeding fearfully.

"Why that girt mortial of a vish as hath his hover in Crocker's Hole. Zum on 'em saith as a' must be a zammon."

Off went Pike with his handkerchief to his mouth, and after him ran Alec Bolt, one of his fellow-pupils, who had come to the shop to enjoy the extraction.

"Oh, my!" was all that Pike could utter, when by craftily posting himself he had obtained a good view of this grand fish.

"I'll lay you a crown you don't catch him!" cried Bolt, an impatient youth, who scorned angling.

"How long will you give me?" asked the wary Pike, who never made rash wagers.

"Oh! till the holidays if you like; or, if that won't do, till Michaelmas."

Now the midsummer holidays were six weeks off—boys used not to talk of "vacations" then, still less of "recesses."

"I think I'll bet you," said Pike, in his slow way, bending forward carefully, with his keen eyes on this monster; "but it would not be fair to take till Michaelmas. I'll bet you a crown that I catch him before the holidays—at least, unless some other fellow does."

PART II

The day of that most momentous interview must have been the 14th of May. Of the year I will not be so sure; for children take more note of days than of years, for which the latter have their full revenge thereafter. It must have been the 14th, because the morrow was our holiday, given upon the 15th of May, in honour of a birthday.

Now, John Pike was beyond his years wary as well as enterprising, calm as well as ardent, quite as rich in patience as in promptitude and vigour. But Alec Bolt was a headlong youth, volatile, hot, and hasty, fit only to fish the Maëlstrom, or a torrent of new lava. And the moment he had laid that wager he expected his crown piece; though time, as the lawyers phrase it, was "expressly of the essence of the contract." And now he demanded that Pike should spend the holiday in trying to catch the trout.

"I shall not go near him," that lad replied, "until I have got a new collar." No piece of personal adornment was it, without which he would not act, but rather that which now is called the fly-cast, or the gut-cast, or the trace, or what it may be. "And another thing," continued Pike; "the bet is off if you go near him, either now or at any other time, without asking my leave first, and then only going as I tell you."

"What do I want with the great slimy beggar?" the arrogant Bolt made answer. "A good rat is worth fifty of him. No fear of my going near him, Pike. You shan't get out of it that way."

Pike showed his remarkable qualities that day, by fishing exactly as he would have fished without having heard of the great Crockerite. He was up and away upon the mill-stream before breakfast; and the forenoon he devoted to his favourite course—first down the Craddock stream, a very pretty confluent of the Culm, and from its junction, down the pleasant hams, where the river winds toward Uffculme. It was my privilege to accompany this hero, as his humble Sancho; while Bolt and the faster race went up the river ratting. We were back in time to have Pike's trout (which ranged between two ounces and one-half pound) fried for the early dinner; and here it may be lawful to remark that the trout of the Culm are of the very purest excellence, by reason of the flinty bottom, at any rate in these the upper regions. For the valley is the western outlet of the Black-down range, with the Beacon hill upon the north, and Hackpen long ridge to the south; and beyond that again the Whetstone hill, upon whose western end dark port-holes scarped with white grit mark the pits. But flint is the staple of the broad Culm Valley, under good, well-pastured loam; and here are chalcedonies and agate stones.

At dinner everybody had a brace of trout—large for the larger folk, little for the little ones, with coughing and some patting on the back for bones. What of equal purport could the fierce rat-hunter show? Pike explained many points in the history of each fish, seeming to know them none the worse, and love them all the better, for being fried. We banqueted, neither a whit did soul get stinted of banquet impartial. Then the wielder of the magic rod very modestly sought leave of absence at the tea time.

"Fishing again, Mr. Pike, I suppose," my father answered pleasantly; "I used to be fond of it at your age; but never so entirely wrapped up in it as you are."

"No, sir; I am not going fishing again. I want to walk to Wellington, to get some things at Cherry's.

"Books, Mr. Pike? Ah! I am very glad of that. But I fear it can only be fly-books."

"I want a little Horace for eighteen-pence—the Cambridge one just published, to carry in my pocket—and a new hank of gut."

"Which of the two is more important? Put that into Latin, and answer it."

"Utrum pluris facio? Flaccum flocci. Viscera magni." With this vast effort Pike turned as red as any trout spot.

"After that who could refuse you?" said my father. "You always tell the truth, my boy, in Latin or in English."

Although it was a long walk, some fourteen miles to Wellington and back, I got permission to go with Pike; and as we crossed the bridge and saw the tree that overhung Crocker's Hole, I begged him to show me that mighty fish.

"Not a bit of it," he replied. "It would bring the blackguards. If the blackguards once find him out, it is all over with him."

"The blackguards are all in factory now, and I am sure they cannot see us from the windows. They won't be out till five o'clock."

With the true liberality of young England, which abides even now as large and glorious as ever, we always called the free and enlightened operatives of the period by the courteous name above set down, and it must be acknowledged that some of them deserved it, although perhaps they poached with less of science than their sons. But the cowardly murder of fish by liming the water was already prevalent.

Yielding to my request and perhaps his own desire—manfully kept in check that morning—Pike very carefully approached that pool, commanding me to sit down while he reconnoitred from the meadow upon the right bank of the stream. And the place which had so sadly quenched the fire of the poor baker's love filled my childish heart with dread and deep wonder at the cruelty of women. But as for John Pike, all he thought of was the fish and the best way to get at him.

Very likely that hole is "holed out" now, as the Yankees well express it, or at any rate changed out of knowledge. Even in my time a very heavy flood entirely altered its character; but to the eager eye of Pike it seemed pretty much as follows, and possibly it may have come to such a form again:

The river, after passing through a hurdle fence at the head of the meadow, takes a little turn or two of bright and shallow indifference, then gathers itself into a good strong slide, as if going down a slope instead of steps. The right bank is high and beetles over with yellow loam and grassy fringe; but the other side is of flinty shingle, low and bare and washed by floods. At the end of this rapid, the stream turns sharply under an ancient alder tree into a large, deep, calm repose, cool, unruffled, and sheltered from the sun by branch and leaf—and that is the hole of poor Crocker.

At the head of the pool (where the hasty current rushes in so eagerly, with noisy excitement and much ado) the quieter waters from below, having rested and enlarged themselves, come lapping up round either curve, with some recollection of their past career, the hoary experience of foam. And sidling toward the new arrival of the impulsive column, where they meet it, things go on, which no man can describe without his mouth being full of water. A "V" is formed, a fancy letter V, beyond any designer's tracery, and even beyond his imagination, a perpetually fluctuating limpid wedge, perpetually crenelled and rippled into by little ups and downs that try to make an impress, but can only glide away upon either side or sink in dimples under it. And here a gray bough of the ancient alder stretches across, like a thirsty giant's arm, and makes it a very ticklish place to throw a fly. Yet this was the very spot our John Pike must put his fly into, or lose his crown.

Because the great tenant of Crocker's Hole, who allowed no other fish to wag a fin there, and from strict monopoly had grown so fat, kept his victualing yard—if so low an expression can be used concerning him—within about a square yard of this spot. He had a sweet hover, both of rest and recreation, under the bank, in a placid antre, where the water made no noise, but tickled his belly in digestive ease. The loftier the character is of any being, the slower and more dignified his movements are. No true psychologist could have believed—as Sweetland the black-smith did, and Mr. Pook the tinman—that this trout could ever be the embodiment of Crocker. For this was the last trout in the universal world to drown himself for love; if truly any trout has done so.

"You may come now, and try to look along my back," John Pike, with a reverential whisper, said to me. "Now don't be in a hurry, young stupid; kneel down. He is not to be disturbed at his dinner, mind. You keep behind me, and look along my back; I never clapped eyes on such a whopper."

I had to kneel down in a tender reminiscence of pasture land, and gaze carefully; and not having eyes like those of our Zebedee (who offered his spine for a camera, as he crawled on all fours in front of me), it took me a long time to descry an object most distinct to all who have that special gift of piercing with their eyes the water. See what is said upon this subject in that delicious book, "The Gamekeeper at Home."

"You are no better than a muff," said Pike, and it was not in my power to deny it.

"If the sun would only leave off," I said. But the sun, who was having a very pleasant play with the sparkle of the water and the twinkle of the leaves, had no inclination to leave off yet, but kept the rippling crystal in a dance of flashing facets, and the quivering verdure in a steady flush of gold.

But suddenly a May-fly, a lucious gray-drake, richer and more delicate than canvas-back or wood-cock, with a dart and a leap and a merry zigzag, began to enjoy a little game above the stream. Rising and falling like a gnat, thrilling her gauzy wings, and arching her elegant pellucid frame, every now and then she almost dipped her three long tapering whisks into the dimples of the water.

"He sees her! He'll have her as sure as a gun!" cried Pike, with a gulp, as if he himself were "rising." "Now, can you see him, stupid?"

"Crikey, crokums!" I exclaimed, with classic elegance; "I have seen that long thing for five minutes; but I took it for a tree."

"You little"—animal quite early in the alphabet—"now don't you stir a peg, or I'll dig my elbow into you."

The great trout was stationary almost as a stone, in the middle of the "V" above described. He was gently fanning with his large clear fins, but holding his own against the current mainly by the wagging of his broad-fluked tail. As soon as my slow eyes had once defined him, he grew upon them mightily, moulding himself in the matrix of the water, as a thing put into jelly does. And I doubt whether even John Pike saw him more accurately than I did. His size was such, or seemed to be such, that I fear to say a word about it; not because language does not contain the word, but from dread of exaggeration. But his shape and colour may be reasonably told without wounding the feeling of an age whose incredulity springs from self-knowledge.

His head was truly small, his shoulders vast; the spring of his back was like a rainbow when the sun is southing; the generous sweep of his deep elastic belly, nobly pulped out with rich nurture, showed what the power of his brain must be, and seemed to undulate, time for time, with the vibrant vigilance of his large wise eyes. His latter end was consistent also. An elegant taper run of counter, coming almost to a cylinder, as a mackerel does, boldly developed with a hugeous spread to a glorious amplitude of swallow-tail. His colour was all that can well be desired, but ill-described by any poor word-palette. Enough that he seemed to tone away from olive and umber, with carmine stars, to glowing gold and soft pure silver, mantled with a subtle flush of rose and fawn and opal.

Swoop came a swallow, as we gazed, and was gone with a flick, having missed the May-fly. But the wind of his passage, or the skir of wing, struck the merry dancer down, so that he fluttered for one instant on the wave, and that instant was enough. Swift as the swallow, and more true of aim, the great trout made one dart, and a sound, deeper than a tinkle, but as silvery as a bell, rang the poor ephemerid's knell. The rapid water scarcely showed a break; but a bubble sailed down the pool, and the dark hollow echoed with the music of a rise.

"He knows how to take a fly," said Pike; "he has had too many to be tricked with mine. Have him I must; but how ever shall I do it?"

All the way to Wellington he uttered not a word, but shambled along with a mind full of care. When I ventured to look up now and then, to surmise what was going on beneath his hat, deeply-set eyes and a wrinkled forehead, relieved at long intervals by a solid shake, proved that there are meditations deeper than those of philosopher or statesman.

PART III

Surely no trout could have been misled by the artificial May-fly of that time, unless he were either a very young fish, quite new to entomology, or else one afflicted with a combination of myopy and bulimy. Even now there is room for plenty of improvement in our counterfeit presentment; but in those days the body was made with yellow mohair, ribbed with red silk and gold twist, and as thick as a fertile bumble-bee. John Pike perceived that to offer such a thing to Crocker's trout would probably consign him—even if his great stamina should overget the horror—to an uneatable death, through just and natural indignation. On the other hand, while the May-fly lasted, a trout so cultured, so highly refined, so full of light and sweetness, would never demean himself to low bait, or any coarse son of a maggot.

Meanwhile Alec Bolt allowed poor Pike no peaceful thought, no calm absorption of high mind into the world of flies, no placid period of cobblers' wax, floss-silk, turned hackles, and dubbing. For in making of flies John Pike had his special moments of inspiration, times of clearer insight into the everlasting verities, times of brighter conception and more subtle execution, tails of more elastic grace and heads of a neater and nattier expression. As a poet labours at one immortal line, compressing worlds of wisdom into the music of ten syllables, so toiled the patient Pike about the fabric of a fly comprising all the excellence that ever sprang from maggot. Yet Bolt rejoiced to jerk his elbow at the moment of sublimest art. And a swarm of flies was blighted thus.

Peaceful, therefore, and long-suffering, and full of resignation as he was, John Pike came slowly to the sad perception that arts avail not without arms. The elbow, so often jerked, at last took voluntary jerk from the shoulder, and Alec Bolt lay prostrate, with his right eye full of cobbler's wax. This put a desirable check upon his energies for a week or more, and by that time Pike had flown his fly.

When the honeymoon of spring and summer (which they are now too fashionable to celebrate in this country), the hey-day of the whole year marked by the budding of the wild rose, the start of the wheatear from its sheath, the feathering of the lesser plantain, and flowering of the meadowsweet, and, foremost for the angler's joy, the caracole of May-flies—when these things are to be seen and felt (which has not happened at all this year), then rivers should be mild and bright, skies blue and white with fleecy cloud, the west wind blowing softly, and the trout in charming appetite.

On such a day came Pike to the bank of Culm, with a loudly beating heart. A fly there is, not ignominious, or of cowdab origin, neither gross and heavy-bodied, from cradlehood of slimy stones, nor yet of menacing aspect and suggesting deeds of poison, but elegant, bland, and of sunny nature, and obviously good to eat. Him or her—why quest we which?—the shepherd of the dale, contemptuous of gender, except in his own species, has called, and as long as they two coexist will call, the "Yellow Sally." A fly that does not waste the day in giddy dances and the fervid waltz, but undergoes family incidents with decorum and discretion. He or she, as the care may be,—for the natural history of the river bank is a book to come hereafter, and of fifty men who make flies not one knows the name of the fly he is making,—in the early morning of June, or else in the second quarter of the afternoon, this Yellow Sally fares abroad, with a nice well-ordered flutter.

Despairing of the May-fly, as it still may be despaired of, Pike came down to the river with his master-piece of portraiture. The artificial Yellow Sally is generally always—as they say in Cheshire—a mile or more too yellow. On the other hand, the "Yellow Dun" conveys no idea of any Sally. But Pike had made a very decent Sally, not perfect (for he was young as well as wise), but far above any counterfeit to be had in fishing-tackle shops. How he made it, he told nobody. But if he lives now, as I hope he does, any of my readers may ask him through the G. P. O., and hope to get an answer.

It fluttered beautifully on the breeze, and in such living form, that a brother or sister Sally came up to see it, and went away sadder and wiser. Then Pike said: "Get away, you young wretch," to your humble servant who tells this tale; yet being better than his words, allowed that pious follower to lie down upon his digestive organs and with deep attention watch. There must have been great things to see, but to see them so was difficult. And if I huddle up what happened, excitement also shares the blame.

Pike had fashioned well the time and manner of this overture. He knew that the giant Crockerite was satiate now with May-flies, or began to find their flavour failing, as happens to us with asparagus, marrow-fat peas, or strawberries, when we have had a month of them. And he thought that the first Yellow Sally of the season, inferior though it were, might have the special charm of novelty. With the skill of a Zulu, he stole up through the branches over the lower pool till he came to a spot where a yard-wide opening gave just space for spring of rod. Then he saw his desirable friend at dinner, wagging his tail, as a hungry gentleman dining with the Lord Mayor agitates his coat. With one dexterous whirl, untaught by any of the many books upon the subject, John Pike laid his Yellow Sally (for he cast with one fly only) as lightly as gossamer upon the rapid, about a yard in front of the big trout's head. A moment's pause, and then, too quick for words, was the thing that happened.

A heavy plunge was followed by a fearful rush. Forgetful of current the river was ridged, as if with a plough driven under it; the strong line, though given out as fast as might be, twanged like a harp-string as it cut the wave, and then Pike stood up, like a ship dismasted, with the butt of his rod snapped below the ferrule. He had one of those foolish things, just invented, a hollow butt of hickory; and the finial ring of his spare top looked out, to ask what had happened to the rest of it. "Bad luck!" cried the fisherman; "but never mind, I shall have him next time, to a certainty."

When this great issue came to be considered, the cause of it was sadly obvious. The fish, being hooked, had made off with the rush of a shark for the bottom of the pool. A thicket of saplings below the alder tree had stopped the judicious hooker from all possibility of following; and when he strove to turn him by elastic pliance, his rod broke at the breach of pliability. "I have learned a sad lesson," said John Pike, looking sadly.

How many fellows would have given up this matter, and glorified themselves for having hooked so grand a fish, while explaining that they must have caught him, if they could have done it! But Pike only told me not to say a word about it, and began to make ready for another tug of war. He made himself a splice-rod, short and handy, of well-seasoned ash, with a stout top of bamboo, tapered so discreetly, and so balanced in its spring, that verily it formed an arc, with any pressure on it, as perfect as a leafy poplar in a stormy summer. "Now break it if you can," he said, "by any amount of rushes; I'll hook you by your jacket collar; you cut away now, and I'll land you."

This was highly skilful, and he did it many times; and whenever I was landed well, I got a lollypop, so that I was careful not to break his tackle. Moreover he made him a landing net, with a kidney-bean stick, a ring of wire, and his own best nightcap of strong cotton net. Then he got the farmer's leave, and lopped obnoxious bushes; and now the chiefest question was: what bait, and when to offer it? In spite of his sad rebuff, the spirit of John Pike had been equable. The genuine angling mind is steadfast, large, and self-supported, and to the vapid, ignominious chaff, tossed by swine upon the idle wind, it pays as much heed as a big trout does to a dance of midges. People put their fingers to their noses and said: "Master Pike, have you caught him yet?" and Pike only answered: "Wait a bit." If ever this fortitude and preseverence is to be recovered as the English Brand (the one thing that has made us what we are, and may yet redeem us from niddering shame), a degenerate age should encourage the habit of fishing and never despairing. And the brightest sign yet for our future is the increasing demand for hooks and gut.

Pike fished in a manlier age, when nobody would dream of cowering from a savage because he was clever at skulking; and when, if a big fish broke the rod, a stronger rod was made for him, according to the usage of Great Britain. And though the young angler had been defeated, he did not sit down and have a good cry over it.

About the second week in June, when the May-fly had danced its day, and died,—for the season was an early one,— and Crocker's trout had recovered from the wound to his feelings and philanthropy, there came a night of gentle rain, of pleasant tinkling upon window ledges, and a soothing pater among young leaves, and the Culm was yellow in the morning. "I mean to do it this afternoon," Pike whispered to me, as he came back panting. "When the water clears there will be a splendid time."

The lover of the rose knows well a gay voluptuous beetle, whose pleasure is to lie embedded in a fount of beauty. Deep among the incurving petals of the blushing fragrance, he loses himself in his joys sometimes, till a breezy waft reveals him. And when the sunlight breaks upon his luscious dissipation, few would have the heart to oust him, such a gem from such a setting. All his back is emerald sparkles; all his front red Indian gold, and here and there he grows white spots to save the eye from aching. Pike put his finger in and fetched him out, and offered him a little change of joys, by putting a Limerick hook through his thorax, and bringing it out between his elytra. *Cetonia aurata* liked it not, but pawed the air very naturally, and fluttered with his wings attractively.

"I meant to have tried with a fern-web," said the angler; "until I saw one of these beggars this morning. If he works like that upon the water, he will do. It was hopeless to try artificials again. What a lovely colour the water is! Only three days now to the holidays. I have run it very close. You be ready, younker."

With these words he stepped upon a branch of the alder, for

the tone of the waters allowed approach, being soft and sublus-
trous, without any mud. Also Master Pike's own tone was such
as becomes the fisherman, calm, deliberate, free from nerve, but
full of eye and muscle. He stepped upon the alder bough to get
as near as might be to the fish, for he could not cast this beetle
like a fly; it must be dropped gently and allowed to play. "You
may come and look," he said to me; "when the water is so, they
have no eyes in their tails."

The rose-beetle trod upon the water prettily, under a lively
vibration, and he looked quite as happy, and considerably more
active, than when he had been cradled in the anthers of the rose.
To the eye of a fish he was a strong individual, fighting
courageously with the current, but sure to be beaten through
lack of fins; and mercy suggested, as well as appetite, that the
proper solution was to gulp him.

"Hooked him in the gullet. He can't get off!" cried John Pike,
labouring to keep his nerves under; "every inch of tackle is as
strong as a bell-pull. Now, if I don't land him, I will never fish
again!"

Providence, which had constructed Pike, foremost of all things,
for lofty angling—disdainful of worm and even minnow—
Providence, I say, at this adjuration, pronounced that Pike must
catch that trout. Not many anglers are heaven-born; and for one to
drop off the hook halfway through his teens would be infinitely
worse than to slay the champion trout. Pike felt the force of this,
and rushing through the rushes, shouted: "I am sure to have him,
Dick! Be ready with my night-cap."

Rod in a bow, like a springle-riser; line on the hum, like the
string of Paganini; winch on the gallop, like a harpoon wheel,
Pike, the head-centre of everything, dashing through thick and
thin, and once taken overhead—for he jumped into the hole,
when he must have lost him else, but the fish too impetuously
towed him out, and made off in passion for another pool, when,
if he had only retired to his hover, the angler might have shared

the baker's fate—all these things (I tell you, for they all come up again, as if the day were yesterday) so scared me of my never very steadfast wits, that I could only holloa! But one thing I did, I kept the nightcap ready.

"He is pretty nearly spent, I do believe," said Pike; and his voice was like balm of Gilead, as we came to Farmer Anning's meadow, a quarter of a mile below Crocker's Hole. "Take it coolly, my dear boy, and we shall be safe to have him."

Never have I felt, through forty years, such tremendous responsibility. I had not the faintest notion how to use a landing net; but a mighty general directed me. "Don't let him see it; don't let him see it! Don't clap it over him; go under him, you stupid! If he makes another rush, he will get off, after all. Bring it up his tail. Well done! You have him!"

The mighty trout lay in the nightcap of Pike, which was half a fathom long, with a tassel at the end, for his mother had made it in the winter evenings. "Come and hold the rod, if you can't lift him," my master shouted, and so I did. Then, with both arms straining, and his mouth wide open, John Pike made a mighty sweep, and we both fell upon the grass and rolled, with the giant of the deep flapping heavily between us, and no power left to us, except to cry, "Hurrah!"

Spare the Rod

Philip Wylie

THE EYES OF Dexter Heath were the most remarkable feature in a rather dashing ensemble—gray eyes, round, penetrating and vigilant. Next was his hair, which was dark and curly, but curly without pattern, and incredibly unkempt; his hair was like a distant view of some irregular object foundering in a stormy sea. The rest of him was normal for a boy of eleven—snub nose, a voice that was invariably an exclamation, although sometimes hushed, and, under his sun-tanned skin, young muscles of which he was proud to the point of racy braggadocio.

On a late summer afternoon, Crunch Adams, coming down the Gulf Stream Dock to minister to his fishing cruiser, was struck by the posture and attitude of Dexter. Balanced on a rail at the end of the dock, with his chin in his hand, the young man was staring ferociously at the universe, not seeing it, but not liking it, either. Crunch pondered the spectacle of fury in equilibrium for a moment, and then, with a grin, interrupted it.

"What's eating you, Dexter?"

The young man budged a little, put down a tentative foot, and looked at the captain. All traces of wrath had been erased by those slight movements. He seemed calm—even bored. "Nothing," he replied. "Nothing."

Crunch persisted. "Don't kid me. If there had been a nail between your teeth, you'd have ground it to filings."

"I was just thinkin'," Dexter responded lazily. And, indeed, he began thinking. Hard. His broken reverie was not a subject he could discuss. There had been sadness in it, and frenzy at the injustice of the world. His mind had been clamorous with ideas which were antisocial, hostile, and, even, illegal. Dexter did not wish to have any of his secret thoughts heckled out of him. It was therefore necessary to dissemble. Earlier in the afternoon he had indulged in a different sort of daydream. He recalled it and drew on it for material: "I was just thinkin' what if a brontosorassus came steamin' up the bay."

"A what?"

"Brontosorassus. Swimmin' like a submarine! Neck out. Fangs drippin' ooze! You couldn't hang him on any fifty-four-thread. But maybe you could hold him on three-hundred-thread. With a fifty-ought reel. You'd have to fight him night and day—for maybe a couple of weeks!"

"Oh," said Crunch. "A dinosaur." He was still grinning, but he fell in with Dexter's mood. He felt that he now understood the savagery which had been on the young man's face. "I guess you could never hang one. And you certainly couldn't boat an eighty-footer in a forty-foot cruiser."

"You could beach him," Dexter said, pleased at this attention from a great man and yielding his inner sorrow to imagination. "Maybe, if they were still plentiful, you'd have to keep a swassy-cans on the dock."

"Swassy-cans?"

"That's French," said the boy with some small condescension. "My father taught it to me. My father knows most languages, I guess. It's the French word for a seventy-five. A gun. You could have one right here—if you put some cement posts under the dock. Then—Wham! Whang! Zowie! Boy! You'd have to mount her like a antiaircraft gun, too, in case any of those big old peterodackles flew by. Wham! Whacko! Blow a wing off one and steam out and polish her off with a lance! Wham! Boom!"

Crunch chuckled. "Guess you're right. Too bad we didn't live in those days. There'd have been some real fishing, hunh?"

"Fishin'," said Dexter, "and huntin'!"

"Like to wet a line now? I mean—I've got a hand line on the *Poseidon*. And some bait. I'd be glad to rig it for you."

Dexter was grateful, but negative. "No, thanks. I don't care much for this old hand-line stuff. But if I ever had a harpoon in any big old brontosorassus . . ."

Crunch nodded and stepped aboard his boat. He had no precise recollection of his own age of dinosaur hunting, but he felt an indefinite kindredship for it. "Maybe," he said as he picked up a square of sandpaper and tore it into suitable sizes, "you'd like to go out with Des and me some day?"

Dexter's head moved forward from his shoulders and his brow puckered. "You mean you'd really take me out?"

Crunch set up a rasp and sizzle on the varnish. "Sure. Sometimes. If I get a couple of nice customers who don't mind."

The young man gasped. Then he controlled himself. Life had taught him not to count too many unhatched chickens. "How soon—how soon—do you think you might possibly run across a couple of people like that?"

"Oh . . . soon," Crunch answered. "Any day."

Dexter had put in frequent appearances at the Gulf Stream Dock before Crunch had made that astonishing offer. But, thereafter, he was the most regular of all the juvenile buffs— boys who wistfully watched the boats go out and who, when the boats came in, identified various fish for less knowing adults, with a marked air of superiority. Dexter scrutinized every party that chartered the *Poseidon*. Sometimes he knew at a glance that the customers were not the sort who would care for an eleven-year-old supercargo. Sometimes he had great hopes. But no invitation was forthcoming.

The truth was that Crunch had forgotten the conversation. Small boys were ubiquitous, indistinguishable, and, on a busy fishing dock, often in the way. The *Poseidon*'s skipper had noticed Dexter closely enough to like him—to be amused by him—and to make a suggestion which had dropped back into his unconscious mind. Dexter, however, was that rather common but always astounding combination of the dreamer and the man of action. His father, who knew all languages, had told him that one of the cardinal virtues was "initiative." He had explained the word. Dexter eventually enlarged upon its meaning.

In consequence, on one blue and golden morning when the *Poseidon*'s outriggers were trailing balaos down the enameled sea, Crunch went below and was startled by the sight of two medium-sized shoes protruding from beneath a pile of pillows, blankets, canvas and gear on the starboard bunk. He grabbed one of the shoes and pulled forth Dexter.

The young man was alarmed, but in control of himself. "I had to do it!" he said. "You invited me! Besides—Mr. and Mrs. Winton fishing out there are two of the nicest people in Miami. My father said so. I heard them charter you last night—so I sneaked here early . . ."

Crunch remembered his offer, then. His first feeling for his stowaway was one of intense sympathy. Mr. and Mrs. Winton would be amused and pleased by the event. There was no doubt of that. But, on the other hand, it had been presumptive of the boy to steal a trip. Crunch had been rather harshly brought up; he felt that contemporary children were less disciplined and respectful than they should be. His father would have given him a good licking for behavior like young Mr. Heath's. Crunch weighed the situation. The corners of his mouth twitched. He hid that reflex with his hand. Sternly, he eyed the boy. "I suppose you realize that what you've done is a crime on the high seas?"

"I just thought—since you'd asked me already—"

"If I had a brig," Crunch went on, "as captain, I could throw you in it. All stowaways are condemned to hard labor. And bread and water—"

"I got my own lunch—right here!" Dexter produced from his blouse a large and messy-looking sandwich which was inadequately wrapped in newspaper. "And I'll be only too glad to work . . ."

Crunch nodded and cast his eye about. The *Poseidon* was spic and span. "You'll go aloft," he said finally, "where my mate can keep his eye on you. Here's a rag and a can of polish. You can shine all the brass till it's too bright to look at. And you can also keep your eye on the baits. If you see anything—don't scream. Just tell Des."

"Gee!" said Dexter. "Golly!" he added. "I was afraid you'd keep me down here!"

Crunch motioned the boy up the companionway and into the cockpit, where the two Wintons regarded his appearance with moderate surprise.

"This," said the captain, "is Dexter Heath. A stowaway. I'm putting him to work polishing brass."

Mr. Winton, who was a big man with white hair and a white mustache, burst into hearty laughter. His wife only smiled, and she regarded the boy's struggle of jubilance and discomfiture with a certain tenderness. "I'm sure he didn't mean any harm, Crunch. How old are you, son?"

"Eleven," Dexter replied.

"Do you like fishing?"

"My father," Dexter said uncompromisingly, "is the greatest fisherman in the world! Sometimes, he takes me. I will be nearly as good when I get that old."

"Your father's a great fisherman," Mr. Winton mused. "Heath. I don't think I've heard about him."

"You would," the boy said, "if—" He broke off. "You can stand a hundred feet from my father and he can cast a plug into your pocket! I guess he knows mostly where every fish lives in every canal in the Glades. He hooked a water moccasin on a plug, once, and reeled it up and killed it with a stick!"

Mr. Winton whistled and shook his head in awe. Crunch turned away his face. "Go and polish that brass," he said.

Desperate received the newcomer placidly. Crunch had yelled up his name and the conditions of tolerance to be applied to him. The *Poseidon* sailed along. Dexter put elbow grease in his work and the results began to show. His eye attention, however, was largely for the baits. He labored perhaps half an hour before he ventured any conversation. Des had been wondering just how long he would keep that humble silence.

"This is the Gulf Stream, isn't it?" the boy inquired.

Des nodded. "Right here, in this dark-blue water, it is. Over yonder, where the water is paler blue, it isn't. You can see the edge."

"Yeah," Dexter murmured. "Like two kinds of tile in a first-class bathroom."

Des pursed his lips, squinted judiciously at the boy, and nodded again. "If you look at that turning buoy out there, you'll see it has a wake behind it. Just as if it was being hauled through the water. But it's anchored. It's the Stream that makes the wake."

"Sure," the boy assented. "I can see it plain." And then, with every atom of energy, every possible vibration of his vocal chords, he bellowed, "Marlin!"

Crunch dropped a bait and stared. Des whirled from the top controls. Mr. Winton sat up straight. His wife said, "Goodness! Where?"

Dexter was pointing with his polishing rag—pointing palely. His knees were knocking together a little. "Right out there!"

Some fifty feet behind Mr. Winton's bait there was, indeed, a fish. Its length lay yellow under the water. A fin stuck darkly from its back into the air. It was obviously following the bait—following it with a speed not greatly in excess of the *Poseidon*'s and with a peculiar wobbling motion, as if it swam in zigzags.

Crunch stepped toward the canopy and peered at his prisoner with annoyance. "I told you not to yell, Dexter. That's no marlin. It's a lousy hammerhead shark. Speed her up, Des, and we'll get away."

Dexter was not dashed. Instead, he seemed rather more interested. "A hammerhead shark!" he repeated. "A real, live one! Boy, look at her cut around that old bait!"

Des notched up the throttles. The shark began to lose the race.

"A real shark,"Dexter went on excitedly. "A man-eater! And I saw it first!"

Then Mr. Winton spoke. Perhaps his words contained the whole truth. But perhaps he understood and shared the feelings of the boy. "What do you say we slow down and let him get the bait? The fishing's slow today, anyhow, and I need a workout. Helen's always telling me to take more exercise."

"Boy!" murmured Dexter, in a low tone, but one that held audible hope.

"If you want to do it . . ." said Crunch, who was not much on fighting hammerheads. Mako sharks, or whites, or threshers, were different. He waved Des to slow down.

Out beyond the *Poseidon*'s wake, the shark was plunging back and forth in an effort to pick up the scent of the bait. When Des slowed the boat, the shark got it, and came boiling through the sea. His ugly, scimitar-shaped foreface broke water as he engulfed the small fish. The line drifted down from the clothespin at the outrigger tip. Mr. Winton reeled until it was taut and he struck hard several times. The shark gradually became aware that there was a thorn in its jaws and a hampering line hitched to the thorn. First he swam off in a logy manner. Then he essayed a short run. After that, he went fast and far.

"I saw him swallow it!" Dexter kept saying.

Mr. Winton screwed up the drag on the side of his reel. The extra tension bent the rod in a bow. The reel kept humming.

"Like a big amberjack," Mrs. Winton said. "Only—not so fast."

"He's got about three hundred and fifty yards," her husband finally muttered. "That's a good deal."

Crunch grinned. "You asked for it."

Presently the run stopped. Hammerheads, as a rule, make one exciting and fairly fast run. After that they merely resist— lunging lazily, throwing their weight around, bracing dead against the angler's pull. They are not sporty fish. They do not jump. They lack flash and fire and heart. But any fish that weighs three or four hundred pounds provides a tussle on twenty-four-thread line.

Mr. Winton worked hard. It was a warm day. Perspiration ran from him. He called for a glass of water. He called for his sun helmet. He dried his slippery hands on his trousers. He rocked back in the fighting chair and winked up at Dexter, who was standing on the edge of the canopy with, as Mr. Winton later said, "his eyes popping and his tongue hanging out."

"I can see him!" the boy presently yelled. "He's turning over on his side!"

And so he was. A moment later, the shark quit. He came in without a struggle—so much dead weight pulled through the water like a boat on a painter. Crunch went to the stern. He picked up a long knife. Dexter was panting—as if he had manipulated the tackle through the whole fight. He saw Crunch grab the leader and shorten it. He saw him reach down to the water. Dexter held his breath. The skipper actually grabbed one of the hideous eye stalks in his bare hand. Then the muscles in his arms and the muscles along his back bulged, and hardened like rocks. He pulled the great fish—a fish which in that instant seemed bigger to Dexter than any "brontosorassus"—at least a third of its length out of water. He hooked one eye stalk over the gunwale and held the other while he plunged the knife deep into the white bellyside. "I hate sharks," he said coldly.

Dexter gasped. The shark trembled as the knife point found its heart. Blood poured from it. But, still calmly, Crunch put down the knife, picked up a pair of pliers, and went after the hook. The curved jaws snapped convulsively inches from the captain's hand. Nevertheless, he got the hook out with a quick, hard wrench, and he let the hammerhead slide back into the water. It sank, trailing crimson, stone dead.

Mr. Winton fanned himself with his helmet. "How'd you like it, son?"

Dexter swallowed. "Gee!" he murmured. "Imagine! Bare-handed! I guess that's about the bravest thing I ever heard of."

Crunch laughed. "Nothing to it—if you know how to handle 'em."

"And," Mrs. Winton added, "if you're as strong as a derrick."

It had been a day for Dexter. A champion day. The fishing had not been much—two bonitos and a mackerel. But they had supplemented his sandwich lunch with a piece of chocolate cake, two pears, three hard-boiled eggs, some pickles and potato chips. They had forgotten, after the fight with the shark, that he was a prisoner. He'd been allowed to troll a feather on a casting rod for more than two hours. He hadn't had a strike, but that did not matter. He'd "fished the Stream." Not many kids could say that. He'd seen a big one take out line by the hundreds of yards. You could tell people that, without adding that the "big one" was just a shark.

As the *Poseidon* came in, the world seemed especially elegant to Dexter. The sun was going down in a yellow sky and the whole bay—the islands, the palms, the buildings, the lawns—

was gleaming in amber opulence. It made reality theatrical, and only the sight of the Gulf Stream Dock brought the boy out of the mood. Then he became quiet. His thanks were effusive, but not as effusive as his day-long behavior had been. He apologized for stowing away. He went ashore rather solemnly. He had to get home for supper, he said.

"I like that kid," Mr. Winton chuckled.

His wife agreed. "He's marvelous. Who are his people?"

Crunch shrugged. "Darned if I know. I like him, too. He's here a lot. The fellows let him fish—and sometimes he makes a nickle running an errand. I think I heard somebody say that his mother is dead."

It was on the next morning that Des missed the rod. The casting rod with which Dexter had fished. But he didn't think of Dexter right away. "I put it in its regular place on the rack," he told Crunch. "I remember doing it. Who'd swipe that? If somebody wanted dough, why didn't they take an expensive outfit? I made that rod myself two years ago—and there were rods worth five times as much hanging there!"

Crunch did not think of Dexter, either. Not then.

They did when the skipper of the *Firefly* happened to say, "That kid you took out was down here looking for you fellows last night. At least, I think it was him. When I called to him, he beat it."

"Was he carrying a rod and reel?" Des asked.

"Couldn't say. He was maybe carrying something. Skulking along out of the range of the floodlights. You missing one?"

Neither Des nor Crunch replied to that. They went back to their boat. "I'd have bet a week's charter that kid wouldn't touch anything," Crunch said.

"I guess he didn't. At least, I hope he didn't. As far as that goes, the whole outfit wasn't worth more than twenty-five bucks. I can easily—"

"I don't like kids that steal," the captain interrupted angrily.

"Still—what can we do? Ask him? Go to his house and ask his father? When you think how he'd feel if somebody else took the rod?"

There the matter dropped. Or, rather, it drifted. Dexter did not show up for three or four days, which was suspicious, but when he did put in an appearance he was as bland and poised as ever. They saw him often, after that. Sometimes he fished for snappers and grunts. Once he did a job of brass polishing on the *Firefly*. Two or three times he hosed down the *Merdora*. But neither Crunch nor Des were happy about the youngster. If he had taken the rod, something should be done about it. If he had not, they would have given a good deal to be certain of the fact. They discussed the situation occasionally, but to no purpose.

It was Desperate's idea to invite him to go fishing again.

"What'll that prove?" Crunch asked.

"I dunno. We'd get to know him better. Kids are funny. We might find that the rod came back all by itself—which would save us buying a new reel and line and me doing a lot of work. Or we might be able to ask him if he took it—and find out he didn't. Which would make me feel a lot better."

"Yeah," Crunch replied. "Me, too. And I'd also feel free to do a little snooping around the dock. There are four or five guys here dumb enough to think we might not recognize that rod if it was rewound and repainted."

"I haven't seen it yet, anyhow," Des said. "If I do! . . ."

"If you do," Crunch grinned, "let me start the trouble."

They asked the Graymonds first. The Graymonds were summer visitors from Tennessee. They'd never fished in salt water. They said they'd be delighted to have an "extra" mate.

Then they asked Dexter.

He was sitting on a soap box at the time, cutting out long, thick strips of bonito belly for Red. He looked at them with an expression which neither could quite analyze. They decided it changed—from a sort of alarm to eagerness.

"I thought you were mad at me," Dexter said.

"What for?" Crunch asked that question quickly.

"Stowing away."

"Oh. No. You worked that out. We'll be going tomorrow at nine, if you'd like to come along. Bottom fishing—down the reef a ways. Anchored all day. You may have a chance to fish. Somebody swiped one of our casting rods, but you could use a hand line."

"I'll go."

He did not seem especially pleased. Crunch said as much.

Dexter gazed at him in a hurt manner. "Can't a fellow be overwhelmed?" he asked tremulously.

"He didn't do it," Des said later that evening.

And Crunch nodded. "Guess not. And that's a relief!"

Mrs. Graymond found the "extra" mate shy and rather uncommunicative.

She was a dark-haired, dark-eyed girl and she had a way with boys. A most successful way, as a rule. She simply treated them as if they were twice their age. But Dexter did not seem to have an opinion about the outcome of the World's Series, he was not expecting to play football in the fall, he had no dog, and he was willing to admit that he liked fishing—but not with any emphasis or detail.

Indeed, after a quarter of an hour of lopsided conversation, Dexter embarrassedly asked Crunch if he could go "up topside" and shine a little brass. Crunch sent him up. And Desperate respected the boy's vast quietude.

It was a very tragic quietude. The one thing Dexter had wanted in his whole life more than the friendship of two such dramatic, important persons as Crunch and his mate, was that rod. He had taken it. Stolen it so craftily that even though he had been spotted on the night of the theft, he was positive nobody could testify he had been carrying away the precious tackle. Indeed, when the skipper of the *Firefly* had called to him, the rod, line and reel had been hidden underneath the dock in a spot from which Dexter had later retrieved it by means of a temporarily borrowed dinghy.

Now—they had taken him fishing. As he polished brass—and glanced up occasionally with sadness at the broad back of the best mate on the Gulf Stream—Dexter reflected that he had sort of hoped they might vaguely suspect him and would in consequence merely become negative toward him. They couldn't prove anything. And he would never tell. He would go on lying, even if they tortured him worse than the Indians. But the fact that they had invited him to go out—and even to fish—was an almost unendurable kindness. It showed they trusted him.

If he had known their true anxiety over the suspicion of his deed, Dexter would probably have tried to slip overboard unnoticed. On the other hand, when his conscience smote him with the epithet of "thief," he did not flinch. He merely stuck out his chin and squinted back any dampness in his eyes. Maybe he was a thief, but there are things worse than robbery.

It was in the company of such fierce feelings that he watched them cut the *Poseidon*'s speed, make ready the anchor, pick an exact spot over a favorite patch of rocks after much searching through a glass-bottomed bucket, and come to an easy rest. In the distance were the V-shaped outriggers of boats trolling the Stream, the spindly legs of Fowey Rock Light, a few sails, and the smoke-plumed hulls of a pair of tankers beating south inside the current. Under the *Poseidon*'s keel were the irregular blurs of a coral bottom—lumps and caverns, miniature mountains and dark valleys of a size to hide groupers, jewfish, sharks.

The baits went overboard and Dexter was summoned from the comparative obscurity of his place aloft. He was given a hand line by Crunch, who said, "Now, son, hang a whopper!" Desperate grinned at him. He wondered how he could stand it all day long.

They fished with dead shrimp and chunks of balao. Mrs.

Graymond used a rod like the one Dexter had stolen. Its twin. Her husband chose a larger rig with a bigger hook, a heavier hunk of bait, and a reel that buzzed instead of clicked. The three lines soaked up salt water.

"Just about like perch fishing, isn't it?" Mrs. Graymond said.

Dexter smiled back at her smile. "Perch?"

"We catch them in Tennessee. And catfish. And bass, sometimes. Quite big ones. Two pounds—even three."

Her husband nodded. "I was thinking the same thing. I'd expected, somehow, that salt-water fishing would be different."

Then—it was different. His rod jerked. His reel whirred. His arms shot up and down. "Whoa!" he shouted. "Must be loose from that anchor! I've got bottom, captain!"

"You've got a fish," Crunch said.

Mr. Graymond opened his mouth as if to make a denial. Then—the grouper really ran. If he'd had bottom, the *Poseidon* would have to have been going at its top speed; even Mr. Graymond could reason that far, although his reasoning processes were seriously compromised by the situation. Crunch set him in the fighting chair and helped to thrust the bucking ferrule of the rod into the gimbal.

It was a pretty fight, though clumsy, and marred by a mild profanity of amazement. Even Dexter almost forgot his burden of trouble. Until Crunch reached over with a gaff and scooped in the fish.

Just an old grouper, Dexter said to himself at that point. His reason was the violent behavior of the Graymonds. *You'd think,* Dexter went on thinking, *it was a blue marlin. Or some kind of swordfish, or something.*

"But it's a monster!" Mrs. Graymond gasped. "A perfect giant! How much does he weigh!"

"Oh," Crunch murmured, "around, say, twenty pounds."

"Why, darling, it's a whale!" She kissed her husband.

Perhaps Mr. Graymond caught sight of Dexter's eyes. "Well,

dear . . . it may not be so big for here. You've got to remember, we're pond and stream anglers." He stared, however, into the fishbox, where the grouper displayed its tweedy pattern of browns and its brilliant fins, spread taut. "Still," he said, "it's a doggone big fish! Doggoned big." He glanced at Dexter defiantly.

But Dexter had lost his cynical expression. Something had hit his line. He was pulling it up, hand over hand, with an expert continuum of effort which gave the fish no slack, no chance to escape. He flipped his fish deftly into the box, without benefit of gaff. The enthralled Tennesseans bumped heads lightly in their eagerness to look. Dexter had caught a pork fish—a vivid yellow chap, eight or nine inches long, with a flat surface and black, vertical stripes.

"It's the most gorgeous thing I ever saw!" exclaimed Mrs. Graymond.

"And good to eat," said Dexter.

She turned toward him with surprise. "But—it's *much* too beautiful for that! It ought to be in an aquarium!"

Dexter went to the box for bait.

And the fishing continued. Every fish, it appeared, was too beautiful for Mrs. Graymond to think of eating. Even Dexter, who was a practical individual, began to see the quarry through the lady's eyes. And they were kind of pretty—mighty bright-colored—when you thought of it. Right down to grunts.

The accident happened in the only way it could have happened. And in a place where even the most nervous boatman would hardly expect anything serious to occur. Dexter, liking the Graymonds almost against his will, and passionately eager to do anything to aid Crunch and Des, had undertaken to remove fish from the hooks and to put on baits for the customers. He was perfectly competent for the chore. He had weeks of dock fishing behind him.

Relieved of the duty, Crunch had gone below to prepare a special chowder from the grouper. Desperate had already occupied himself with the rearrangement of gear on the foredeck. Thus the two novices and the youngster were left alone. Mrs. Graymond hooked a fish. Dexter went to her side to give advice. It was a pretty good-sized fish—a snapper, he hoped—and his attention was entirely focussed, on the lady.

Mr. Graymond also hooked a fish. Not wishing to disturb his thrilling wife, and imagining himself by then a fairly proficient fisherman, he fought the creature in silence. It ran and it shook and it bent his rod but he dragged it to the surface. Then, seeing that Dexter was still busy, he undertook to copy the boy's trick of flicking his quarry aboard. He wound the line up to the swivel, blocked the reel spool with his thumb, braced his feet, and gave a tremendous heave. His fish was yanked out of the water. It rose into the air, writhing. It landed in the cockpit. It spat out the hook. And Mr. Graymond yelled.

Crunch and Des, separately, interpreted the yell as evidence of another triumph. It was not. It was a yell of sheer horror.

For the thing in the boat was horrible. A thing like a fat snake, five feet long, a sickly rich green, with a sharp, reptilian mouth, terrible teeth, and brilliant, evil eyes. Even as Mr. Graymond yelled, it slithered into a knot and struck like a rattlesnake, at the support of a chair. It bounced from that and struck again, biting fiercely on a glove. Dexter wheeled and saw it and turned ash-pale. Mrs. Graymond also saw, and she tried to scream and could not. She tried to move, but her legs would not budge.

"Keep away from it!" Dexter said hoarsely. "It'll bite! It's deadly poison!"

That it would bite was obvious. It was, even then, striking a pail. That the green moray is poisonous is a technical problem, since the toxicology of slimes and fish poisons is an unfinished science. Certainly morays make bad wounds that are slow to heal. Certainly men have suffered fearful infections from their bites, or from bacteria that entered the bites. Certainly all the boatmen in Florida waters would be hard put to choose between

a big moray and a rattlesnake, if one had to be let loose in a
cockpit.

Dexter's husky advice was heeded by the terrified man. He
jumped backwards mechanically and found himself, somehow,
standing on one of the couches. But his wife was still transfixed.
The moray saw her—and started for her.

Dexter had been standing behind her. He came around in
front. In coming, he grabbed the only thing handy—a gaff. The
moray turned toward him. As it struck, Dexter clipped it with
the gaff. Savagely, the green, repugnant monster plunged again
and the boy hit it again, knocking it back. His gaff was too short
for such work, and he knew it. He knew that if he missed, the
moray would not. But he struck a third time. Mrs. Graymond
came to galvanic life. She realized the boy had made a place
which would permit her to jump to the side of her husband. She
jumped. And, at last, she screamed.

Seeing that the lady was clear, Dexter lost no time in leaping
up on one of the fishing chairs.

Then Crunch came, fast. He had recognized the scream as one
not of exultation. He snatched up the long-handled gaff—which
Dexter hadn't been able to reach—and he broke the moray's
back with it.

It took two hours and a half, together with one of the tastiest
dishes in all the experience of the Graymonds, to start the fishing
again. They called Dexter a hero and the bravest kid they had
ever seen and Mr. Graymond patted his back and Mrs. Graymond kissed him. There were long discussions of the venom-
ousness of the big eels, and there was a brief but tense
altercation between husband and wife over the uncourageous
behavior of the former. Dexter noted a look in Crunch's eye
which eased away a full half of his sadness. Then the lines were
wet again, no more morays were caught, and Mr. Graymond
made no further attempts to fling fish aboard unaided.

It turned out to be a good day, with a fine catch of panfish, and two more groupers. A day marked by An Adventure to Tell People Back Home. The Graymonds began to refer to the battle in that fashion. Dexter slipped back into his melancholy. The sun moved down. The anchor went up. And, in the purpling evening, the *Poseidon* hummed paint-slick down the Government Cut toward home.

Dexter was sitting alone on the canopy top when Mr. Graymond came up beside him. He didn't say anything. He just shook Dexter's hand, and his own head, and went away. But he had left something in Dexter's palm. The boy looked at it. And—for him—the sun shone brightly, the sea was perfumed, there were flowers on every tree. It was a five-dollar bill.

His first impulse was to shout for Crunch. Five dollars was a fortune. It would pay for the rod. But Dexter was a youth accustomed to consideration. Maybe four dollars would foot the bill. Or even three. His ideas about money, in sums larger than ten or fifteen cents, were not merely vague. They scarcely existed. If three were enough . . . what he could do with the other two would be! . . . But he sturdily thrust back temptation. He leaned over the cockpit.

"Captain Adams," he said in a low tone, "would you come here a minute? It's important."

Crunch recognized the tone. He had been hoping to hear it all day. "Take over," he said quickly to his mate. "I'll see the kid."

He climbed up on the canopy. He sat down beside the boy. He was smiling. "O.K., Dexter. What's important?"

Dexter handed him the five dollars. "That's for the rod I stole."

Crunch took the money. "Oh," he said somewhat numbly. "Where'd you?—"

"Mr. Graymond gave it to me. A reward, I guess, for saving that Mrs. Graymond's life, or maybe her leg."

"I see. Yeah. Look, Dex. About swiping the rod. Why?"

Dexter was crying a little, then. Things had broken too well for a man to bear. But he started to talk. Every sentence made the going tougher. Crunch didn't interrupt. He just sat there, watching the causeway slide past, watching the boat swing as Des prepared to back her in.

"I had to," the youngster began. "You gotta believe I had to! If you didn't, I'd about die!" He swallowed. "Look. You know about 'business reverses'? Pop's been having what he calls that. It really means we don't have any money. Until they started, we had enough. We had a wonderful time! We'd get up together, and I'd help get breakfast, and eat lunch at school, and evenings, we'd cook at home and sometimes we'd go out for dinner to a real restaurant! Then . . . when Saturday came . . ."

Dexter had to pull himself together. "When—Saturdays came— he'd take me out in the Glades—fishing in the canal! We'd drive in our car, and I'd fish a jack pole and he'd cast plugs. I—I—I told you he could put one in your pocket a hundred feet away. It's true! Then—when we had to sell the car—we couldn't go so far and we had to fish in places that weren't so good—but we hardly never missed a Saturday! He's—he knows all the birds— and how to catch snakes—and we saw deer and 'coons and possums! And then . . ."

The boy's voice went lower—close to inaudibility. His words ran fast. "School was coming. I had to have shoes and knickers and books and things—and Pop sold his rod and his reel and his tackle box and he had about a million plugs and he sold them and said he didn't care to fish with an old jack pole so we didn't go out together any more. He didn't tell me he sold those things to get my school stuff ready—but I found out from the man that bought them. Pop had a chance to sell—and he knew we'd have to buy all my stuff in a few weeks. I found that out. So I knew."

He didn't get any further than that. He couldn't. But there was no need of it.

The *Poseidon* was edging toward the dock. Crunch jumped to the top controls while Des made fast the bow lines. Crunch didn't particularly want Dexter to see him at that instant, anyway. His jaw was set like steel. When the *Poseidon* was snug, Crunch looked at the hunched back of the boy. Then his eye traveled ashore, and he saw a man standing there. A medium-sized man, an unimportant-looking man, with a good face, full of worry. The man's eyes were hurt, and in his hand was the rod Des had made—the one his son had stolen.

Des helped the passengers ashore. Immediately afterward, the man—Mr. Heath—accosted the mate. He spoke rapidly, nervously. "My boy must have stolen this. He left it in my room a few days ago with a note saying he had found it. As soon as I had time—I traced it—through the tackle shops. Somebody recognized your work . . ."

Des just stood.

But the boy heard his father's voice. He leaped up with a tearing, ecstatic cry. "It's all right, Pop! It's yours! I just paid five bucks for it!"

The man, gray, embarrassed, gazed at his son. He spoke the first words that came into his head—spoke them bitterly. "Five bucks—when it's worth twenty-five! See here, son! . . ."

Dexter slid down into the cockpit. He was not breathing, or even seeing. He was sick. Sicker, perhaps, than he would ever be again in his life. He leaped ashore and eluded Desperate's panicky effort to catch him. He ran away down the dock—to be alone.

Crunch dropped down, also, and came ashore. The Graymonds were waiting for their catch to be put on the fish rack. They realized something was wrong. They stood by, puzzled and unhappy.

Crunch took the gray-faced man by the arm. It was quivering. "Look," he began urgently. "I can't explain now. But you've got to believe me, Mr. Heath! This is a mighty important moment in your kid's life! He's a fine kid, Mr. Heath! I only hope mine grows up half that swell! But I want you to let me handle this my way. I want you to keep that rod—"

"I couldn't, Captain! I—I'm kind of broken up about it. I came home that night to tell my son I had found a job—a good one—and there was the stolen rod and the lying note! I've tried to teach him—about stealing—lying—and it half killed me! I decided not to say a thing about the job, till my boy confessed the theft. He—" Mr. Heath stammered. "He did it—for me. That is—for motives which were decent. If you . . ."

Crunch squeezed the father's arm hard. He also swallowed. "Look, Mr. Heath. I know all that! You keep the rod. Do you hear me? You've gotta! You've got to trust my judgment!" His blistering blue gaze held on the gray eyes of the other man.

"All right," said Mr. Heath, sighing. "All right. I'll trust you. I'm sort of mixed up—anyway . . ."

Crunch raced away—butting into people on the dock. He found Dexter hiding, on the ground, under the truck that took away fish carcasses. Dexter was racked by crying. Crunch seized his foot, pulled him out, and stood him up.

"Go away!" Dexter said in near strangulation. "I don't want any favors! I thought that five bucks was plenty."

Crunch shook him. "Listen!" His own voice was wild and tight. "Listen, Dex! I want you to get square with me! You gave that rod to your dad. He's gotta keep it. You got to pay for all of it. That's what I'm here to tell you."

"How can I? Twenty-five!—"

"I told you to shut up! Now, shut up! I'm doing the talking! You owe me twenty bucks. All right. There's just about twenty days before school begins. From now on—every day—you're working for me all day. A dollar a day. And lunches," Crunch added hastily. "A dollar a day and lunches. If you don't earn all of it—if you're a couple of days short—then you can go out a few Saturdays! You shine brass, and watch baits . . ."

Dexter shook his head miserably. "I—I ain't no good! You know that! I steal, and I think hammerheads are marlins. . . ."

"No good?" The man's voice was incredulous. "No good! Son,

you got bait eyes like a hawk's! You can see a fin before even the fish knows he's coming up! You're the rarin'est, tearin'est moray fighter I ever saw milling in a cockpit! No good! Why—you're worth any three eighteen-year-old mates on the Gulf Stream Dock! Now! You working for me—or not?"

Dexter had listened. He wiped a wet sleeve wetter. "Gee!—" He hesitated, and dared it—"Gee, *Crunch*, you're a swell guy!"

Crunch slapped his shoulder and caught up his arm.

They went back along the dock together in a swift, easy lope, taking care not to butt into anybody.

The Thrilling Moment

Henry Van Dyke

Every moment of life, I suppose, is more or less of a turning-point. Opportunities are swarming around us all the time, thicker than gnats at sundown. We walk through a cloud of chances, and if we were always conscious of them they would worry us almost to death.

But happily our sense of uncertainty is soothed and cushioned by habit, so that we can live comfortably with it. Only now and then, by way of special excitement, it starts up wide awake. We perceive how delicately our fortune is poised and balanced on the pivot of a single incident. We get a peep at the oscillating needle, and, because we have happened to see it tremble, we call our experience a crisis.

The meditative angler is not exempt from these sensational periods. There are times when all the uncertainty of his chosen pursuit seems to condense itself into one big chance, and stand out before him like a salmon on the top wave of a rapid. He sees that his luck hangs by a single strand, and he cannot tell whether it will hold or break. This is his thrilling moment, and he never forgets it.

Mine came to me in the autumn of 1894, on the banks of the Unpronounceable River, in the Province of Quebec. It was the last day, of the open season for ouananiche, and we had set our hearts on catching some good fish to take home with us. We walked up from the mouth of the river, four preposterously long and rough miles, to the famous fishing-pool, "*la place de pêche à Boivin.*" It was a noble day for walking; the air was clear and crisp, and all the hills around us were glowing with the crimson foliage of those little bushes which God created to make burned lands look beautiful. The trail ended in a precipitous gully, down which we scrambled with high hopes, and fishing-rods unbroken, only to find that the river was in a condition which made angling absurd if not impossible.

There must have been a cloud-burst among the mountains, for the water was coming down in flood. The stream was bank-full, gurgling and eddying out among the bushes, and rushing over the shoal where the fish used to lie, in a brown torrent ten feet deep. Our last day with the land-locked salmon seemed destined to be a failure, and we must wait eight months before we could have another. There were three of us in the disappointment, and we shared it according to our temperaments.

Paul virtuously resolved not to give up while there was a chance left, and wandered down-stream to look for an eddy where he might pick up a small fish. Ferdinand, our guide, resigned himself without a sigh to the consolation of eating blueberries, which he always did with great cheerfulness. But I, being more cast down than either of my comrades, sought out a convenient seat among the rocks, and, adapting my anatomy as well as possible to the irregularities of nature's upholstery, pulled from my pocket *An Amateur Angler's Days in Dove Dale*, and settled down to read myself into a Christian frame of mind.

Before beginning, my eyes roved sadly over the pool once more. It was but a casual glance. It lasted only for an instant. But in that fortunate fragment of time I distinctly saw the broad tail of a big ouananiche rise and disappear in the swift water at the very head of the pool.

Immediately the whole aspect of affairs was changed. Despondency vanished, and the river glittered with the beams of rising hope.

Such is the absurd disposition of some anglers. They never see a fish without believing that they can catch him; but if they see no fish, they are inclined to think that the river is empty and the world hollow.

I said nothing to my companions. It would have been unkind to disturb them with expectations which might never be realized. My immediate duty was to get within casting distance of that salmon as soon as possible.

The way along the shore of the pool was difficult. The bank was very steep, and the rocks by the river's edge were broken and glibbery. Presently I came to a sheer wall of stone, perhaps thirty feet high, rising directly from the deep water.

There was a tiny ledge or crevice running part of the way across the face of this wall, and by this four-inch path I edged along, holding my rod in one hand, and clinging affectionately with the other to such clumps of grass and little bushes as I could find. There was one small huckleberry plant to which I had a particular attachment. It was fortunately a firm little bush, and as I held fast to it I remembered Tennyson's poem which begins

"Flower in the crannied wall,"

and reflected that if I should succeed in plucking out this flower, "root and all," it would probably result in an even greater increase of knowledge than the poet contemplated.

The ledge in the rock now came to an end. But below me in

the pool there was a sunken reef; and on this reef a long log had caught, with one end sticking out of the water, within jumping distance. It was the only chance. To go back would have been dangerous. An angler with a large family dependent upon him for support has no right to incur unnecessary perils.

Besides, the fish was waiting for me at the upper end of the pool!

So I jumped; landed on the end of the log; felt it settle slowly down; ran along it like a small boy on a seesaw, and leaped off into shallow water just as the log rolled from the ledge and lunged out into the stream.

It went wallowing through the pool and down the rapid like a playful hippopotamus. I watched it with interest and congratulated myself that I was no longer embarked upon it. On that craft a voyage down the Unpronounceable River would have been short but far from merry. The "all ashore" bell was not rung early enough. I just got off, with not half a second to spare.

But now all was well, for I was within reach of the fish. A little scrambling over the rocks brought me to a point where I could easily cast over him. He was lying in a swift, smooth, narrow channel between two large stones. It was a snug resting-place, and no doubt he would remain there for some time. So I took out my fly-book and prepared to angle for him according to the approved rules of the art.

Nothing is more foolish in sport than the habit of precipitation. And yet it is a fault to which I am singularly subject. As a boy, in Brooklyn, I never came in sight of the Capitoline Skating Pond, after a long ride in the horse-cars, without breaking into a run along the board walk, buckling on my skates in a furious hurry, and flinging myself impetuously upon the ice, as if I feared that it would melt away before I could reach it. Now this, I confess, is a grievous defect, which advancing years have not entirely cured; and I found it necessary to take myself firmly, as it were, by the mental coat-collar, and resolve not to spoil the

chance of catching the only ouananiche in the Unpronounceable River by undue haste in fishing for him.

I carefully tested a brand-new leader, and attached it to the
line with great deliberation and the proper knot. Then I gave my
whole mind to the important question of a wise selection of flies.

It is astonishing how much time and mental anxiety a man
can spend on an apparently simple question like this. When you
are buying flies in a shop it seems as if you never had half
enough. You keep on picking out a half-dozen of each new
variety as fast as the enticing salesman shows them to you. You
stroll through the streets of Montreal or Quebec and drop in at
every fishing-tackle dealer's to see whether you can find a few
more good flies. Then, when you come to look over your
collection at the critical moment on the bank of a stream, it
seems as if you had ten times too many. And, spite of all, the
precise fly that you need is not there.

You select a couple that you think fairly good, lay them down
beside you in the grass, and go on looking through the book for
something better. Failing to satisfy yourself, you turn to pick up
those that you have laid out, and find that they have mysteriously vanished from the face of the earth.

Then you struggle with naughty words and relapse into a
condition of mental palsy.

Precipitation is a fault. But deliberation, for a person of
precipitate disposition, is a vice.

The best thing to do in such a case is to adopt some abstract
theory of action without delay, and put it into practice without
hesitation. Then if you fail, you can throw the responsibility on
the theory.

Now, in regard to flies there are two theories. The old,
conservative theory is, that on a bright day you should use a
dark, dull fly, because it is less conspicuous. So I followed that
theory first and put on a Great Dun and a Dark Montreal. I cast
them delicately over the fish, but he would not look at them.

Then I perverted myself to the new, radical theory which says that on a bright day you must use a light, gay fly, because it is more in harmony with the sky, and therefore less noticeable. Accordingly I put on a Professor and a Parmacheene Belle; but this combination of learning and beauty had no attraction for the ouananiche.

Then I fell back on a theory of my own, to the effect that the ouananiche have an aversion to red, and prefer yellow and brown. So I tried various combinations of flies in which these colours predominated.

Then I abandoned all theories and went straight through my book, trying something from every page, and winding up with that lure which the guides consider infallible,—"a Jock o' Scott that cost fifty cents at Quebec." But it was all in vain. I was ready to despair.

At this psychological moment I heard behind me a voice of hope,—the song of grasshopper: not one of those fat-legged, green-winged imbeciles that feebly tumble in the summer fields, but a game grasshopper,—one of those thin-shanked, brown-winged fellows that leap like kangaroos, and fly like birds, and sing *Kri-karee-karee-kri* in their flight.

It is not really a song, I know, but it sounds like one; and, if you had heard that Kri-karee carolling as I chased him over the rocks, you would have been sure that he was mocking me.

I believed that he was the predestined lure for that ouananiche; but it was hard to persuade him to fulfill his destiny. I slapped at him with my hat, but he was not there. I grasped at him on the bushes, and brought away "nothing but leaves." At last he had made his way to the very edge of the water and poised himself on a stone, with his legs well tucked in for a long leap and a bold flight to the other side of the river. It was my final opportunity. I made a desperate grab at it and caught the grasshopper.

My premonition proved to be correct. When that Kri-karee,

invisibly attached to my line, went floating down the stream, the ouananiche was surprised. It was the fourteenth of September, and he had supposed the grasshopper season was over. The unexpected temptation was too strong for him. He rose with a rush, and in an instant I was fast to the best land-locked salmon of the year.

But the situation was not without its embarrassments. My rod weighed only four and a quarter ounces; the fish weighed between six and seven pounds. The water was furious and headstrong. I had only thirty yards of line and no landing-net.

"Holà! Ferdinand!" I cried. *"Apporte la nette, vite! A beauty! Hurry up!"*

I thought it must be an hour while he was making his way over the hill, through the underbrush, around the cliff. Again and again the fish ran out my line almost to the last turn. A dozen times he leaped from the water, shaking his silvery sides. Twice he tried to cut the leader across a sunken ledge. But at last he was played out, and came in quietly towards the point of the rock. At the same moment Ferdinand appeared with the net.

Now, the use of the net is really the most difficult part of angling. And Ferdinand is the best netsman in the Lake St. John country. He never makes the mistake of trying to scoop a fish in motion. He does not grope around with aimless, futile strokes as if he were feeling for something in the dark. He does not entangle the dropper-fly in the net and tear the tail-fly out of the fish's mouth. He does not get excited.

He quietly sinks the net in the water, and waits until he can see the fish distinctly, lying perfectly still and within reach. Then he makes a swift movement, like that of a mower swinging the scythe, takes the fish into the net head-first, and lands him without a slip.

I felt sure that Ferdinand was going to do the trick in precisely this way with my ouananiche. Just at the right instant he made one quick, steady swing of the arms, and—the head of the net broke clean off the handle and went floating away with the fish in it!

All seemed to be lost. But Ferdinand was equal to the occasion. He seized a long, crooked stick that lay in a pile of driftwood on the shore, sprang into the water up to his waist, caught the net as it drifted past, and dragged it to land, with the ultimate ouananiche, the prize of the season, still glittering through its meshes.

This is the story of my most thrilling moment as an angler.

But which was the moment of the deepest thrill?

Was it when the huckleberry bush saved me from a watery grave, or when the log rolled under my feet and started down the river? Was it when the fish rose, or when the net broke, or when the long stick captured it?

No, it was none of these. It was when the Kri-karee sat with his legs tucked under him on the brink of the stream. That was the turning-point. The fortunes of the day depended on the comparative quickness of the reflex action of his neural ganglia and mine. That was the thrilling moment.

I see it now. A crisis is really the commonest thing in the world. The reason why life sometimes seems dull to us is because we do not perceive the importance and the excitement of getting bait.

Brannigan's Trout

Nick Lyons

AFTER THE CRACKUP, he was hospitalized for six months. Twice the doctors warned Jane that they might lose him. Then, when they saved him, they warned that there was probably brain damage. When he was released, in November, they told him he'd be paralyzed on his right side for life. Four doctors confirmed the verdict.

There was nothing for it.

Perhaps there was a slight chance, but not likely, that regular exercise, steady exercise over a period of several years, might restore some small portion of his mobility. Not much. Possibly none. Frankly, Brannigan was not inclined to try. Why go through all the effort? So he sat silent and sullen in the wheelchair that grey afternoon and allowed the men in white to push him to the car, lift and place him into the front seat, collapse the chair and put it in the back, then tell Jane how he was to get in and out, how she was to rig the contraption and place it for him. Like a baby.

He said not a word on the long trip through the sere, dead

countryside. Jane told him about the boys, and which friends had called; Mike Novak might come over that evening. He didn't even nod. His great black-haired head thrown back and tilted to one side, he watched with dead eyes the fleeting fields of withered cornstalks, leafless trees, dark scudding clouds. There was nothing for it. He was forty-six and it was over. He couldn't sell books or anything else anymore; he didn't know whether he could drink beer with his friends, chop wood, tend his garden, drive, smoke, sing, read, write; and certainly the fishing season was over for him. Permanently.

The crash in all its stark detail, the fluky chance of it, kept flashing through his brain: Johnny Wohl driving, across the seat from him, saying seconds before, "Well, Billy, we made a day of it, didn't we? I never saw the river so alive." And Mike in the back, laughing wildly and about to say something about having caught three Hendricksons. Then the rasp of brakes, the black car coming just that moment smoothly out of the side road, the jolt of fear, his hands flying up, his back thrusting backward against the seat, then hurtling forward—and darkness, and stabbing, raw pain in his shoulders, his head. Then nothing. Johnny Wohl and the two teenagers in the black car had been killed instantly. Mike came out of it with his right pinky broken. Well, good for him. Good for old Mike.

As for himself, it would have been better to have had it over then, right then when it happened. Quick. No more pain to die than to live, then. He need merely not have come out of the coma. After that first, searing pain, poof. For good. And they all said he'd only lived because he wanted to live. So he lived—like a half-squashed worm.

He saw suddenly in his mind the 20-gauge shotgun in the cabinet in his den. Would Jane have removed it? This was no time to ask. That night, when the boys were doing their homework, he'd wheel in by himself and just take a look-see. He'd take it out, break it open . . . take a look-see.

At dinner, Jane talked constantly—about the Murphys' new Brittany spaniel; the good batch of slab wood Frank had hauled from the lumber yard, piece by piece, and cut himself; the threat of an early snow. Brannigan looked up now and then from his plate, spread his lips slightly in the best he could do for a smile, and nodded. He said nothing. He was still not sure what the cracked, alien sound of his voice—what remained of speech— would be to these people, whether he could put together all the words needed for one whole sentence. Whenever he raised his head and looked toward one of his sons, Frank to his right, fifteen, Junior on his left, a year older and dark-haired too, rebellious, they were looking at their own plates. They knew everything. When he looked back at his own plate and prepared his next strategy to get a piece of meat to his mouth, he thought he saw, peripherally, their heads raise slightly and turn toward him. He didn't think he could bear it. Not that. He'd come through Normandy without a scratch; he'd never been seriously ill in his life.

Working diligently with the fork in his left hand, like they'd taught him in the hospital, he speared a piece of the steak Jane had cut for him, shifted the fork carefully in his hand, and brought it to his mouth. He chewed the chunk of meat slowly for a few moments, then lowered the fork to get another. But the prongs pressed against the gristle, slipped, and flicked the meat onto the floor. Brannigan looked after it, heard Jane say, "I'll pick it up later, dear," then slammed the fork down on his plate. Frank and Junior raised their hunched shoulders and looked up sharply. Jane took a deep breath.

"Nuff," muttered Brannigan. "Nuff." He pushed the wheel-chair away, turning it, and, his hand on the wheel-rail, glided into the living room and toward his den—hearing Frank say something low that ended with "like that," and Junior's heavier voice, and then Jane telling them in a normal voice to finish quickly and go upstairs: they'd talk of it later.

He negotiated the living room and came to the door of his den. His room. The door was closed but he came against it sideways, took his left hand from the wheel-rail and reached out for the knob. As he did so, the chair slipped back a few inches and he was only able to touch a bit of the knob. He gritted his teeth, pounded his left hand down on the armrest, wheeled himself close again, and tried another time. Again the chair slipped back a bit and he couldn't, hard as he strained, even touch the knob. *Damned. Damned.* He sat in the chair, breathing heavily for a few moments, then tried again, got it, flung the door open, gave the wheel-rail a sharp thrust forward, and was in his room. *His* room.

God, how many good hours he'd spent there. The soft old armchair. His own mount of the four-pound brook trout he'd caught in Canada that summer with Mike and Johnny. The humidor with those long black dago-ropes he loved so much. Fireplace. Little fly-tying table—just like he'd left it. Silver rod cases in the cabinet he'd built himself. The old black-bear rug he'd bought, over Jane's hilarious objections. *His room.*

It was a room to which he slunk after a knockdown argument with Jane, a lousy road trip; he went there to plan his selling strategies, realign the world, read quietly in the evening or tie flies. He'd had most of his serious talks with his boys in this room; and he'd laughed and drunk beer and told stories half the night with Johnny and Mike here. Useless now. There was not one thing in the room, as he looked around, that he wanted.

The shotgun.

His eyes shifted sharply to the oak cabinet with the V-back that fitted into the corner so snugly. It was there. He went to his fly-tying table, opened the middle drawer, and felt with his hand among the capes and bobbins until his fingers found and closed tightly around the long brass key. Then, holding the key in the palm of his left hand, he used his fingers to push the chair over to the cabinet.

He had only that one gun, a beautiful 20-gauge with polished walnut stock, grey shoulder cushion, twin slate-grey barrels. He liked the feel of it in his hands, the power with which it jerked back when he shot. He'd gotten his first grouse with it last winter. Sam, Johnny's Brittany, had frozen on a point, Johnny had called for the flush, and the grouse, a single, had exploded with a whirr from the underbrush. "Yours!" shouted Mike, and he'd swung, led, and watched the bird pause, sputter, and fall. He remembered the deep satisfaction he'd felt from that connection, that force which shot out from him and dropped that bird.

The shotgun.

Another moment and he'd have it in his hands, feel its sleek powerful lines, its smooth stock. The gun held power, energy, force; merely to have it in your hands was to feel some electrical current, some charge of strength shot into your veins, your body. "Look-see," he said, flinching at the cracked, strange sound of his voice, inserting the key into the lock and turning, then opening the cabinet door slowly.

It was not there. The cabinet was empty.

His eyes blazed and he slammed the door shut. It was not there. She had taken it. Grasping the wheel-rail he thrust downward and began to roll across the carpet toward the closed door to the living room. She had taken it. "Gun," he said, his voice a rasping growl. "Gun. Gun." Then, opening the door, he let his head fall, and he muttered, "Did she . . . really . . . think . . ."

"So the point is that *I* asked Jane for your goddamn shotgun because mine is at the gunsmith and I ain't got one to use next week," Mike said ten minutes later when they were alone in the den. "She didn't want to let me have it. Nope. 'Mike,' she says, 'Billy loves that rifle.' That's what she called it, a rifle, 'and I don't think I can let you have it.'"

Brannigan frowned. He looked intently at the bronze, hearty face of his friend, that bullish chest above toothpick legs, the straight black, always greasy and carefully combed hair, the mechanic's hands, stained black.

"I says: 'Look, Janie, he may not be out until after Christmas and I know he'd want me to put a few notches on it for him. One thing about Billy, he don't like a good rod or shotgun lying around. Offends his Scotch-Irish blood.'"

"Lie."

"I was going to take it out to the range, test it on clays, but if you'd like it back, got some special use for it, I'll . . ." He broke off, lowered his voice, and said: "It's been rough, ain't it, kiddo?"

"Ruh-uf."

"Yeah," said Mike, turning his back and walking across the room to look at the big, bright male brook trout on the wall. "Remember when you got that one, Billy?" he said without turning around. "You'd cast that big funny fly from New Zealand, the Red Setter, looked like a whore's hairdo, into the swirls below the falls. I was behind you. I'd gotten one about three pounds that morning and you was burning mad. Didn't even speak to me at lunch. Well, maybe I was being a bit rotten about it." He came and sat down in the soft old armchair. "I must've turned and the next thing I know your rod's bent like a crescent moon and you're yelling like a banshee. Johnny thinks you've fallen in or got bit by a snake, so he comes running up, and by this time there's the goddamnedest smug look on your face! You've got the fish well hooked, you've seen him roll, and you know the size of him—and you know you got the greatest audience any mug ever had."

He watched Brannigan's eyes. They changed as he told the story.

"You're using this ten-pound-test leader and can't possibly lose that fish unless it gets into the rapids, and you're acting just as cockeyed cool as a cock of the roost. Johnny and me, we may be a little green around the gills but we're sitting polite as you please, murmuring a few friendly words of praise now and then—like, 'Did *that* lemon have to get it?'—and you keep playing him gently, making maybe a bit too much of a show of fear when it heads downstream. Cool. Very cool, Billy. And when Johnny wants to net him for you, with the big net, what do you do? Wave him away, and fuss with that minnow net you carry."

The faintest trace of a smile began to struggle around the corners of Brannigan's twisted mouth and eyes.

"So this absolute monster of a brookie, the biggest trout any of us has ever seen, is beat, and over on its side, and you're swiping at it with your net—probably trying to get it to rush off so's the show can go on—and first you get the tail in, right?"

Brannigan nodded.

"Then when it flops out, you try to bend it in, from the middle, but the monster won't be bent, so you go for the head, which barely fits into that guppy net, and then you've got it head first to about the gills and sort of clamp your hand down on the rest and come yelping out of the water, the line and rod and net and you all tangled together, and you fall on it. God, that fish was gorgeous—and there he is. That the way it happened, Billy? Something like that?"

Brannigan raised his left hand in a little shrug. "Ha-pinned . . . like . . . that."

"So the point is, you got one. You got one bigger than any of us ever got, even Johnny, God rest his soul, and now you figure, 'The big bird's crapped on me. I've caught my last big fish and shot my last grouse.' That it?"

"Tha-z-it."

"Johnny doesn't make it and you ain't satisfied to be here. Instead of being pleased I come tonight, passing up some very possible quail, you're going to stew in your own bile, right?"

"Rrr-ight."

"There's no one in particular to hate for it, so you figure you'll spread the hate around, to Jane and the boys, and especially yourself, and maybe you'll get lucky and not be around too much longer to be a burden to anyone. Well, I see your point, Brannigan. Lot of logic to it. They say maybe there's a chance in a couple hundred thousand that you get anything back on that right side, so you say, 'Bad odds.'" He walked to the fly-tying table, picked up one of the capes, a pale ginger, and bent back the hackle of one feather. "A good one, Billy. First-rate dry-fly neck. Good small size, too." Then he went to the humidor and drew out one of the twisted black cigars. "You don't mind?" Brannigan, watching him closely, did not change his expression. Mike put the cigar in the center of his mouth, struck a match, and got the tip of the cigar glowing like a little coal. "Good cigar, Billy." He puckered his lips, held the cigar in three fingers, and took a long puff.

Brannigan kept watching him. He had not moved his chair from the moment Mike had come in. *Quail. Big trout. A grouse or two. Lives for that. Two wives, maybe have ten more. Funny guy. The way he holds that cigar—like he owned the world, all of it. Shotgun. Ask.*

"So the point is, it would break my sweet heart if you wasn't around, kiddo. Know what I mean? You know what I did when they told me you was"—he put out his hand, palm down, and rocked it slightly—"maybe not going to make it? I prayed. Me. Prayed. I said, 'Oh, God, let old Billy come through with *anything*, any goddamit thing at all, so long as he's here and I can brag to him now and then about what quail I'm snatching—anything, God, just so long as he's here where I can see his ugly black-haired head now and then'"—he puffed hard on his cigar—"when the quail ain't flying and the trout is down. It's rough, right?"

Ask about shotgun.

"Suddenly the rules is all changed."

The gun.

"So the point is," he said, puffing hard, exhaling three times in rapid succession—"Hell, I don't know what the point is, Billy, but it will be awfully lonely next May when the Hendricksons start popping not to . . . Here, catch this"—and he tossed a softball, underhand, directly at Brannigan's chest. The left hand went up and forced the ball against the right shoulder. The right shoulder, limp and loose, twitched ever so slightly toward the ball. Brannigan held the ball for a moment, then took it in his left hand and tossed it back. Then he felt his right shoulder and slowly dug his fingers into the muscle. "Not . . . much-left."

"You'll cast lefty," said Mike. "Once knew an old poacher name of Sven who had to learn because there was bad brush on the right side. Dry-fly purist of a poacher." And the story went on for twenty minutes, and included a patrol dog named Wolf, five pound rainbows, two delicious young women, the true origin of "Sven's left curve drop cast," which only lefties could use, and then, just before the point of it all, Mike simply said, "It's eleven. The quail will have flown. I'll bring the 20-gauge tomorrow, eh?"

Brannigan smiled, a slow, deep smile that spread into his cheeks and eyes, and stayed, even when the twitch started. He nudged his right hand out with his left, so Mike could take and hold it, and Mike took it and held it in both of his own, rubbing the lifeless thing vigorously, then turning quickly for the door. Before he got there, Brannigan said: "The gun . . . yours."

The limbs remember, he thought, working the rake lightly across the soil he'd just fitted with seed, *and so does the earth. It remembers what it must do to these seeds, and the seeds, someplace deep within them, knew what they must do.*

Back and forth he moved the rake, holding it firmly in his left hand, using his nearly useless right to steady it. The May sun was warm but not bright, and kneaded his broad naked shoulders. He could walk without the cane now—somewhat. With that bizarre arc. His hair had gone snow white, which he liked, but otherwise, if he didn't move and didn't talk, he looked nearly the same.

Everyone else had planted a week or two ago but he'd worked more slowly, as he had to—long patient hours, setting his fertilizer, running the hand plow steadily across the small garden he'd staked out last spring, seeding the soil. This would be a good year. He could feel it. He'd learned how to coax green from the brown soil, how important it was, always, to be patient—to lay the proper foundations, however long that took, before you could expect anything to grow. Tomatoes, cucumbers, carrots, radishes, onions—he'd had these last year; now he added kale, zucchini, tarragon, other herbs. Each day now he would work on his garden for several hours, bending down to it, plucking, feeling, watering, watching. It all mattered. Even the watching. Every day. He'd increased the size of his garden by a third this year. It would require more work but he could do it. He still forgot many things—names, events, people he had known; but he forgot nothing connected to his garden. It would be a good garden this year, as fruitful as anyone's garden. Maybe better.

Got it all in now, he thought, leaning against the rake, *and Mike will be here soon to take us a-fishing.* It would be good to be in the car, on a trip, listening to Mike's excited patter; it would be good to try the river again. Mike had said the Hendricksons had started.

Three years. Days, weeks, months had ticked by, minute by minute, and imperceptibly the changes had come. The insurance had kept them from bankruptcy, Jane had begun to work for a real-estate agent in town—and had blossomed with it. Junior was earning his way in college, his own man, and Frank was a senior in high school and working part-time at Mike's garage. They didn't need what he'd once earned; he knew that what they needed most he could give them only after he had given it to himself.

He had done the exercises the men in white advised, with barbells and bicycle—over and over and again; he hated to do them and stopped when it came time to work in his garden. Several times last spring Mike had taken him to the West Branch, which they'd often fished together, before he got wrecked. At first he merely found a rock, sat down, and watched. But he had not been able to resist the tug, deep inside him, to be on the stream, part of it, fishing. Wasn't that *really* why he'd done all those endless, tedious exercises, up and down, back and forth, hour after hour, all those months?

It had been impossible at first, after nearly two years. He had slipped twice on the rocks before he even reached the river. Even with the cane his right leg would not hold on broken terrain. Then he slipped again when he took his first tentative step into the water, careening badly, catching himself on his left arm. "No help, no help," he'd said when Mike stepped toward him. Then he'd been unable to strip line and cast left-handed, and finally, after several mad minutes he had given it up and fallen again on his way out, slamming his chin into a rock, cutting it sharply. No it was not possible. He could not do it.

But it was a warm May morning and Mike would be there soon and it would be better this year. He'd earned it. Perhaps he'd even take his first trout since the crash.

Mike came promptly at twelve, and in a few minutes they were in the car racing toward the West Branch. "Magnificent day, Billy," Mike said, pushing the pedal harder. "The Hendricksons will be on in all their glory. They'll be popping out and the birds will be working, and we're going to get us a few. The cornfield run. I can feel a certain fat old brownie just waiting for you there today."

Mike parked along a small dirt turnoff and they got out and began to rig their rods, put on their waders. Mike was suited up and ready before Brannigan had worked one leg into his hip boots. "Go on, Mike. I'll be there . . . when I'm there."

"So you're tired of my company. Fine. I'm going upstream, you take the middle of the run, where the current slows. Take your time: we're a half hour early. Lousy luck, kiddo."

Brannigan watched him stride off, his bull back bouncing even in waders. Then he finished raising his boots, strapped them to his belt, and got out his vest. He could use his right hand as support now, to hold one section of the rod firmly enough for his left to insert the other section; he managed it, with guides aligned, on only the second try. Then he strung the line slowly through the guides until the end of the fly line and all of the leader were outside the tip top. It was well he had practiced all winter.

He got out a Hendrickson he'd tied before the crash, kept in mothballs, and held it as firmly as he could with his right fingers. Then he tried to insert the point of the leader. It would not go. He kept shoving it off to the side, or shaking the fly. Finally he dropped the fly in the grass and had to bend down, slowly, to look for it. When he found it, he stayed on the ground in the shadow of the car and held the fly up to the sky so that the light-blue would show through the hole and he could better fit in the leader. The operation took him five minutes.

As he began to walk along the edge of the cornfield toward the river, his right leg came up in a large, jerky arc, and then down again, one step after the other. Slowly. There was no rush. There was plenty of time. Mike had coaxed him out several more times last summer and fall, and each time he fell but there was some slight improvement. Not much. Not enough for him to know he could do it, like he could garden, not enough to get a line out far enough to tempt a trout—but some. You had to connive. You had to be cunning and crafty, and to forget how it once was. You had to remember always that it would not all come back, not ever. You had to work within the fixed knowledge that you could continue to improve, always, and that this counted, but that even at your very best, some day, you would be, by the world's standards, a lemon.

Perhaps he'd get one today. His first. It would be wonderful if he could get into a really large trout, perhaps seventeen or eighteen inches. You didn't have to make many casts, just the right one at the right time. He'd practiced on the lawn and he knew he now could get enough distance to reach the lip of the current in the cornfield pool. He'd once fished it many times. There was room for a decent backcast, and the shallow bar on his side of the run was hard earth and rubble, with only a few rocks that might trip him up. Mike had made a good choice; he'd be fishing upstream, in the fast water where the Hendricksons hatched, but there'd be plenty of fish falling back into the pool to pick up the duns as they floated down, especially once the hatch really got going.

One step at a time—the right leg out first, and down, out and down. No hurry. You couldn't rush a walk anymore than you could a garden. You couldn't rush anything. Anyway, you saw more when you walked this slow—those crows pecking at corn seeds, that huge growth of skunk cabbage, lush and green and purple, the fuzzy green on the boughs of the willows. A gorgeous day, only slightly overcast now, perfect for Hendricksons.

As he neared the row of trees that bordered the river, he could see Mike upstream, wading deep; his rod was held high and had a sharp arc. *Good old Mike. Got one already.* Up and out, then down. Then again. And again. He worked his way through the alders to the edge of the river. The water was perfect—dark and alive, flecked with bubbles and eddies where the current widened and slowed. Like he'd dreamed it all winter. Yes, that was a fish. And another. He looked to the sky and saw four or five tan flies flutter and angle off into the trees. *Yes. Yes.*

He took a tentative step into the water and felt a touch of fear as he left the firmness of the earth. No matter. It would pass. All the old feeling was there; he could still feel, deep within him, something in him reaching out to the life of the river—its quick faceted run above, the long flat pool below; its translucent dark green and gliding shadows. Flowing, always moving. Changing. The same and not the same. He picked out a dun and watched it bound, like a tiny tan sailboat, over the tail of the riffle, then swirl and float into slower water where it vanished in a sudden pinching of the surface.

Yes, they were moving today. He could see six, seven fish in fixed feeding positions, rising steadily. There was plenty of time. *Don't rush. Do it very, very slowly*. They'd be going good for another hour; he wanted to pick out one good fish, near enough for him to reach with his short cast. Only one good fish. He didn't want a creelful. Only one.

Upstream, Mike was into another trout, and a few minutes later, while Brannigan still eased slowly, steadily into deeper water, inch by inch, Mike had another. *We've caught one of those magical days,* he thought. *Another foot or so* . . . At last, deep as he dared go, he stood on firm hard rubble in water up to his thighs. He stripped line deliberately by raising and lowering his right hand; then, holding the loose line as best he could, he made an extremely short cast. *Good. Much better this year.* Then he stood, rod poised, watching the spreading circles of feeding fish. There were two twelve-inchers in the middle current lane, feeding freely, and two small fish back ten feet; he couldn't reach any of those anymore, though they'd once have been easy enough casts. He could never have fished to that rise in the far eddy, though: the currents were too tricky, the cast too long. Too bad. That was a large fish.

Then he saw the steady sipping rise directly upstream from him, not thirty feet away. Sometimes the largest fish rose like that, but so did fingerlings. It was time to try. He could reach that fish.

His first cast was too short and too hard. His next was off to the right and too hard. The next two were not bad but the fish both times rose to a natural a second before his fly floated past. On his next cast, the trout rose freely, took, and, gripping line and handle with his left hand, as he'd practiced, he struck and had the fish on. A good one. A bright, large leaper that came out, shaking its spots at him and falling back, and then streaking up into the current, across to the far bank, boring deep, and then leaping again.

"Mike!" He usually didn't talk while he fished but he wanted his friend to see this. He hadn't shouted very loud and above him, Mike, busy with still another fish, did not hear. Again the fish came out. "A beauty," he said audibly. "A fine brown." Again the fish raced across the current, stripping line from the reel, arching the rod sharply. *Got to get it. Can't lose this one.*

In ten minutes he could tell the trout was tiring. But it was still on the opposite side of the current. As he began to retrieve the line slowly, the fish came into the current and allowed itself to be carried downstream. Then, suddenly, it bolted directly toward him and the line went slack. "No, no," he said, struggling but unable to strip back line quickly enough.

When he regained control, the fish was gone. He drew the line back slowly until he could see the bedraggled fly. The fish had merely pulled out on the slack line—because of his goddam right arm. His right arm—which might as well not be there.

He was sitting in the car, all his equipment packed away, when Mike came back. Mike had caught seven fish, all of size but none as large as the one Brannigan had lost, and said it was the best day he could remember, except of course the day he'd gotten the three-pound brookie in Canada and Brannigan that lucky male. Brannigan offered a weak smile but said nothing, and Mike looked at him and then said nothing as he took off his vest and waders.

In the car, heading home, he turned to Brannigan and asked quietly, "How'd you do, Billy? Take any?"

"I lost one . . . Mike. Pretty good fish. Then I decided I'd better quit because at least I hadn't fallen in. Like every other time. So I headed . . . out. Slowly. Praising myself all the time . . . that at least I hadn't taken . . . a bath this time."

"You took some bad ones last year, Billy."

"I'd lost a good one, a really good fish, and that didn't make . . . me feel too cheery . . . Yet I'd hooked it and played it a long time . . . which I . . . never did before, not since I got wrecked, and I figured . . . if I could get out without a spill, I'd . . . still be ahead."

"Was it a really good fish, Billy?"

"Big. Very big brown."

"Sixteen inches?"

"More."

"That's a big fish."

"So I was one step or two from the bank, smiling and praising myself . . . that I . . . hadn't fallen, when . . . I went into a pothole."

"Hell!"

"So I went down and over, ass . . . over teakettle. Almost drowned."

"Billy!"

"Almost. My head went under . . . and I was on my right side and couldn't . . . get leverage, and sort of forced my head out, and went under again, and gagged. Knew I was going to die. I felt the rasp of brakes . . . in my brain. I suddenly . . . did not want to die. The water was shallow . . . but it was deep enough. Deep enough, Mike. I did not want to die," he said quietly. "So finally I managed to twist over onto my left side. Broke my rod. Slammed my bone badly. Barely . . . got out of it."

Mike looked over at his friend who had lost his fish, nearly ended it all. He had not one word to cheer him with. Brannigan was sitting in the same seat he'd been in when the accident smashed him, and there was a curious grin on his face. "Maybe we . . . really shouldn't go anymore, Billy," Mike said soberly. "Know what I mean?" He had hoped desperately that Brannigan would get one good trout, that this day might be a new beginning. He had for three years said everything he knew to say. He had no words left.

Faintly, as a slight pressure first and then a firm grip, Mike felt his friend's left hand on his shoulder. "No," he heard Brannigan say. And when he turned: "We're going . . . to keep going . . . back."

Giant
Nova Scotia Tuna

~~~~~~~~~~~~~~~~~~~

Zane Grey

IT SEEMED A far cry from Avalon, California, to Liverpool,
Nova Scotia. And at the beginning of the best swordfish time on
the Pacific, to leave for the doubtful pursuit of giant tuna off the
Atlantic coast was something extremely hard to do. Had I not
made plans a year ahead, I probably would have taken the easy
course of postponement.

We were to find that the physical effort alone was enough to
daunt most anglers. The climate of Avalon is the finest in the
world. We had become used to cool atmosphere with a tang of
fog. The Pullman car was a furnace; the Mojave Desert a glaring
waste of hot rock and sand; at Needles the mercury stood at 115
degrees. Arizona gave us a most welcome respite and we reveled
in the green uplands of cedar and sage, the panorama of clouds
and dropping veils of rain, and rainbows curved over the purple
horizons. Kansas was dust and heat; Chicago humid and muggy,
and an infernal place of noise and fury and gasoline; and not
until we left Boston to cross the Bay of Fundy did we get any rest
and comfort.

An angler should not mind the discomforts of travel, weather, and crowds, but while these things are omni-present, he has to think pretty hard of clear swift shady streams and limpid lakes and the cool heaving sea in order to convince himself that he is a rational being.

My plans of several years' development and a year of fixed purpose made it impossible to give up this Nova Scotia trip or regard it in any way except with thrilling zest.

Captain Laurie Mitchell of Liverpool, Nova Scotia, had inspired me to this undertaking. He had fought between fifty and sixty of these giant tuna, and had succeeded in catching one, the largest on record, seven hundred and ten pounds. This fish dragged him nine miles out to sea, and halfway back. It measured ten and one-half feet and was as large round as a barrel. J. K. L. Ross, another Canadian angler, who lives at St. Ann's Bay, has caught several of these great mackerel, all from four to six hundred pounds in weight. He, too, had lost at least seventy-five. Two others of these fish have been caught by an English angler, Mitchell Henry; and these few comprise the total that have ever been landed.

The game was a new one, with no very satisfactory method of pursuing it yet devised. Its possibilities seemed most remarkable. Its difficulties appeared almost as unsurmountable as broadbill swordfishing, though a great difference existed between these two strenuous types of angling.

I determined to go as fully equipped as was possible, and to try out the Nova Scotia method of fishing from a skiff, and also what I called a mixture of Florida and California methods.

Captain Mitchell had constructed for me two light skiffs, one eighteen and the other twenty feet in length, two-oared, sharp fore and aft, and round as a spoon on the bottom. My Florida boatman, Robert King, had a launch built for me in Fort Myers, following the model used by the skillful Florida mullet-fishermen. It was twenty-five feet long, seven and one-half beam, light and strong, and was equipped with two engines, two propellers and two rudders. It was guaranteed to make eighteen miles an hour, and turn round in its own length, at full speed. I had this launch shipped to Liverpool, with the special Catalina revolving chairs furnished with rod-sockets. One of each of these was to be installed in the launch and the two skiffs. Then I brought the tackles I had especially made for taking these great fish.

I was certain that these Coxe reels, Murphy hickory rods, and Ashaway linen lines were the very finest and most enduring which could possibly be built. This question of tackle is a most important one, and must of necessity come up often. Many bitter controversies have been waged by fishermen over the respective merits of light and heavy tackle. My contention has always been that the fair and sportsmanlike method is to use tackle strong enough to subdue the fish, and not to break off a number of hooked fish in endeavor to catch one on a lighter tackle. All hooked fish that break away become prey for sharks, or they die. The slogan of many anglers, "Lighter tackle, fewer fish!" is very impressive and fine-spirited to the inexperienced angler. But in this case the truth is this: "Fewer fish brought in to the dock, but many more dead in the sea!"

I was not yet in any position to write authoritatively about tackle and fishing for these enormous tuna, so many of which have been broken off. If hundreds of them have broken tackle and only about ten been caught, the per cent of loss runs very high. My swordfish tackle should be strong enough, provided the boat can be maneuvered very skillfully. But in any case, if this king of the mackerel family cannot be fairly beaten with the tactics I shall employ (and that means without breaking off many) I shall be inclined to give it up as a bad job. Sea fish no doubt grow too large to be whipped on any rod and reel. If the water is not shallow along this coast, so that it is impossible for tuna to sound, fishing for them with rod and reel would be ridiculous and cruel. It may be that anyway. But I have great hopes of finding it possible to consider this large tuna fishing in a class with broadbill swordfishing. No higher place could be given it.

At Yarmouth we encountered heavy fog, and to me it was like meeting an old friend from across the continent. Long before we ran into this lowering silver bank of fog I could smell it. Probably all fogs are alike. Surely they are all cool, wet, silent, strange, mysterious; and they hide everything from the sight of man. It is a fear-inspiring sensation to go driving over the sea through a dense fog. The foghorns, the whistles, the bell buoys all have a thrilling, menacing sound.

Here we disembarked and took a train, without being able to see what the port looked like. Some ten miles on we ran out of the fog into bright sunshine, and I found the Province of Nova Scotia to be truly of the northland, green and verdant and wild, dotted with lakes and areas of huge gray rocks, and low black ranges covered with spruce, and rivers of dark clear water.

As we progressed these characteristics enhanced. What welcome relief to eyes seared by sight of barren desert and hot cities! The long grass, the wild flowers, the dense thickets of spruce, the endless miles of green were a soothing balm.

Liverpool proved to be six hours' journey from Yarmouth, and turned out to be the very prettiest little town I ever visited. The houses were quaint and of an architecture unfamiliar to me, very inviting to further attention. Everywhere were huge trees, maples, ash, locusts, and they graced ample yards of luxuriant green. A beautiful river ran through the town, and picturesque fishing smacks lined its shores.

We were met by Captain Mitchell, and also my two boatmen, who had come on in advance. My party included my brother R. C. and my boy Romer and an Arizonian named Jess Smith. Out of these three I hoped to have a good deal of fun, besides the considerable help they could give.

We spent that afternoon unpacking our innumerable bags and grips and in trying out the Florida launch on the river. Bob King and Sid Boerstler, my boatmen, found out a good deal that did not suit them; and as often before, their incomparable value to me manifested itself. Sid held a high diploma for engineering ability, and Bob naturally and by long experience was an adept with tools, mechanics, and everything pertaining to boats. He had spent all his life fishing, living by the rivers and bays of Florida. He had a genius for catching fish. He made an art of it. They changed everything in that little launch. Nothing suited them. My boy Romer, who has begun to show marked interest in the mechanics of automobiles, hydroplanes, boats, and all manner of apparatus, had a very great deal to say about what should and should not be done, much to Bob's amusement. He said: "Romer, the trouble is this boat is all right, only it's wrong." To me Bob said: "That boy's smarter than an Everglade Indian."

Later that day we gave the launch a final try-out. I could not have hoped for more. It was fast, easy, comfortable, and could turn quicker than any boat I had ever been in. The self-starters worked admirably. It took about one second to get into motion. In fact, it started so abruptly that it threw me into a corner of the cockpit, and Jess nearly went overboard.

"Hey, cowboy," yelled Sid, testily, "trim the boat! This ain't a bronc!"

"Wal," drawled Bob, "she only makes aboot fifteen miles. She rides too high. The engines should have been forward. But I reckon we can chase these big tuna to a funeral."

Sid was even more pessimistic, mostly relating to the engines. He confounded me in technical complaint about gaskets, controls, levers, spark-plugs, and what not. Then at the conclusion of this tirade he added: "But she's pretty good. I'll soon have her so she'll ball the jack out of here like a scooter duck."

It is interesting to state, in passing, that Bob and Sid had a remarkable flow of language, highly edifying to me and a source of infinite amusement, but unfortunately most of it unprintable.

That evening we went down to the dock to see the native fishermen come in and unload their catch for the market. Docks are always fascinating places for me. This one appeared especially so. The brown river ran between green banks, with farms and cottages on the west side, and low rising piny hills beyond. On the town side a line of old weather-beaten storehouses stood back from the plank dock. You did not need to be told that Liverpool was a fisherman's town and very old. The scent of fish, too, was old, almost overpoweringly so. Two small schooners were tied up to the dock, the *Ena C.* and the *Una W.* What beautiful names are given to Englishwomen and flowers and boats! One of these small ships, a two-master, had a crew of six, sturdy brown seamen, clad in rubber overalls. They had been out three days and had a catch of 16,000 pounds, codfish, halibut, and two swordfish. I surely had a thrill at sight of the broadbills. These were small fish compared with most I had seen during June and July on the Pacific. The codfish averaged twenty to thirty pounds. They had a number of halibut, several over two hundred pounds.

This schooner, with its weather-and-service-worn appearance, its coils of heavy hand-line, its skiffs dove tailed into one another, its rope and barrels and paraphernalia scattered about on the deck, and the deep hold from which the fishermen were pitchforking cod out on the dock, and the rude pulpit built out over the bowsprit, from which swordfish were ironed—all these held great interest and curiosity for me, filling me with wonder about the exploits of these brave simple men who lived by the sea, and emphasizing again the noble and elemental nature of this ancient calling.

We inquired to find out if any tuna had been seen lately. Several weeks ago, they told us, tuna had been plentiful in the bays and inlets. They had come with the first run of herring. But none had been seen lately. The first run of herring was earlier than usual. A big season was expected. Sometime round the middle of August the great mass of herring would arrive. These were the species that spawned along this shallow Nova Scotia shore. They were larger than the present fish. The schools of tuna followed them. We were a little early.

We engaged two natives to accompany us—Pence to run the large launch, and Joe to make himself generally useful. Both men knew the coast and all the fishermen.

Next morning we were up before five, and on the water in half an hour. When we turned the corner of high land, where the quaint white lighthouse stood, and I saw down the widening bay, I was charmed. The shore lines were rugged clean boulders that merged into the dark spruce forest. As we glided down the bay I saw green and black hills rising to a considerable height, and here and there white or gray cottages shone in the sunlight. Toward the mouth of the bay we entered the zone of the nets. They were stretched all along the shore, and the bobbing floats could be seen everywhere, from a quarter to a half mile out. We discovered several traps, which were likewise nets, but operated differently from the gill-nets. These had circles and lines of corks on the surface, marking the trap, and long wings leading off to each side. Captain Mitchell explained that the fishermen had just begun to put in their traps, and that around these the tuna would come and stay, and that was where there was the best chance of hooking one.

We ran up to one boat, to which two fishermen were hauling their gill-net. I saw herring shining in the water and being picked out of the net by the fishermen. We bought a bushel of them for chum and bait. This variety of herring was a beautiful little fish, nearly a foot long, shaped somewhat like a trout, only with smaller head, and colored brilliantly, dark green on the back, silver underneath, with sides that glowed opalescent. We proceeded along these nets, to a point opposite Western Head, a bold cape jutting out, and asked all the fishermen if they had discovered any tuna. But no one had seen any for over a week.

Then we ran outside the bay, round a picturesque lighthouse, into the ocean. I was amazed at the smooth, calm sea. R. C. and I could not believe our eyes. Was this the Atlantic? The gray old stormy sea we had fought so long! Captain Mitchell assured us that it was and that we would see many such fine days in this latitude. There was no swell. The water scarcely moved. The coast line appeared to be wonderfully indented by bays and coves and inlets, and marked by beautiful islands, dark with spruce, and hold headlands, rugged and gray. Low clouds of fog shone white in the sun. We ran through some of them, and between islands, and along the shore for fifteen miles to a place called Cherry Hill. Off this point Captain Mitchell had won his memorable fight with his 710-pound tuna. We met and talked with several net fishermen, none of whom had seen any fish that day. So we ran out a few miles, and then circled back toward Western Head. We sighted some schools of pollack feeding on the surface, but no other kind of fish. The sea remained tranquil all day, and when we entered the bay again, late in the afternoon, there was only a gentle ripple on the water. Then we ran in, and so ended our first day, August 1st.

That night we heard of tuna having been seen ten miles west, at Port Mouton, and decided to go there next day. We made the same early start. The day equaled the one before, and the shore line proved remarkably beautiful. High wooded hills, green slopes, gray rough banks, rose above the sea. We wound, at length, in between gemlike islands, where the channels were calm and clear, and the round bays like glass, and the sandy beaches burned white in the sunlight. Port Mouton was a little fishing village with gray weather-worn houses facing the sea. We landed at a dock where fishermen were unloading tons of herring. Many of these were being salted in barrels for lobster bait. It was a crude, primitive place, singularly attractive with the weather-beaten huts, boats, docks, its bronzed fishermen, its air of quaint self-sufficiency. We were told that tuna had been seen two days before off the island and eastward from the nets. There was a wreck that marked the locality. The leader of this fisherman squad talked interestingly:

"Our methods are crude," he said. "We have no money to buy proper equipment. We could do ten times as much. Herring fishing is but in its infancy. The supply is enormous and inexhaustible. The sea is a gold mine."

I agree with him about the sea being a treasure house, but I could not believe the supply of herring inexhaustible. I had seen the bluefish, the menhaden, the mackerel, the white sea bass and albacore, all grow scarce where once they had been abundant. Herring, however, may be different. I heard of schools twenty miles in extent. In fact, I received an impression of the marvelous fecundity and vitality of this species. The whole south shore of Nova Scotia lived by the herring.

These fishermen called the tuna by the name of albacore. That was a surprise to me, for they certainly are not albacore. Horse-mackerel and tunny are two other names, characteristic of the Jersey shore and of the Mediterranean.

We found the place to which we had been directed, off a wild and lonely shore, where the ocean boomed and a great iron steamer, broken in the middle, gave grim evidence of the power of the sea in storm. The current was swift here. We anchored, and tried chumming for a few hours. But we raised no tuna. The wind came up strong and on the run back we sent the spray flying. The air grew chill. When the sun went under clouds I felt quite cold, despite my warm woolen clothes; and I was glad to get back.

Next day was Sunday. The Nova Scotians keep the Sabbath. They do not fish on the seventh day of the week. I am afraid they made me feel ashamed of my own lack of reverence. More and more we Americans drift away from the Church and its influence. Perhaps that is another reason for our lawlessness, our waning home life, our vanishing America. I should never forget that some of Christ's disciples were fishermen, and since then all fisher folk have been noted for their simplicity and faith. Liverpool was to awaken in me something long buried under the pagan self-absorption of life in the United States. When I was a boy I had to go to Sunday school and to church. It made me unhappy. I never could listen to the preacher. I dreamed, mostly of fields, hills and streams, of adventures that have since come true. As I grew older, and learned the joys of angling, I used to run away on Sunday afternoons. Many a time have I come home late, wet and weary after a thrilling time along river or stream, to meet with severe punishment from my outraged father. But it never cured me. I always went fishing on Sunday. It seemed the luckiest day. I do not consider it wrong. But I shall respect the custom of the Nova Scotians and stay quietly in the hotel on that day. Full well I know there will come a Sunday when the tuna will run into the bay and smash the water white.

Monday was cool and rather dark, with a southwest wind that made me favor the protected places in the sun. We anchored off Western Head, chummed and fished awhile, then ran out to sea several miles to try for halibut. About noon we returned and anchored in the bay opposite one of the traps, and tried again. The water grew rough and the wind cold.

Upon our return, rather late, we found most thrilling news awaiting us. All the herring fishermen are eager to help us find tuna and report every evening. One of them had three tuna under his boat all the time he was hauling his net. Two of the fish were very large. A *small* one usually runs about five hundred pounds. These tuna rushed for every herring that slipped away from the net.

Another fisherman found a hole in his trap, assuredly made

by a big tuna. Then late this evening a third man reported seeing a large school of tuna near Coffin Island. All this is thrilling and exciting news. The presence of these great fish near at hand is something momentous. I have no idea how sight of one is going to make me feel. But it will be a tremendous experience. And to hook one—what will that be?

The weather is threatening to-night, cold, windy, dark, and the air seems storm-laden.

During the night I was awakened by the patter of rain on the roof. What a welcome sound to a traveler from California! The wind wrestled in the trees, moaned and soughed. I lay awake for a long while. Morning disclosed gray skies and copious showers. We had to forego our fishing. And we talked fish, tackle, past performances, especially those that concerned the tuna angling on the Nova Scotia coast.

Captain Mitchell had a hurry call on the telephone from Homans, a fisherman of Port Mouton. Homans sent information that tuna were thick in Jordon Bay, near Lockeport, some thirty miles from Liverpool. This was most alluring news. We decided to leave at once, sending the boats with the boatmen, and the rest of us traveling by auto. Meanwhile the skies cleared and the sun came out bright and warm. The ride down through the forest was both beautiful and hideous; it depended on where fire had been. Sable River attracted my fisherman's eye. It was a rock-lined, hemlock-shaded stream of clear dark water, almost black. The driver said it contained fine trout.

As we neared Lockeport I caught glimpses of the ocean, and a blanket of white fog far out, drifting toward shore. That worried me. I was afraid the boats would have to put in.

The fishing settlement, a small town, was located on an island to which we crossed over a bridge, and it was surrounded by islands, little and big, and a ragged stretch of mainland, where the breakers crawled foaming up the rocks. I heard the melancholy wash of the surf, and presently espied a beautiful curved beach of sand, very broad and smooth, upon which little lines of shallow breakers rolled.

We found comfortable quarters, and at once set out to learn something about the tuna. We were overjoyed to find out that Jordon Bay was full of tuna. Many had gotten into the nets and a few had been harpooned. There was no market for them here. Our design to catch tuna on rod and reel excited no little interest.

After supper we went out to be surprised and dismayed to find the fog had drifted in. It was not heavy, but it obscured the sea and islands, and gradually the houses at a distance. I was discouraged. What was worse, we received a telephone message from Port Mouton informing us that our boats had to put in there on account of the fog.

Just before dark young Romer disappeared. We looked every- where for him, and at last Jess found him way out on one of the fish docks, all by himself. Jess said: "By golly! it was so foggy I couldn't see very far. Nearly fell off the dock. I yelled and he answered. Then I found him fishing. He had caught fifty-seven pollack, several as long as his arm, and he was shore excited. He was throwing them back. He made me stay long enough to catch one myself. I reckon Romer is a chip off the old block."

That sort of pleased me. Romer had been rather trying with his incessant energy and mischievousness. The fish dock had to be approached by narrow alleys, running round behind fish houses and big gloomy buildings. It was a lonesome and a weird place, shrouded as it was in thin fog. I would not have cared to spend any time there. I certainly marked this incident down to the lad's credit.

Before going to bed I walked out upon the porch. The little fishing hamlet was wrapped in silence and gray obscurity. No lights showed. A few dim shapes of houses loomed darkly.

Somehow it was oppressive. To think these people lived here, half the time unable to see across the road!

Morning brought no change. A heavy fog mantled the port. There was no help for it. My impatience and eagerness must be endured. About eight-thirty the fog lightened somewhat and a pale sun, just visible, shone through. I went down to the dock.

It was a bustling place. The herring boats were coming in from the nets to unload the morning's catch. Some boats were half full of the beautiful silver-green and pink fish; others had not so many, and some only a few bushels. These boats and the fishermen who manned them certainly showed the labor and travail of their calling. Yet how picturesque they seemed! The men were hardy, rough, genial, clad in rubber, covered with fish scales, and redolent of the sea. The wharf where they discharged their cargo was a busy scene, just as hard and crude as their boats. I was tremendously interested to see what became of the herring. Since the magnificent tuna fish followed the herring, lived off them, the same as the fishermen, I wanted to know all that was possible about them.

Information obtained from H. R. L. Bill, owner of the fish market, Lockeport, Nova Scotia:

Kippered herring are shipped mostly to upper Canada and Vancouver—season starts in September.

New York handles a lot of Scotch cured herring with the heads on—cheap way of preparing. They are stripped, only insides removed, not split, and salted—60 pounds of salt to the barrel. Also called Matjes herring—much used by Jews in New York.

Kippered herring are pickled for one hour—smoked one night— only 24 hours old when smoked. 9x18 ft. smoke house—fires of hard wood and sawdust—smoked one night on racks in the ceiling.

Split herring—Fat herring are best in July—cured 10 days, packed filled with salt.

No. 1 herring are eleven inches and up.

July and August are the hot months in the United States and when there is most fog. Fog caused by the warm waters of the Gulf Stream coming into the cold water of the Atlantic.

About one hundred small motor boats have lain about the wharf at Lockeport, laden with cod, at one time. Usually eighteen vessels a day in winter—able to fish only about one day a week in winter.

Lockeport, Nova Scotia. Information from H. R. L. Bill on fish and fishing:

Most winter fish are shipped fresh—what they can't ship are made into fillets—also the small "scrod"—all kinds of small fish are made into fillets and salted down.

The "pine-tree cod" are caught in the fall on the shoals. They have a design on their sides that looks like a pine tree.

Fish caught on kelp bottom are red cod and other fish caught in shoal water are yellow.

One day 15,000 pounds of halibut were boxed on Mr. Bill's wharf in one morning.

The town of Lockeport handles 5,000,000 pounds of cured fish in one season.

It takes 360 pounds of fresh fish to make one cantle (112 lbs).

Sixty pounds of smoked finnan haddie are obtained from one hundred pounds of fresh haddock.

Thirty-five pounds of fillets from one hundred pounds of fresh fish.

Two boxes of dried herring (40 fish each) from one bushel.

One barrel of split herring from four and one-half bushels.

They use ocean salt—Mediterranean. The best is from Trapenay (an island off the coast of Italy).

Bill's firm uses 10,000 bushels of salt. West Indian salt also used—from Turk's Island. Trapenay salt contains no lime, but West Indian salt does. Therefore the former is best for fish.

I met some of these fishermen, all of whom were eager to give me information or help me to succeed. Most of them were doubtful. All were sure I would hook many tuna. But to land one on a rod was improbable. They told me about ironing (harpooning) these monsters and fighting them on a rope. Their boats would be towed for miles, at first very swiftly. One fellow lost five tuna in succession the same morning. Another had a tuna that broke through all the nets in the bay and finally got loose.

"The albacore are there," said another. "I saw some and heard a lot of them this morning. Splashing round the nets. It was too foggy to see clearly."

I talked with the native fisherman who was Whitney's guide when he fought a large tuna. It whipped him and also his comrade. They chased it around until it lodged on a rock, and finally the boatman harpooned it.

At four o'clock Captain Mitchell and my boatmen arrived to report a most difficult trip from Port Mouton. They had to follow the buoys, and finding each one in the dense fog was no easy matter. We planned to go to Jordon Bay to-morrow, in any event.

To-night, about six, the fog settled down so thick it could be cut. It was heavy, wet, and most depressing to a Californian. I could not accustom myself to the gloom, the spectral shapes, the silence, the dampness, the inscrutable mystery. I love the fog in California, but this Nova Scotia brand is another matter. I can hear the drip, drip, drip of heavy drops on the porch outside, the low sad wash of the surf, and the moan of a distant fog whistle. Yet somehow all this is thrilling. Contrasts are helpful. I cannot understand how people could choose to live in a country where fog predominated over sunshine, but it serves to make me appreciate my own country vastly more.

Next morning Lockeport was so thickly muffled that you could not distinguish one house from another. Hours we wandered round, waiting. It was most trying. Never before had I known what it meant to be fogbound. About ten o'clock it lifted enough for us to see the wharves, the boats, and some of the capes, all dim and weird. We decided to run to East Jordon Bay, some eight miles round the headlands. This was a dangerous passage even in fair weather, for anyone who did not know the coast. Some of the fishermen disclaimed any wish to pilot us. Finally one of the dealers let us have his skipper, a man who had navigated this coast for twenty years. With him we set out. In ten minutes we lost sight of the town and could see only a few rods all around us. Sid and Bob, with R. C., kept close behind in the launch. Sometimes we could not discern the rocky bluff. I could hear the wash of the sea when the land was invisible. Occasionally dim slopes loomed up ahead. I could see them grow out of the gray gloom. How indistinct and far away they seemed! But they were close. Rocks! Ugly, jagged rocks, they looked like sea demons rising out of the water to smash us. We managed to elude them. Beyond we encountered a heavy swell. Our boats rocked and tossed. Soon I could hear the mournful whistling-buoy. Bob called it "Groaner," and indeed that was felicitous. Soon a dark wall loomed through the fog. It was the headland we had to pass. The sea boomed against it. I could see the dim white breakers dash upon it, and climb. What a frightful place to pass! Suppose our engine went dead! We would have been lost. When we rounded that forbidding point, begirt with thundering surges, it was none too soon for me.

Inside the bay the water was calm and the fog thinner. Several times we saw land, and one of these points was Blue Island. It towered like a mountain. We traveled on for an hour or more, and finally reached a ruined lighthouse and a dilapidated breakwater. Through the fog I discerned the dim outline of a house, and boats, and net racks. This was East Jordon. We tied up to the dock.

A fisherman named Sears lived there. He and his men kept a weir, for the purpose of catching herring. He was a huge man and looked the lifetime he had spent there. He said the bay was full of albacore and that two had been caught in the weir the day before. He expected the weather to clear. Naturally we were cheered, and we waited another two hours until the fog lifted somewhat. A breeze sprang up, rippling the bay. Across from us rose a wooded ridge, wild and ragged, and behind us sloped a verdant farm, with a generous sprinkling of evergreens.

We ran out with the two boats to a point halfway between the shores, and anchored the big boat, to which we tied. Then we began to chum. The herring ground to bits made a slick in the water. It drifted away across the bay, toward the weir. The breeze strengthened until there was a noticeable ripple. I was watching a dark shadow on the water, wondering what it was, when R. C. and Bob yelled in unison: "Tuna! Tuna!"

I nearly fell off my seat. The dark shadow had been a school of fish. We all yelled at the sight of fins. Slim dark sharp fins unmistakably those of tuna. The fish did not show well nor long. After that we kept on chumming. Soon Bob sighted a second school coming down the bay. It crossed the slick, to our great excitement. But nothing happened. The slick did not hold them. I was the lucky one to sight the third school of these huge fish. Two more schools followed, and not one of them paid any attention to our chum. Finally when we were out of chum and had left only a few herring for bait, I decided to troll before these tuna, after the manner in which we feed a bait to a swordfish.

We had no difficulty getting in front of a school, although they swam swiftly. We ran beyond them and stopped the engines of the launch. Bob began to throw herring in front of the tuna. Suddenly the water roared. It seemed a swirling hole sucked down a herring. Frantically I wound my bait to get it near. We all shouted. But the tuna did not take another bait.

Then, after that school disappeared, we ran around searching for another. It did not take long to find one. We tried the same method, which this time did not work so well. But a third school gave us a better chance, and again we saw the huge swirl as one of the giant mackerel took a bait. R. C. and Bob wished for a kite to fly, after the Pacific method of getting a bait to tuna, but Sid and I were at first rather doubtful about the possible success of that.

At last we had to quit, owing to lack of bait. Moreover, the fog had begun to shut down. We ran back to the breakwater and held a council of war. I had sent for two cars to meet us at this point, and had intended to return to Liverpool that night and have the boats follow as soon as permitted by fog. But now I decided to send R. C. and Jess and the boy back, and remain myself.

They left at four-thirty, with the understanding that they were to return the next day with food supplies and some camping equipment. I walked up and down the long breakwater, hungry and tired. We had little to eat, and nothing that I wanted.

Between six and seven o'clock the fog lifted again, so that we could see objects low down. One of the native fishermen was out in a skiff to look into the weir. For the first time then I paid some attention to this contraption. When he rowed back and shouted, "Two albacore in the weir!" I was tremendously excited.

Sid and Bob rowed me out to the weir. It had a long wing reaching out from the bank two hundred yards or more. The construction was simple, consisting of thin saplings of spruce driven down into the mud. They were a foot apart, and at the low-tide level and also high-tide level were pieces nailed cross-wise for strength. No wire or net of any kind! This long wing led out to a large heart-shaped corral open at the apex for about fifteen feet. Then from the other side of this corral extended a large wing, curved deeply back toward the straight line and working away from it. The corral was built after the same fashion, of saplings a foot apart. There was nothing else to stop the fish. Herring and mackerel could have swum through these fences as easily as through unobstructed water. But the strange fact was they did not. A school of herring would come down with the tide, strike the wing, and follow along it to enter the mouth of the heart-shaped corral. Then they would circle to the left. They would keep on circling and circling until the men came out with a net and surrounded them with it. I could scarcely believe the fish were so stupid. As for tuna staying in that place—I scouted the idea.

We rowed round the inclosure of thin poles, very curious and skeptical. Suddenly Bob yelled: "Wow! Look at that boil!"

Then I saw an enormous swirl and an eddying of the water such as could only be made by the tail of a powerful fish. We stood up in the skiff, and clinging to the poles we peered through, as if we were watching for a tiger. Twice more the big swirl appeared.

"He's thar," vociferated Bob, "an' he's a humdinger. They'll ketch him easy. Funny about fish in a trap. They're all alike except mullet. You can't keep mullet millin' round."

It was an astounding thing for me to ascertain there was really a tuna inside that weir and he would not go out the way he came in. When we saw the fishermen rowing out in their big sharp-nosed yawls we went round the weir beyond the curved wing to meet them. Sears invited us to go inside to see the fun.

"There's not much money in it for us," he said, "but we got to keep the albacore out of the weir, else the herring won't come in. Sometimes we drive one out. We're going to kill these and ship them."

We remained just outside the mouth of the heart-shaped corral, while the fishermen fastened their net to the left side, and then began pulling the boat round by holding to the poles. They let the net out of the boat as they worked round. Big corks kept the top of the net afloat. "Sometimes a smart albacore will hug the poles and we'll fail to get him in the net. Then we have to try over. We made six hauls the other night, before we got one."

When they had half circled the inclosure and had drawn the net away from the opening, we rowed inside. Presently they joined the ends of the net and hauled the purse strings. That closed the net at the bottom. The circle of corks was now perhaps fifty feet in diameter. Sears kept to the outside in his boat, while his three men fastened their boat to the weir and gradually drew in the net, narrowing the circle. Suddenly I saw a blue flash in the middle of the net circle. It was followed by a roar in the water and a tremendous white splash. We were fully fifty feet back, yet the splash reached us.

"Got a netful!" yelled Sears, above the sound of thumping water.

We rowed closer, and I stood up to see better and to take pictures. The inside of that net then became a threshing cauldron. I could make out huge fins and blue gleams and silver flashes. Presently by looking deep in the water I could see a tuna plunge against the net, then slide along. He gleamed like an enormous silver-green shield. The tuna had no room to get headway. It looked easy for them to leap out or slide over the net, but not one made the attempt. As the net was drawn closer and closer the mêlée increased, and for a few moments there was a tremendous splashing.

"They'll give up quick," said Sears. "Sometimes, though, we get hold of a fighter. Not long ago one sank our boat, tore through the net and got away."

I hoped these would all escape. It was an exciting and painful spectacle for me. Presently the fury of plunging eased and then I could see the huge fish piling over one another. Their round backs were like barrels. They lifted their great heads out and gaped with wide mouths. The action was really a gasp. Soon they were so constricted that they could only roll, and beat with mighty tails.

"Only four of them," said Sears. "I thought there were more. They'll give up soon now."

Indeed it seemed so, except in case of the largest. The folds of the net meshed them so they could hardly move. Then two of the fishermen stood up in the skiff. One was armed with a mattock having a spike fully a foot long. The other had a huge mallet, almost too heavy to swing, I thought. It sort of paralyzed me to see these two men prepare for action. What Bob and Sid said was funny, but would not do for publication. When one of the huge tuna rolled his head out the man with the mattock struck him, imbedding the iron several inches in his head. Then the man with the mallet drove the iron mattock clear to the end. It took five powerful strokes. Then they served two more of the tuna in the same way. The water turned red. This work seemed on the moment a horrible butchery to me. It made me sick. Those wonderful beautiful fish!

"Well, it's their country and their work," said Bob, meditatively, as if trying to excuse it to himself. "They have to keep this trap clear for the herring."

The fourth and largest tuna did not give up. Scarcely had his three companions been dispatched when he began to beat with his tail. Faster and faster! He carried net and boats away with him. The roar of water was like that from a huge propeller. He churned a space half as large as the inside of the weir. The yells of the men and their strenuous efforts to hold him proved the resistance of that fish. But they drew the bag of the net closer and closer until he was rolled up in it, and then hauling him to the surface they mattocked and malleted him to death.

Then the fishermen towed their catch ashore and tied them in shallow water. The last act of the day was to chop open their throats with an ax, so they would lose all their blood.

"Wal, then albacore are stupid as pigs an' they shore get treated like pigs," was Bob's last comment.

We rowed back to the boats. I did not eat any supper. I walked the long breakwater from the lighthouse to the shore. The fog shut down thick and wet. It seemed a gloomy hard place, with none of the charm of the south. There were teeth in this northland country. At dark I crawled into one of the little bunks and went to sleep. Several times during the night I awoke, cold and wet. At intervals I heard the low strange moan of the whistling-buoy at the mouth of the bay six or eight miles out. It seemed to harmonize with the surroundings.

At dawn the fog was thicker than ever. We could not see fifty feet. Moreover, we heard the rumble of thunder. A storm was coming down on us. The thunder grew heavier, and at last lightning penetrated the thick mist. What a ghastly phenomenon—lightning-illuminated fog! Then it began to rain. It poured. And gradually the deluge beat down the fog, so that we could see the land with its dark fringe of spruce trees. It rained for three hours, then let up to some extent, so that we could get out and move round.

And presently we took the boats and made for the middle of the bay. The water was dead calm, except where ripples and wrinkles and waves showed the presence of tuna. All the bait we had been able to procure was a bushel of small herring, not very good for our needs. But we used them, anyway. We chummed, and I sat with a bait out. Then it began to rain, and it rained hard for two hours. All this while I sat there hoping for a strike. I got cold and wet, though I had on heavy woolen clothing and rubber coat. The fog drifted by to quell the rain; then the rain clouds got the upper hand of the fog. At last we used up our bait. We ran back to the breakwater, where I dried my clothes and shoes by the little stove in Captain Pence's boat. The rain pattered on the roof. At two o'clock it ceased and all around the fog curtain lifted. For the first time I saw down the bay to Blue Island and Gull Rock, and then on to West Headland. The scene was superb.

I had three hours to wait for the car that was to come for me. So quite naturally I decided to get some bait and fish some more. We took the launch and crossed the bay and ran down six or seven miles. We sighted some fish-net buoys, then some store-houses on the shore, and finally fishermen. Here we obtained a bushel of herring that had just been salted. With these we proceeded to where the schools of tuna had been sporting. Sure enough, they were still there.

We planned to work in front of a school and beyond it, then stop the engines. I was to throw my bait out, and the boys were to throw herrings. The very first school of tuna presented favorably. I could see four or five fish, tails and dorsals out, but there were surely a dozen or more in this school. The leaders pushed waves a foot high ahead of them. They made identically the same waves as the Pacific tuna, only larger. What a thrill I had as they came on! I could hear the soft swish of the water.

When the leaders were perhaps fifty feet from the launch I pitched my bait fully halfway to them. Then Bob and Sid threw out herring. I saw a wide slow swirl, then a rising wave.

"He's got your bait!" yelled Bob.

Quick as a flash I leaped down to straddle my rod and grasped it. The line whizzed off the reel. I meant to let the fish take time with the bait. But he let go. Instantly I saw my mistake. Had the drag of the reel been set that tuna would have hooked himself!

"You should have soaked him," said Bob. "Say, but he was quick. I saw him take that bait. He'd have hooked himself. Some fish, I'll tell the world!"

My bait was the only herring taken by this school. Much excited and encouraged, we hunted for more tuna. We ran from one bunch to another, and sometimes consumed moments in heading the leaders, and we tried to work the same method that had earned my first strike from a Nova Scotia tuna. We had no more such luck. We counted four herring taken by tuna, but not one of these baits had my hook in it. At last we drove them all down for the time being, and once more the fog set in, lowering, drab, cold, dismal. I was in a glow of excitement and had forgotten mist, rain, everything but tuna. It was after four o'clock and the car was waiting for me. I left the boats there and started for Liverpool, with the intention of coming back next day. The farther I rode from East Jordon the clearer grew the weather, and at Liverpool the sun was shining and clouds were all golden. R. C. and Romer listened to my story with bated breath.

"We're going to catch one of those birds," avowed Romer.

I wondered, and felt a rush of thrilling hope, tinctured by doubt. When I remembered the majestic motion of that grand tuna, his swift yet ponderous action, the vast shining green-silver bulk of him, and the swirling waves he shoved ahead of him, I was only a humble and longing fisherman.

On Sunday afternoon we left Liverpool for East Jordon, and had a different and more entertaining ride through wide country, woods and moose meadows, and thick brush. We emerged from this at Jordon Falls. From that point to the lighthouse on the bay was only a short run.

The sun had shone all afternoon, up until now, and at four o'clock the fog began to roll in. Joe reported sighting numerous tuna around the weir on Saturday, but none on Sunday. After supper I walked along the lonely beach, and could not see far through the gloom. The shore was lined with huge gray boulders and fringed with stunted spruce trees. The time and place were not conducive to cheer.

R. C. and I made our beds in the launch, there being just room for one cot and a bed on the floor. We both slept well. At five o'clock all was mantled in thick gray fog. We could not see the lighthouse from the shore. We had breakfast, and then there seemed only waiting. But at seven-thirty I decided to go in the launch after herring. We towed the skiff, and crossed the bay in the fog. Finally we saw shore, and soon encountered several fishermen, from whom we bought a barrel of bait. One of them said there ought to be tuna at his nets, and I hired him to go with us. One of his companions went also, which made us eight in the launch. Too many! As we ran down the bay the fog began to whiten and thin. Soon we saw net-buoys, then Gull Rock, and at last Blue Island. The sun shone pale through the fog. I began to reproach myself for complaints that the fog would never lift.

We found the fisherman's nets full of herring, and Romer and Joe began to pick herring from the meshes. They were still alive, caught behind the gills. Presently another fisherman came along in his boat and told us he had just been feeding herring to a big albacore round his net. I hired him to take us over there and to stand by.

The distance was short. Soon we were tied to the net-buoy and chumming. I put a bait over, rather with a feeling that there was not much chance of a tuna coming along. But in less than five minutes I had a terrific strike, and I jerked with all my might, yelling: "*Strike! Strike!*"

Excitement reigned on that boat. The tuna lunged, dragging my tip into the water, and he ran off away from that net toward another. Sid had the engines going and we were after him with wonderful quickness. I could not believe that I was hooked to a tuna. My legs shook as they used to shake years ago when I had my first swordfish experiences. But gradually I recovered, and as we went after the fish, and I pumped and wound in line, there was hilarity added to the excitement on board. The tuna ran round a net-buoy and fouled the line. I loosened the drag, then while the boys frantically endeavored to free my line the tuna went off on his first terrific rush. He took two hundred yards off the reel. Suddenly I felt my line free of the buoy. Bob had cut the rope on the buoy. We were free, and away we sped after him! The fisherman followed in his launch.

There was sunshine around us, and the shore glimmered through fog. I fought this fish pretty hard while he was taking us up the bay. Sometimes he towed us. The little launch handled perfectly. We were a wildly excited crowd. I endeavored to calm myself and to face the fact that the tuna would probably get away.

Meanwhile the sun came out and we could see everywhere. It was beautiful alongshore. The fish had taken us four miles up the bay. In an hour he appeared to be slowing down and getting tired.

Then he made for shore. Ugly rocks stuck up all around us. The fisherman was of the opinion the tuna had gone in there to cut the line on the rocks. But I did not take this seriously.

R. C. stood up on the bow, and presently he yelled: "I see him! A whale! He'll go five hundred!"

This at once terrified and elated me. I worked as hard as I could. The tuna kept ahead of us, and he turned every way. The leader got tangled round his tail. At first we welcomed that, as we thought it would soon exhaust him. But it did not. He swam near the surface and kept among the rocks. Once Captain Mitchell said: "We'd better lead him out of here." But he would not lead, and we followed him round. When he swam quickly to one side, dragging the line under the boat, I jumped up, threw off my drag, and poked my rod down in the water clear to the reel. I had not yet realized the hazardous position into which the fish had dragged us. I was not worried. In fact I had begun to feel he was weakening and that I would get him.

It began to dawn upon me presently that there was something most unusual and sinister in the action of this fish, turning and wheeling for the rocks. I could not see those rocks deep under the surface, but I heard the boys yell: "Look out! Slack off! Rocks! Starboard!" and various other alarms. When, however, the fish ran straight for a black-nosed reef that was wreathed in foamy breakers, then I gave way to panic. We turned and tacked this way and that. Time after time the big mackerel ran under the boat, and I had to leap up, throw off my drag, and plunge the rod into the water. Seven times I did this successfully. But it was risky business. We followed him in and out, round the black rock, through channels, over shoals, and toward the beach. Then he swept out a couple of hundred yards. I began to breathe easier. But my relief was short-lived. Again he made for the rocks.

"Say, we're following him too much!" shouted R. C.

That warning fell upon deaf ears, for still I had no consistent fear he would cut off on the rocks. We got in a bad position, nearly sliding upon a flat rock we had not seen. The tuna went round it and we had to navigate between the rock and the breakers in order to free the line.

"Go to it!" I yelled, above the roar. "We can swim if we have to!"

Romer, whose face I happened to see, was white and rapt, perfectly wild with excitement and joy. He kept shouting advice to me. R. C. looked stern and grim as he stood upon the bow and waved Sid to steer to port or starboard. Once he called to me, "Good night!" and pointed to a green curling breaker with its white crest. How it boomed! Fifty feet in shore! With the tuna going strong! Still something happened to save us, and we ran round the bad rock away from the heave of the swell that raced toward the ledge. I had a few moments of comparative relaxation.

But when the stubborn tuna deliberately swerved back for the rocks I realized that he was not lunging for shoal water by accident. He had tried every means in deep water to dislodge the infernal thing that held him, and failing, he had headed for the rocks. How strange I had not believed this before! But it was hard to fight the fish and think deliberately at the same time. I had called these giant tuna stupid, an accusation made without careful consideration, and I was now compelled to retract it. At least this tuna was keen, cunning, resourceful, and probably unbeatable. It was instinct that guided him.

Suddenly he made a quick surge on the surface. I saw him—huge, blue-moving mass! It shook my heart, that sight. He swept round, and again the line went under the bow. I leaped up, and threw off my drag. Too quick! As I plunged my rod down into the water I saw some loops of slack line drift back toward the tip. I was frightened. I feared they would catch on the guides. They did catch. I felt a powerful pull—then the rod shot up. My line had caught on the tip and cut off on a guide!

Perhaps I had suffered more at the loss of a great fish—years ago. But not lately. I was stunned. Poor Romer looked sick. R. C. swore roundly and said we had bungled by letting the fish stay in the shallow water. For my part I did not see how we could have helped that. Bob thought we might have dragged him, turned him. And so did Captain Mitchell. We saw him twice after he was free, a blur of blue, moving ponderously away. I felt weak and had a nausea.

"Two hours and ten minutes," reckoned R. C. "And you had him coming! Rotten luck!"

"Well, it was my fault," I replied, finally. "There's nothing to do but swallow it—and try again."

We made our way back to the point between Gull Rock and Blue Island. It was clear and sunny now. What a magnificent view! I put R. C. on the rod to try his luck, and I rested and watched. I was wet with sweat and somewhat shaken by emotion. All the preparation and thought could not do less than have me roused to a high degree of feeling.

The sea was running high, with big swells and waves, yet it was not uncomfortable. Gull Rock, a bare gray steep rock, was chafed by contending tides. Blue Island was a long wild strip of timbered land, with a bluish color. Far beyond, the great white rollers dashed upon West Head, and across the bay on the other headland rose the white spire of a lighthouse. Fishermen were working at their nets. Up the bay the green and gray shores smiled under a belated sunshine, and the cottages of the fishermen stood out upon the hills.

"There's a tuna!" yelled R. C.

I came to with a jump, just in time to see a swirl in our slick. We waited with beating hearts. R. C. sat rigid, ready to strike back, should one of these giants take hold. But nothing happened.

We did not see any more tuna, and used up most of our herring. Then we ran up the bay to try again. We chummed another hour. R. C. sighted a tuna, Captain Mitchell another. They were isolated fish. Evidently no schools were running. So at five o'clock we came ashore.

After resting awhile and having supper I found I was pretty tired. My arms and wrists ached. My head ached, too. It appeared then that I had worked harder on this fish than I realized at the time. We talked over the whole event from all angles, and we certainly marked our mistakes. Mine seemed the most inexcusable. Yet how swiftly it had happened! And that was the first time such a thing had ever happened to me.

By way of a happy change we had the first clear late afternoon, with breeze in the west, and that in itself meant much to me.

Toward sundown I noticed signs of an unusually vivid promise of color in the west. And I wandered out to the end of the long breakwater and sat beneath the old deserted lighthouse. Sure enough, the sunset was beautiful, the first I had seen in Nova Scotia. The west appeared to be sheeted over with a belt of clouds and these all turned from rose to flaming red. It made a glorious blaze over water and land, until the whole world seemed on fire. The freshness and vividness of the color struck me singularly. It took some of the somberness and the cold hard gray quality out of this northland. I watched it until the shadows of dusk at last subdued the afterglow.

Next morning I was up at four-thirty. There were gray clouds in the east and patches of sky, colorless, like the hue of a moonstone, very soft and misty. The air was cool, sweet, damp, laden with mingled scent of sea and forest. How strange to have my view unobstructed by fog! Far down the bay I could see the points of the headlands, and two islands, one large and one small, that I at once recognized, though I had not seen them at this distance. We had breakfast at five o'clock. When we came out again the east was a wonderful delicate gold, too exquisite to attempt to describe.

Soon we were off down the bay, the launch leading the way to pick up the native fisherman who had piloted us to his nets. The water was as level as a mirror and as reflective. The delicate gold suffused all the soft misty clouds, growing stronger as I watched, until at length the sun burst forth gloriously, a golden fire, bathing forest, bay, and meadow slopes in a wondrous luster. Fire at sunset and gold at sunrise! After all the gloomy foggy weather I had been rewarded. It gave me such a different feeling toward this rugged land of seashore and rock-ridged forest.

In less than half an hour we had reached the first of the nets, and soon after that arrived at a point between Gull Rock and Blue Island where the morning before I had hooked my first tuna. How different a scene now! Gentle heaving sea, sparkle of water, bobbing boats of fishermen lifting their nets, the tang of salt, fresh from the vast open space beyond, the clear outline of Gull Rock, a desolate, forbidding gray stone, the swelling rise of Blue Island, green and dark, and bathed in sunrise gold, and then out over the promontories a low belt of land fog—these met my roving glances and gave me the delight that makes so much of the worthiness of fishing and the good fortune which befalls the early angler.

We procured a basketful of herring from the fisherman who had accompanied us down the bay. Then we ran on to the next fisherman, who had seen one tuna about his net, but not for some time. Nevertheless we tied on to his buoy and began to grind chum and throw out herring. I put a bait over and waited with my heart in my throat. One tuna strike had prepared me for a second.

"Look down there!" exclaimed Captain Mitchell.

"By Jove! that fisherman is punching at a tuna near his boat."

It did seem so. I saw the man strike with an oar, saw the splash, and then when he poised, as if waiting for another chance to hit something, I yelled out:

"Let's get there pronto."

And in less time, almost, than it takes to tell it we were on our way. Captain Pence, however, with R. C. and Romer on board the large boat, did not follow at once.

We ran straight down on the fisherman we had watched and hauled in close.

I made eager query: "Didn't we see you hit at a fish?"

"Yes. There are two albacore round; one of them's a big one. He was stealing herring almost out of my hands."

We explained our intentions and asked if we could tie to his buoy. He nodded, and grinned when he said he hoped we would hook on to the big one.

No doubt of our excitement! The certainty of a strike made it impossible to be calm. In less than two minutes I was holding tenaciously to my rod and watching the shiny slick float down along the net.

"Bad place to hook one, if he runs up the bay," warned Captain Mitchell, pointing to the net-buoys. Indeed the lane between them was tortuous and narrow. My feeling was one of dismay at that prospect; my hope was that if I hooked one he would run out to sea.

"*Oh-h!*" yelled Sid, hoarsely, in most intense excitement. At the same instant I heard a tremendous splash. Wheeling, I saw white and green water settling down near the net, not fifty yards from us.

"That was a tuna!" exclaimed Captain Mitchell. "Did you hear the smash? He was after a herring."

Sid jabbered like a wild man, until finally I made something of his speech: ". . . big blue tuna! He had a back like a horse! He came half out!"

Bob's eyes flashed like keen blue fire. "I saw him. Some he-scoundrel, that fish!"

"You'll get a strike in no time," added Captain Mitchell. "If only he doesn't run up the bay!"

My state was one of supreme rapture, dread, and doubt combined. I really was not a rational being. There I sat, left hand holding about four feet of loose line off my reel, my right clutching the rod, my eyes everywhere. I saw the net, the slick, the drifting particles of chum Bob was grinding, the shiny floating herring Captain Mitchell threw in, the bright green water, the buoys and boats and fishermen. R. C. and Romer sat perched upon the deck of their boat, perhaps a quarter of a mile distant. Romer was watching us through glasses. How long would I have to wait? Five minutes seemed an age.

Suddenly the loose line whipped out of my hand and ran through the guides on the rod.

"There!" I whispered, hoarsely.

My line swept away, hissing through the water. Gripping rod with both hands I jerked with all my might. What tremendous live weight! Again—two—three—four times I struck, while my line whizzed off the reel. Hard as I jerked I never got the curved rod upright.

"You've hooked him!" yelled Captain Mitchell, with great elation. Both the boys yelled, but I could not tell what. The rush of the tuna wheeled me in the revolving chair, dragged me out of it, with knees hard on the gunwale. My rod made rapid nods. But despite the terrific strain I got the drag off. Right there began a demonstration of the efficiency of the great Coxe reel.

The tuna had run round the net, on the ocean side, and had headed toward Blue Island. I had heard the scream of a reel, the rush of flying line, but that run beat any other I ever saw. An ordinary reel or line would have failed. Of course I had wet my line. I felt the fine spray hit my face stingingly. I could judge yards only by space on the reel, and this fish took off two hundred or more in what seemed a single flash. If he had kept on! But he ended that rush. And in two more seconds the engines were roaring and the launch was wheeling. We were after him with half my five hundred yards still on the reel.

"How about it?" shouted Sid, red-faced and fierce, bending over the open engine box.

"Slow down! Plenty of line!" I called back.

Then we got settled. The surprise of the attack had not upset us, but it had surely been electrifying. Many times on the *Gladiator,* while roaming the sea for swordfish, had R. C. and Sid and Bob and I talked over the way to meet just such a strike and rush as this.

I sat facing the bow, rod high, line taut for several hundred feet out of the water. The tuna headed for Blue Island, about a mile away. We were leaving the dangerous labyrinth of nets. All was serene on board then.

"Some run, I'll tell the world!" rejoiced Bob. "Makes a tarpon look slow!"

I had, of course, put my drag on when the fish had slowed and we had started after him. We were running seven or eight miles an hour, and the tuna was taking line slowly off the reel. This chase extended in a straight course for some distance and it was singularly exhilarating. We all complimented the work of the little launch. The quick start was what had saved us.

"I had both engines going before you got through hooking him," boasted Sid.

When half the line had slipped off my reel I said: "Run up on him. Let me get back the line."

Sid speeded up, and I worked swiftly and hard to pump and reel, so as to recover line and not allow any slack. When I got back all that was possible at the time I was sweating and panting. Then we slowed down again.

My tuna headed up the bay and ran a mile or more before he turned. We did not want him to go up the bay, and welcomed his swerving. But when he pointed us toward the nets I was suddenly filled with dread.

"Port, Sid," I called, sharply. "Sheer off a little. We'll quarter with him and head him out to sea. . . . Or lose him right here!"

"That's the idea," replied Captain Mitchell. "Fight him now. We've got two miles before he reaches the nets."

So we ran with him yet a little to his left while I pulled with all my might and used all the drag I dared. He took line—one hundred yards—two hundred yards—three hundred yards. Still he did not turn. But he slowed down. Dragging three hundred yards of thirty-nine line, and the launch besides, told perceptibly upon his speed.

Meanwhile our other boat, with R. C. and Romer wildly waving, joined the chase, and falling in behind us kept close as possible. It was a grim ticklish time. I hated to risk so much. But that was the game—to keep him out of the nets or lose him.

"Shore he's headin' out!" yelled Bob.

That was good news, but I could not see it. Bob, however, knew more about lines in the water than I, as presently I saw proved. My tuna was slowly turning away from the dreaded nets.

"Close in, Sid. Help me get back some line," I said.

Still keeping that strain on him, we narrowed the distance between us until I had all the line back except a hundred yards or so, and with this we were well content. When we had him headed straight for the open sea we gradually moved over to a point behind him. Then I eased the drag, let him set a pace, which we adopted; and he led us out to sea. It was a great situation. The sun had come out, not bright, but enough to make the water glimmer and the distant headlands show distinctly. The lighthouse on the southwest point gradually faded; then Western Head blurred in the pale land fog; only Gull Rock and Blue Island remained in sight. We passed a bell buoy some five miles outside the bay. A foghorn bayed in faint hoarse notes its warning to mariners.

"What time did we hook up with this fellow?" I inquired.

"Seven-ten," replied Sid, consulting his watch. "It's now eight-thirty."

"Wal, I reckon it's aboot time to settle down to a fight," drawled Bob. "He's shore well hooked."

"All right. Get my coat off and put the harness on," I said.

I had never gotten much satisfaction or help out of any harness we had ever bought or made, but I expected much of the one Coxe had constructed for me. Mr. C. Alma Baker, the English angler, had liked it so well that he ordered one. It was made of leather, and like a vest with the front cut out. Straps hooked on to my rod below my reel. It felt good. I could pull with my shoulders. Thus equipped, and with gloves over thumb-stalled fingers I settled down to the grim job.

With slow steady sweeps and swift winds of reel I went through the usual procedure of fighting a heavy fish. But I could gain line only when Sid ran the boat faster than the tuna swam. Nevertheless I slowed him down in his headlong flight toward the open sea. Otherwise I could not see that I had made the slightest impression upon him. Time flies while one is fighting a fish. I was amazed when Sid sang out: "Ten-thirty—and all's well!"

There was no wind. The sea resembled a dimpled mirror. The sun shone through pale gray clouds and it was warm. The land fog began to encroach upon the sea, hiding the headlands under a silver belt. Only the dark shore line of Blue Island showed us the direction of the bay.

We were eight miles off before I stopped the tuna and turned him. I was not in the best of condition for a hard, grueling battle, as I had fought only one fish during the summer—a 413-pound broadbill swordfish. I had tried to keep fit, but there is nothing like actual work with a rod on a fish to keep an angler hard and strong.

At the end of three hours I was wet and hot. All this time, even when I had pulled my hardest, the tuna had continued to tow the launch. Sometimes more slowly than at others, but always he towed it, bow first! Most of this strain had fallen upon my back and shoulders, where the harness fitted so snugly. And about this time I made the discovery that, if I held high on the rod and let all the strain come on it instead of the harness, I could stand the mighty pull for only about two minutes at a stretch. Then I would have to transfer the strain back to the harness. Which of course meant to my shoulders! I felt chafed under the arms and I ached a little, but otherwise did not appear to be suffering any great discomfort from this unusual demand on my muscles. It struck me forcibly, however, that the tuna was towing the launch absolutely by pulling against my back. What amazed me was the great value of the Coxe harness. During all this time, which seemed short, the fight itself and the remarks of my comrades, especially the droll speech of my Florida boatman Bob, kept me in a state of excitement. Probably I could not have felt even an injury at that stage.

All fights with big fish have stages, and this one was no exception. The great tuna came to the surface, and abandoning a straight course out to sea he began to swim in circles. He was still fast, still strong. But he had shown his first indication of weakening. He had lost sense of direction. He was bewildered. He pushed a wave ahead of him and left a wide wake behind.

"Bob, get up on the bow and watch him," I ordered. "Never take your eye off him!"

An experienced fisherman such as Bob, if he could see a fish, could tell exactly what he was going to do. It turned out that I had chosen wisely to give this scout duty to Bob. The tuna was in front a couple of hundred feet and half as far to starboard. He was deep under the surface, so that I could see only the waves he started in motion. But to Bob he was visible. Suddenly he shouted, piercingly: "Look out!"

I saw a surge in the water and a pale gleam, incredibly swift, right at the boat. Leaping up, I threw off the drag and plunged my rod deep in the water. Not a second too soon! All I saw was the bag of line shoot under the boat. Then I felt a lunge on my rod, and the whir of the reel. Sid had been as swift with levers and wheel. Bob and Captain Mitchell were leaning over the gunwale.

"All clear!" sang out Sid.

"Son-of-a-gun!" ejaculated Bob. "Talk about puttin' it in high!"

"Splendid work!" declared Captain Mitchell, rising. "By jove! but he made a dash!"

I lifted the dripping rod and reel, fell back in the seat, jammed the butt in the socket, and tightening the drag I faced about to look for the tuna. What a cunning wonderful rush that had been! If Bob had not been standing on the bow I would never have perceived that action in time to avert disaster. A bagged line floating on the surface and dragged under a boat oftener than not will cut off on the propeller. It had been a narrow shave.

"Boys, we've got to get mad or he'll fool us, same as that one did yesterday," I said.

We all grew silent and watchful then. I began to conserve strength, to leave more to my reel, to study every move of the tuna, to make absolutely sure he never had an inch of slack line. As he circled here and there at random, sometimes in wide curves, at others in short turns, he always towed the launch. I kept on a good stiff drag, but not strong enough to break the line, should he suddenly rush. And the line paid off the reel slowly as he dragged the launch. Sid said he towed us four miles an hour, but I thought that a little too much. But he kept us moving. Gradually he drew us back toward the bell buoy, and round this he hung, near or far, as it happened. During this strenuous hour he never sounded once. Always that bulge on the smooth surface and the swelling wake behind! These were new and fascinating tactics in a game fish.

About at this period of the battle the physical man began to rebel. There is a limit to the time emotion and imagination can make a man oblivious to pain and fatigue. Long had I been tired, but it was a tired feeling I rather reveled in. It had not made any difference. But suddenly I was made to realize that something was wrong. My hands, wrists, arms were still strong, and I felt that I had reserve in them for what we call the finish of a fight, sometimes the most strenuous part. My shoulders likewise seemed as good as ever. But my back, low down where the harness fit so like a glove, had begun to hurt. I thought about this carefully. We never mind pangs. It would not be any achievement to catch a great fish without toil and sweat, endurance and pain. Anybody can catch some kind of a fish without these. But no one will ever catch a great tuna without them. Accidents happen, and the lucky-fluke captures of giant game fish are on record. But I never had one and I do not take any account of them. So up to that point I had not paid any particular attention to my growing discomforts. I decided the pain in my back was due to a different kind of pull. In fact, my whole body was pulled. It was harnessed to that tuna. But I could stand the strain, and so entered upon the second half of the struggle.

The weather grew even better, if that were possible. The sea appeared flat without heave or swell. Not a breath of wind stirred. The transparent film of cloud let sunlight through, but little heat. It seemed a wonderfully lucky day.

R. C. and Romer in the large boat followed us, plying cameras and motion-picture machines with great assiduity. Sometimes they came within a hundred feet behind us or off to one side. I could hear the boy's shrill voice: "Some fish! Hang on, dad! You

can lick him! Don't work too hard! Let him pull the boat!"
Occasionally R. C. yelled a word of encouragement. I waved to
them once in a while until the time came when I forgot
everything but the tuna.

While I went through the labored motions with rod and reel
I waited and hoped for some expression from Bob that we had
a chance to whip this fish. Bob knew fish nature as well as Sid
knew the workings of an engine. And I knew I could absolutely
rely on what Bob said. But what a long time I waited! He stood
balanced on the bow, his keen profile against the sky, his eyes
glued to the shadowy blue shape of the tuna.

"Wal," he said, finally, "if the hook doesn't tear out we'll lick
him."

That gave me renewed life and energy.

"If he ever heads this way yell to me, so I can release the
strain," I replied. "We just won't pull the hook out."

Captain Mitchell sat or stood at my side all the while,
sometimes silent, often giving a quiet word of praise or encouragement. He was always optimistic. "You're going to kill this
tuna," he averred. "I'm a lucky man to have in the boat." He was
particularly keen to observe our handling of the launch and
manipulation of tackle; and it was plain he was deeply and
favorably impressed.

"We always have a long double line above the leader," he said.
"Then when we get the end of that over the reel we hold hard
and let the tuna tow the skiff around. When it's safe to do so we
have the boatmen row against the fish."

"But, Captain, wouldn't a tuna like this one tow a skiff all day
and all night?" I queried.

"I'm afraid so. He's a mighty game fish and a big one. Some
tuna give up quicker than others. One now and then is a terrific
and unbeatable fighter. This fellow amazes me. He's a stubborn
devil."

I had an eighteen-foot leader and double line about the same length. It was an occasion for cheers when I got the end of the double line up to the tip of my rod the first time. But I could not get it over the reel. After several more attempts and aided by Sid slipping in closer on the fish, I did get the double line over my reel. That was a signal victory which we all celebrated. Also we saw the end of the leader. These things marked another stage in the fight—hopeful ones for me. I had most trouble in going slow, in holding back, in maintaining patience. It must necessarily be a very long contest. But to know this and to practice it were vastly different things. The sweat from my forehead ran down in my eyes and over my nose.

To and fro over the unruffled ocean we glided, seldom under our own power. Now and then Sid would throw in the clutch of one engine to help me get back some line. Bob stuck to his post on the bow and had nothing to say. Captain Mitchell did not let me grow discouraged.

"He's shoving a bigger wave all the time," he said. "That means he's swimming higher. Soon his fins and tail will show."

Sure enough they did. His ragged dorsal, and the long curved yellow spike behind it, and then his blue-black tail, at last cut the calm surface of the water. Yells from the other boat attested to the close attention and pursuit our comrades were giving us. During the next half hour we sighted his fins many times, always within a hundred feet. I could have held him at that distance just as long as my strength would stand it, but when we got him close so he saw the boat he would move ahead. A hundred times more or less we ran him down and I dragged him within thirty feet of where Bob stood. Gradually he got used to the boat and always he tired almost imperceptibly. All I could see was the last third of his body, the huge taper of his blue bulk, decorated with the little yellow rudderlike fins, and his wagging tail. But of course Bob could see every inch of him. At length I had to yell:

"Say, Bob, how big is he?"

"Huh! I'm shore afraid to say," replied Bob.

"Tell me!"

"Wal, it'll do you more good not to know."

"Where's he—hooked?" I panted.

"Deep, I reckon. I see the leader comin' out of his mouth on this side."

"Is he wearing out?"

"He can't put it in high any more, that's shore. Just hang on an' save yourself for the finish."

"But I won't—have—much to save."

Time and again the tuna got the leader round his tail. This made the rod wag up and down in a kind of weaving motion, and it lifted me to and fro in my chair. So far as we could see, it did not inconvenience the tuna in the least. When a Marlin or broadbill gets tangled in the leader, he cannot fight until it is free again. But not so with this tuna!

"Sid, ease in behind him," I called. "I'm going to pull the leader up to Bob. Captain, you go forward and get ready for a possible chance to gaff him."

"Not yet! It's too soon," replied Captain Mitchell.

"It may not come soon. But I want you there. . . . Bob, grab the leader and hold it—not stiff—but just enough to let it slip. We'll see. Now, all do as I say—and if we lose him I'll be to blame."

I shut down on the drag and began to haul and wind with all I had left. Of course, without Sid's help I never could have pumped the leader out of the water, not at that time. No man unaided could have pulled that tuna toward him. In a few moments Bob's eager sinewy hands closed on the end of the leader just below the ring. He never uttered a word, but I saw his tense expression change. The others whooped. That relieved me of the terrific strain. It was such a change that for an instant my head swam.

The tuna did not like it. He lashed the water white. He towed us faster. Then he pulled the leader away from Bob.

"Boys, we'll try that," I said, doggedly. "We'll keep at him. Be quick, careful. Do the right thing at the right time."

"Reckon it's our chance," replied Bob. "I'll shore handle that leader easy. It'll work if the hook doesn't tear out."

Then I had the task of hauling that leader back to Bob. It took moments of strenuous work. Bob stood far out on the bow, reaching for it. The double line passed him. It would have been risky at that stage to have trusted to the double line. When he got hold of the leader I had another little rest. What welcome relief! I was burning, throbbing, aching. Still both hands and arms were strong. I felt that I could last it out. The tuna lashed the water and sheered to starboard. Sid had one engine in reverse, the other full speed ahead, and he was working the wheel. Quick as we turned, however, we could not keep the leader from being torn out of Bob's hands. The tuna made a roar on the surface and sounded. He went to the bottom. I had the pleasant job of lifting him. As a matter of fact I did not budge him an inch. But I pulled as mightily as I could and persuaded him to come up again. Then we went after him. I got the leader to Bob, and once more was free of that awful drag at my vitals. Bob held the fish rather longer this time, and Sid threw out the clutches.

We warmed to these tactics, for in them we saw sure capture of the tuna, if the tackle held. My task seemed tremendous. When the tuna sheered away, tearing the leader from Bob, I had to haul it back. I could turn the fish now and move him a very little. But oh, what a ponderous weight! When he shook his head I thought he would crack my back. Many times we tried this, so many that after fifteen I quit counting them. But they worked. The tuna was weakening. If I did not give out first we might get him. Every time now I could see him, and the sight seemed to inspire me momentarily with the strength of Hercules. It was that sight of him, marvelous blue massive body and tail, and the short rest following my getting the leader to Bob, which kept me up.

After what seemed a long while Bob was able to hold to the leader while the tuna towed us round and round. Then began another stage, that of hauling him closer. At first it would not work. When Bob hauled away hand over hand, very cautiously and slowly for a few feet, then the tuna would lunge and break away. By degrees, however, this method worked as had the mere holding of the leader. The awful thing for me was that now when the fish tore the leader out of Bob's hands he would sound and I had to pump him up. There was nothing else to do. I had to do it. Both my excitement and agony augmented, yet somehow I was able to carry on and keep a cool head.

When Bob finally turned to us with his keen blue eyes flashing I knew something was up.

"I can hold the leader an' drag him. If we all work right now he's marchin' to his funeral."

How cool he was! I knew he lent us all confidence. Sid had surely had his hands full at the wheel and clutches. I was worn to a frazzle. But Bob's patience and endurance seemed to grow. He looked at me.

"A few more times an' he's a lost fawn-skin," he said, tersely. "Don't let him rest. Haul him up to me."

"Bob—your—words—sound—like music," I panted. "Sure— I'll haul him—right up."

My tuna was down deep. He had become almost a dead weight. Yet every wag of head or tail had irresistible power. Fortunately his wags had become few. I had now to favor my lame back. I pulled with my arms, lifted with my knees. Only such a tackle as this could ever have lifted this fish. I was afraid something would break. But reel, rod, line, all held. At last I heaved him out of the depths. When Bob got the leader again I gasped.

"Hang on—till I come to!"

Then Bob began what turned out to be the greatest performance I had ever seen. He held the tuna. Sometimes he would let a yard or two of the leader slip through his hands, to relieve the strain of a roll or lunge, but he never let go of it. He was pulled from side to side as the fish wagged across the bow; sometimes on his knees; again straddling the leader; often bent forward almost ready to let go. His face was sharp and stern and full of tense cords of pain. It must have hurt to hold that wire. Sid's motions were no less active and tense. According to Bob's signs, which came mostly through nods of his head, Sid had to throw the clutches in or out, reverse one and full speed ahead on the other, all the time working the wheel. The launch spun like a top; it never went straight any more. How the two of them kept that tuna from running under the boat was astounding to see. But they accomplished it. I was on edge, however, ready at a second's notice to act my part and plunge the rod overboard to save the line from fouling on the propellers. I had also to keep the line from catching on the bow or the gaff in Mitchell's hands, and as much as possible out of Bob's way. This strain was almost as hard to bear as had been the one of weight.

Thus the fight narrowed down to the climax. Many times the huge tuna rolled within reach of the long gaff. But I wanted a sure chance. Bob knew when far better than I, and he never said a word. Captain Mitchell leaned over one gunwale, then the other. Sid had begun to wear nervous under the strain. He talked a good deal, mostly to himself. He had many things to operate all at once, and to do so without mistake required tremendous concentration. Back and forth he swiftly bent from wheel to clutches.

The tuna heaved on the surface, he rolled and gasped, lunged out his huge head with jaws wide and black eyes staring—a paralyzing sight for me. Then he wagged toward the bow, his wide back round and large as a barrel, out of the water.

"Gaff him!" I yelled, hoarsely.

Captain Mitchell reached over him and hauled on the big gaff. It did not even stick in the fish for a second. I could not speak. I expected the tuna to smash our boat and break away. But he only rolled wearily, and Bob dragged him closer. Captain Mitchell tried again with like result. I feared he did not know how to use a detachable gaff such as we had built for swordfish. I yelled for Sid to try. He leaped over the engine box, attached the gaff to the pole, and extended it out. The tuna was rolling alarmingly. My heart stopped beating.

"Take time. He's all in," shouted Bob, cool and hard.

Sid dropped the wide hook over the broad back and lunged back with all his might. He pulled the tuna against the launch. Bang! Slap! The big tail jarred me almost off my feet.

"Shiver our timbers!" yelled Bob. "That gaff won't go in his body. It's too big."

Sid hauled the gaff in, and plunging over the gunwale he caught the fish on the side of the head. It did not go deep, but it held. Still if the tuna had been capable of violent action he would have torn away. Captain Mitchell as quickly put the other gaff in the mouth of the fish and jerked it through his jaw. Then Bob followed that action with a rope, slipping it through the ring on the gaff. When I saw the great fish had finally and surely been captured I flopped back in my chair, dizzy, reeling, scarcely aware of the acclaim about my ears.

We towed him back to the bay and up to the lighthouse. In lieu of a flag we flew a red kite, by way of celebration. My aches seemed strangely trivial.

It took five men to haul that tuna out on the bank. I shall not soon forget the eyes of my son Romer, or his wild whirling words, when he saw my tuna close at hand. R. C. stood in mute admiration. Sid and Bob were more elated than I had ever seen them. The native fishermen marveled at such a catch on a rod and line. Captain Mitchell radiated delight and congratulations.

"Gamest tuna I ever saw or heard of!" was his praise of the fish.

He measured 8 feet 4 inches in length, 6 feet 2 inches in girth, and weighed 684 pounds.

It took me a long time to realize the actual fact of his capture. But by gloating over him and photographing him and hanging around him I at last arrived at some sane appreciation of his tremendous bulk and remarkable beauty.

He was built like a colossal steel projectile, with a deep dark blue color on the back, shading to an exquisite abalone opal hue toward the under side, which was silver white. He blazed like the shield of Achilles. From the edge of his gill cover to the tip of his nose was two feet. He had eyes as large as saucers. His gaping mouth was huge enough to take in a bucket. His teeth were like a strip of sand paper, very fine and small. The massive roundness of his head, the hugeness of his body, fascinated me and made me marvel at the speed he had been capable of. What incalculable power in that wide tail! I had to back away to several rods' distance before I could appreciate the full immensity of him.

Then when the men hung him up! I could not believe my eyes. He seemed another and vaster fish, with a beautiful broadness, depth, fullness, all that signified the wonder of his growth and the mysterious power of the sea that had nourished him.

The fine weather did not last long. About four o'clock the sky darkened over and a wind from the east brought scudding gray clouds and a fine rain. The native fishermen predicted a northeaster. By five o'clock wind and rain had increased and before dark we were storm-beaten. R. C. and I had our beds in the launch, his on a cot and mine on the floor. We expected the canvas hood to protect us. It might have served for an ordinary rain, but not for the deluge that descended upon us. It roared on the canvas and leaked through. The bilge filled rapidly. We could hear the water splashing. I was too tired and full of aches to care what happened. The boys were very solicitous and said I would drown if I stayed on the floor of the launch. But I went to sleep in the midst of the storm and did not awaken until I was rested, some time in the early morning hours. The storm had slackened, yet the rain still fell, in drizzles and gusts. I could hear the boom of the surf on the island out in the bay, and the hoarse bellow of the foghorn. My bed was wet outside, but warm and dry within, and I enjoyed the sound of the elements.

Morning brought lowering fog and drab, somber surroundings and more rain. We were hard put to it to pass the time. Bob, however, had a task to skin the big tuna for mounting. At intervals the rain ceased. We saw tuna out in the bay, and during the afternoon tried to get a bite out of one. Captain Mitchell and R. C. saw a much larger tuna than mine. He passed directly under the boat. They estimated his weight at over a thousand pounds. But though tuna appeared plentiful, they were not feeding. Then the fog and rain rolled in again, blanketing us for another uncomfortable night. It rained all night.

Next morning the storm was gone, the wind had veered, and there were indications of clearing weather. At six o'clock we started down the bay, very glad for a little pale sunshine. A heavy swell was running. Great white breakers dashed up on the rocky shores.

When we got to the fishing grounds we found the fishermen at their nets, evidently unconcerned about the heavy sea. The swells were mountainous. The first fisherman we accosted said there had been a tuna at his net a little while before. We bought a bushel of herring and set about fishing, with R. C. at the rod.

Soon another fisherman hailed us. We ran over to his boat and saw the huge swirl of a tuna on the surface. I was thrilled with the certainty that R. C. would soon get a strike. Several times this fish swirled on the surface. Captain Mitchell saw him pass near our boat. But nothing happened there, and soon another fisherman called us over to try for a tuna round his net.

"Only a few round this morning and they're not hungry," he said. "They'll take a couple of herring, then leave. Yesterday morning we saw a good many."

Later two other of the herring fishermen beckoned for us, and when we hastened to them informed us there was a tuna there. We saw one swirl. But we could not get a bite for R. C. The sea grew rough and we decided we could not very well fight a fish if we did not hook one, so we returned to the breakwater.

I took advantage of the opportunity to drive back to Liverpool for mail, supplies, and to send telegrams relative to my lucky catch.

The driver carried me over another road, part of which led through what was called Nine-Mile Woods. After the heavy rains the wild country appeared intersected by running streams. It was a moose country, green and flat in places, meadows alternating with heavy spruce forest, and in some places very rough and rocky. The streams were beautiful. Gold-brown water swirled and glided out of the dark wet woods. Spots of white foam floated along; waterfalls roared and foamed; still black pools gleamed under the dense foliage; white flowers bordered the brooks; ferns and grasses waved in the edge of the current. Big gray boulders, amber with moss, broke the level monotony. Spruce trees, maples, ash, pine, lined the narrow wet road. Arbor vitæ and huckleberry bushes spread thicker covering over the open patches. How green, cool, wet, mossy, fresh with rain and sparkling with dewdrops! It was a country used to water. The verdure grew heavy, thick, dark. What a contrast to the desert! I bathed my eyes in a soothing balm of nature. After the red and yellow wastes of Arizona, and the glaring openness of the Pacific, where I had spent the last three months, this green and verdant northland was most satisfying and welcome.

The driver of the car told me an interesting thing, which later I verified. Several years ago Mr. Whitney broke off a tuna. The following summer this same fish was caught in a net and was identified by the leader and hook still attached. This seems a remarkable circumstance. I am inclined to believe it singularly unusual. Most fish that get away with hooks in their gullets become prey for sharks or die. These giant tuna, however, might present an exception to this rule. They are so tremendously big, virile, and powerful that it takes more to affect them than in the case of ordinary tuna or other fish. I have not seen a shark in these waters, though the fishermen say there are a few here. Most probably this icy water, straight from the Arctic seas, is too cold for the warm-water shark. The temperature is about fifty degrees. It is a beautifully clear green water, not like the blue of the Pacific. It makes me think of glistening green-white icebergs, and most assuredly it feels as if it had lately been closely associated with them.

Upon my return to East Jordon, wind and sea had fallen and the sun shone warm. It was an afternoon to bask in the warmth on the breakwater, drying blankets, clothes, cameras, fishing lines, and everything else that was wet. Not a tuna had been seen during the day; though a close watch was kept. The fishermen seemed to have an idea herring and albacore were leaving the bay. They had been here in abundance for five weeks. Nevertheless we had great hopes of raising one for R. C. on the morrow, and made preparations to get up at four o'clock.

Toward morning the air grew frosty. I was awake on and off, and by four o'clock, which was the hour for arising, I felt quite ready to crawl out. R. C. was slow. I heard Bob say: "Wal, when it gets to makin' frost it's time for me to stick a feather in my hat an' beat it for home."

The moon was a pale bright silver, and the sky a steely cold blue. The morning star burned with the same hue. Indeed it was the northland. A soft pearly-gray fog hovered over bay and forest; and the wild fringed horizon seemed unfamiliar and strange to me. While I took some brisk exercise along the breakwater the east brightened and presently it was daylight. Still there was no color anywhere. All pale gray, somber, cold tones! We had breakfast, and were gliding down the bay before five o'clock.

Gradually the pale east took fire and glowed, the clouds changing, until the sun rose, golden red, throwing a glimmering track upon the water. I saw the lighthouse on the headland to the south, and it blinked like a great star. Gull Rock and Blue Island appeared begirt by white surges, and a dull steady roar came from shore.

Four boats bobbed upon the water. The first fisherman we approached said he had seen a tuna about daylight. We bought a barrel of bait from him, and were soon ready. Two near-by fishermen beckoned to us, and we ran over to where they were hauling their net. One of them threw out a herring and pointed. Immediately I saw a huge boiling bulge on the water. I yelled, and at once excitement claimed us. We fastened to their buoy. R. C. threw out his bait and Captain Mitchell threw out herring. I was standing high on the bow.

Suddenly a shield-shaped blaze of silver-green flashed through the water. It came from a great tuna. He took the loose herring and made a heavy break on the surface. All of us except R. C. were shouting at the same time. The next herring Captain Mitchell threw out did not sink. A huge shadow loomed out of the green water. Smash! The tuna lunged on the surface. I saw his broad blue back, his fins, his tail. He missed the herring. His quick movement amazed me. He was as fast as a trout. Next time he got the herring, leaving a swirling eddy behind. But for me, this time, the light was bad and I could not see him. We expected him to take R. C.'s bait, but he so plainly avoided it that we made certain he was a cautious tuna. Captain Mitchell kept throwing out herring and the great fish kept rising out of the green depths to take them. It was as exasperating as it was thrilling. Once he flashed by broadside to us, only a few yards away and a few feet under the surface. I saw every line of him, clear-cut, green and gold. He was enormous. His big black eye showed distinctly. I saw him open his mouth wide and gulp the herring. He closed his jaw and swept away. The whole motion seemed just one flash. How perfectly incredible!

He took every herring we threw out, except the one on R. C.'s line. Finally Captain Mitchell threw out R. C.'s bait and another herring at the same moment. Both sank slowly. Then—up flashed the monster, swift as light. He made a mistake in his choice of the two herring. He got R. C.'s hook. The line swept out and R. C. lunged back on the rod.

I turned to throw off the buoy. Sid jammed at the self-starters. In a second we were moving. That fish cleared the net and headed inshore, going like a bullet. We followed at top speed, the water flying from our bows. Still he took line. When we had two hundred yards off the reel the strain slackened. We thought he had fouled the line on a buoy rope and broken off. But it turned out he had wheeled back on us, gaining slack line, and the hook had come out. We were pretty hard hit, but went back hopefully to try over again.

Another fisherman signaled us. Before we reached him we saw a boil on the water near his net, and that revived all the thrilling sensations. Here we employed the same tactics. The second time R. C.'s bait was thrown out the tuna came up for it. I could not see well. But Captain Mitchell saw it. R. C. jerked with all his might. There was a screech from the reel—then the hook pulled loose. More bad luck! It seemed to hurt me more than any of the others.

"You tried to hook him too soon," I argued. "Let him have a little line."

Bob backed me up in this. Captain Mitchell said he never let tuna have any line, especially when only one was working round the boat. But with all due respect to the Captain's practice I insisted that R. C. give the next fish a chance to move away

with the bait. R. C. said this was what he had wanted to do in the
first place, but our differing suggestions had upset him.

"Three bites!" I ejaculated, incredulously. I could not realize it,
and perhaps I felt all the more because of the actuality of it.

Then my roving eye caught sight of a fisherman waving to us,
some two hundred yards away. We were quick to run his way.
Long before we got near I saw an enormous splash, right under
his gunwale. The water flew over the boat. The fisherman threw
out another herring. Smash! The tuna had it.

We soon tied on to the buoy, and as the fisherman's boat
drifted off we began to chum, throw in herring, and let out
R. C.'s bait in the midst of it. This tuna rose like a bass to take a
grasshopper on the surface. *Wop!* His mouth opened and sucked
in the herring, and a cloud of silver scales floated away in the
green water. We were all on the *qui vive* for another bite, and
surely expected it. I stood on the bow, heedless of the launch
rising on the huge swells, and watched with strained eyes. The
sun had come out brighter, so that I had a much better chance
to see under the surface. Again Captain Mitchell threw out a
herring.

"There he comes!" I yelled. "Oh! did you see him take it?"

"Did we?" they all answered together, and even R. C. joined it.
His eyes were ticking out. No wonder! Of all the fish sights I had
ever seen, this one was the greatest. Blue, silver, green, gold—
how the colors shone! The ponderous grace of the fish, the
gliding action, the single wave of his forked tail, the little fringe
of yellow rudders, the savage gap of his mouth as he seized the
herring, the turn and the flash—these features I seemed to take
in all in a glance. Then he was gone. But he rose again to the
next herring. Again and again he took loose bait. But he would
not take R. C.'s. He moved the leader as he swept by it. And we
fed him herring, one after another, marveling at the magnificent
sight of him flashing in the sunlight, sheering down to vanish,

until he would not rise any more. Then we chummed for a while.

All the boats except one had left the fishing grounds. This was Saturday, and preparatory to Sunday the fishermen took up their nets and left. The one man left had shown us more than one favor, and I kept watch on him hopefully. Suddenly I espied him raise a piece of canvas and wave it. The distance was far and some of the boys thought I had made a mistake. But I knew I was right, and soon we were flying back up the bay toward this last boat. A mass of floating sea grass surrounded him. Before we reached him I saw boils on the surface.

"Hey! they're here—a lot of them!" he called, as we drew near.

We were soon in position, as before, except that Bob held to the stern of the fisherman's boat. R. C. threw over his bait, and Captain Mitchell stood with herring poised, ready to cast it. But he never did. I saw a green shadow come out from under our boat. I would have yelled wildly if I had not been paralyzed. The beautiful fish showed every line, every spot and feature. He moved easily, opened his mouth, took in the bait, closed his jaws on it, and glided on, flashed, gleamed, faded, vanished. R. C. let him take line off the reel—ten—twenty—thirty feet. Then he shut down on the drag and struck mightily. What a lunge! R. C. was lifted out of his seat. I whirled to throw off the buoy. It got tangled on our line and I took some valuable seconds releasing it.

Sid and Bob were yelling. I heard the engines roaring. But we were not moving right. Too slow! And R. C.'s line was whizzing off the reel. I did not know what was wrong, but something was.

"Quick there! Get after him!" I yelled.

"Doing our best," yelled back Sid. "Propellers caught in sea grass."

R. C.'s line went out with a rapidity that appalled me. Three hundred yards—four hundred! When only a little line was left and I was about ready to succumb the propellers cut loose from the sea grass, and we shot ahead so swiftly that all of us except R. C., who was sitting down, were thrown off our balance. I fell off the bow. Wonder indeed that I fell into the boat instead of out of it! When I recovered my equilibrium the boys and Captain Mitchell were shouting at the top of their lungs. R. C.'s face was a sight to behold! All of us had given up that tuna and line. I leaped back on the bow.

We were now running almost at full speed and it was hard to stand up there. I grasped the bow rope with my left hand and rose to my feet. We could not gain an inch on the fish. The line was stretched like a banjo string, and as it cut the water it picked up strands of sea grass. Bob leaned over and tore this grass off, and as fast as another bunch collected he removed that also.

"He's shore got it in high!" he yelled.

This run discounted any other I had ever seen. Straight up the bay the tuna led us a mile—fully three miles—then inshore another mile, before we began to gain on him.

"If he doesn't break off, that run will kill him!" shouted Bob.

R. C. looked both rapt and grim.

I saw that there were still fifty or more yards on his reel, and I was not worried now. We were holding our own. How the rod nodded and the line sang! R. C. began to try to recover line. He hauled far back, and swinging forward tried to wind the reel. In vain! He could not get an inch.

"Sid, have you any more speed?" I called.

"A little. But we're going like h——now. I'm afraid I can't stop her quick enough," he replied.

"We'll take a chance."

Then the chase was truly wonderful. Our motor launch, with two engines at full speed, roared across the bay, leaving a huge V-shaped wake. We had outrun our other boat. This accelerated speed soon brought the desired results. R. C. began to recover line. Gradually he worked half of it back, and then just when we began to feel safe again the tuna ended that extraordinary run. Sid slowed up. R. C. pumped and reeled like a swift machine. Soon with four hundred yards back on the reel we burst into acclaims, each in his own particular feeling for the moment.

"That run would kill any fish," called Bob, quick and sharp. "R. C., you hand it to him for all you're worth, before he gets his wind! I tell you—shore as you're born he's a lost fawn-skin."

He was so electrifying in his keen spirit and assurance that R. C. set to work with might and main, exerting himself to the utmost, saving nothing. My task was to watch the line, to make sure which way the tuna turned. As I was high up I could see fully fifty feet of the line after it entered the water. He was swimming high. Often I would look back to get a glimpse of R. C. He never varied that tremendous winchlike action of shoulders and that whirl of the reel. He was red-faced and sweating, with the white shadows showing under his eyes, always a mark of great exertion in him. The engines were running, but the clutches were out. R. C. and the tuna together made the launch sail through the water. The moments seemed as nothing.

Four times R. C. got the double line over the reel, only to lose it. The fifth time he held it and gained more. Then I saw the tuna. He was laboring, fighting that tremendous strain. He had not yet gotten his wind.

Suddenly I discerned a green-white wavering shape. I feared more keenly. The tuna was swimming on his side.

"Work hard!" I burst out. "He's coming!"

Foot by foot the double line slipped by me. At last I saw the leader. Then the fish turned farther on his side. R. C. was dragging him. The launch was slipping closer. There! I saw him closer. There! I saw him clear. He gaped. He rolled. Oh—fish of fishes!

"Just what I said!" yelled Bob, leaping up beside me. And in a second more he had the leader.

I picked up the small gaff and turned, finding something of coolness at the finish.

"Steady, R. C. Look for a rush! . . . Sid, throw her out and grab a gaff."

When I faced forward again the tuna was rolling and gasping on the surface, just under the bow, a terrifying and magnificent sight.

I fell down and leaned over with the gaff. What would happen to me? I reached for him.

"Careful! Quick! In the mouth!" called Bob's keen voice in my ears. He was kneeling over me. Quickly I slipped the gaff into the wide-open jaws and jerked hard. The tuna wagged his tail. What an awful wrench he gave my arms! I thought they would be torn out by the roots. My feet went high in the air. Bob's powerful hand clutched my shirt. I did not go overboard nor release the gaff. Then Sid plunged the big swordfish gaff into the tuna.

For a little while then all was roar and splash and straining arms. It took the three of us to hold him. But at last he was overcome. Then with a rope round his tail we fell back into the launch to gaze amazedly at each other.

"Once in my life I had some good luck!" ejaculated R. C. "Another half hour of that and he would have cracked my spine!"

We towed him up the bay, having only a mile to go to the breakwater. He had been hooked seven miles down the bay. Many and various were the remarks made by us upon that triumphant procession. Not one of us had remembered to take note of the time he was hooked. But the whole performance fell short of an hour. Bob had been right. That terrific run had taken his strength for the time being.

"All mackerel are alike," declared Bob. "A long run takes their wind."

This is true of Pacific tuna, and seemed to have been so in the case of R. C.'s tuna. But I was inclined to say that a combination of this remarkable run and R. C.'s Herculean exertion had accounted for the unparalleled record time for a fight with such a fish.

We hauled him out on the grass—a spectacle for anglers. Length, 8 feet 7 inches. Girth, 5 feet 10 inches. He was therefore a longer slimmer fish than mine. But the bulk of him, hung up, looked vastly otherwise than slim. He weighed 638 pounds.

The afternoon passed swiftly enough, with photographing R. C.'s fish, care of tackle and launch, and talking about the performance of the several tuna we had hooked.

The wind died away early and there was a promise of an unusual sunset. It turned out to be strikingly beautiful. Scattered clouds to north and west quickly changed from white to gold, and then to rose. As I had noted before, the color was exquisitely fresh and vivid, and magnified by reflection in the water. I sat beneath the old deserted lighthouse and tried to absorb the beauty and glory of it all. The water changed even more vividly than the clouds, and when the sun sank to give place to the afterglow there was no adequate expression for the blaze and the shimmer of the bay. There were spaces of purple and violet, dark as the sky at midnight, and supremely mysterious with shadows and depths. Northward where high amber clouds shone lustrously the reflection on the water resembled myriads of quivering jewels, such as opal and topaz. To the south the bay seemed a rippling lake of rose, delicate and dark, conforming strangely to hue and line of clouds. This colorful pageant lasted a long time, only very gradually losing its brilliance, and dying at length into the cold clear northern twilight.

During the night the wind veered to its old quarter, the southeast, and it brought back the fog and the rain. Some little boys visited us and I noted that they had on rubber boots and slickers. I asked them if they wore these to school and they answered in the affirmative. It gave me an inspiration.

We left the boats and motored back to Liverpool, where we purchased rubber boots, coats, pants, and hats called southwesters. Now let it rain!

Reports as to fish around Liverpool were not encouraging. But few herring had been brought in, and no tuna had been seen. The main body of herring, the second run, had not yet begun. We spent Sunday motoring inland to Annapolis, to see a three-masted schooner that I contemplated purchasing, and returned late at night.

Next morning a pall of dark cloud and rain had settled down, as if to discourage us for good. But we went on with our plans just the same. The ride back to East Jordon was made through teeming rain and over flooded roads. About four o'clock the storm let up, and there seemed some indication of a shift in the wind.

Schools of tuna had been seen in the bay on Saturday afternoon, and none since. The herring had become scarce. I rowed the skiff round for an hour, trying to keep warm. Upon my return to the boats I observed the men loading a half dozen cans of gasoline from the wharf to the deck of the larger boat. I thought at the moment some of the cans might slip overboard. Our small launch was moored next to the large boat. The canvas hood was up. Bob was tinkering around the engines. Sid, all bundled up in heavy clothes, and with his rubber things on over them, was moving about on the deck. I tied the skiff to one of the piles. Suddenly a heavy sodden splash alarmed me.

"There goes our gasoline!" I shouted as I looked up.

The launch appeared to be righting itself from a violent lurch. Bob was bending over, performing some unusual gymnastics.

"Save the funnel! Save the funnel!" he yelled to somebody.

Then I was certain the cans of gasoline had fallen overboard. But further heavy splashing between the boats added curiosity to my alarm.

"Say, Bob, what on earth's happened?"

"Nothin'. Sid just fell in!" he replied.

Then a sputtering voice followed: "Can't swim . . . Help me—out!"

Whereupon I got out of the skiff and ran along the wharf, in time to see Captain Pence haul Sid out of the water into the boat. Bundled up as he was, he afforded a spectacle calculated to excite mirth in anyone. I had to sit down.

"Where have you—been—Sid?" I asked.

"—— ——fell in!" he choked, indignantly. "Bob's fault. When I jumped on to the launch—he must have done somethin'. Because she careened over. I couldn't hold on. I fell in. And I sank like lead. Thought I'd drown sure, before I could kick up. . . . Then that darned Florida mullet-fisherman yelled. 'Save the funnel!' . . . When I was drownin'. . . . Oh, boy, it was cold! We don't know what ice water is in California."

"Save the funnel!" I echoed. "By golly! that's immense!" And I had the heartiest laugh for many a long day.

Rain and fog soon drove me to shelter under the awning of the launch, where, snug in the blankets, I was soon asleep. I awoke at different times during the night. The rain had ceased. Morning disclosed a northwest wind and a promise of clearing weather. At five-thirty we were on our way to the fishing grounds. Blue sky showed in the west, and the east lightened. I saw to my satisfaction that a good day was at hand.

But we did not find any net fishermen out between Gull Rock and Blue Island. There were no nets set. Finally inshore beyond Gull Rock we saw some boats and we ran in on them, to find several fishermen making for home. They had only a few herring. Reported the fish very scarce.

We ran inshore with them, where we bought a couple of bushels of bait, in fact all that had been caught that morning. One of the fishermen said there had been tuna round his net that morning. We ran back. Meanwhile the sun had come out bright and warm and the sea was rippling and sparkling.

R. C., who was on the big boat, had seen a tuna during our absence. We picked up one of the net-buoys and began to churn right there. But no tuna came. Then we ran out beyond Gull Rock, to the nets anchored off toward the lighthouse. An hour's chumming brought no reward in the way of a strike. Whereupon we made our way back to our former location and tried for another hour. Disappointment replaced our hopes.

R. C. and Captain Mitchell had taken their boat into Green Harbor, on the other side of Blue Island. They reported that one fisherman over there had seen a couple of tuna.

The herring were no longer abundant and had changed their locations. Some of the native fishermen were of the opinion that the fish were leaving and might not return. Others said the herring followed the bait off-shore when the wind blew from the north, and that the tuna went with them. We quit for the day.

Later we drove over to Lockeport to make inquiries there. The run of herring had slackened. The best ground at this time was between Blue Island and Western Head, and this was the place about which R. C. had been told. I was informed that a week ago one fisherman had reported a huge tuna round his net every morning. It was very tame and would just about eat out of his hand. In size it was twice as large as any seen thereabouts for some time. This was happening some six or eight miles from us, and we did not know. What an opportunity! But it seemed ungracious of me to want so much. One of an angler's weaknesses is to yearn to be in two places at the same time. I have never yet discovered any way to accomplish this. On thinking it over, however, I put this down as a natural eagerness to see more of these great tuna, and not as a dissatisfaction. The game is very hard. I would not want it otherwise. It would not be a real test of an angler to catch some of these wonderful fish without great expense, labor, discomfort, and agony.

Sunset was a flare of red and gold, herald of a fair to-morrow. During twilight I watched several nighthawks wheeling to and fro over a swale back of the wharf. The tide was low and this hollow had only a little water. Flies or gnats of some kind must have been hovering over this particular spot. The birds flitted like streaks across the shadowy space, out over the bare bank, and all around. They came within a few feet of me, so near that I could see the white spots on their drab wings. Wonderful, graceful, eerie creatures! They did not make the slightest noise as they cut the air. They darted, whirled, flitted, infinitely faster than swallows. The irregular flight was owing to their pursuit of the gnats. They would swoop low along the ground, like an arrow, then suddenly dart upward, poise an instant, and shoot on again. As a boy I had been mystified by these strange birds. In Ohio we called them bull-bats, and they greatly resembled whippoorwills.

It struck me that I had almost forgotten my propensity to wait and watch for wild creatures. But these huge giant mackerel fish had obsessed my mind. I had forgotten that we had seen three deer on our way here. They were almost yellow, viewed against the bright wet green background, and the largest deer I had ever seen. Indeed I thought, when I sighted the first one, that it was a cow moose. But when it moved, leaping across the banks, I at once recognized that it was a buck deer. The Arizona deer are a blue-gray at this season; and these red-gold species were strikingly new and beautiful to us.

Before I turned in for the night I sat awhile in the dark over by the bridge over the cut where the tide ran in and out. It was a lonely place and quiet hour. I heard katydids up in the woods. Lonesome and weird, they reminded me of October—of the melancholy autumn nights of Lackawaxen. Then, as if this was not enough, a frog began to boom his croaky song. He seemed to be aware of the cold and that he could not much longer bemoan the death of summer.

At three-forty-five I awoke the boys. It was cold. The moon shone with a pale brightness over the bay. There was no wind. The sea swelled in calm and peaceful movement, without any wash. The morning star burned white and large in the east, the Orion showed pale by comparison.

We had our meager breakfast, and before five o'clock were on our way down the bay. Daylight came soon. The sky was softly gray, with an open space low down in the east where the blue was kindling. Presently the gray tinged to pink and then to red. All around us the broad bay gleamed mistily, like a moving jeweled medium, and the clouds in the west took on golden crowns.

At five-thirty the sun burst up over the black forest ridge, too dazzling for my gaze. It blanched the water and caused the moon to dim. I climbed up on the bow and held to the towrope. We had reached a point between Gull Rock and Blue Island where the great swells came heaving in. How wonderful to rise on them, high and higher! We would shoot down the far slope, gliding like an arrow. Those moments were full of reward. The break of day was fair, promising. Sea and land welcomed the sun. What joy there seemed in the hour, alone there on this isolated bay, seeing and feeling the everyday life of the native fisherman!

Only two boats sighted here between the islands, and they reported few herring in the nets and no sign of tuna. We ran on round Gull Rock, out into the open sea. Here the swells lifted us seemingly on hills of sunglazed water. The surf pounded on the gray rocks. Gulls screamed and wheeled around and over us, and the snowy white-breasted gray-backed terns welcomed us as if they remembered how we had dispensed manna on the waters.

I saw seven boats between Gull Rock and Shelberne Lighthouse, but they were really beyond the mouth of the bay. We approached them. Herring showed plentifully in their nets. "They've come back," said one fisherman. Another informed us no tuna had yet been sighted. We bought our usual quantity of bait, and asked the men to wave to us if anyone saw a tuna. In one boat there were two men and a boy, a bright-faced lad, very curious about us. I asked him how the herring were running.

"Pretty good. We've got several bushel out of three nets. And we have eight more nets to pick."

"Have you seen any tuna?" I asked.

"Not yet. But yesterday there were six around our boat all the time we hauled. I hit one with an oar. He was a big fellow. I'd like to see you hook him."

I knew by the way he smiled at me that he could anticipate nothing but disaster for me.

"Well, if you see one this morning you wave your cap," I told him. "Perhaps you will have some fun watching me."

We proceeded then toward the end of the net zone, where our other boat had halted. Suddenly I saw R. C. and Captain Mitchell waving to us.

"Hook her up, Cap!" I shouted.

"Shore there's somethin' doin'," remarked Bob.

It did not take many moments for us to reach the boat. R. C. yelled and pointed. I turned to see two net-boats near at hand, and a fisherman in one of them waved to us, at the same time throwing herring overboard. Instantly a boiling swirl appeared on the water just where the herring had alighted.

"Say, did you see that?" queried Bob, turning his sharp blue glance at me.

We sped over to this boat, and Bob lifted the net-buoy out of the water and up on our bow.

"Big albacore here," said the fisherman. "He's taken two herring. I saw his head and his eye."

"Thanks for waving to us," I replied. He was a tall lean chap, dark and weather-beaten, and as he stood there in his old boat, holding the net in his hands, with fish scales shining all over his rubber clothes, I paid him a silent tribute. There is something great about fishermen who live by the sea. His boat was a low-lying launch, black with age, wet as if it had been under water. The engine box was situated in the middle. I saw scattered herring on the floor, an old oar, and a net-scoop, and several round baskets, low and flat, and ready to fall apart. All this I took in with one swift glance.

Then I threw my bait overboard, and let it drift away and sink until I could not see the end of the leader. Sid had stopped the engines. Bob was already grinding chum. I coiled fifteen feet of line on the stern, and held it in my hand, while I straddled my rod, and gazed into the beautiful green depths with fascinated eyes. I was looking to see the tuna show again. Something would happen soon, but I hardly thought I would have a bite. We all expected to see the fish come up to take one of the herring the fishermen threw out.

R. C. and Captain Mitchell and Romer stood on the deck of the other boat just outside the zone of nets, and they were observing us. The morning, the place, the situation seemed perfect for some extraordinary adventure. I felt it. Three of the fishermen's boats were near us, one just a few yards away. The men had stopped work to watch us, very curious, jovial, and with good-natured unconcealed doubt. They thought I was in for an albacore bite–and broken tackle.

Suddenly I felt a strong slow tug. The line slipped through my hand.

"He's got it!" I called. I flashed a quick glance at R. C. He waved. His sharp eyes had seen the line pay out. All the coiled line slipped overboard. I sat down, and stripped off several yards

more. It was a slow sweeping movement of line. When it
straightened out I jerked with all my weight and strength. The
response was a tremendous downward pull on my rod. My arms
cracked. My body, braced as it was by my feet against the boat,
lurched over hard. Sid had the engines roaring and the launch
moving. The fishermen cheered us. My line slipped off the big
reel. But it did not fly off, as in the former runs. This tuna
showed no lightning-swift movements at the onset. What was
worse, however, he ran straight inshore toward a net. He took
about two hundred feet of line before we got going satisfactorily
after him. We were not saying anything. If I had spoken I could
have voiced only fears. The excitement of the strike had not left
me. Besides that, I had a horrible expectancy of some sure and
quick calamity.

The tuna sheered just short of the net. Probably he ran to it
and turned. Then he headed toward another. In fact we were
hemmed in on three sides by nets. They were all within two
hundred yards.

"He'll go out to sea. Don't worry," yelled Bob.

As my tuna had headed straight for another net I could not
accept Bob's optimistic assertion. The action of the fish was not
slow, yet it did not compare with that of the first runs of the
others. We even gained a little line. When I was about to give
way to despair the tuna sheered abruptly to the right. This
brought our launch toward another net—the third. We had
headed back almost toward the boats and the spot where I had
hooked him. Hope revived in me. He might be looking for a
place to get out to sea.

As good fortune would have it this tuna made another swerve
away from a net, and found the lane that led out to open water.
I had to whoop.

"What'd I tell you?" shouted Bob. "He didn't want to run in
them nets any more than we wanted him to."

Sid bent a beaming red face upon me. "What's your legs

wabbling for?" he queried. Indeed my legs were shaking, especially the right one. My knees seemed to have no bones or muscles in them. No feeling! I had not observed this proof of unusual agitation until Sid called my attention to it. But it was an old affection, not experienced for long, and it returned with a vigor and familiarity calculated to make up for absence.

The tuna got up speed; still he did not compel us to race after him. He took a couple of hundred yards of line before we regulated our pace to his. And instead of heading out to sea he took a straight course across the mouth of East Jordon Bay. It was three or four miles wide. The nets to our left were close to Gull Rock, and we soon passed them. All seemed clear sailing now. My feelings underwent change and I felt as strong as a horse. I worked so hard that the boys expressed some little fear that I might break him off.

"No danger!" I declared. "It's the lightning-swift runs that scare me. This fellow acts different. He swims deep and doesn't change his pace. But, oh! he's heavy!"

"Reckon he's a buster," observed Bob. "Suppose you try to lead him out to sea."

Whereupon we got the tuna on our port side, and while Sid edged the launch quarteringly out to sea I hauled strenuously on the rod. I lost line. Then we changed our course until I had recovered it, and tried over again. For all I could tell I did not budge him an inch from the bee line he had taken toward Blue Island. When we had covered three miles or more, and were slowly approaching the ragged black reefs reaching out from this island, I began to grow alarmed. Captain Mitchell and R. C., following us within hailing distance, waved and yelled for us to turn the fish out to sea.

"Turn this fish!" I yelled. "Ha! Ha!"

When we arrived within a half mile of the point of Blue Island we abandoned any hope of heading the tuna out to sea. He was well inside the reef now, and he might be turned up the bay.

"Boys, we'll take a chance," I decided. "If he means to go for the rocks we'll have it out with him."

Bob shook his head dubiously. He was plainly worried. Sid showed more signs of perturbation. This magnificent tuna fishing had some features not calculated to be good for one's heart.

"Run up on him," I ordered.

We closed in on the fish, and I hauled and reeled in line until we were perhaps less than two hundred feet from him. Then I shut down on the drag and set determinedly to the task ahead. The setting of this angling adventure was something on a tremendous scale, consistent with the nature of this giant tuna fighting. The south side of Blue Island showed its naked black teeth wreathed in white. Already we were lifted on the ground swells that heaved us slowly and gracefully. We were riding hills of green water. Even the fear that had begun to grip me could not wholly kill my mounting exhilaration.

Bob stood in the bow, like a mariner searching ahead for reefs. He made a strong figure standing there, his sharp-cut profile expressing courage and intelligence.

"Shore we'll stay with him," he said. "I'm not worryin' about hittin' a reef. It's the line that bothers me. If it touches a rock—snap!"

"I'll go so far and no farther," replied Sid, stubbornly.

"But, man, you've got two engines heah, an' a boat followin'!" expostulated Bob. Then they argued while I toiled on that irresistible tuna. I had begun to sweat, perhaps from fright as much as exertion. For it was cold sweat! But the time and place lent me more strength than I had ever possessed before. I bent the big Murphy hickory double. I put arms, shoulders, back, and weight, with all the bracing power in my legs, into united effort to work slowly up to my limit. No sudden violence would have changed that fish. It would only have broken the tackle. My plan was to keep at him slowly and hard, all the time.

When we were a quarter of a mile off the end of the island, with my tuna heading straight in, the situation narrowed down to the climax. I had no thought then of the dramatic side of it. But I was filled with emotions freed by this struggle and the hazard, and the physical things impossible not to see and hear and feel.

Blue Island seemed a mountain, green on top, black at the sea line, a bleak jagged precipitous shore against which the great swells burst ponderously. The white spray shot high. I saw the green swells rise out of the calm sea and move in with majestic regularity, to crash and boom into white seething ruin. Then the water falling and running back off the rocks sounded like the rapids of a river. The feel of the sea under me was something at that moment to take heed of. If I had not been hooked to what must be a gigantic tuna, I would have grown panic-stricken.

"So far and no farther!" called out Sid.

"You'll do as I tell you," I replied, sharply.

"All right. If we smash it won't be my fault. I can swim," he said.

"Swim! It'd sure do you a lot of good heah," retorted Bob. "But I'm tellin' you we're safe. The big boat is just behind. Captain Mitchell is out in the skiff. Let's stay with this son-of-a-gun. He must be some fish!"

"Boys, I feel him slowing up," I called out, eagerly. "He's bumped into the bottom."

"Work all the harder then," advised Bob.

I gazed behind me to see Captain Mitchell perhaps a hundred feet from us, and beyond him the big launch rode the swells. R. C. stood in the bow. Romer waved from the deck. I could hear his shrill wild cry above the roar of the surf. Whatever else the moment held, it surely was full of stinging excitement.

We reached a point perhaps a hundred yards from the shore. It seemed closer because of the thunder of water and the looming rocks. The reef on the point stood out to our right, beyond us. Far to our left another reef extended out. Low, sharp, ugly rocks showed at times, cutting the white water.

"It's now or never," I yelled to the boys. "This is no fun. But we're in it. Now let's do the right thing and still hang. . . . Sid, edge her off a little. We'll head him out of here or break him off."

Still I did not mean to break the tuna off. I could trust that line so long as it did not touch a rock. Putting on the small drag, something I had never done before, and screwing the larger one tighter, I increased my exertions. I determined to turn that tuna. Somehow I had not shared the opinion of the boys that the fish had gone inshore to cut off on the rocks. I pulled until at the end of every sweep I saw red. Gradually the line slipped off the reel. Gradually the launch worked her bow out from the shore. Gradually the tuna responded to the great strain put upon him. Of course the elastic rod and the perfect reel saved the line from parting. It slipped off the drags just short of the breaking point. All I had ever learned in swordfishing, about the limit of tackle strength and the conserving of muscular force, came into play here. Had I not had such long experience the task here would have been hopeless. It was a terrific fight. We dared not go any closer to where the swells smashed in green-white mounds on the rocks. I did not seem to be conscious of weakness, but I was of strain. Never had I subjected my body to such concerted and sustained effort. When I heard Bob yelling I knew we were turning the fish, though I could not hear what he said. The roar was almost deafening. Our launch glided and rose, glided on and fell, with easy motion. The violence of the seas was all inshore. Across my taut line, that sang like a telephone wire in cold wind, I saw the notched noses of the black rocks, the white seething rise and fall of foamy waves, the angry curl and break, the short spurts of water. Beyond the reef tumbled the breakers along the inside of the island. Never had a given point in my angling experiences seemed so unattainable. Only a few hundred yards! How slowly we moved! Could I last it out? I had begun that climax of this part of the fight within two hundred feet of my fish. As I worked I had lost line until over seven hundred feet were off the reel. The more feet out the more pressure on the line! It looked like a wet fiddle string and it twanged off my thumb and flipped a fine spray into my face. But hopeful indications were not wanting. The launch was not outside the danger zone, beyond the end of the reef, even if we ran straight. But the tuna had been turned broadside to the shore. That sustained me. What I had gained I would not surrender. I held to that slow, ponderous, terrific regularity of heave and wind. My sight grew dim. My heart seemed about to crack. My breast labored. My back had no sensation. I could no longer feel the bind of the leather harness.

There seems no limit to human endurance. Always I could hang on a moment longer. And I held on until my tuna rounded the end of the reef. Bob whooped the glorious news. Then I released the drags and lowered my rod to rest on the barrel of bait in front of me. Bob had stacked cushions on it. What unutterable relief! I seemed numb all over. I heard the line running off the reel, and also the accelerated working of the engines.

"Careful—slow—till I—get my breath," I panted.

"Shore. Let him have line. He's runnin' to his funeral now," shouted Bob.

The din of the surf subsided. Where dark rocks and white waves had obstructed my vision I now saw with clearing sight the wide shining waters of the bay and the beautiful forested shore line. My tuna took four hundred yards of line, with our launch going fairly fast, while I was recovering myself. Then I approached further work gradually. In half an hour I had all the line we wanted back on the reel, and we were four miles farther up the bay.

Here the large boat, with R. C. and Romer and Captain

Mitchell gayly industrious with cameras of all kinds, cruised round us and up alongside.

"Must be a whopper!" yelled Romer. "Don't work too hard, dad. Don't let him get away. Don't give him any rest."

Impossible as it was to follow so much varied advice, it struck me as being sound. I recovered surprisingly, considering the effort I had made, and soon got down to hard work again. This tuna had somehow inspired me with a conviction that he was bigger than the others. I must not spare anything. How strange it was to feel him at the end of my line, to know he was monstrous, almost unconquerable, to realize that he was indeed a tuna, though I had not had one glimpse of him. He swam deep. He never made a wave on the surface. While I fought him to the best of my reduced strength he towed the launch. Oftener and oftener Sid threw out the clutches. Then he shut off the engine entirely.

"Shore that'll take the sap out of him," declared Bob.

We seemed to be a ruthless combination of skill, cunning, experience, and strength, equipped with special instruments, all for the destruction of that poor luckless tuna. The incongruity, the unfairness of it struck me keenly. Why did I do this sort of thing? I could not answer then any more than at other times when the vexatious problem had presented itself—always at the extreme moments of the struggle. Afterward, when I asked myself the same queries, I could answer them to my satisfaction. But just then the sport seemed inhuman and unjustifiable. The psychological changes an angler goes through while fighting a fish adversary vastly his superior, the capture of which seems a vital thrilling need, are varied and extreme, some swift as flashes of emotion, and others long drawn out and compelling.

"That's a big fish," observed Bob for the twentieth time. He said it meditatively and seriously, as if talking only to himself. Bob was always thinking fish.

My tuna had developed into a more important possibility than

that of the first one. I was intensely curious to have a look at him
and bewailed his deep-fighting temper. He crossed the bay with
us, rather close to the Two Sisters, the only reefs in the upper
waters of this harbor, and if he had turned in their direction we
would have had more serious work cut out for us. But he passed
by them and turned again toward the sea. This was eminently
satisfactory. He took us back down the bay straight for Gull
Rock. Three more miles of stubborn flight! When we got within
a mile of the nets off the rock we all agreed that it was high time
for us to contest this flight back toward open sea. The brunt of
such contest fell upon me. So we fought it out right there in that
wide space of deep water, and I was the vanquished one. In the
end I had to give in to him and let him tow us, while I confined
my efforts to turning him from a straight course.

The bay here was as smooth as a mill pond, waved only by
gentle swells. My tuna came up. What a wave he pushed ahead
of him! Then he roared on the surface, showing first his sickle
dorsal fin, then his black wide tail, then the blue bulge of his
back, round as a huge tree trunk, and at last his magnificent
head, out of the water to his eyes.

"Oh! Oh!" bawled Sid, wildly.

"Some socker!" ejaculated Bob. "I said he was a big fish."

To me he seemed enormous, supremely beautiful and unattainable. He flashed purple, bronze, silver-gold. When he went
under he left a surging abyss in the water, a gurgling whirlpool.
This sight again revived me. I was a new man, at least for a little
while. I turned that tuna round. I pulled the launch toward him.
I held him so that he towed us stern first. In short I performed,
for the time being, miraculous and hitherto unknown feats of
rod endurance. I would cheerfully have walked overboard into
the sea for that fish. All the same, he took us gradually toward
the nets.

"They don't worry me none," said Bob, seeing my growing
anxiety and dismay. "We'll go under or cut through. I was afraid

of nets at first. But one end of them is free. It drifts with the tides. We can go through a dozen nets. Just you hand it to that tuna and never worry about nets."

Nevertheless I did worry, and I worked to the extent of all left in me. If I had not been able to slow him up, turn him from side to side, I could not have found the heart to keep it up. Many times he swerved to the surface, raising a wave that thrilled me every time I saw it. It was not a wave, but a swell. Next to that the boils that rose to the surface never ceased to fascinate me. These were new in my experience. They came when he was swimming along deep, and they would rise to the surface as far as a hundred feet behind him. They were swirls, eddies, powerful circles beginning with a small radius, and spreading until they were whirlpools six feet in diameter. More than any other single detail these breaks on the surface impressed me with the extraordinary tail power of these tuna.

I got the double line over the reel—lost it—won it back again—watched it slip away once more—heaved and wound it in—again, again, again, until my thumbs stung through gloves and stalls and my wrists and arms were pierced by excruciating pains. Still I heaved on. The ring in the wire leader came out of the water and spun round. How the leader vibrated! Bob leaped on the bow and reached for it. One last supreme effort! It took all I had left. Bent and tense, with bursting heart and failing sight, I got that leader to Bob's eager hand. When the strain was released I fell back, spent and shaking, hot and wet, absolutely all in, and most assuredly conscious of the worst beating ever given to me by a fish. I was thoroughly whipped, and so exhausted that my nerve wavered.

But seeing Bob hang to the leader reinspirited me, and so roused my thrilling wonder and speculation that I forgot my pangs. Bob would not let go. The great fish rolled and soused on the surface, thumping the water heavily. He too was tired. He could just wag his tail. But the effect on that wag pulled the launch round and round. Sid was helping to make it spin by running the engines full reverse and working the wheel. The tuna had his head toward us, and he was almost within reach of a gaff. We had to back and go round with him to keep him from going under us. Bob would haul in six or eight feet of the leader, then lose it a little at a time. I stood up the better to see. The tuna rolled on his side. And then I had my most electrifying shock. He looked as wide as a door and as long as the boat. His color was a changing blaze of silver, gold, amber, purple, and green. He seemed at once frightful and lovely, fierce and pitiful, a wild creature in the last act of precious life.

Then he changed these tactics. Righting himself, he sheered ahead and with fin out of the water he began to tow the launch. I could not see plainly. But it was evident that he could not swim otherwise than in a circle. The launch was dragged round at a fairly rapid rate, as if it were at the mercy of a strong eddy. Finally the tuna pulled the leader through Bob's hands, so that he was holding by the double line.

"Let go, Bob!" I shouted. "I'll work the leader back."

"But we'll shore have that all to do over again," objected Bob.

"No matter. Let go. I know it's tough, when you had him so near."

Bob did as he was bidden, and again the issue lay between the tuna and me. If I was weaker, so was he. I held him on the double line, so that only a few inches slipped off the reel. And he towed the launch around precisely the same as when Bob had held the leader. He came up about forty feet away, a little to the right of our bow, and turned on his side. Pale green, wonderful shieldlike shape! He was first weakening, and that recalled my vanished strength. I thumbed the reel-drag tight as I dared, and with left gloved hand I held to the line. It cut through glove and burned my palm. But I held him. Strangely, we were all quiet now. We had seen him close. I could not look up to see where our other boat was, but I heard the beat of its engine and the cries of my faithful comrades. I could see only the shining oval fish-shape, sailing, gliding like a specter under the smooth surface. The bow of the boat and Bob's crouched form showed in the tail of my eye.

"That fish's a lost fawn-skin," yelled Bob. His quaint mode of speech and Southern twang had never struck me more forcibly. And I shared his conviction about the tuna. I felt that he was beaten. Letting go of the line, I set to heaving on the rod and whirling the reel. I could hold him, move him, drag him.

"Grab the leader, Bob," I shouted. "Sid, get ready to jump for the gaff."

A few powerful pulls brought the leader to Bob. He held it. The magnificent fish creature rolled and gaped on the surface. Bob drew on the leader, inch by inch at first, then, when he got the tuna coming, foot by foot, until he was close to the bow, head toward us, swimming on his side while Sid backed the boat. When I gave the word Sid threw out the clutch, leaped over the engine box, and grasping the gaff he leaned far over—and lunged back. The detachable gaff pole came loose, leaving the rope in Sid's hands, but the pole hit him hard over the head. He yelled lustily, as mad as if one of us had done it with intent. I could not see the tuna now, but I heard him begin to splash and pound, harder, faster, until the water flew above us and I could scarcely see Bob.

"Did he make a good job of it?" I yelled, fearfully.

"Shore. We got him. An' I'll have a rope round his tail in a jiffy," replied Bob.

That gave me license to sit down and let go of the rod, so suddenly a burden. The other boat came up and we were hailed and cheered. Captain Pence waved the British flag. Presently Bob had the tuna safely lassoed and tied to our stern, where the ponderous thumps from a mighty tail splashed water over me.

"Three hours an' ten minutes!" exclaimed Bob, consulting his watch.

"Seemed a year to me," I replied, but I did not tell them then how that tuna had punished me.

"Well, let's go home," spoke up Sid, brightly. "The little launch and the big tackle sure are the dope."

"Wal, where do we all come in?" drawled Bob.

It took us nearly two hours to tow our catch back up the bay to the breakwater. Every time I looked at him I was sure he grew larger in my sight. When we reached the wharf our eager comrades almost fell overboard to see that fish.

We rigged up three poles with block and tackle, and prepared to haul the tuna up on the wharf. I told Captain Mitchell that I had beaten his world record of 710 pounds. I had no way of knowing, yet somehow I felt absolutely sure of it.

"I hope you have," replied Mitchell, studying the blue-and-silver monster lying in the water.

The men had a hard time hauling the fish up, and as he came more and more into sight his enormous size grew manifest. Moreover, for me there was something appallingly beautiful about him. At last they had him high enough to lower on the wharf. Then I was mute! I could not believe my own sight.

"What a grand tuna!" ejaculated Captain Mitchell, in heart-felt administration and wonder. "Indeed you have beaten my record. . . . Old man, I congratulate you. I am honestly glad."

They all had something fine to say to me, but I could not reply. I seemed struck dumb by the bulk and beauty of that tuna. My eyes were glued to his noble proportions and his transforming colors. He was dying, and the hues of a tuna change most and are most beautiful at that time. He was shield-shaped, very full and round, and high and long. His back glowed a deep dark purple; his side glanced like mother-of-pearl in a lustrous light; his belly shone a silver white. The little yellow rudders on his tail moved from side to side, pathetic and reproachful reminders to me of the life and spirit that was passing. If it were possible for a man to fall in love with a fish, that was what happened to me. I hung over him, spellbound and incredulous.

"Well, I always said it was coming to you," averred R. C., and I gauged his appreciation by his tone and the significance of his words.

The native fishermen who lived near the breakwater came down to see the tuna. I was most eager to get their point of view. Frank Sears had been there for fifteen years and had been recommended to me as a man of integrity and intelligence. One of his men had fished for herring along that coast all his life. These fishermen had seen thousands of albacore, as they called the tuna. They walked round him, from one side to the other, and the more they gazed the keener were my thrills and anticipations.

"Biggest albacore I ever saw," said Sears, at length. "He's got a small head. He's all body, and big and thick clear down to his tail. We have shipped over two hundred albacore to the markets and have had hundreds in the traps and weirs. But that's the biggest I ever saw. You might fish for ten years and never see another like it."

Sears's man was even more gratifying. "I can say the same. He'll go over eight hundred pounds. Fish are my business and I'm not given to overestimating. . . . You certainly must have caught the big one that's been seen around Western Head for a month or more."

When I exhibited my tackle to these fishermen their interest and amaze knew no bounds. They could hardly believe so huge and powerful a fish, the kind that had often smashed their boats, gone through net and weir, could have been held and subdued on that little line. In truth the thirty-nine-thread line did look small, but its strength was mighty.

My tuna was 8 feet 8 inches in length, 6 feet 4 inches in girth. His head measured 2 feet and 5 inches in length. Yet Sears had called his head small. He weight 758 pounds.

Perhaps my son's remark pleased me most of all:

"Sure is some fish! Biggest ever caught on a rod, by anybody, any kind of a game fish. . . . And I was here to see you lick him, dad!"

Mr. Sears signed an affidavit for me, substantiating his statements above, and Captain Mitchell wrote another for me as follows:

EAST JORDON, NOVA SCOTIA,
August 22, 1924.

To ANYONE IT MAY CONCERN:

This is to certify that I was one of the eight men who saw Mr. Zane Grey's 758-pound tuna fought, landed, and weighed. It broke my record tuna weight, 710 pounds, which I have held for some years. And I confirm the statement made by Sears and the native fishermen here.
(Signed)   CAPTAIN LAURIE D. MITCHELL.

That evening there was a rather pale and threatening sunset. The bay became as calm as a mill pond. But before dark a slight ripple moved from the southeast and a damp wind followed it. Then a ring appeared round the moon. We were in for more weather.

And the next day it rained. Moreover, although it rained hard all day it did not really get started until night. Then there was a deluge. We passed a most uncomfortable night.

The following morning fog and rain obscured all but the closest objects. During the afternoon rain fell at intervals, drizzling and misty, and the fog curtain blew in, sometimes dense, at others permitting sight of the island and headlands. We put in the time as best we could, mostly playing checkers with the insatiable Romer. He succeeded in beating all of us once, to his great joy.

The next morning we had fished in the fog. Herring had become very scarce, and likewise tuna. Later in the day we learned that some fishermen had taken a good number of herring off Blue Island, and one of these men reported having tuna around his boat. The fishermen between Gull Rock and Shelberne Light caught no herring at all, and were convinced the run was about over. We were inclined to agree with this opinion, but decided to try another morning off Blue Island.

During the afternoon the fog lifted somewhat and we had a few hours of less depressing weather. Upon returning from a walk I found Romer fishing, and as I approached I saw him haul a small, big-headed fish up on the wharf, very gingerly detach it from his hook, and cast it back into the water. Then he flipped his bait back. As his action was unusually interesting I went over to his side with a query as to his luck.

"Sculpin! Darndest fish I ever saw!" he ejaculated, disgustedly.

"How so?" I inquired.

"I've caught that sculpin five times. He's a big hog and a damn fool, I'll say."

"Romer, surely you are mistaken! You haven't caught the same fish five times?"

"You just bet I have," he declared. "See here! Look! . . . There! I've got him again."

Whereupon he jerked out the queer, ugly, misshapen fish about a foot in length, gray and black, with large head and enormous mouth. Somehow the name sculpin seemed felicitous. Romer had the fish hooked squarely through the thick jaw. He handled it most carefully, explaining to me that the sculpin had poisonous spines, very dangerous, the sting of which had cost boys loss of arm and even life. His hook was large and not easily extracted.

"Now, watch," he said, throwing the sculpin back into the water and dropping hook and bait after it. I did indeed watch, and I saw the fish swim round with slow motion, apparently unconcerned about having been hooked and hauled out six times. Romer edged his bait near where the sculpin was circling, not far under the surface. When it saw the bait it promptly opened that huge mouth. I was amazed. That sculpin showed no instinct of self-preservation except the one of feeding. It took the large bait ravenously. Romer jerked hard and hauled the crazy fish up for the seventh time.

"Say, what do you know about that?" he inquired.

"Well, to tell the truth, Romer, I don't know anything," I replied. "That is a stumper. I wonder what naturalists would say. No doubt the sight of food acts so powerfully upon the senses of a sculpin that no other reaction is possible. . . . Throw him back again."

The identical performance was repeated for my benefit, and to my further mystification and wonder. There are many low forms of life in the sea, and a sculpin, although he is a fish, must indeed belong to one of them. Stupidity would seem to be his dominant characteristic, and hoggishness his strongest instinct. It would be interesting to learn what enemies a sculpin has, if any, and how he reacts to them.

Next morning we were up at four, in the cool damp dark grayness. The fog had raised. I could see the black fringe of the forests. But the stars were obscured. At daylight we were bound across the bay to meet a native fisherman, Harold Locke, who had left out a herring net in our interest. He was waiting for us on his little dock, beneath a tiny gray cottage on the hill. He lived, indeed, beside the sea and by the sea. I liked his clean-cut lean face, tanned by exposure, and his tall form, clad in soiled rubber overalls. He was not optimistic as to the herring. And indeed his net yielded only a few bait.

We ran round to the net-buoys on the other side of Gull Rock. The nets had been taken up. Much disappointed, we crossed the mouth of the bay, pushing into an incoming bank of fog. Only one fishing boat could we find, and the men in this informed us that the herring and albacore had gone out to sea. So we gave up and decided to return to Liverpool.

On our way up the bay we ran out of the fog into bright sunshine, a very welcome and beautiful change. But the wind appeared to be rising. After putting Locke ashore we turned back down the bay. Blue Island and Gull Rock were disappearing in a low silver fog bank. But as it looked broken and moving out to sea we ventured to go on. What a strange difference when we entered that gray, cool, mystic medium! It changed all. Here it was thick and there thin. Sometimes the sun would shine through and again we were engulfed in a heavy wet blanket. We followed the shore line, however, all the way out to Western Head, and as we rounded that low dark booming point we ran into thick mist. We should have turned back. But as we had run into and out of fog I decided we might risk it by laying a course for the whistling-buoys along the coast.

Captain Pence laid his course, but it led us straight into the reefs. And it was my sharp eye that first espied the dim black edges of rock. We slowed down, changed our course, and then ran between and around the rocks, out to sea. I shall not soon forget that strained two hours.

Again we came out of the fog bank, so that we could see the rocky shore line. All seemed well then. We ran on. But the sea began to rise with the wind, and in an hour it was rough, too rough for our small launch. We could not have fought our way against it. With a following sea, however, we bowled along, shipping only a little water.

Good luck could not stand by us. The large boat, which we had engaged solely as a safeguard for our little launch, slowly dropped astern and finally stopped. Something was wrong. Bob and Sid certainly said some things about the single-engine in that boat. But danger or no danger, we had to put back to their aid. The way we tossed on the huge waves frightened me. We managed to reach them and take off R. C. and Romer. Captain Pence yelled that his engine would not run and he could not start it. Bob boarded the boat and soon yelled to us: "Out of gas!" That was not all he yelled.

There was nothing to do but attempt to tow the boat. I knew it would not be easy. When Sid asked me for orders I realized the danger. We got a long line to them, and then ran before the sea. The towline broke our stern gunwale and pulled out the braces, so that we had to tie to the fishing chair. I feared the strain would pull out the whole back end of the launch. But it held. We headed in for the entrance of the harbor of Port Joli, the place so famous as a winter feeding grounds for wild geese.

When we finally entered the harbor and were sighted by fishermen from shore, my relief was immense. Gas was procured, and the trip to Liverpool made without further mishap.

It rained hard that night. And next day was dismal, wet, dark. Toward evening the wind increased and the rain beat. When I went to bed it was pouring. About one o'clock I was awakened by the shaking of the house and the roaring of wind. A storm had burst upon us. I could not go back to sleep. Indeed, in an hour I did not want to. The lights went out, so that the whole place was in total darkness. I lay listening to the lash of rain, the roar of wind, the crash of breaking branches and falling trees. And presently I realized that it was a hurricane. I remembered then that I had seen the dock lined by fishing smacks which had run in that day. But surely all boats and ships had not made some safe port. I knew that somewhere out there in the roaring ebony blackness mariners and fishermen were at the mercy of the elements.

I lay awake until dawn, when the fury of the storm abated. It had lasted four hours and had been the worst in my experience. When I went out I found the streets almost impassable for wires and fallen trees. Much damage had been done. I walked down to the park, where the little lighthouse stood, and there I gazed out over the bay toward the open sea.

A pale sun was rising. The black clouds were sweeping away

before a shifting wind. On the reefs great combers were breaking, green and white. The cold bright Atlantic Main! I did not on the moment feel any love for it. It cleared off and the day became fine, with a brisk northwest breeze.

Not until next day did we learn much of what a fearful storm it had been. Then tales of wrecked ships and missing men came in, all the way from Halifax to the Bay of Fundy. That jagged shallow shore, cut like the teeth of a saw, and the fiercest driving sea seen for years, had exacted a frightful toll of loss and life. I read of several wonderful rescues by shore fishermen, one particularly filling me with awe and reverence for the single fisherman who at terrible risk of his life had saved the crew of a trawler. And it is the modern trawlers that are driving the shore fishermen out of business. How heroic, such a man! But somehow it is good to know. This storm made clearer to me the lives of these fishermen. I understood then the quiet lean faces, the pondering brows, the sad eyes, the lack of something that I might call joy of life. For them life was as hard as the relentless sea. It made them pay.

After the storm the weather cleared beautifully. Today, which is the third since the havoc wrought by wind and sea, the fishermen came in from their nets and traps with boatloads of mackerel and the first of the spawning herring. Tuna were reported at the mouth of the harbor.

Several other ambitious anglers have arrived from Boston and New York. They have come poorly equipped, and like all former anglers who have visited Nova Scotia, they have no idea of the difficulty of this game. I tried not to discourage them. It is always a delicate matter—trying to advise anglers. I never do it any more unless requested, and even then I am reluctant. Fishermen are queer. They are fundamentally egoists. They cannot, as a class, be instructed. Those who excel, that is to say, who learn to fish, do so through a long, slow, painful process. Salt-water

fishing for huge fish is not casting a salmon fly or sitting on a
green bank with a pole and line. It is strenuous, and this Nova
Scotia tuna angling is extraordinarily trying. One angler said:
"Oh, I'll be satisfied to break a few off!" Another expressed the
amazing opinion that it would be well to have a long lever
attached to a reel, so that by a forward and back movement the
line could be drawn in. And then one of the Liverpool boatmen
told how the angler he had taken out several years ago, and who
had lost so many tuna, had hooked his fish, or had claimed to
hook them. He used a cork on his line some four feet above the
leader. An ordinary small net cork, about five inches in diameter! According to this angler, when a tuna took his bait and
pulled the cork under, the cork hooked the fish. This was an
actual statement. It rendered me speechless. You could not drive
a nail into the jaw of a tuna without a hammer and considerable
force. My brother, using a heavy tackle, and striking with all his
great shoulder strength, had failed three times to see the hook in
the jaws of these tuna.

I may have some remarkably interesting things to record here
before many days pass.

Next morning we were up at four-thirty, and on the way
down the bay before sunrise. The morning was clear, crisp, cool,
with rosy east and sky a pale blue.

We found fishermen pulling their nets and traps, but herring
were scarce. At length we obtained half a bushel or more, and
went to chumming near a trap where the men were taking off a
good catch of mackerel. The swells rolled in from the open sea,
not by any means comfortable. In fact this place was almost out
in the open.

We saw a tuna smashing the water near the trap next to the
one where we were anchored, and we made haste to run over
there. Two of the anglers mentioned above were near by in
boats, and evidently sighted the tuna also, for they made for the

trap as quickly as possible. Whereupon we were soon all fishing for that tuna.

"Reckon there'll be a tackle funeral round heah if business picks up," observed Bob.

Soon we left to run over behind Coffin Island, a very felicitously named rock-bound bit of treacherous land, catching fairly the brunt of the sea roll. We tried here awhile, and then ran to a point off Port Medway, where Captain Mitchell had done most of his fishing. He showed us the place where he had hooked his 710-pound tuna. We anchored outside another trap, a large one, and began to chum as usual. The sun shone bright; the gulls screamed and laughed; the terns flitted about for bits of our ground-up herring. The sea was heaving and as clear as crystal. What a spectacle it would have been to see a tuna rise for a bait in this clear water! But it was not to be.

This trap interested me. It was made of seine twine, with corks and buoys keeping it afloat. The body lines somewhat resembled a huge figure 8, two hundred feet or more in length. The wings extended a long way obliquely from the trap. When herring or mackerel encountered these wings they swam along them, and so entered the small hole into the maze of net partitions, and seldom or never found their way out again. The same could be said of the tuna that entered. These trap fishermen, however, preferred to open the nets and let out the huge fish. It was cheaper to allow them to escape. It took six men in three boats to tend the trap. They reported a few mackerel and no herring or tuna.

On the way back to Liverpool Bay we passed a storm-battered fishing smack, returning home from the banks. She certainly showed scars of struggle with the hurricane. We learned, later, that one man had been lost overboard. Two schooners came into Lunenburg that day, with flags at half mast, and both captains reported loss of life and much damage in the worst storm of their sea experience. A number of fishing schooners had not yet been heard from. Assuredly some of them had been lost. It struck me to the heart, the tragedy of these fishermen's lives. Yet they are not hardened. They are serious seafaring folk, religious and simple in their lives, as indeed are most men who live in the open and fight the elements. I could not help but try to picture in mind the fury of the storm, the black night, and the terrible white horses of the sea, crashing over the vessels and carrying away boats, spars, and men. These heroic fishermen faced death every time they left home. And some of them had met it. Man overboard! Perhaps he was not even missed in the grim wild moment. But he knew! When he was swept away into the black night, on the crest of a crashing wave, he knew his doom. How tremendous and sickening to think of, and yet how splendid! He was washed overboard. He would swim and fight for his life, as a brave man, when all the time he would know. Surely he would pray. There would be thought of home, wife, children. . . . And then!

On Sunday morning I arose early and went out for a walk. It was a quiet, peaceful, beautiful morning. The streets were deserted. Not a sign of life! I walked to the park at the end of the street, and sat near the lighthouse, facing down the bay.

At once I was struck with the remarkable tranquillity and repose of the scene. Never had I seen such an unruffled surface of water. It was like silk. Only at the shoals near the beach did any motion show, and that was a gentle, almost indistinguishable swell. The bay shone a dark pearl-gray color, mirroring the clouds. Had it not been for the dark-green rugged shores stretching away to the east, and the lighthouse marking the headland, there would not have been any telling sea and sky apart. Not a breath of wind! How strange that seemed after the recent hurricane! It was only another mood of the inscrutable ocean. Almost I loved it then. But I could not forget. I think the ocean fascinates me, draws me, compels me, but not with love.

By listening intently I caught a faint low roar of surf far outside the headlands, and then the moaning of the whistle buoy, and at last the melancholy ring of a bell buoy. The spell of the scene gripped me and was difficult to explain. There was no sign of sunrise, though the hour was long past. A pale purple bank of cloud rose above the dim horizon line. Toward the south it broke and lightened, until a clearer space shone with some hue akin to rose and pearl. The whole effect seemed one of lull before a storm, and I was reminded that another hurricane had struck off the Virgin Islands and was reported traveling north. While I sat there, watching, listening, feeling, a strong desire to return to Nova Scotia at some future time moved me to vow that I would. It was indeed a far cry from California. Nevertheless I found myself planning another trip to this land of spruce forests and rock-lined streams of amber water, to this wild storm-bound coast with its beautiful bays and coves, its thundering reefs and lonely gale-swept headlands.

Dark
on the Water

～～～～～～～～～

Roderick L. Haig-Brown

Early morning and late evening are supposed to be great times for the fisherman. Generally, I have not found them so. There are exceptions: maturing Pacific salmon, for instance, are very likely to take best in salt water toward change of light; there may be rare circumstances, such as the movements of Corethra and other light-hating creatures, which make early-morning trout fishing not only profitable but almost essential; and after a hot, bright summer day the gentle evening light is reassuring to almost any creature. Dawn can be a beautiful time on the water, and I am glad I have tried early-morning fishing as often as I have and in as many different places; but I am glad, too, that I know it is seldom necessary for a fly-fisherman to get up early to catch fish, because early rising tends to make work out of pleasure. I like to start comfortably after a good breakfast and that, perhaps, is why I can make the broad generalization that the best fishing hours are likely to come between 10:30 A.M. and 4:30 P.M.; certainly a fisherman will be doing his own best work then, and that is at least as important as the mood of the fish; moods are changeable and skillful fishing can sometimes change them.

Evening fishing is important, though, traditionally, aesthetically and actually. The hot summer months are the time for it, July, August and early September, and it is no effort then to stay out until the last light is gone. The hours of a summer evening from seven o'clock onward are an exciting time; the day's work is done and man's world is very peaceful, but other creatures begin to move. I have seen many things at that stealthy time. Once a family of coons, working their way in playful hunting along the river's edge, came past where I was standing, less than half the river away from them, and went on round the upstream bend without noticing me. Once a cougar came silently from heavy timber onto a railroad track that I was following toward a good pool; he saw me, stopped for a moment, then went on across the track and disappeared to his hunting. Several times I have seen beaver, out in the quiet hour before their night's work of harvesting willow and alder; several times otters, sleek bodies sliding from rock or dirt into the water, little quick-eyed heads held low in swimming; and many times bear and deer moving with a calmness and a sense of right that forsake them in full daylight.

If land creatures move to their feeding at that time, perhaps it is not unreasonable to suppose that trout also will move then. Sometimes they do; often the dusk of a hot day brings flies down to the water, spent after their mating flight, and the trout move up to take them. Nearly always the quiet light of dusk brings fish into the shallows and stirs them to greater activity than during the day. Again and again one sees the still surface of a lake, scarcely broken by movement all through the day, marked by a thousand rings at sunset.

A fisherman is always hopeful—nearly always more hopeful than he has any good cause to be. He is probably most hopeful of all when he goes out in the early dawn, feeling that he has stolen an hour on his brothers and earned himself a reward by sheer virtue and fortitude. But the hope of the evening rise is a darker, more powerful hope; it is a mysterious time, when miracles may happen: a big fish, stirred from the hidden depths of a dark pool, may be under that tiny rise in the shallows; heavy gut and a clumsily cast fly may not matter; perhaps the sedges will be out and the fish will forget all caution to come to them. At worst it is a different time, quiet and strange, and it may well be that something stirs in a fisherman to give him a kinship with the time, just as something in the slant of the sun and the length of the shadows moves the cougars and coons to their hunting.

Generally the great hopes one has of evening fishing are not fulfilled, the imagined shapes of huge fish do not materialize. But it scarcely matters. Whatever affinity with the time may stir in a man, it is not hunting lust, but something far gentler. I remember the good evenings I have fished, even the ones that realized material hopes, not by the fish that came to the fly, but by the color and movement of water and sky, by the sounds and scents and gentle stirrings that were all about me.

There was a strange and beautiful evening once, below Theimar Falls, when the creek poured over into the slack of a small full tide. It must have been late in the year, for the coho salmon were running, but it was a warm evening and the sun went down red and the clouds grew mauve and gold behind it, as they often do over Johnstone Strait. I was not expecting much, a cutthroat or two, perhaps, and possibly a coho if a school chanced to turn in. I reached a fly across the foot of the falls, well into the eddy on the far side, felt the current draw the line tight, then knew I was hooked to a twenty-inch length of silver that leaped in brightness from the eddy. In six casts I had hooked six of them, precocious male cohos, coming in a year early to spawn with the rest of the run. They were larger than any I have seen before or since, the smallest of them over two pounds, and they were so clean and bright that I knew they must have found the creek only that day.

By the time I had landed the last of them, the light was only a reflection from the pale sky, but it was reflected again from the smooth water of the strait and I could see well enough to keep fishing. I had worked well down and was dropping my fly where the fresh water spread invisibly into the open strait when I felt the solid, heavy stop of a big fish taking. He ran out and fought without showing, except when the stir of his tail broke and made the light strike from oily swirls on the surface; he fought slowly and sulkily, and the lights came gleaming on in the bay across the strait. He took out my poor little forty yards of backing till there were only a few turns left on the reel; and I heard the solemn, throaty diesel of a purse seiner very clear and close across the silent water. My fish began to give a little, to come back, and I heard the heavy splash of another fish jumping far out of the water. The moon was up when I slid mine to the beach, and I heard a dog barking in the woods behind me and knew that Ed and Scraps were coming down to look for me. I took the fly out gently, turned him and slid him back, for we had no need of a fish like him, a great cock coho, clear silver still, broad sided, heavy shouldered with a strength that would surely take him to his spawning.

I have fished many evenings on lakes and had great pleasure from them, but a lake is not so good as a river unless one is waiting on some known shoal for some known monster to come up to his feeding. Evening salt-water fishing has its peaceful beauty, the quiet fading of the distant mountains, the blackening of the nearer hills, and distant sounds clear across the water. Once or twice I have caught feeding spring salmon until nearly midnight, when the full moon was the only light. But sea fishing is not river fishing, and night fishing it not evening fishing at all. I remember that I used to think that as evening fishing might yield stranger miracles than day fishing, so night fishing would

be yet more powerful than evening fishing. We used to try this
theory on the Frome, poaching the deep dry-fly pools with
silver-bodied salmon flies in black darkness, but we caught only
half-pounders and grew discontented in the darkness as one
seldom does while there is still light in the western sky.

There is a little river that flows down Elk Valley from Summit
Lake to Upper Campbell Lake. It is a beautiful river, or was while
the heavy timber still stood along it, very clear and very cold,
cold enough to make your legs ache after a long spell of fishing
even on a summer day. The fish do not spread through it until
late July or August, and Buckie and I went there in 1937, at
what should have been just the right time. The first afternoon
we fished was hot and sunny, too bright really, but we covered
a lot of water and saw very few fish. I wondered a little if it might
be a late year and hoped not, because Buckie had come a long
way to fish with me.

We went back to camp for supper and afterward went down
to the big pool just below camp. It is a very fine pool, the head
of it a smooth, swift run on a sixty- or seventy-degree curve,
good current sliding beyond the curve, past the narrow entrance
of a little slough, spreading wide at the tail, but still three or four
feet deep and deeper than that under the bushes on the far side.
There was nothing moving in the pool when we came to it, so
we sat with our rods on the gravel bar on the inside of the curve
and watched the water. A few flies were coming down and
many were playing above the water. "We ought to see a few
rises," I told Buckie. "It's a perfect place and a perfect evening."

Then I saw a single quiet rise right under the bushes on the far
side. Buckie hadn't seen it, so I went down to try the fish,
wondering if I could reach him well enough to bring the fly over
without drag. The pool was even wider than I thought, and I
dropped the first cast well short; but the second reached him,
and he took the sedge gently as it slid along just short of the
bushes. Elk River fish fight well for their size, and he did his best;

but there was little to help him in the open water at the tail of the pool, so I led him to the net fairly quickly.

The sun was almost gone behind the mountains, but there was still a warm light on the pool and the flies still danced in it. Then a fish rose at the end of the curving run, another rose above him, one rose at the head of the run, and suddenly they were rising all along it, beyond it in the mouth of the slough and below it in the tail, where I had hooked the first fish.

Buckie started in to work up the run with a dry sedge, and it was all so peaceful and lovely that I simply stayed to watch. He waded well out and fished steadily up the center of the run. He was fishing a short line, covering the rises as they came, and the fish took him well, accepting the sedge as calmly as they were accepting every natural that drifted down. Once or twice I helped Buckie with the net, but after that I left him on his own and just lay back on the gravel while he caught six or eight good fish one after another. It was quick and almost automatic— certainly rhythmic: a rise, a cast, the float of the brown-hackled fly against the light water, its sharp disappearance in the confident swirl of a solid rise, the strike, and then the quick active fight of a good little trout in perfect condition.

There were two or three fish cruising in the slack water at the mouth of the slough, rising steadily, and another, taking everything that came to him, on the far side of a broken tree branch just below the slough. I had been watching them for some time when the fever of evening fishing came suddenly upon me. It was getting dark, but I wanted those fish. I had a feeling that they might be big; watching the rises in the half light, considering the places they had chosen, I felt sure they were big.

So I went down into the water and cast for the fish behind the branch. He had to take it the first time, to save my fly from the branch, and he did. I tightened on him and saw that my line bent around the branch, as I had known it was bound to unless he chose to run upstream immediately he felt the hook. Perhaps it's foolish to try for fish in places like that. Some good fishermen think so, I know, and leave them alone unless they can come at them from some other angle. But I always do try for them and only begin to worry about getting them out when the hook is set. This time, as nearly always happens, the fish solved the problem for me by running hard for the far bank. I worked upstream a little, keeping the line tight on him and my rod high in the air, held by the butt at the full extent of my arm. Nothing happened, so I slacked the strain, gave the line a flip, tightened again and saw it slide easily over the backward curve of the branch and come free.

The fish didn't weigh quite a pound, but I still thought the others in the mouth of the slough were good ones, and I waded over as far as I could to try for them. My first cast reached the slack water, but the fly was well short of the nearest rise. I waded a step farther and felt the icy water pouring in over my boots; I could reach the fish then and I did, dropping a slack line across the current so that the fly held for a moment without drag. The next rise came within an inch of it, but left it floating. I knew the drag was coming, held my rod far downstream to delay it, then there was another rise and this time the fly went down. I caught three fish from the slough before it was too dark to see the fly, not one of them over a pound.

The evening rise is very often like that, many fish, feeding well and taking well, but the big ones are not always up, or else one does not happen to find them, in spite of high hopes. But it is still a magic time, even on western rivers, where big trout are reckless enough in broad daylight. On the English chalk streams it is almost a holy time, not only because there is a real chance of finding a big fish in a foolish mood, but because a summer evening in English water meadows has a rich and gentle love-liness that is quite different from the quality of our own newer, harder country.

It was a July evening in 1930 when I last went up to Stratton

Mill. The day had been very hot, not oppressively hot but with a pouring-on of heat from a hard, bright scorching sun. During the late afternoon I had worked my way slowly and rather carelessly along a small and difficult carrier, finding few fish moving and fewer still that I could approach and cover. When I came to the mill, I had risen only two good fish; one of them had come short and gone off upstream from my strike, throwing a startled bow wave that put down two more feeding fish, and the other had buried himself in a weed bed and, in the mysterious way that chalk-stream trout seem to understand so well, left my fly holding nothing livelier than a strand of milfoil.

Stratton Mill is not an especially attractive or pretty building, but it settles comfortably enough into the meadows, and its red brick is mellowing to a good color that is soft and pleasant even now in an evening light. The meadows are not very wide here; the little river, the Wrackle, runs past Chick's Farm some two hundred yards from the mill and the ground climbs quickly from its far bank to the churchyard and the center of the village. On the other side, the Frome is only thirty or forty yards away, and beyond the river the ground climbs again. The millstream is cut away from the Frome at a big hatch pool above the mill, runs down past the wheel and curves on to join the river again some way farther down. This leaves a long oval island of meadow between the Frome and the millstream, and it was from that island I meant to fish the evening rise.

There were very few fish moving when I first came there, and I felt it was the pause between the sparse hatch I had fished in the carrier during the afternoon and what Hills calls the "casual rise" at six or seven o'clock; so I went on up to the hatch pool and sat there, looking upstream and across to the wider meadows where Farmer Chick's beautiful Devon cattle were feeding. There is no pasture land in the world richer than the Dorset water meadows; even in July they are knee-deep to cattle in heavy, dark-green grass, scented and full of moisture. Chick's animals showed the quality of it, straight-backed, slow-moving, rich-red creatures, sleek with well-being, yet proud and almost light with the grace of their long curving horns. Man has developed no creature more beautiful than the dairy cow, building her deep-bellied and heavy-uddered, calm-eyed and with a slow wisdom for her own deep business of production. I have felt a powerful admiration in me for many handsome cows, Holstein, Jersey and Guernsey, but for none more than the red Devon.

A fish rose in the deep, smooth water above the hatches, where I did not mean to fish, and I turned to look below me at the pool. There was a good run of water through the hatches, and two or three small fish were rising where the run of it spread in the pool, but there were no fish up on the bar yet and none moving in the slower water along the sides. It seemed time to go down, since I meant to fish all the way up, and I picked up my rod and went. There was little water passing through the milltail, but I stopped there and found a good fish cruising slowly in the shallow water five or six yards below the wheel. I watched until I thought I knew his line, then dropped a hackle olive near him, somehow too clumsily, because he turned at once and went down into the depths of the pool, leaving me to feel ashamed and awkward.

I went straight down then, a little angrily, right to the down-stream tip of the island. Just below is a beautiful strip of wide, clear water that runs between weed beds over pale-golden gravel. I looked down over it, wishing I could fish it, and saw a big, wide-backed trout rise gracefully a long cast below me. As he hovered there, waiting for the next fly, the evening light seemed to slide under him, pick him up and hold him invisibly suspended, so that I knew everything about him—his size, his shape, his depth and thickness, his very spots. He rose again and I wanted more than anything to see him rise to a fly of mine. I could have one cast, I knew. It must fall just short of him, with two feet or so of slack in twenty yards of line. I should probably put him down with the cast or, if not, then with the drag as the line came tight in the current; and if all went well I should miss him on the strike. A really respectable dry-fly fisherman would have left him in peace. I didn't. The fly dropped perfectly, drifted, drifted—and a moment before the drag came, he took it. I tightened slowly, my hand quivering on the rod, and came solidly into him. He jumped once in shocked surprise. Then the light showed him to me, every run, every twist, every struggle toward every weed bed, through a long five minutes while I brought him up to the net. I measured him against the handle of the landing net, fifteen inches, light-backed, golden-bellied, the deep-red spots sharp and clear on his sides.

I became orthodox then, working upstream, waiting for my rises, considering them, covering them if I judged the fish worth while. The light began to fade, so I broke off the olive after a fish had let it drift past him twice and tied on a ginger quill. He took that at the first cast and made the fourth fish in the bag. I was pleased with them because they were a level lot, all within an inch of the length of that first one.

It was some little while before I found another good one rising, and then I spoiled the chance he gave me by striking too hard and breaking off the fly. It was too dark to think of threading another ginger quill, so I mounted the heavier cast I had ready with a silver sedge tied on it. There were sedges on the grass and in the air, and I felt that the fish would be coming to them on the water very soon. I was opposite the mill again now, at a sharp bend in the river where strong current ran against the low branches of an alder tree. A fish rose close to the branches, and I felt certain that he was a good one. I made the first cast well outside him and found I could see the big fly perfectly against the water. I cast for him and hooked an alder branch. A gentle pull showed that the fly was fast. Then the fish rose again, and I still thought he was big. I pulled hard and knew that the gut had broken. It took me a long, agitated five minutes to tie on a new sedge, but my fish was still rising, and I covered him, rose him, hooked him—and found he was barely ten inches long.

I followed the river through two bends, hoping for a rise that I could know was a big fish. But the light was wrong, and the water was dark until I came to the short stretch that runs east and west just below the curve from the hatch pool. Two mallards rose from the hatch pool, climbing almost straight in the air on short quick beats of their strong wings, bodies and stretched necks black against the light sky. The water reflected the lightness of the sky almost perfectly now, and I could see the dark dots of the sedges against it and fish rising to them everywhere. One fish showed head and tail as he rose, and I thought for a moment he was big, then remembered how deceptive the show of a trout's tail can be in half-darkness. There was a tiny quiet rise, steadily repeated, close against a long island of weeds near the head of the stretch. I liked the look of that one, went up to fish it, then was sorry. Another ten-incher, I told myself. But I wasn't sure and I made the cast. Something went wrong, and the fly hooked weed just below the fish. I pulled and it came free, dragging horribly. Something splashed fiercely and heavily near it. I struck blindly, and the fly whipped back, caught in the grass at my feet. As I freed it, the little rises began again, a quiet nose poking the surface softly almost against the weed. I didn't know, I told myself; he could be big; he might have turned to make that heavy splash at the dragging fly and the surging boil that cut away from it. The next cast was right, and the fly slid along so close to the weed bed that I could scarcely judge where it was in the short shadow. The little rise came again. I tightened to it and the reel screamed like torn cloth. Foolishly I checked him, held him at last and turned him. He came back toward me, swimming slowly and dangerously, then ran again, straight for the weed bed. This time I had to turn him and I did, just enough to force his run straight upstream instead of across.

He came to the tail of the hatch pool, rode over the shallows in a great sweeping wave and went down into deep water. I went down into the river myself, wading the shallows right out to the center of the stream. He was boring up into the deep water, still strongly, swinging over to the bank I had just left. There was an alder tree there and behind that the stakes of rotten cribbing against the bank. He hadn't quite the strength to reach them and in a little while I netted him, gratefully. The poplars on the far side of the pool were dark against a dark sky now and it was time to go home. But I had my limit of six fish, all of them good fish for the water and the last one, the only one that had come on the sedge hatch, nearer two pounds than anything else.

Fly-Fishing Alone

Thaddeus Norris

WITH MANY PERSONS fishing is a mere recreation, a pleasant way of killing time. To the true angler, however, the sensation it produces is a deep unspoken joy, born of a longing for that which is quiet and peaceful, and fostered by an inbred love of communing with nature, as he walks through grassy meads, or listens to the music of the mountain torrent. This is why he loves occasionally—whatever may be his social propensity in-doors—to shun the habitations and usual haunts of men, and wander alone by the stream, casting his flies over its bright waters: or in his lone canoe to skim the unruffled surface of the inland lake, where no sound comes to his ear but the wild, flute-like cry of the loon, and where no human form is seen but his own, mirrored in the glassy water.

No wonder, then, that the fly-fisher loves at times to take a day, all by himself; for his very loneliness begets a comfortable feeling of independence and leisure, and a quiet assurance of resources within himself to meet all difficulties that may arise.

As he takes a near cut to the stream, along some blind road or cattle-path, he hears the wood-robin with its "to-whé," calling to its mate in the thicket, where itself was fledged the summer before. When he stops to rest at the "wind clearing," he recalls the traditionary stories told by the old lumbermen, of the Indians who occupied the country when their grandfathers moved out to the "back settlements," and, as he ruminates on the extinction, or silent removal of these children of the forest, he may think of the simple eloquent words of the chief to his companions, the last he uttered: "I will die, and you will go home to your people, and, as you go along, you will see the flowers, and hear the birds sing; but Pushmuttaha will see them and hear them no more; and when you come to your people they will say, 'Where is Pushmuttaha?' and you will say, 'He is dead:' then will your words come upon them, *like the falling of the great oak in the stillness of the woods.*"

As he resumes his walk and crosses the little brook that "goes singing by," he remembers what he has read of the Turks, who built their bowers by the falling water, that they might be lulled by its music, as they smoked and dreamed of Paradise. But when the hoarse roar of the creek, where it surges against the base of the crag it has washed for ages, strikes his ear, or he hears it brawling over the big stones, his step quickens, and his pulse beats louder—he is no true angler if it does not—and he is not content until he gets a glimpse of its bright rushing waters at the foot of the hill.

Come forth, my little rod—"a better never did itself support upon" *an angler's arm,*—and let us rig up here on this pebbly shore! The rings are in a line, and now with this bit of waxed silk we take a few hitches backward and forward over the little wire loops which point in opposite directions at the ends of the ferules, to keep the joints from coming apart; for it would be no joke to throw the upper part of the rod out of the butt ferule, and have it sailing down some strong rift. The reel is on *underneath,* and not on top, as those Bassfishers have it, who are always talking of Fire Island, Newport, and Narragansett Bay.

What shall my whip be? The water is full, I'll try a red hackle, its tail tipped with gold tinsel; for my dropper, I'll put on a good sized coachman with lead-colored wings, and as soon as I get a few handsful of grass, to throw in the bottom of my creel, I'll button on my landing-net and cross over, with the help of this stick of drift-wood, for it is pretty strong wading just here. Do you see that rift, and the flat rock at the lower end of it which just comes above the surface of the water, and divides the stream as it rushes into the pool below? There's fishing in rift and pool both; so I'll begin at the top of the rift, if I can get through these alders. Go in, my little rod, point foremost; I would not break that tip at this time to save the hair on my head;—hold! that twig has caught my dropper—easy, now,—all clear—through the bushes at last.

When I was here last July, and fished the pool below, there was no rift above, the water hardly came above my ankles; now it is knee-deep; if there was less it would be better for the pool; but it makes two casts now, where there was only one last summer, and I have no doubt there is a pretty fellow by the margin of the strong water, on this side of the rock,—an easy cast, too,—just about eight yards from the end of my tip. Not there—a little nearer the rock. What a swirl! He did not show more than his back; but he has my hackle. I had to strike him, too, for he took it under water like a bait—they will do so when the stream is full. Get out of that current, my hearty, and don't be flouncing on top, but keep underneath, and deport yourself like an honest, fair fighter! There you are, now, in slack water; you can't last long, tugging at this rate; so come along, to my landing-net; it's no use shaking your head at me! What a shame to thrust my thumb under that rosy gill! but there is no help for it, for you might give me the slip as I take the hook out of your mouth, and thrust you, tail-foremost, into the hole of my creel.

You are my first fish, and you know you are my *luck*; so I would not lose you even if you were a little fellow of seven inches, instead of a good half-pound. I imbibed that superstition, not to throw away my first fish, when I was a boy, and have never got rid of it. Now, tumble about as much as you please; you have the whole basket to yourself.

Another cast—there ought to be more fish there. He rose short,—a little longer line—three feet more will do it—exactly so. Gently, my nine-incher! Take the spring of the rod for a minute or so—here you are! Once more, now. How the "young 'un" jumps! I'll throw it to him until he learns to catch; there, he has it. No use reeling in a chap of your size, but come along, hand-over-hand; I'll release you. Go, now, and don't rise at a fly again until you are over nine inches.

Not a fly on the water! So I have nothing to imitate, even if imitation were necessary. Take care! that loose stone almost threw me. I'll work my way across the current, and get under the lee of that boulder, and try each side of the rift where it runs into the pool below the flat rock. Not a fish in the slack water on this side; they are looking for grub and larvae in the rift. Now, how would you like my coachman, by way of a change of diet? There's a chance for you—try it. Bosh! he missed it; but he is not pricked. Once more. Oh, ho! is it there you are, my beauty? Don't tear that dropper off. Hold him tight, O'Shaughnessy; you are the greatest hook ever invented. How he runs the line out, and plays off into the swift water! It would be rash to check him now; but I'll give him a few feet, and edge him over to the side of the rift where there is slack water. That's better; now tug away, while I recover some of my line. You are off into the current again, are you? but not so wicked. The click of this reel is too weak, by half—he gives in now, and is coming along, like an amiable, docile fish, as he is. Whiz! why, what's the matter, now? Has "the devil kicked him on end?" as my friend with the "tarry breeks" has it. He has taken but two or three yards of line, though. How he hugs the bottom, and keeps the main channel! Well, he can't last much longer. Here he comes now, with a heavy drag, and a distressing strain on my middle joint; and now I see him dimly, as I get him into the eddy; but there's something tugging at the tail-fly. Yes, I have a brace of them, and that accounts for the last dash, and the stubborn groping for the bottom. What a clever way of trolling! to get an obliging Trout to take your dropper, and go sailing around with four feet of gut, and a handsome stretcher at the end of it, setting all the fish in the pool crazy, until some unlucky fellow hooks himself in the side of his mouth. How shall I get the pair into my basket? There is no way but reeling close up, and getting the lower one into my net first, and then with another dip to secure the fish on the dropper; but it must be done gently. So—well done; three-quarters of a pound to be credited to the dropper, and a half-pound to the stretcher—total, one pound and a quarter. That will do for the present. So I'll sit down on that flat rock and light my dudeen, and try the remainder of the water presently. I'll not compromise for less than four half-pound fish before I leave the pool.

These are *some* of the incidents that the lone fly-fisher experiences on a favorable day, and the dreams and anticipations he has indulged in through the long gloomy winter are in part realized. "Real joy," some one has said, is "a serious thing," and the solitary angler proves it conclusively to himself. He is not troubled that some ardent young brother of the rod may fish ahead of him, and disturb the water without availing himself of all the chances; or that a more discreet companion may pass by some of the pools and rifts without bestowing the attention on them they deserve; but in perfect quietude, and confidence in his ability to meet every contingency that may occur, he patiently and leisurely tries all the places that offer fair. What if he does get hung up in a projecting branch of some old elm, that leans over the water? he does not swear and jerk his line away, and leave his flies dangling there—it is a difficulty that will bring into play his ingenuity, and perhaps his dexterity in climbing, and he sets about recovering his flies with the same patient steadiness of purpose that Cæsar did in building his bridge, or that possessed Bonaparte in crossing the Alps, and feels as much satisfaction as either of those great generals, in accomplishing his ends.

If he takes "an extraordinary risk," as underwriters call it, in casting under boughs that hang within a few feet of the water, on the opposite side of some unwadeable rift or pool, and his stretcher should fasten itself in a tough twig, or his dropper grasp the stem of an obstinate leaf, he does not give it up in despair, or, consoling himself with the idea that he has plenty of flies and leaders in his book, pull away and leave his pet spinner and some favorite hackle to hang there as a memento of his temerity in casting so near the bushes. Far from it; he draws sufficient line off his reel and through the rings to give slack enough to lay his rod down, marking well where his flies have caught, and finds some place above or below where he can cross; then by twisting with a forked stick, or drawing in the limb with a hooked one, he releases his leader, and throws it clear off into the water, that he may regain it when he returns to his rod, and reels in his line; or he cuts it off and lays it carefully in his fly-book, and then recrosses the river. A fig for the clearing-ring and rod-scythe and all such cockney contrivances, he never cumbers his pockets with them. Suppose he does break his rod—he sits patiently down and splices it. If the fracture is a compound one, and it would shorten the piece too much to splice it, he resorts to a sailor's device, and *fishes the stick*, by binding a couple of flat pieces of hard wood on each side.

Captain Marryatt, in one of his books, says, a man's whole lifetime is spent in getting into scrapes and getting out of them. This is very much the case with the fly-fisher, and he should always curb any feeling of haste or undue excitement, remembering at such times, that if he loses his temper he is apt to lose his fish, and sometimes his tackle also.

My neighbor asked me once if Trout-fishing was not a very unhealthy amusement—he thought a man must frequently have damp feet. Well, it is, I answered; but if he gets wet up to his middle at the outset, and has reasonable luck, there is no healthier recreation.——But I have sat here long enough. I'll fill my pipe again and try the head of that swift water—If this confounded war lasts a year longer "Lynchburg" will go up to three dollars a pound, but it will be cheap then compared with those soaked and drugged segars that are imposed upon us for the "Simon Pure," under so many captivating names. At all events *this* is what it professes to be, good homely tobac——Whe-e-euh! What a dash! and how strong and steady he pulls; some old fellow "with moss on his back," from under that log, no doubt of it. Is it line you want?—take it, eight—ten—fifteen feet—but no more if you please. How he keeps the middle of the rift! Don't tell me about the "grace of the curve," and all that sort of thing; if the bend of this rod isn't the line of beauty I never saw it before, except of course in the outline of a woman's drapery. Speaking of lines, I'll get a little of this in as I lead the fellow down stream, even at the risk of disturbing the swim below. It is the best plan with a large fish; I have Sir Humphrey Davey's authority for it, although I believe with Fisher, of the "Angler's Souvenir," that he was more of a philosopher than an angler. Talk of "dressing for dinner," when the fish are rising! Steady and slow, my boy, you are giving in at last—two pounds and a half or not an ounce! now I see you "as through a glass, darkly"—a little nearer, my beauty—Bah! what a fool I am! here a fish of a half-pound has hooked himself amidship, and of course offering five times the resistance he would if fairly hooked in the mouth, and no damage to his breathing apparatus while fighting, either; for he keeps his wind all the while. If he had been regularly harnessed, he could not have pulled with more advantage to himself and greater danger to my tackle in this rough water. I thought I had been deceived in this way often enough to know when a fish was hooked foul.

Now I call it strong wading coming down through that dark ravine; I must take a rest and put on a fresh dropper. And so my friend asked me if it was not very lonesome, fishing by myself. Why these little people of the woods are much better company than folks who continually bore you with the weather, and the state of their stomachs or livers, and what they ate for breakfast, or the price of gold, or the stock-market, when you have forgotten whether you have a liver or not, and don't care the toss of a penny what the price of gold is; or whether "Reading" is up or down. Lonesome!—It was only just now the red squirrel came down the limb of that birch, whisking his bushy tail, and chattering almost in my face. The mink, as he snuffed the fish-tainted air from my old creel, came out from his hole amongst the rocks and ran along within a few feet of me. Did he take my old coat to be a part of this rock, covered with lichens and gray mosses? I recollect once in the dim twilight of evening, a doe with her fawns came down to the stream to drink; I had the wind of her, and could see into her great motherly eyes as she raised her head. A moment since the noisy king-fisher poised himself on the dead branch of the hemlock, over my left shoulder, as if he would peep into the hole of my fish-basket. The little warbler sang in the alders close by my old felt hat, as if he would burst his swelling throat with his loud glad song. Did either of them know that I am of a race whose first impulse is to throw a stone or shoot a gun at them? And the sparrow-hawk on that leafless spray extending over the water, sitting there as grave and dignified as a bank president when you ask him for a discount; is he aware that I can tap him on the head with the tip of my rod?—These are some of the simple incidents on the stream, which afterwards awaken memories,

"That like voices from afar off
Call to us to pause and listen,
Speak in tones so plain and childlike,
Scarcely can the ear distinguish
Whether they are sung or spoken."

But I must start for the open water below—What a glorious haze there is just now, and how demurely the world's great eye peeps through it! Trout are very shy though, before the middle of May, even when the sun is bright. I have sometimes taken my best fish at high noon, at this season of the year.—I am as hungry as a horsefly, though it is only "a wee short hour ayont the twal." So I'll unsling my creel by that big sycamore, and build my fire in the hollow of it. If I burn it down there will be no action for trespass in a wooden country like this.

What boys are those crossing the foot-log? I'll press them into my service for awhile, and make them bring wood for my fire. I know them now; the larger one has cause to remember me "with tears of gratitude," for I bestowed on him last summer a score of old flies, a used-up leader, and a limp old rod. He offered me the liberal sum of two shillings for the very implement I have in my hand now; and to buy three flies from me *at four cents apiece*.—Halloo, Paul! what have you done with the rod I gave you—caught many Trout with it this season? Come over the creek, you and your brother, and get me some dry wood, and gather a handful or two of the furze from that old birch to light it with. I'll give you a pair of flies—real gay ones.

Dining *alone* may be counted almost the only drawback to one's taking a day to himself, and you are glad of any stray native who is attracted by the smoke of your fire. Your whiskey is beyond a peradventure, better than he has in his cupboard at home; he is invariably out of tobacco—a chew or a pipeful, and a swig at your flask, will make him communicative. If he has not already dined, he will readily accept a roasted Trout and a piece of bread and butter, and while eating will post you as to all the Trout-streams within ten miles. It is, therefore, a matter of policy to cultivate the good feeling of the natives, the boys especially, as stones are of very convenient size along the creek to throw at a surly fisherman. A few of "Conroy's journal-flies," which have occupied the back leaves of your fly-book for long years are profitable things to invest in this way, for three boys out of four you meet with, will ask you to sell them "a pair of fly-hooks," which of course results in your giving them a brace or so that are a little the worse for wear, or too gay for your own use.

If the fly-fisher, though, would have "society where none intrudes," or society that *won't* intrude, let him take a lad of ten or twelve along to carry his dinner, and to relieve him after the roast, by transferring part of the contents of his creel to the empty dinner-basket. The garrulity and queer questions of a country boy of this age are amusing, when you are disposed to talk. Any person who has sojourned at my friend Jim Henry's, and had his good-natured untiring boy Luther for his *gilly*, will acknowledge the advantage of such a "tail" even if it has not as many joints as a Highland laird's.

If there *is* an objection to a Trout-roast, it is that a man eats too much, and feels lazy after dinner. But what of that? it is a luxurious indolence, without care for the morrow—Care! why, he left that at home when he bought his railroad ticket, and shook off the dust of the city from his hob-nailed boots.

What pretty bright Trout there are in this bold rocky creek! it would be called a river in England, and so it is. We Americans have an ugly way of calling every stream not a hundred yards wide, a creek. It is all well enough when the name is applied to some still sedgy water, which loses half of its depth, and three-fourths of its width, at low tide, and is bank-full on the flood. But speckled fellows like these don't live there. De Kay must have received some inspiration at a Trout-roast, when he gave them the specific name of "Fontinalis," and they are truly the Salmon of the fountain; for a stream like this and its little tributaries, whose fountains are everywhere amongst these rugged hills, are their proper home. What an ignorant fellow Poietes was to ask Halicus if the red spots on a Trout were not "marks of disease—a hectic kind of beauty?" Any boy along the creek knows better. And what a pedantic old theorist Sir Humphrey was, to tell him that the absence of these spots was a sign of high condition. Well, it may be in England, for the river Trout there, are a different species from ours. But I'll bet my old rod against a bob-fly that there is twice as much pluck and dash in our little fellows with the "hectic" spots. I don't wonder that Trout like these so inspired Mr. Barnwell, who wrote the "Game Fish of the North," when, with his fancy in high feather, he mounted his Pegasus and went off—"How splendid is the sport to deftly throw the long line and small fly, with the pliant single-handed rod, and with eye and nerve on the strain, to watch the loveliest darling of the wave, the spotted naiad, dart from her mossy bed, leap high into the air, carrying the strange deception in her mouth, and, turning in her flight, plunge back to her crystal home."

Julius Cæsar! what "high-flying" Trout this gentleman must have met with in his time. Now, I never saw a Trout "dart from her mossy bed," because I never found Trout to lie on a bed of that sort; nor "leap high into the air, and turning in her flight plunge back," as a fish-hawk does. In fact, I may safely say I never saw a Trout *soar* more than eight or ten inches above its "crystal home." I honor "Barnwell" for the Anglomania which has seized him—he has been inoculated with a good scab, and the virus has penetrated his system: but I can't help being reminded by his description, of the eloquence of a member of a country debating society in Kentucky, who commenced— "Happiness, Mr. President, is like a crow situated on some far-distant mountain, which the eager sportsman endeavours in vain to no purpose to reproach." And concluded—"The poor man, Mr. President, reclines beneath the shade of some wide-spreading and umbrageous tree, and calling his wife and the rest of his little children around him, bids their thoughts inspire to scenes beyond the skies. He views Neptune, Plato, Venus, and Jupiter, the Lost Pleides, the Auroly Bolyallis, and other fixed stars, which it was the lot of the immorral Newton first to depreciate and then to deplore."

But a gray-headed man who cannot tie a decent knot in his casting-line without the aid of his spectacles, should forget such nonsense. There is one consolation, however, that this "decay of natur," which brings with it the necessity for glasses in seeing small objects within arm's length, gives in like ratio, the power of seeing one's flies at a distance on the water; there was old Uncle Peter Stewart who could knock a pheasant's head off at fifty yards with his rifle, and see a gnat across the Beaverkill, when he was past sixty.

Here is the sun shining as bright now as if he had not blinked at noon, and such weather, not too hot and not too cold; I must acknowledge, though, my teeth *did* chatter this morning when I waded across at the ford.

> "Sweet day, so cool, so calm, so bright,
> The bridal of the earth and sky;
> The dew shall weep thy fall to night.

I'll start in here, for it appears there is always luck in the pool or rift under the lee of the smoke where one cooks his Trout. It is strange, too, for it seems natural that the smoke would drive the flies away, and as a consequence the fish get out of the notion of rising. But no matter, here goes. Just as I supposed, and a brace of them at the first cast. Come ashore on the sloping gravel, my lively little fellows,—eight and nine inches—the very size for the pan; but who wants to eat fried Trout after cooking them under the ashes or on a forked stick?

There are no good fish here; the water is not much more than knee-deep, and they have no harbor amongst those small pebble-stones. I have thrown in a dozen little fellows within the last ten minutes. I'll go to the tail of that strong rift below the saw-mill. The last time I fished it was when that lean hungry-looking Scotchman came over here from Jim Henry's; he had been sneaking through the bushes and poaching all the little brooks around, where the fish had run up to spawn, with his confounded worm-bait. This stream was low then and the fish shy; I had approached the end of the rift carefully and was trying to raise them at long cast in the deep water, when he—without even saying "by your leave"—waded in within a few yards of where they were rising, and splashed his buck-shot sinker and wad of worms right amongst them. I said nothing, and he did not appear to think that interfering with my sport so rudely was any breach of good manners, or of the rules of fair fishing. A Scotchman, to catch Trout with a *worm!* Poor fellow! his piscatory education must have been neglected, or he belonged to that school who brag *only* on numbers. I know a party of that sort who come up here every summer from Easton and bring a *sauer-kraut stanner* to pack their Trout in, and salt down all they take without eating one, until they get home. They catch all they can and keep *all* they catch, great and small. Bah! a poor little *salted* Trout—it tastes more like a piece of "yaller soap" than a fish. Such fishermen are but one remove from the bark peelers I found snaring and netting Trout in the still water below here, last August. I can just see their shanty from here. "Instruments of cruelty are in their habitations. O my soul, come not thou into their secret; unto their assembly, mine honor, be not thou united!"

There is the sawyer's dog; if he comes much nearer I'll psychologize him with one of these "dunnicks"! But he turns tail as soon as I stoop to pick one up. Now for it—just at the end of the swift water—ah! my beauty—fifteen inches, by all that is lovely! He threw his whole length out of water—try it again—I can't raise him. This won't do. Am I cold, or am I nervous, that I should shake like a palsied old man because I missed that fish? Fie on you, Mr. Nestor, you who have run the rapids at the "Rough Waters" on the Nipissiguit, in a birch canoe, with a Salmon at the end of sixty yards of line, and your pipe in your mouth; I thought you had gotten past a weakness of this kind. But it will only make bad worse, and convince that Trout of the cheat to throw over him again; so I must leave him now, and get back to the log on that sunny bank and compose myself with a few whiffs, while I change my flies. It will be just fifteen minutes until I knock the ashes out of my pipe; by that time my vaulting friend will likely forget the counterfeit I tried to impose on him, if I offer him something else.

Now Dick gave me this for a meershaum, and I have no doubt Mr. Doll sold it for one in good faith; but it is a very "pale complected" pipe for one of that family. I have smoked it steadily for a year, and there is only the slightest possible tinge of orange about the root of the stem. It is hardly as dark as this ginger hackle in my hat-band. However, it is light, and carries a big charge for a pipe of its size, and the shortness of the stem brings the smoke so comfortably under the nose—a great desideratum in the open air. The pipe must have been instituted expressly for the fisherman; it is company when he is lonesome, and never talks when he wants to be quiet; it concentrates his ideas and assists his judgment when he discusses any important matter with himself, such as the selection of a killing stretcher. No wonder the Indians smoked at their council-fires; and, as for the nerves, I'll put it against Mrs. Winslow's soothing syrup. What a pity it is that infants are not taught to smoke! What shall my stretcher be; that fish refused Hofland's Fancy; now let me try one of my own fancy. Here is something a great deal prettier; a purple body in place of a snuff-brown, and light wings from a lead-colored pigeon instead of a sober woodcock feather. What a pretty fly—half sad, half gay in its attire, like an interesting young widow, when she decides on shedding her weeds, and "begins to take notice." I'll change my dropper also—here it is; body of copper-colored peacock hurl, wings of the feather of an old brown hen, mottled with yellow specks. What a plain homely look it has; it reminds me of "the Girl with the Calico Dress." You are not as showy, my dear miss, as the charming little widow, but certain individuals of my acquaintance are quite conscious of your worth. Let me see which of you will prove most attractive to my speckled friend. So here goes—two to one on the widow—lost, by jingo! He looked at her and sailed slowly away. Has he ever heard of the warning that the sage Mr. Weller gave his son "Samivel?" Perhaps, then, he will take notion to "the girl with the calico dress." Once more—now do take care! Ah ha! my old boy, you would be indiscreet, after all, and the widow has victimized you. Now she'll lead you a dance! Don't be travelling off with her as if you were on your wedding tour, for I know you would like to get rid of her already; but there is no divorce beneath the water,—you are mine, says she, "until death us do part!"

There you are, now! the three-minutes' fight has completely taken the wind out of you. That's the last flap of your tail; the widow has killed you "as dead as a mackerel." Acting the gay Lothario, were you? I know some scaly old fellows why play the same game ashore, stealthily patronizing Mrs. Allen, subsidizing the tailor, bootmaker, dentist, and barber, and slyly endeavoring to take off a discount of twenty-five per cent, from old Father Time's bill. But that won't do, for folks of any discernment know at a glance those spavined, short-winded shaky old fellows, who trot themselves out, as if they were done-up for the horse-market. Lie there, my Turveydrop, until I move down a little, and try under the bushes, on the opposite side.

With this length of line I can just come close enough to the alders to miss them. Dance lightly, O my brown girl, and follow in her wake, dear widow, as I draw you hitherward. Ah, ha! and so it is: there is one dashing fellow who sees charms in your homely dress. How he vaults!—nine rails, and a top rail! Did you ever know Turney Ashby? Not Beau Turner—I mean Black Turner. Did he ever straddle a bit of horse-flesh with more mettle? None of your Conestogas. There he goes again! How long have you belonged to the circus? But he can't run all day at that gait; he begins to flag, at last, and here he is now, coming in on the "quarter stretch." There you are, at last—died as game as a Dominica chicken. Once more, now. I knew it.—And again.

Three times my brace of beauties have come tripping home across the deep whirling rapid, and three bright Trout lie on the gravel behind me. I begin at last to long for the sound of some friendly voice, and the sight of a good-humored face. I must keep my appointment with Walter at the foot-bridge; so I am off. Some of the "Houseless" don't like this solitary sport. I know one of them who would as soon be guilty of drinking alone; but *he* is not a contemplative angler, and has never realized how hungry some folks get through the winter for a little fishing. May-be he has never read what William Howitt says, in his "Rural Life in England," about fishing alone. It will come home to every quiet fly-fisher. See what an unveiling of the heart it is, when the angler is alone with God and Nature.

"People that have not been innoculated with the true spirit may wonder at the infatuation of anglers—but true anglers leave them very contentedly to their wondering, and follow their diversions with a keen delight. Many old men there are of this class that have in them a world of science—not science of the book, or of regular tuition, but the science of actual experience. Science that lives, and will die with them; except it be dropped out piecemeal, and with the gravity becoming its importance, to some young neophyte who has won their good graces by his devotion to their beloved craft. All the mysteries of times and seasons, of baits, flies of every shape and hue; worms, gentles, beetles, compositions, or substances found by proof to possess singular charms. These are a possession which they hold with pride, and do not hold in vain. After a close day in the shop or factory, what a luxury is a fine summer evening to one of these men, following some rapid stream, or seated on a green bank, deep in grass and flowers, pulling out the spotted Trout, or resolutely but subtilely bringing some huge Pike or fair Grayling from its lurking place beneath the broad stump and spreading boughs of the alder. Or a day, a summer's day, to such a man, by the Dove or the Wye, amid the pleasant Derbyshire hills; by Yorkshire or Northumbrian stream; by Trent or Tweed; or the banks of Yarrow; by Teith or Leven, with the glorious hills and heaths of Scotland around him. Why, such a day to such a man, has in it a life and spirit of enjoyment to which the feelings of cities and palaces are dim. The heart of such a man—the power and passion of deep felicity that come breathing from mountains and moorlands; from clouds that sail above, and storms blustering and growling in the wind; from all the mighty magnificence, the solitude and antiquity of Nature upon him—Ebenezer Elliott only can unfold. The weight of the poor man's life—the cares of poverty—the striving of huge cities, visit him as he sits by the beautiful stream—beautiful as a dream of eternity, and translucent as the everlasting canopy of heaven above him;—they come, but he casts them off for the time, with the power of one who feels himself strong in the kindred spirit of all things around; strong in the knowledge that he is a man; an immortal—a child and pupil in the world-school of the Almighty. For that day he is more than a king—he has the heart of humanity, and faith and spirit of a saint. It is not the rod and line that floats before him—it is not the flowing water, or the captured prey that he perceives in those moments of admission to the heart of nature, so much as the law of the testimony of love and goodness written on everything around him with the pencil of Divine beauty. He is no longer the wearied and oppressed—the trodden and despised—walking in threadbare garments amid men, who scarcely deign to look upon him as a brother man—but he is reassured and recognised to himself in his own soul, as one of those puzzling, aspiring, and mysterious existences for whom all this splendid world was built, and for whom eternity opens its expecting gates. These are magnificent speculations for a poor, angling carpenter or weaver; but Ebenezer Elliott can tell us that they are his legitimate thoughts, when he can break for an instant the bonds of his toiling age, and escape to the open fields. Let us leave him dipping his line in the waters of refreshing thought."

Thus writes William Howitt. But there is the foot-bridge, and here are my little friends, the Sand-pipers. How often the fly-fisher sees them running along the pebbly margin of the Trout stream (as Wilson truly says), "continually nodding their heads;" sometimes starting with their peculiar short shrill note, from their nests in the wave-washed tufts of long grass, flapping along the creek sideways, as if wounded in leg or wing, to decoy the fancied destroyer from the nest of downy little snipelings. And there, where the waters of the noisy rapid finds rest in the broad shallow below, is one perched on a big gray boulder, as gray as herself. How lonely she seems there, like the last of her race, were it not that her constant mate is on the strand below, busily engaged picking up larva and seedling muscles for its little ones in the nest up the creek.

May and the Mayfly

~~~~~~~~~~~~~~~~

John Waller Hills

Pan doth pipe to us anew,
Reedy calls and catches,
So we'll go and throw a fly
Dainty, delicate and dry,
Forty miles from Waterloo—
Where the May-fly hatches.
The Trout Fisher.
PATRICK R. CHALMERS, 1914

THE COMING OF the mayfly is more than an incident in the fisherman's year. It is an event of nature. The sight of it carries the mind to other countries and throws it back to earlier times. Few of us are lucky enough to have seen the great movements of wild animals which still take place even on our restricted globe. The migration of the caribou in the Barren Lands of Labrador, the herds of antelope described by the old African hunters, even the incursion of swarms of the little lemming into Norway, are sights which not many can witness. But though, as continent after continent gets enclosed and cultivated, the range of animal life gets restricted, and many species languish or die, the air is still free to all. Its inhabitants can range at will. The air has no oceans and no continents, and it remains unfenced and unharvested. Even now, in this populous land of ours and this civilised century, the migrations of bird life which occur every spring and autumn are nearly as great as ever they were. It is still possible for a slender bird like the chiff-chaff to pass the winter in Persia and the spring in Hampshire, and for the willow wren to travel every year the long road to and from Cape Colony. And in a humbler plane there still occur, every year, the birth, the life, the mating and the death of innumerable mayfly; and though it sounds a fanciful confession, I never look at the process without comparing it to those larger movements of more important creatures which I have not been so fortunate as to see.

It is in this spirit that I would have you approach the mayfly, and let me therefore announce the good news that it is increasing on the Test. Its history is a series of ups and downs, of growth year by year up to immense numbers, and then a gradual falling away until it almost disappears. Some of these processes we can follow. For instance, in 1853 it began to lessen at Stockbridge, as indeed it did also on the Hampshire Avon: in 1856 and 1858 it got fewer and fewer, and Halford in his *Autobiography* quotes a writer who in 1875 considered it doomed. But then it began slowly to increase, and by 1890 the hatch at Stockbridge was the greatest ever known. Then it got less once more, and by 1893 the Houghton Club were importing it from the tributary Dun, which flows in at Kimbridge, and in 1899 from the Kennet also. But this did little good, for the fly got scarcer and scarcer until in 1906 it was completely absent and, for the first time in the club's history, not a single fish was killed on it. Many were the reasons assigned for this, and learned writers blamed late frosts, weed cutting, mud clearing and even swifts and swallows, forgetting, or perhaps not knowing, that the same thing had happened before. Anyhow, the fly was believed to be in process of extinction. Nor was the loss confined to the Test, for all south country rivers suffered, and on many a stretch of the Itchen where the fly was formerly abundant it became unknown. The disaster seems to have fallen somewhat later on the Kennet, for when I first fished at Hungerford, in 1901, mayfly was present in

such countless thousands that it is difficult to believe it was ever
more plentiful. But here too it began to diminish, and on some
of the upper waters of that river it had disappeared entirely by
about 1910. By then an added reason could be assigned, and
there was dark talk of road tar and oil and petrol. But it began to
reappear, and by 1922 was nearly as strong as ever. The same is
the case with the lower Test: the hatch in 1924 was enormous,
and anyone who saw the immense falls of spent fly which came
down for several days round about 30th May—fly, be it noted,
all of which had escaped the ravages of trout and swifts and had
propagated their race—need have little fear for the future,
provided no abominable poisons are allowed to pollute the river.
The truth is that mayfly, like all wild species, is subject to cycles
of increase and diminution of which we know nothing. These
revolutions take many years to work out: we see a slow death
and we shake wise heads and assign our puny causes: but then
again we see a slow rebirth, and we have to invent new theories,
till finally we realise that we are in touch with a great fact of
nature, working itself out on lines unknown to us. And, at the
moment, let us be of good cheer, for the curve is an ascending
one.

Mayfly fishing is proverbially uncertain. You get days when
trout will take anything, when the most dreadful bungle will not
put them down, and when they mind neither thick gut, bad
casting nor wretched imitations. But such days are rare. Looking
back over many years, I can only remember a few. And, to put
against such days, I remember many more when trout were
wonderfully difficult, when fish were feeding steadily and yet
accurate and delicate fishing met with scanty reward. I am
talking, be it noted, of days when all is in the fisherman's favour,
when there is not too much fly and trout appear hungry and
eager. But you have even greater obstacles to overcome when
there is a glut of fly. Both the newly hatched and also the spent
insect sometimes come down in masses which no one would

believe possible who had not seen them. The water is covered, trout are not taking one fly in a hundred, your artificial has to float among droves of naturals, and there seems no imaginable reason why the fish should ever take it.

Now though the fly lasts a fortnight or more, and though on any of those fourteen days you may if you are lucky kill some heavy fish, there are not much more than two dates on which fishing is really good, and on the rest it is often most disappointing. My experience has been so unvarying, that if I were told I was to have only two days' fishing during the period, I should choose my days with every confidence. I should ask the date on which the fly first hatched in quantities (and this date varies little from year to year, whatever the weather) and I should select either the fourth or the twelfth day after that. By the fourth day trout have acquired the taste of the newly hatched fly and are taking it confidently, no longer regarding it as a thrilling but somewhat alarming incident. The big fish are moving by then, and have not been much fished for and are not shy. Nor have they been pricked, as numberless fish are pricked during mayfly fishing. That is the first great chance, the fourth day. And the next is the twelfth day, by which time the fly is going off and trout know it, and are making the most of the short time remaining. They are feeding steadily on spent fly, and, moreover, the big fish who have been hooked and lost earlier have forgotten all about it and are on the move again. Your best chance of a big fish is either the fourth or the twelfth day.

In my experience this has worked out with a certainty almost mathematical. A few years ago I wanted to give some mayfly fishing to a friend, who had taught me dorado fishing in South America, and the date had to be fixed some time beforehand. On the water to be fished—not the Test—the fly appears on 5th or 6th June. Accordingly I arranged for us to go there on the 9th. We could not get on the river till eight at night, but we found the fish rising madly, walloping at the fly, occasionally jumping to catch it in the air. They took anything, and hardly a rise was missed. We got ten fish between us in an hour and a half. And next day, my chosen fourth day, no fly appeared till seven, and yet my friend during a short rise got four excellent trout. The same thing happened at Mottisfont in 1924. The fly appeared in force on 20th May. Good fishing was had on the 24th, the fourth day, when a fish of 3 lb. 11 oz. was killed, and one of 3 lb. 14 oz. on the following day. Moreover, the only other three pounder was got on the spent gnat on 1st June, the twelfth day from the beginning of the rise.

There is also a third occasion when you may get a big one, but it is an event about which it were wise not to prophesy, lest we be guilty of insolence. Do not expect it: if it happens, accept it with humility and gratitude. Sometimes a belated company of mayfly will drift down after the season is past, and then if all goes right—if these happen to come over a fish and if you happen to be there—you may catch something large. Trout have not forgotten the taste, and rise eagerly. I fished the Hungerford water in 1901. The first mayfly appeared on 30th May, the usual date, and the first good hatch was on 3rd June. By the 18th the season was considered over. Yet as late as the 22nd, when we were using red quills on drawn gut and trout were beginning to take an interest in sedges, by good fortune I chanced to be watching a place where a powerful fish had broken two anglers during the fortnight. Suddenly what should appear but mayflies, mayflies in some quantity, freshly hatched and seductive, sailing down the slow current: and something which might be a big trout, or might be a small one, began to cruise about and eat them, one after another. By the time the third had disappeared I was nipping off my red quill and knotting on a mayfly, and before I quite realised what had happened I was playing a fish which seemed immense. He weighed 3 lb. 14 oz. That, however, was a piece of good luck which does not happen often.

Why is it that mayfly fishing, except on selected days, is so disappointing? I do not know, but it is. Partly, no doubt, it is due to too much fly. Fish get gorged, they allow natural after natural to float past them, and inducing them to take an artificial is a long business. Many casts have to be made, and the fisherman gets careless and makes a mistake, or when the rise comes at last it comes unexpectedly, and he strikes either too quickly or too hard, with dreadful consequences. I can assure the non-fisherman that it is exciting work attacking a fish whom you know to be over three pounds weight and who may take you at any moment. After an hour of such business your nerves get frayed, you are tired, and you may do something quite silly. But though I invariably do the wrong thing, I will tell fishermen what they ought to do, for I know what that is, though I do not do it. There is a fatality about fishing which makes most people, myself certainly, do what we know to be inept. Fishing faults are incurable. So though I shall proceed to lay down the law in pontifical fashion, pray do not think that I am one of those impeccable individuals whom we read about, for no one sins so often against the light.

Strike slowly, you can hardly be too slow, and, if a floating fly is refused, try a hackle one, waterlogged. Use fine gut. When I go into a London tackle shop and ask for a mayfly cast, I am continually astonished at what I am shown. Some of those produced would terrify a tarpon. On a fine, still day use 3x: as a general rule, 2x: on a very windy day, or at dusk, or when trout are mad, and it is silly to handicap yourself, you can put on something with which you can hold fish hard, and keep them out of weed. But never, if you take my advice, descend to a point thicker than 1x, and only use that occasionally. Many a salmon has been killed on finer gut. Why, just read a book which came out a few years ago by Mr. E. R. Hewitt, the *Secrets of the Salmon*. It is a revelation of what the dry fly will do for salmon in low water. He fishes sometimes with a point .004 diameter, on which he kills fish up to 10 lb. I reckon that gut of .004 inches is finer than 2x by our scale, so you need not be afraid of 3x: indeed he who cannot kill a three pounder on it 'deserves not the name of an angler,' to quote Charles Cotton.

But, when all is said, however good your tackle, whatever you do, however accomplished you are, and however long your experience, trout on the mayfly are extraordinarily hard to hook. This remains the eternal difficulty of the mayfly. I think the reason is partly because of the stiff whole-feathers with which most patterns are winged. If you change to a soft hackled variety you often hook more. A stiff fly is hard to suck in. Partly too, no doubt, the difficulty is due to the fact that so large an insect takes time to eat: partly to the trout's fear that it is something dangerous: and partly, perhaps, to his over anxiety to secure it. But a sedge is as large, and more difficult to catch, and with no fly do I hook so many rises as with the sedge, while with no fly do I miss so many as with the mayfly. With no fly do you get so many false rises. Some of them are not rises at all, for though the fish comes at the artificial, often with a splash and a wallop as though he had been looking for it all night, he never really takes it in his mouth. Or he seems just to mouth it, not closing his jaw firmly. Or he takes hold and quickly lets go. And the strangest part of the business is that he will vary his habits, even during the same day.

In the life cycle of the mayfly there are three occasions on which trout devour it: the first when, newly hatched, it sits on the water, the second when the female fly is laying her eggs, and the third when it floats down dying or dead. You get heavy hatches of the fly on the Test: but, large as they are, nothing on it, nor I believe on any other English river, can compare with the Kennet. The hatch of mayfly at Hungerford in the old days is difficult to write of without seeming to exaggerate. As you went down from London in the train you saw the river and carriers covered with fly as with a mist: the engine was plastered with their bodies: your carriage got full of them, blown in through the window: as you drove from the station your horse's hoofs stamped them into the road. I remember particularly 7th June 1901. It was a warm cloudy day with a violent north-east wind. No fly appeared till six in the evening, but between then and nine they came up in incredible numbers. They floated down in flocks, almost touching: as you looked into the air the droves of them carried along by the wind gave you the impression of being out in a very heavy snow storm: your clothes and your hat were covered: they perched on your rod: as you walked the bank you had the feeling that you were pushing your way: the greedy trout were gorged, and the greedier swifts retired replete. Nothing made any impression on their numbers. They were there in hundreds of thousands, and still they kept hatching out and still the surface got thicker and thicker with them.

You do not do much in these great falls. Indeed, the appearance of them paralyses you. Why, when trout are refusing thousands of natural insects, should they eat your clumsy imitation? But the mayfly season is full of continual surprises; the unexpected always happens. So I will give an account of two days, not unlike in character, but very different in result. The first was the 31st May 1924 at Mottisfont. On the previous evening trout had had a terrific gorge on spent gnat, and on the 31st I went down to the river expecting to do nothing until it came down again, but hoping to catch something then. And truly, at ten in the morning the river had a dissipated, 'after the party' appearance. Two fish, lying near the top in the fast water of the Oakley Stream, refused mayfly and spent gnat, but took, capriciously enough, a jenny spinner: however, I do not think they meant business and neither was hooked. I then walked across to the main river, where I found a mass of fly life such as you rarely see out of a chalk country. Iron blues and pale watery duns were tripping down in little fleets, convoyed by an occasional tall mayfly, looking like some lateen-rigged piratical craft carrying off smaller vessels. Caperers, in their russet coats, were sitting on the surface or trying to reach the shore by short, clumsy jumps. In the reeds bordering the river were clouds of alders, restlessly flickering about, taking aimless journeys through the air, running nervously up grass stems, or tumbling into the water like careless children. But in spite of all this quantity of insects, there was a jaded air over the world of the river. An occasional fish rose, one, indeed, at an artificial mayfly, but was not hooked. Mayflies decreased, and iron blues increased, so I put on 4x gut and a hackle iron blue, 000 in size; I rose a fish, landed and returned a small one, and then hooked and lost a very good one. After that an absolute deadness fell on the water and its inhabitants, and nothing stirred till two o'clock. At last I found a trout rising under my bank. He took my iron blue well, but I missed him: he did the same at an alder: but then, as I was waiting to give him time to recover, to my delight he ate a natural mayfly. Aha, I thought, you are mine. And so he was. I whipped off my alder and knotted on a partridge hackle mayfly, which he seized the first time it came over him, and was landed. He weighed 1 lb. 12 oz. Nothing else seemed likely to happen for some time, so at three o'clock I went home in order to have a meal and be able to stay out late. I started back at five; and long before I reached the river I knew the fly would be there in quantities.

As I walked there, all along the hedges, round the bushes, over the willows and the tall trees were clouds and clouds of the male fly, rising and falling in their dancing flight. They were like swarms of bees, seen everywhere as far as eye could reach, in numbers uncountable. Through the day you might have found them clinging to grasses or reeds or sedges, quiescent and torpid: but now at evening they had awakened and collected together and resumed their dances. The air was full of drifting female fly too, and as one was carried by the wind past any of these assemblages, she would immediately be seized and mated. When mated, she makes her way to water; for the last two stages, the laying of the eggs and the death, take place on the river, and I should see them later. They had not begun when I got there. Instead a few of the newly hatched fly appeared now and again. The wind had dropped, the river world had come to life and lost its jaded look, and as I sat down to watch I felt confident that it would not be long before I was up and doing. Nor was it. A fish rose twice in midstream, and I caught him, then I missed two, then caught another and missed another. The pair I had captured weighed 4 lb. 9 oz. between them. But now it was past six o'clock; and the spent fly began to come on the water. All over the surface mayflies were to be seen; they were in clouds in the air above, busy egg-laying, now dipping down and just touching the top of the stream, then rising in the air, then dipping again. They got thicker and thicker, and so did bodies of dead mayflies floating down. If your eye followed an individual egg-layer, you noticed, if you could pick her out from the swarms of her companions, that her trips through the air got shorter, and her visits to the water more frequent, and that, instead of just brushing the surface in order to lay her eggs, she began to sit for a second or so upon it, until the time came when she could rise no more. Then, her work done, her store of six or seven thousand eggs safely laid, the future of her race assured, she settled on the surface and sailed down upright; but soon she would give a shiver, one of her wings would collapse on the water, until finally she died and fell flat, wings extended in the form of the cross. Thicker and thicker grew the mass of fly over the water, more and more numerous those carried down by the current. At first those floating were present in all stages, sitting upright, or half collapsed, or dying, or dead: but soon the dead predominated, until all that could be seen were their bodies, the dead fly, the spent gnat. These came down in ever increasing quantities. In the backwaters and eddies they were packed nearly solid. In the main current, the quick swinging stream of the lower Test, they were separated only by inches. All the broad river was covered, and bore them seawards like a moving carrier. Now all these had escaped the attacks of trout and grayling, and swifts and swallows and martins and wagtails and warblers and chaffinches and many other birds which prey on them: all of them had escaped, and had reproduced their species: when you looked at the countless thousands which floated down in the small time during which you saw only a small part of the river, you realised that the quantities of them which had survived were so vast that the assaults of all their enemies made no appreciable impression on their number.

By seven o'clock on this day, therefore, I was in a happy situation. I had landed three fish, weighing well over six pounds. The spent fly was beginning to come down and the real rise to start. I had two hours of daylight ahead of me, and one of the finest stretches of the lower Test to fish. Can it be wondered that the capture of three more trout, to make up my three brace, seemed such a certainty that the only matter of speculation was what they would weigh? But how often do you seem on the edge of great things, and yet do not attain them! How often do you believe you have surmounted the difficult part of your road and have your foot firmly planted on the land of desire, only to be thrown back and thwarted! And so it happened. Nothing else did I get. Though spent fly appeared in unimaginable numbers, very few trout rose. A short time before, when there was little fly, trout had eaten every one, and had taken every artificial put over them properly. Now, when an immense meal was provided, they suddenly changed, they only took one fly in a hundred and almost disregarded the artificial. In fact it was difficult to find any good fish rising at all. At last I settled down to a big one who took an occasional spent gnat. He took mine, but only after incessant spells of casting, of resting, and of fly drying, and after one of the valuable daylight hours had gone: and then I missed him, alas, alas! I struck too soon, probably. After that I spent some time over another, and did indeed hook him, but he turned out to be a big chub. And then the rise was over. Fate, I felt, was unkind: if I had to miss one, why could I not have missed the chub and hooked the trout?

The second day was 22nd May 1927 at Stockbridge. It was a good day, succeeding where the other day failed.

You usually get the heaviest hatches of new fly in the afternoon, sometimes as late as five o'clock. A big morning hatch is not so common. As a rule you can look for fly any time after four, and what with the newly hatched and the spent insect, you ought to be on the water from then until ten at night. Now, some time you must eat something. If you go from breakfast till ten without anything except sandwiches, you get irritable and fish badly. At the same time it is maddening to miss the rise for a wretched meal. After some experience I have found the safest time to be away is between three and four, summer time. By three the morning hatch should be over, and by four the afternoon one has not begun. So, if you take my advice, you will eat little luncheon, and will have a real meal at three o'clock. It sounds barbarous, but you have no idea how soon you get used to it.

It is hard to write with any confidence about patterns, and my advice is to carry a good many. Those with wings of light mallard, dyed green or yellow, or of dark mallard, undyed, are successful—and so are others. Perhaps the French partridge hackle fly is best of the hackle patterns. At any rate I kill more fish on it, but then I fish it more. But I often find that it pays to change your pattern constantly. If he refuses one, give him something quite different: it can do no harm, and at least you fish it with more confidence. The best patterns of spent gnat are the light grey ones, not those usually sold in the shops, whose wings are made of almost black hackles. And never forget that trout will sometimes take the caperer better than the mayfly.

Good or bad, disappointing or successful, a mayfly season is always enjoyable. You often have quite bad days. Fishing with olives is more amusing and more delicate. But the mayfly is more romantic. Anything may happen. Unknown monsters may appear from the depths. The excitement is always kept up. Fishermen may despise it: it may be unscientific angling: but I sincerely hope it will last out my time. Apart from fishing, it is a spectacle of unrestricted natural life. Such sights are becoming so rare that we cannot afford to lose any of them.

Discovery

Ben Hur Lampman

A LEAF FROM FRENCH EDDY

A GOLDEN-VEINED LEAF of scarlet, enclosed in a letter, is said by the writer of the note to be "part of a day's catch at French eddy." And the letter asks if one ever has been to French eddy, where the leaf was picked. Yes, often, but not often enough. It is said that we tire soon of all things that grow commonplace to us, and in tiring grow indifferent to their virtues, as children weary of playthings to which they are long accustomed. But it is not to be imagined that one would tire soon, or at all, of that broad and secret pool, with the current racing beyond it, which lies cupped in the hand of the hills. Of itself the eddy is sovereign for weariness. And part of the catch at French eddy always is more than trout.

Long and long ago, when the mail was fetched up the river by boat, through the green swift reaches and over the shallows of sun and shadow, French eddy—so they say—was the upper terminal of the service. This margin, where the water ouzels come to beg dole of fishermen, has long been familiar to people, and once it was of truly utilitarian importance. The eddy had an official status in those times. Now it is only a fishing hole on the excellent river that creates it. But to a great number of people, when they fall to thinking of rivers—which is one of our devices for enumerating the days that have mattered—this loitering of waters where the trout assemble must symbolize their river, their own especial river. For when you think of rivers, there is one river that runs before all. And that sort of spell was cast, long ago, when the river carved its channel, at French eddy.

"There is," said the letter, "a ghost of a forest across the stream. The mists lift from the top of Euchre mountain, and the hills are as clean as a window newly washed." Yes, it would be like that, on a fall day between rains. The hills are quite breathlessly cleansed. In their breathless quietude the hills almost are exclamatory. But have ever you been at French eddy when the hills send tribute to the river, by their thousand minor watercourses that are affluents of the great stream, and the haste of the river is jeweled with dancing rain, and the driftwood begins its final pilgrimage—down and down to the sea? Then is a very good time for fishing at French eddy, and to taste rain on one's lips, and to be driven back, and back, by the rising river, while the trout are elate and hungry. The eddy is famous in those parts for the steelhead trout that swing valiantly in from the current, on such a day, to explore the gravel they knew in infancy.

Of course, and surely, one has been to French eddy, and often—but not often enough. There is ever something more in the catch, at French eddy, than the trout that come to the creel, or the steelhead that are beached gleamingly in the rain. An artistry touched those secret swift fishes, and lingered over their modeling, the hue of their flanks. It was, it must have been, akin to that instruction which taught the water ouzel how to walk upon the silt, with the stream flowing round and over. And in the half of a minute the hill, that dark pagan, with mists at his head, will speak with a voice, and the words will be wisdom. For manifestly the hill has something in thought that requires to be said. Have ever we been to French eddy? Why, surely. But send no scarlet leaf from that place to us, until we may go again.

THIS FISHING!

It is remembered as clearly in every essential detail as though it had been yesterday. Over the planks of Poskin's dam, and these were painted a dull green with water mosses, the stream trickled thinly. There were willows, quite as a matter of course, and the bank was lush with the tenderest of clover, cropped close by cattle. And where the water fell into the pool, there was carried, down and down, an interminable outpouring of false pearls that rose streamingly to the surface and fizzed into nothingness. Save for this the pool was forbiddingly dark and mysterious, yet it exercised a spell not all unpleasing. It held a promise, it extended an expectancy, that I have since remarked in many waters. And somebody said, with the least trace of mature impatience, sharply, urgently:

"Pull him in! Land sakes! You got a bite!"

I pulled. Upward along the line, through my fingers, and thence to every dancing nerve, tingled the message of my captive, struggling in the dark water beneath Poskin's dam. And my heart sang to his strugglings and magnified his might. Out of mystery he rose, gnomish of aspect and mildly blue of eye, with every barbel waving, and pectoral spines fiercely set, that singular catfish we called bullhead—seven tremendous inches of him. He shone on the clover as ebony would, and leviathan seemed not more vast to the ancient father who fleshed the first harpoon. I was seven and this my maiden fish.

I hold it to be a goodly heritage that wherever water is found, salt or fresh, land-girt or sweetly flowing, there fish are to be had in nearly every instance. Nor can there be a loneliness more inconsolable than that of some desolate lake which, heavily burdened with minerals, may not be host to fishes, but lies barren and lamenting, with never a scaled flank to flash above it, and never a fin to cruise casually amid its secret places. To harbor fish is the proper heritage of every water, and foremost among the rights of man, all landed proprietors to the contrary, with a plague on placards of trespass, is the right to wet a line and take a fish.

It is pleasant to observe that the eldest and most democratic of all fraternities is that of the fishermen, wherein membership is shared by the veriest aboriginal and the most cultured of cosmopolites. These speak a kindred language and are never at loss to comprehend one another when the theme is fishing. What is this fishing?

One has no difficulty in distinguishing mere anglers from your true fisherman. Though it is possible for the individual to be both angler and fisherman, or almost, it is a phenomenon of great infrequency for any fisherman to be an angler or to wish to become one. The fisherman is artlessly gratified by the simpler expressions of the urge to fish. He will fish, doggedly, happily, with the aptness of the perfect convert, in waters where a strike is extremely improbable, and at seasons when every natural sign is against him. He will fish when thunders are above, and lightnings streak the sky. He will fish with the sleet in his face and the wind chilling him to the marrow. He will fish with a knotted cord of cotton and the crudest of hooks. It is true that the finer gear of the craft, superlative, beautiful, masterly, is very dear to him—but the urge to fish is dearer. He fishes because he must fish.

So, as I have said, it began for me with the capture of a catfish—the most personable and handsome catfish—in the black pool below Poskin's dam. I drew from the earliest water something more than a catfish—a charmed creature, weaving spells. If I required his life of him, he in his turn exacted a tribute that has not wavered. The sorcery of him has led me to my armpits in frigid mountain water, of which I derived twinges that linger; and to shores of summer where the sun flayed me, face and arm—and shall lead again. I, too, am well content.

I would pass rapidly on, for the sin of fishermen is that of tedium, to the adventure of the floating island, which befell a few years later. The lake is in Wisconsin, and for all I know to the contrary the selfsame islands cruise it yet. They were masses of treacherous bogland, half peat, half deeply rooted waterplants thriving in their own decay, and they floated heavily over the lake and the wind's will, now here, now miles away. Only boys, with the casual bravado of their kind, fished from the treacherous vantage of these wanderers.

Each island reared a numerous brood of black frogs, and it followed that each island was ringed with watchful eyes. That incautious frog who quitted the quaking mass, though ever so briefly, was seen no more by his fellows. In a gleam and a swirl the bass or pickerel struck, and where the swimmer had been there was only a momentary eddy with a bubble whirling on its rim. Of boats we had none to command, but when an island came within tempting distance of the mainland we pushed out on logs and gained it, and at sunset were known to walk through town with such strings of mighty fish, and mostly of bass, as brought the loungers to attention. But these were our islands and we did not tell. So long ago and far away.

*   *   *

And three of us voyaged one day not to a single island only, but to all three of them, for the weather was auspicious and the log extraordinarily obedient. It was so that the forebears put out from shore. We had reversed the record and were again at the beginning of things. Here and there, on the two islands first visited, and from the log in mid-lake, we took fish—bass with the scent of sweet herbes rising from their fat sides, lean, savage pickerel mottled and barred, and that fish called the wall-eyed pike, which when taken from a certain bottom is golden as a coin. Yet the catch had been but a fair one when we moored the log insecurely to the third island and tossed our frogs beside its rushes.

The island lay near the mouth of a river and the swing of the waning current played with it musingly. Deep and deeper sank my frog, till white stomach was lost to view in green shadow, and I began—for it was our custom to kill this bait before we used it—that jerking motion of the 5-cent cane, which caused the luckless batrachian to seem to swim. There was a reluctance manifest. The line drew slowly outward and downward, and, lacking the refinement of a reel, I moved the tip toward the surface and thrust it under, and still under, until my eager wrist was in the water. And I struck.

A fisherman would know, and an angler might know—though I doubt many anglers have fished after that fashion. The vibrant, furious berserk rage of him! The whiteness of his flanks, far down, far down. The rush that sent him twisting into the June sunshine. The dread that swept me, lest he should be lost. And at long last, by the clemency of those fates that watch over fishermen, and give particular heed to boys, the drawing forth of a great pike or pickerel that weighed unbelievable pounds, and that was borne home between two of us on a stout stick as becomes a mighty fish who has fought the good fight and can no more.

Does pride know a summit loftier than this? Or fullness of heart a deeper, more pervasive content? Why, sir, I assure you that even an angler might have been dislodged from his studied nonchalance by the taking of that magnificent specimen of its species.

The time came for the catching of my first trout, and this is always a memorable experience. For the trout, of whatever kind, is not appraised for weight alone, but for those finer values which are found in fluent outline, in grace, and glow and all of beauty's attributes. He who catches a trout has in the rough, mortal hand of him one of nature's poems, a creature of a comeliness so rare, so strange, so patrician, as to touch the heart of the captor with pity and praise. And they who take tarpon, I dare say, those vast and valorous herrings that are silver as a shield, do not take with their tarpon that certain something which every fisherman takes with his trout, though the fish be no longer than a stretched finger. This trout of mine, this first trout, was taken in the creek we knew as Four-Mile.

Thickets of hazel and sumac pressed close to Four-Mile, and willows waded lithely into its sweet current, and in all it was such a stream as is hard to come at, and such a one as you might cross almost at a stride. In that creek, I remember, I first saw the miller's thumb, that universal ugliness, that finned belly, which is the bane of bait fishermen. He came squattering over the bright sand, as he were come from the moon, strange, lunar, outlandish. I drew the grasshopper from his gullet, and kept the miller's thumb, for fish are fish to a boy. And very stealthily I moved toward that place where Four-Mile made music under a hanging sod. Within the music were trout, many trout, untaught, uncaught, and uncommonly hungry. Ha! He was fast. He was forth. He was mine.

And thus, by this and by that, and here and there, in one hundred waters, I became an indifferent but incurable fisherman, such as must fish when the wind fares from the wrong quarter, such as yearn from a train toward the merest shimmer of a creek through the first, such as brood hopefully beside pasture ponds, and are guided by an innocent faith which passes understanding.

ALMOST TIME FOR TROUT

There are reasons for this and for that, and we hear much of their openings, but really there is only one season that matters to many men at this time of the year. Looking out of office windows. Driving along in trucks. Handling freight down at the yards. Or walking a beat in the rain. There is one season that is best of all. That, of course, is the trout season which is to open very soon. It is good to live in a land where there is plenty of trout fishing. You never tire of it, and never does the season open without the old tingling, the old response.

People try to explain it, although this is unnecessary, but nobody ever has been quite able to do so, not even Walton. But most fishermen are agreed there is a quality in trout fishing that approaches the ideal. It is like the pursuit and realization of a pleasing dream. The trout is its symbol of abundant reward. It is something like this: We know, of necessity, that we can never have all to which we aspire, and we realize, too, that the dreams of aspiration have a way of fading, and yielding, until they are gone beyond recovery, and we have but memories of them. Is it sad? No. That isn't it. This is the common experience of mankind. We are reconciled to it, or nearly so. Yet men must dream of a time, if it be no more than a single day, when their dreams shall come true, even as they dreamed them. Now the virtue of trout fishing is that it, of all pursuits, rewards the dreamer with realization of his dream. The trout are more beautiful than he remembered them as being, and the day, the scene and the occupation are at harmony. That is why men go trout fishing.

It has often been remarked by trout fishermen that when they are about the affairs of stream and rod, the events of yesterday and the necessities of tomorrow are singularly dwarfed in importance. They seem somehow to lack for real significance. The beauty of stream and forest, the beauty of the fish, the agreeable nature of the employment—these are real. All else appears to be of little moment, and to wear an aspect of trickery, as though men were both betrayed into and by it. It is for this reason that men go trout fishing, vowing that they prefer it to other recreations. Physically weary as they are before the sun is high, the truth is they are resting. They have rediscovered the escape. The stream they fish is running through their hearts to bear away the frets and worries of yesterday and tomorrow. All fishermen will know how it is, though it is uncommonly difficult to explain.

If any city dweller could enumerate at this moment the citizens, working and dwelling within a dozen miles of him, whose thoughts are fixed upon the opening of the trout season, he would be astonished at the number of them. And if he might, at the same time, appraise the gentleness and innocence of their reflections, he must be even more astonished by the essential boyishness of their natures. A recreation which sets aside the usual desires, and banishes the common thought of gain and selfishness—as any true recreation should—must be of important benefit to the people that practice it, and therefore to the commonwealth. The state could make no sounder investment than in trout. Such fishing is beneficial to the nature of the citizen. Anything that will persuade a great number of people to think sanely, and decently, and happily, though it be but of a favorite recreation, is of great importance to society.

But no trout fisherman is thinking of this, and small blame to him. He has more important matters to ponder. He must think of his flies and his tackle. He must speculate upon the probable condition of the water. He must recall, and this effortlessly, the very look and laughter of the stream to which he will be going. Mr. Coolidge says that fishing improves the republic, and Mr. Hoover holds the same view. But though we applaud their discernment, we submit that they have told us nothing not already known. There's a stream down toward the coast that should be right, as trout fishermen say, just right, in a day or so.

OPENING DAY

Where shall we go, you say? Let's go back to the place where the tall fern is parted under the first at the brink of the canyon, and the black trail plunges down, with handholds of sapling and root, to white water—down, down to the South Fork. With the salmonberry blooming, and the blue grouse hooting, and somewhere a wild pigeon mourning its heart out. The voice of the South Fork comes up from the canyon till the air pulses with it, and as you go down, down, where the deer have gone, you glimpse the tossed swiftness of the long rapids. Now the last few yards of the trail are steep as a church roof—but here, gray-walled and clamoring, unforgotten, with a hatch dancing above the green swirl by the black rock, here is the South Fork. Do you remember? Let's go back.

Do you remember? Yonder's the log jam that was many a freshet in making, and the green water lifts without foam as the river slips under the barrier. If trout come out from under the satiny weave of it, they are likely to be large fish, and from much dwelling in shadow are apt to be darkly gleaming. And they will strike where the water lifts—instant and visible and strong. It is a place where the water ouzel sings, as once we heard him; a place where the swifts hunt the little wind of the canyon, for the fly hatch, as once we saw them. It is a place where the mink stares at you, wonderingly, glistening. How far, how very far above, the canyon's brink seems. How small the firs and how foreshortened. The hawk calls as he crosses over. And wild, and fond, and far the place is, and beyond the log jam is the great bar and the long riffle. Let's go back.

Where shall we go, you say? Let's go back to the place where the paunchy, lithe, shining grandfather of all trout rose thrice, and at the third rise struck smashingly—to leap unbelievably! The reel sings. Not under the trailing branch! Not there! Back to the place where you beached the big trout, bigger even than he had seemed, and the sunshine that fell on the sandbar warmed the rose of his flanks and his cheeks, and the green, and the gold, and the silver and all the glory of him. And plain on the sand is the print of the cougar's great paw. So that one looks at the tangled steepness, up and up to the brink of the canyon—looks and wonders. And here a trout and there a trout, and each of us wet to the armpits, and a sort of feeling that we have come home again. Let's go back.

Do you remember? Well, then, let's go back to the canyon of the South Fork—or someplace—where we used to go. To get so tired from the fishing, but never of fishing, that the very ache of our tiredness is good to feel. Back where we used to go. Let's skirt the black cliff again hazardously—watch out for that rodtip!—and fish once more to the bend and then take time off to make coffee over a driftwood fire. And lie on the sand with a tussock of clover for pillow and from under the brims of our hats watch the high clouds wander over. And lie on the sand and talk, or keep silent, and wonder about how far the car is. And count our trout, maybe, and clean them. It is odd about happiness. The hour glass that measures it is both swift and slow. Do you remember the place where we used to fish? Let's go back.

The Intruder

~~~~~~~~~~~~~~

Robert Traver

(from "Trout Madness")

IT WAS ABOUT noon when I put down my fly rod and sculled the little cedar boat with one hand and ate a sandwich and drank a can of beer with the other, just floating and enjoying the ride down the beautiful broad main Escanaba River. Between times I watched the merest speck of an eagle tacking and endlessly wheeling far up in the cloudless sky. Perhaps he was stalking my sandwich or even, dark thought, stalking me. . . . The fishing so far had been poor; the good trout simply weren't rising. I rounded a slow double bend, with high gravel banks on either side, and there stood a lone fisherman—the first person I had seen in hours. He was standing astride a little feeder creek on a gravel point on the left downstream side, fast to a good fish, his glistening rod hooped and straining, the line taut, the leader vibrating and sawing the water, the fish itself boring far down out of sight.

Since I was curious to watch a good battle and anxious not to interfere, I eased the claw anchor over the stern—*plop*—and the little boat hung there, gurgling and swaying from side to side in

295

the slow deep current. The young fisherman either did not hear me or, hearing, and being a good one, kept his mind on his work. As I sat watching he shifted the rod to his left hand, shaking out his right wrist as though it were asleep, so I knew then that the fight had been a long one and that this fish was no midget. The young fisherman fumbled in his shirt and produced a cigarette and lighter and lit up, a real cool character. The fish made a sudden long downstream run and the fisherman raced after him, prancing through the water like a yearling buck, gradually coaxing and working him back up to the deeper slow water across from the gravel bar. It was a nice job of handling and I wanted to cheer. Instead I coughed discreetly and he glanced quickly upstream and saw me.

"Hi," he said pleasantly, turning his attention back to his fish.

"Hi," I answered.

"How's luck?" he said, still concentrating.

"Fairish," I said. "But I haven't raised anything quite like you seem to be on to. How you been doin'—otherwise, I mean?"

"Fairish," he said. "This is the third good trout in this same stretch—all about the same size."

"My, my," I muttered, thinking ruefully of the half-dozen-odd barely legal brook trout frying away in my sunbaked creel. "Guess I've just been out floating over the good spots."

"Pleasant day for a ride, though," he said, frowning intently at his fish.

"Delightful," I said wryly, taking a slow swallow of beer.

"Yep," the assured young fisherman went on, expertly feeding out line as his fish made another downstream sashay. "Yep," he repeated, nicely taking up slack on the retrieve, "that's why I gave up floating this lovely river. Nearly ten years ago, just a kid. Decided then 'twas a hell of a lot more fun fishing a hundred yards of her carefully than taking off on these all-day floating picnics."

I was silent for a while. Then: "I think you've got something there," I said, and I meant it. Of course he was right, and I was simply out joy-riding past the good fishing. I should have brought along a girl or a camera. On this beautiful river if there was no rise a float was simply an enforced if lovely scenic tour. If there was a rise, no decent fisherman ever needed to float. Presto, I now had it all figured out. . . .

"Wanna get by?" the poised young fisherman said, flipping his cigarette into the water.

"I'll wait," I said. "I got all day. My pal isn't meeting me till dark—'way down at the old burned logging bridge."

"Hm . . . trust you brought your passport—you really are out on a voyage," he said. "Perhaps you'd better slip by, fella—by the feel of this customer it'll be at least ten-twenty minutes more. Like a smart woman in the mood for play, these big trout don't like to be rushed. C'mon, just bear in sort of close to me, over here, right under London Bridge. It won't bother us at all."

My easy young philosopher evidently didn't want me to see how really big his fish was. But being a fisherman myself I knew, I knew. "All right," I said, lifting the anchor and sculling down over his way and under his throbbing line. "Thanks and good luck."

"Thanks, chum," he said, grinning at me. "Have a nice ride and good luck to you."

"Looks like I'll need it," I said, looking enviously back over my shoulder at his trembling rod tip. "Hey," I said, belatedly remembering my company manners, "want a nice warm can of beer?"

Smiling: "Despite your glowing testimonial, no thanks."

"You're welcome," I said, realizing we were carrying on like a pair of strange diplomats.

"And one more thing, please," he said, raising his voice a little to be heard over the burbling water, still smiling intently at his straining fish. "If you don't mind, please keep this little stretch under your hat—it's been all mine for nearly ten years. It's really something special. No use kidding you—I see you've spotted my bulging creel and I guess by now you've got a fair idea of what I'm on to. And anyway I've got to take a little trip. But I'll be back—soon I hope. In the meantime try to be good to the place. I know it will be good to you."

"Right!" I shouted, for by then I had floated nearly around the downstream bend. "Mum's the word." He waved his free hand and then was blotted from view by a tall doomed spruce leaning far down out across the river from a crumbling water-blasted bank. The last thing I saw was the gleaming flash of his rod, the long taut line, the strumming leader. It made a picture I've never forgotten.

That was the last time ever that I floated the Big Escanaba River. I had learned my lesson well. Always after that when I visited this fabled new spot I hiked in, packing my gear, threading my way down river through a pungent needled maze of ancient deer trails, like a fleeing felon keeping always slyly away from the broad winding river itself. My strategy was twofold: to prevent other sly fishermen from finding and de-flowering the place, and to save myself an extra mile of walking.

Despite the grand fishing I discovered there, I did not go back too often. It was a place to hoard and save, being indeed most good to me, as advertised. And always I fished it alone, for a fisherman's pact had been made, a pact that became increasingly hard to keep as the weeks rolled into months, the seasons into years, during which I never again encountered my poised young fisherman. In the morbid pathology of trout fishermen such a phenomenon is mightily disturbing. What had become of my fisherman? Hadn't he ever got back from his trip? Was he sick or had he moved away? Worse yet, had he died? How could such a consummate young artist have possibly given up fishing such an enchanted spot? Was he one of that entirely mad race of eccentric fishermen who cannot abide the thought of sharing a place, however fabulous, with even *one* other fisherman?

By and by, with the innocent selfishness possessed by all fishermen, I dwelt less and less upon the probable fate of my young fisherman and instead came smugly to think it was I who had craftily discovered the place. Nearly twenty fishing seasons slipped by on golden wings, as fishing seasons do, during which time I, fast getting no sprightlier, at last found it expedient to locate and hack out a series of abandoned old logging roads to let me drive within easier walking distance of my secret spot. The low cunning of middle age was replacing the hot stamina of youth. . . . As a road my new trail was strictly a spring-breaking broncobuster, but at least I was able to sit and ride, after a fashion, thus saving my aging legs for the real labor of love to follow.

Another fishing season was nearly done when, one afternoon, brooding over that gloomy fact, I suddenly tore off my lawyer-mask and fled my office, heading for the Big Escanaba, bouncing and bucking my way in, finally hitting the Glide—as I had come to call the place—about sundown. For a long time I just stood there on the high bank, drinking in the sights and pungent river smells. No fish were rising, and slowly, lovingly, I went through the familiar ritual of rigging up: scrubbing out a fine new leader, dressing the tapered line, jointing the rod and threading the line, pulling on the tall patched waders, anointing myself with fly dope. No woman dressing for a ball was more fussy. . . . Then I composed myself on my favorite fallen log and waited. I smoked a slow pipe and sipped a can of beer, cold this time, thanks to the marvels of dry ice and my new road. My watching spot overlooked a wide bend and commanded a grand double view: above, the deep slow velvet glide with its little feeder stream where I first met my young fisherman; below a sporty and productive broken run of white water stretching nearly a

half-mile. The old leaning spruce that used to be there below me
had long since bowed in surrender and been swept away by
some forgotten spring torrent. As I sat waiting the wind had
died, the shadowing waters had taken on the brooding blue
hush of evening, the dying embers of sundown suddenly lit a
great blazing forest fire in the tops of the tall spruces across river
from me, and an unknown bird that I have always called simply
the "lonely" bird sang timidly its ancient haunting plaintive
song. I arose and took a deep breath like a soldier advancing
upon the enemy.

The fisherman's mystic hour was at hand.

First I heard and then saw a young buck in late velvet slowly,
tentatively splashing his way across to my side, above me and
beyond the feeder creek, ears twitching and tall tail nervously
wigwagging.Then he winded me, freezing in midstream, giving
me a still and liquid stare for a poised instant; then came
charging on across in great pawing incredibly graceful leaps,
lacquered flanks quivering, white flag up and waving, bounding
up the bank and into the anonymous woods, the sounds of his
excited blowing fading and growing fainter and then dying
away.

In the meantime four fair trout had begun rising in the
smooth tail of the glide just below me. I selected and tied on a
favorite small dry fly and got down below the lowest riser and
managed to take him on the first cast, a short dainty float.
Without moving I stood and lengthened line and took all four
risers, all nice firm brook trout upwards of a foot, all the time
purring and smirking with increasing complacency. The omens
were good. As I relit my pipe and waited for new worlds to
conquer I heard a mighty splash above me and wheeled gaping
at the spreading magic ring of a really good trout, carefully
marking the spot. Oddly enough he had risen just above where
the young buck had just crossed, a little above the feeder creek.
Perhaps, I thought extravagantly, perhaps he was after the

deer. . . . I waited, tense and watchful, but he did not rise again.

I left the river and scrambled up the steep gravelly bank and made my way through the tall dense spruces up to the little feeder creek. I slipped down the bank like a footpad, stealthily inching my way out to the river in the silted creek itself, so as not to scare the big one, *my* big one. I could feel the familiar shock of icy cold water suddenly clutching at my ankles as I stood waiting at the spot where I had first run across my lost fisherman. I quickly changed to a fresh fly in the same pattern, carefully snubbing the knot. Then the fish obediently rose again, a savage easy engulfing roll, again the undulent outgoing ring, just where I had marked him, not more than thirty feet from me and a little beyond the middle and obliquely upstream. Here was, I saw, a cagey selective riser, lord of his pool, and one who would not suffer fools gladly. So I commanded myself to rest him before casting. "Twenty-one, twenty-two, twenty-three . . ." I counted.

The cast itself was indecently easy and, finally releasing it, the little Adams sped out on its quest, hung poised in midair for an instant, and then settled sleepily upon the water like a thistle, uncurling before the leader like the languid outward folding of a ballerina's arm. The fly circled a moment, uncertainly, then was caught by the current. Down, down it rode, closer, closer, then—*clap!*—the fish rose and kissed it, I flicked my wrist and he was on, and then away he went roaring off downstream, past feeder creek and happy fisherman, the latter hot after him.

During the next mad half-hour I fought this explosive creature up and down the broad stream, up and down, ranging at least a hundred feet each way, or so it seemed, without ever once seeing him. This meant, I figured, that he was either a big brown or a brook. A rainbow would surely have leapt a dozen times by now. Finally I worked him into the deep safe water off the feeder creek where he sulked nicely while I panted and

rested my benumbed rod arm. As twilight receded into dusk
with no sign of his tiring I began vaguely to wonder just who
had latched on to whom. For the fifth or sixth time I rested my
aching arm by transferring the rod to my left hand, professionally shaking out my tired wrist just as I had once seen a young
fisherman do.

Nonchalantly I reached in my jacket and got out and tried to
light one of my rigidly abominable Italian cigars. My fish,
unimpressed by my show of aplomb, shot suddenly away on a
powerful zigzag exploratory tour upstream, the fisherman nearly
swallowing his unlit cigar as he scrambled up after him. It was then
that I saw a lone man sitting quietly in a canoe, anchored in
midstream above me. The tip of his fly rod showed over the stern.
My heart sank: after all these years my hallowed spot was at last
discovered.

"Hi," I said, trying to convert a grimace of pain into an amiable
grin, all the while keeping my eye on my sulking fish. The show
must go on.

"Hi," he said.

"How you doin'?" I said, trying to make a brave show of casual
fish talk.

"Fairish," he said, "but nothing like you seem to be on to."

"Oh, he isn't so much," I said, lying automatically if not too
well. "I'm working a fine leader and don't dare to bull him." At
least that was the truth.

The stranger laughed briefly and glanced at his wrist watch.
"You've been on him that I know of for over forty minutes—and
I didn't see you make the strike. Let's not try to kid the Marines.
I just moved down a bit closer to be in on the finish. I'll shove
away if you think I'm too close."

"Nope," I answered generously, delicately snubbing my fish
away from a partly submerged windfall. "But about floating this
lovely river," I pontificated, "there's nothing in it, my friend.
Absolutely nothing. Gave it up myself eighteen-twenty years

ago. Figured out it was better working one stretch carefully than shoving off on these floating picnics. Recommend it to you, comrade."

The man in the canoe was silent. I could see the little red moon of his cigarette glowing and fading in the gathering gloom. Perhaps my gratuitous pedagogical ruminations had offended him; after all, trout fishermen are a queer proud race. Perhaps I should try diversionary tactics. "Wanna get by?" I inquired silkily. Maybe I could get him to go away before I tried landing this unwilling porpoise. He still remained silent. "Wanna get by?" I repeated. "It's perfectly O.K. by me. As you see—it's a big roomy river."

"No," he said dryly. "No thanks." There was another long pause. Then: "If you wouldn't mind too much I think I'll put in here for the night. It's getting pretty late—and somehow I've come to like the looks of this spot."

"Oh," I said in a small voice—just "Oh"—as I disconsolately watched him lift his anchor and expertly push his canoe in to the near gravelly shore, above me, where it grated halfway in and scraped to rest. He sat there quietly, his little neon cigarette moon glowing, and I felt I just had to say something more. After all I didn't *own* the river. "Why sure, of course, it's a beautiful place to camp, plenty of pine knots for fuel, a spring-fed creek for drinking water and cooling your beer," I ran on gaily, rattling away like an hysterical realtor trying to sell the place. Then I began wondering how I would ever spirit my noisy fish car out of the woods without the whole greedy world of fishermen learning about my new secret road to this old secret spot. Maybe I'd even have to abandon it for the night and hike out. . . . Then I remembered there was an unco-operative fish to be landed, so I turned my full attention to the unfinished and uncertain business at hand. "Make yourself at home," I lied softly.

"Thanks," the voice again answered dryly, and again I heard the soft chuckle in the semidarkness.

My fish had stopped his mad rushes now and was busily boring the bottom, the long leader vibrating like the plucked string of a harp. For the first time I found I was able gently to pump him up for a cautious look. And again I almost swallowed my still unlit stump of cigar as I beheld his dorsal fin cleaving the water nearly a foot back from the fly. He wallowed and shook like a dog and then rolled on his side, then recovered and fought his way back down and away on another run, but shorter this time. With a little pang I knew then that my fish was a done, but the pang quickly passed—it always did—and again I gently, relentlessly pumped him up, shortening line, drawing him in to the familiar daisy hoop of landing range, kneeling and stretching and straining out my opposing aching arms like those of an extravagant archer. The net slipped fairly under him on the first try and, clenching my cigar, I made my pass and lo! lifted him free and dripping from the water. "Ah-h-h . . ." He was a glowing superb spaniel-sized brown. I staggered drunkenly away from the water and sank anywhere to the ground, panting like a winded miler.

"Beautiful, *beautiful*," I heard my forgotten and unwelcome visitor saying like a prayer. "I've dreamed all this—over a thousand times I've dreamed it."

I tore my feasting eyes away from my fish and glowered up at the intruder. He was half standing in the beached canoe now, one hand on the side, trying vainly to wrest the cap from a bottle, of all things, seeming in the dusk to smile uncertainly. I felt a sudden chill sense of concern, of vague nameless alarm.

"Look, chum," I said, speaking lightly, very casually, "is everything all O.K?"

"Yes, yes, of course," he said shortly, still plucking away at his bottle. "There . . . I—I'm coming now."

Bottle in hand he stood up and took a resolute broad step out of the canoe, then suddenly, clumsily he lurched and pitched forward, falling heavily, cruelly, half in the beached canoe and half out upon the rocky wet shore. For a moment I sat staring ruefully, then I scrambled up and started running toward him, still holding my rod and the netted fish, thinking this fisherman was indubitably potted. "No, no, no!" he shouted at me, struggling and scrambling to his feet in a kind of wild urgent frenzy. I halted, frozen, holding my sagging dead fish as the intruder limped toward me, in a curious sort of creaking stiffly mechanical limp, the uncorked but still intact bottle held triumphantly aloft in one muddy wet hand, the other hand reaching gladly toward me.

"Guess I'll never get properly used to this particular battle stripe," he said, slapping his thudding and unyielding right leg. "But how are you, stranger?" he went on, his wet eyes glistening, his bruised face smiling. "How about our having a drink to your glorious trout—and still another to reunion at our old secret fishing spot?"

Dud Dean and
the Enchanted

Arthur R. MacDougall, Jr.

THE LADY WAS a most alert and intelligent person. I met her at a bookstore in modern Babylon, where she presided over books, clerks, and cash registers. And she asked, "Where can I find a professional guide in Maine who knows how to prepare a palatable meal, make a bough bed, paddle a canoe, and where to find the white orchid, *Cypripedium acaule albiflorum?*" Before I could attempt to answer the question, the lady added, "He must *know* the wilderness, and above all, he must be a gentleman."

I looked at the lady, who was neat and trim but forty years old plus ten. And it seemed to me that she need not worry about men who were not gentlemen. And then, while I sought for words that would not betray my private amusement, I thought of Dud Dean, who would have replied to a question with such stipulations in a courtly manner.

"Lady," I said, "there are doubtless scores of such men who are registered guides in Maine, but I only know one of them. He is much older than you and I, and his mind and personality are more mature. He knows the birds and flowers by their names, although he often calls them names that are not found in the books. And he is a gentleman with the best of manners."

"And what are the wages one must pay such a paragon?"

"Wait a moment. I only told you that I knew such a guide. I didn't say that he was available. Dud Dean picks and chooses his clientelle. One must persuade Dud that he is worth the while. Your money would be a secondary consideration."

"You intrigue me," the lady said. "And how do I approach this Dud? And is he none other than the lauded Dud Dean of your stories? And would he really know where *Cypripedium acaule albiflorum* grows?"

"Dud would call them lady's-slippers or white moccasins. And I am sure that he would know a score of places where they bloom in June."

The lady tapped her white teeth with the rubber end of a pencil. "Now that I have gone so far," she said, "I should tell you the rest. I expect to attach myself to a man in June. The gentleman grew up in Maine. The white moccasin flowers are only an aside. One can buy almost anything in this city, but if it had a glory, that is soiled or dead. We, this man and I, have a hunger in us, not so much to see the rare white orchid as to keep a tryst where such a triumph of the ancient earth survives. It isn't easily said, and I wonder if you understand."

I assumed that I did understand. And I said, "If you will come to Bingham, I will take you to Dud Dean's house, and then you and he can talk about the project to your heart's content. If you are fortunate enough to enlist Dud Dean, he can make your dream come true."

When I had told Dud about the lady and her projected vacation and her projected husband, he smiled quizzically. Then he said, "Nope. I'm too old to lead honeymooners eround.

Besides, I long ago had to give up guidin' parties with women-folks. Nancy's jealous."

Nancy Dean had been washing dishes, and of course Dud had made the speech for her to hear. She came from the kitchen to the sitting-room. Nancy is one of those rare persons who grow more and more attractive as they ripen in wisdom, and with charity for all. Now she came to us smiling.

"To the contrary," she said, "I have always wanted Dud to guide ladies. They have a most delightful effect upon him. He calls to mind all his old gallantries. He gets his hair cut and his mustache trimmed. Furthermore, it has been a long time since the opportunity came to guide honeymooners. Why, I would love to go myself, if I were a guide! And I think, Dudley, that it was kind of Mr. Macdougall to think of you, and to recommend you to these people."

"Pshaw, Nancy, how many times have I heard you say that a man sh'ud keep his eyes on Greeks that come bearin' gifts? Mak's like all parsons. Thar's sunthin' up his sleeves. Besides, w'ud yer trust him to size up a strange woman? Like ducks yer w'ud. What erbout her man? Has he got fallen arches? Can he take blackflies an' bog water? Can he sleep with the stub end of a fir bough in the small of his back? Er is he old enough to know better, but don't?"

"They grew up in little Maine towns," I said. "He came from a little village in Washington County. She grew up in Aroostook. And they are dreaming about white moccasins, and all that."

"Crotch. Is that supposed to prove sunthing, Mak?"

"Dudley," said Nancy.

"Hump. Wel-el, no harm if I talk with them. When they come to Bingham, bring 'em eround. My garden is planted. Chores purty well caught up. Bring 'em up here. Nancy will size 'em up, and if she decides that I am good enough fer sech folks I have no doubt that I'm their man."

Five weeks after that day, the lady, Mrs. Pendmaster Davis, wrote a letter to me, and that is the rest of the story.

Dear Mr. Macdougall,

I am happy! Your friend was the most delightful and entrancing man! To that, we both agree. Pend and I have reviewed our honeymoon and the endless little delights that Dud contrived for us. We have them like a rosary to tell over and over—and I am not irreverent.

First thing. Dud asked us, "Which is most important—the lady's-slippers er *trout?*"

I said, "Trout," because I knew how dearly Pend loves to fish for trout. And he has caught them in England, Scotland, and in the Pyrenees, as well as almost everywhere in North America.

But Pend said, "The lady's-slippers. There is no question about that."

Honestly, I think that your old friend was pleased. But he almost insisted on giving us physical examinations. How careful and wise he is! When at last we convinced him that we really wanted to go afoot into a remote corner of the wilderness, and that I was prepared to undergo the torments of the blackfly, and what else, he said:

"C'ud you even stand bein' lost? Reason I ask is that I've got a sartin place in mind which I hain't seen fer fifty years. Since then, thar's been a big fire in thar, an' since the fire it's been logged over. So I might have to poke eround afore we got thar. But I am mortally sure that we can find your white moccasins, an' find them no end. And thar's bound to be some trout to catch. But to git thar, we'd have to go to Big Enchanted Pond, cross it, and then climb up into Bulldog Mountain."

"Enchanted!" Did anyone ever have a honeymoon in a more fittingly named place? Of course we were enthusiastic. Pend said, "I have been lost with men in whom I had less confidence. And, by gosh, I managed to enjoy it. As for our lady, she has already risked more than that. Lead on, MacDuff."

Then the men bought our supplies. And your Mr. Dean loaned Pend one of his huge packbaskets. They carried fifty pounds each. All because Pend was determined that a honeymoon would be spoiled unless there was plenty to eat.

I do not believe that Dud Dean was even puzzled about where he was or where to go ahead. I know that Pend did not worry for a moment. He said to me, "This man is the genuine old guide. We need not fret." And yet, Dud had not gone that way for fifty years. Think of it, a lifetime!

We walked from the road that goes to Spencer Lake. What a breathless beauty there is in all that country! The Upper Enchanted! Verily. Dud told us about the terrible forest fire of 1895—the very year Pend was born. Dud showed us huge pine trunks that still lie where they fell after that fire. Pend cut into one with his axe. It was still sound under the outer grey shell. And Dud called to our attention the marine rock at the height of land—as one goes down to Enchanted Pond. That man is a matchless entertainer, because his own interests are so varied.

Dud told us about the legend that Enchanted Pond is bottomless beneath its deepest water. He pointed out the place at the lower end where some old lumberman had built a dam between those magnificent granite mountains.

And Pend caught three gloriously colored trout in that blue water, while Dud rowed us to the Bulldog Mountain shore. By the way, Pend did not keep those trout. I have had so much to learn about men and fishermen in these few weeks—things I might have learned years ago, if Pend had come into the store for a copy of your book, *Dud Dean and His Country*, years ago instead of a few months ago. Dud Dean! And His Country! We'll never forget that man or his country—not ever.

The mountain was steep. Did you know that once there was a profile of a bulldog on the east end, until it slid off and away during a springtime deluge? What a savage name, Bulldog! Must there be a bulldog in the Enchanted Country? No. The Enchanted is rid of that. I am glad it is gone. But there is a great raw scar where the profile was.

Now we come to our weather. That old joke about the Maine man who said to the tourist who had complained about the weather, "What kind of weather do yer want? We've got all kinds," is no whimsy. There never was a lovelier day than when we started up the mountain. The sky was as blue as the ribbon that Alice wore into Wonderland. Then, as if by magic, the cumulus clouds grew forebodingly dark. It was as if the demons were angry because we had invaded their mountain. And how it rained!

Dud explained, with that solemn face he puts on, that it does not rain cats and dogs in the Enchanted—not even bulldogs. Instead, according to Dud, it rains rain, although sometimes it rains lady's-slippers—white fer when she gets up in the morning, gold fer when she eats her dinner (at noon, of course) and pink fer when she goes to dance across the sunset. And then he added that he had known it to rain *trout* in the Enchanted, but that kind, he said, hardly ever take a fly, unless a fellow has the Pink Lady.

"I have a Pink Lady," said Pend. And I guess that I was, after such an interpolation!

Dud pretended not to comprehend the implication. He said, "Then I guess, maybe, yer c'ud git some trout if yer sh'ud try real hard. But yer know, thar was once a tribe of Indians that lived up an' down the Kennebec. And among them was a girl so purty that they called her 'Flower-of-the-rising-sun.' Of course, all the young fellers loved her. One of them was a big, tall chap who went by the name of Moxie, an' he courted her morning, noon, an' almost all night. So they were wed. Then the young man made a terrible mistake. Took his young wife with him when he went into the Enchanted to fish fer trout. Fer a little time they was happy an' contented—until early one morning, when Moxie woke up. He looked fer his wife. She had left his side. He hurried outside the wigwam, and thar he saw her walkin' over the lake, where the risin' sun made a path.

"Moxie called to her, but she did not hear him. He ran to the lake, and went after her in his birch canoe. No use. She jist went away, up the mountain, an' thar she vanished out of mortal sight. Poor Moxie! Not even a yeller leaf was turned upside down. Not even a twig had been rolled on its side. An' he never found her. So after a while he left the Enchanted; wandered off, down country, an' where Moxie Mountain is he died of a broken heart. Yer can see him any clear day, with his great shoulders an' chest heaved up ag'inst the sky.

"But what the Enchanted did with Flower-of-the-rising-sun, no man knows. Yer see, it ain't safe in here, but the trout don't know it. As fer fishermen, what do they know but trout?"

Of course, your old friend was talking to help us forget the drenching rain. Once he turned to look at us, and asked, "W'udn't you rather go back to the camps on the big lake? They're nice an' comfortable. We c'ud sleep dry, an' then come up here tomorrow."

Pend looked to me. And I said, "No."

"Ye're sure?"

I was. But I was weary and very, very wet. At noontime we stopped at a little spring. And there Dud and Pend cooked our dinner. The rain continued. And once more Dud asked me, "Don't yer want to go back to the camps?"

I am so glad that I refused to turn back. So glad!

When we went on, Dud said, "Mind now, that I'm goin' it purty blind. Maybe I can't find that pond tonight. It's a small mark in this big country. And maybe it ain't thar anymore, like Flower-of-the-rising-sun. Queer things happen up here, an' ordinary things happen queerly. Even the trout, in this pond I'm lookin' fer, is strange. Some folks declare that thar ain't a trout in it to go over half a pound. An' some persons have fished in here to go back home vowin' that thar's no trout at all. And a few folks whisper erbout tremendous trout that haunt the place."

Pend asked, "But what do you say?"

"I say that it strikes me as odd that when I come in here fifty years ago, the weather was jist like it is this very afternoon. We was young fellers, Mat Markham an' me. Thar was mighty heavy timber up here on the mountain. Take that an' the rainstorm, an' the light was dim. Arter a while, we both figgered that we was good an' lost. So we started settin' a line—yer know, pickin' out a tree straight ahead of us, goin' to that, an' then pickin' another. Mat was kinda superstitious. He still is. I 'member that he said, 'If I ever git out of this godforsaken place, I'll never set foot on it ag'in.' And b'crotch, he was as good as his word, becuz he's never been in here since that time. I've always wanted to come in here, but until now this an' that has lured me elsewhere.

"When Mat an' me had gone over the divide, an' started down, the rain kinda pindled—good deal as it's doin' now. Mat kept on moaning, but I didn't pay much attention of course. All of a sudden, I seen a big round raft of fog, like an old circus tent, but kinda moving, writhing, an' rolling. I scootched down, so's I c'ud see under the fog, an' then I seen the pond, level, an' lookin' like an old kitchen floor that has been scoured with sand an' mopped an' mopped fer a hundred years by generations of peeticular women.

" 'Look,' I says to Mat, who was still grumblin' erbout the rain an' foolish fools like us. 'Look,' I says. An' then I p'inted like this—"

Mr. Macdougall, your Dud is a magician. When Pend and I looked where Dud had pointed, just as he had pointed for his friend fifty years ago, we saw a pond, or part of a pond. And there was a cloud of fog lying over it, like a circus tent!

"Great guns, man," exclaimed Pend. "You have an instinct for the abrupt. Is that the pond you were looking to find?"

"Don't know yit. Maybe. Anyhow, it's a pond. Or will it fold up in that cloud an' vanish away?"

Pend said, "We will soon find out!"

So he ran down to the shore of the pond, where he splashed his right hand in the water. "It's real," he said, while laughing back at us.

"C'ud be," said Dud.

But what a ghost of a pond it was, under that weird raft of mountain fog. It was grey and lonely. And for a moment, no more, I wished that I were back on Madison Avenue. And then I remembered how unearthy the skyscrapers look in fog and storm. One sees a few lower stories, but the rest are swallowed up, as if the building were immaterial or upside down in a vague, formless sea.

"Fust," said Dud, "good sense makes camp. Let's see . . . Ayah, over this way thar's a spring, er thar was fifty years ago."

We followed Dud.

"Here," he said. And I saw the sweetest little spring that came as by kindly magic from under a mound of soft moss. "And thar," said Dud. And I saw a single plant of *Cypripedium acaule* with ten blossoms on the one plant.

Dud smiled at me. "Ye'll have to excuse us, becuz they're only pink ones. An' I don't mind if yer laugh at me, when I tell yer that they was here fifty years ago."

Pend had brought that tent with the wonderfully light but waterproof material—floor and all. And he and Dud were only a few moments setting it up.

"There is plenty of room for the three of us," I said.

Dud Dean laughed at me. "If yer don't mind," he said, "I will put up my own shelter-half where Mat an' me built us a leanto so long ago. Now, when we're all shipshape, why not cook up sunthin' until it's real hot. I'll go explore to see if them cedars still grow near the south shore, where Mat an' me made our raft.

Say, do yer know this is the most fun I've had since the day Mat fell inter a springhole on the shore of Middle Carry Pond. We was hedgehoggin' erlong the shore, lookin' fer a boat that had come up missing, as Mont Spinney said when his wife run off with the butter money. The shore, yer see, looked all firm an' trustworthy, but when Mat stepped in that place he jist went out of sight inter a deep springhole. An' the poor feller was so cold when he wallowed out that he kept saying, 'Colder'n hell, colder'n hell,' till Mak give him a lecture fer what he called apostasy.

" 'What d'yer mean by that?' says Mat."

" 'I mean that hell is *not* cold,' says Mak."

Pend and I began to unpack. And in a few moments we heard Dud's axe. He had found the cedars. Pend explained to me that cedar was a light wood, and that it made a buoyant raft.

When Dud came back, he was poling a large raft. And he had a bundle of dry kindling wood tied and fastened on his shoulders. The fire was quickly kindled, and I am sure that mortals never ate more delicious food than our hot biscuits and beef stew. And then we went to bed. And then we slept like small children—children in the Enchanted Country!

Dud awakened us. And I smelled bacon and coffee. "I figgered," he said, "that it w'ud be all right to wake yer up, becuz the weather has improved. Besides, the trout are puddlin' out front."

Did you ever try to dress in a sleeping-bag? There are difficulties. Dud called again. "I wish that ye'd hurry. Thar's an old she otter and her kits out in the pond. It's int'restin' to watch 'em cut up."

I just wrapped a blanket around me and went out. What a handsomely graceful creature an otter is. There were four of them, diving, rising, and chasing each other in the water. How could one ever forget that strong, swift gracefulness!

At the further end of the pond (it was shaped like a football) the trout continued to rise. "Puddling" Dud called it, "becuz they're only takin' nymphs near the surface."

Otters, trout, nymphs, and the earliest daylight in the Enchanted!

Of course, breakfast was delicious. "Coffee," said Dud, "must be part good spring water—none of your chemically diluted, polluted stuff that is as vile as bogwater! But, as Mat says, 'To make good coffee, fust take some coffee, put it in a *coffee-pot* full of b'ilin' water, an' then let it be so long as it takes to whistle, *Comin' Through the Rye.*'"

Pend and I decided to christen the pond "Ghost Lake." And then we embarked on Dud's raft. Of course I should have died if they had made me stay ashore, although I offered to do so, nevertheless. But the men insisted that I should go.

Pend fished with flies. And I was so proud to observe that Dud Dean approved of Pend's skill. It was all so beautifully done. The dry flies appeared to be so small and fragile—number twelves and fourteens, I think. Pend cast into the circles made by the feeding trout. And those vividly colored fish rose with astonishing savageness. And when hooked, they fought with all the grace of the otters.

When one went free, Pend would say, "Bully for you, mister." Then Dud Dean would chuckle. I counted all the fish that Dud actually netted to remove the flies. There were forty of them— "none under half a pound, an' some of 'em almost big e-nough to scare a hot-house trout to death."

They saved one, an unimaginably beautiful thing. "Plenty fer three of us," said Dud. "An' now, let's go find the lady's-slippers, if yer really meant what yer said."

The sun had risen. The pond was a strange pale green and warm with a golden light when we left the camp. It was amusing to me to witness Dud's apologetic way when the first lady's-slippers that he found were a great bed of *Cypripedium calceolus pubescens*, the big yellow moccasin. "Y'know," he said, "I had fergotten all erbout them yeller slippers. Yer don't see 'em very often."

As a matter of fact, I had never seen them growing in the wild way. The large bed was mixed with ferns. The blossoms were like pure gold in that damp, dark setting of forest shadows. And there were so many of them! So amazingly abundant in that lavish place that I could not believe my eyes.

But all that was only to prepare us for the white slippers around the little lost bog, where like figments of utter beauty the enchanted white moccasins grew. When your raw-boned old friend pushed a screen of ferns aside to show us the first patch, I loved him . . . that greatly simple man.

"Here they are," he said. "And to me, it seems as though I had only left them here a few hours ago. But it was fifty years ago. Ask Mat Markham." Then I detected an anxiety in his voice. "I 'spose that ye'll want to pick some?"

"Just one," I said.

I thought for a moment that he was going to hug me. "Glory be!" he said. "I reckon that the Indian girl c'ud spare yer more than that."

Pend and I took color shots, as we had of the yellow moccasins. We have shown the slides to our friends. The question we always expect never fails to be asked: "Where are they?" And I do not need to pretend vagueness to protect the stand, because I only know that they are somewhere on the other side of a mountain— somewhere in the Enchanted.

"B'fore we go back to camp," said Dud Dean, "I'd be pleased to have the lady try my little flyrod down here off the old beaver dam at the foot of this little bog. The trout in thar are little fellars, but the Lord has dressed 'em up real purty."

That was my first lesson in fly fishing. And the fly was a Red Ibis. I loved fly fishing in spite of the blackflies that beset us. Dud Dean was patient and cheerful when I tangled the line in cedars that grew too near the water. What fun it was to catch those handsome little trout.

And that was how our week began! We fell in love with your friend. He is a great soul and a charming gentleman. He is a mystic, but his big hands were made to hold an axe. He is a big, rawboned weather-beaten man, but he can remember where he saw white lady's-slippers growing fifty years ago.

Our days in that Enchanted Country were too swift, as I suppose days are sure to be when one is altogether happy and content. The last night was clear and lighted by a full moon. And is there a place on earth where the moonlight falls so magically as near a mountain top! Dud came to us where we sat looking out on the little lake. And he said, "If the idea sh'ud appeal to you folks, I w'ud like to show yer sunthin' strange and beautiful."

A pleasant sense of excitement filled me. Pend whispered to me, "I have an intuition that we shall never forget this, whatever he has in mind."

We followed Dud along the west shore of the pond—no flashlights, because Dud said, "They'd be handy, but I w'udn't dare."

He led us to the strangest thing—an old dead pine (very ancient) that seemed to be fast in the soft soil of the shore, but lying its full length out in the pond.

"It's always been here," he said. "The water is real shallow, an' the bottom is hard shale and sand. So if anyone fell off, 'tw'udn't do 'em any harm. Matter of fact, we c'ud wade to the end of the log, if that was necessary. But the pine is as stidy as a board walk."

And then he walked out. I did not think that I could do it in that half-light, but with Pend's help I did. Dud was waiting for us at the end. And he whispered, "Look at the bottom."

The bottom was silver white.

"Sand," said Dud. "In the daytime yer can see it bubbling.

Thar's a tremendous spring here, but it's always gentle—no gushing. Now, jist keep still an' watch."

As I watched, the water seemed to become clearer, or the moonlight brighter.

"Now," whispered Dud.

A school of little trout swam over the white sand, turned, and came back.

"Not yit," whispered Dud, "It haint' here yit."

Pend whispered in my ear, "I suspect that I know what he wants us to see. Watch."

Suddenly, as if they had been summoned from far away, the small trout were gone. And, without a visible approach, I saw a huge fish posed motionless over the sand. And I felt that queer excitement that is older than our Race. And I saw the larger stripe of white-white on the creature's pectoral fins. I saw its eyes!

"Wait," whispered Dud.

And there, beside the first trout, lay another giant. They lay side by side, and I saw that they were perfectly matched.

"Wait," whispered Dud.

And there were three more, and then I saw another. There were six immense trout—as if they had materialized from the clean water and the white sand. My eyes began to doubt, or I to doubt my eyes. I moved nearer to Pend, to touch him for assurance. And the trout were gone!

Dud chuckled. "It w'ud always be that way," he said.

We walked back to the camp without speaking. Dud placed wood on the red coals. It caught fire, and the yellow light was welcome.

"Were they real?" I asked, feeling silly to do so, but unable to keep back the question.

"Of course they were real," said Pend.

But Dud Dean chuckled. "Speakin' fer myself, I'll have to say that I don't know. All I know is that's what I saw off that log when it was full moonlight fifty years ago. I was there to git a pail of water, but I went back after Mat Markham. And I know what Mat said. He says, "Be you tryin' to fool me? Nobudy ever catched a trout that big. Nobudy ever heard of a big trout bein' catched in this pond. It's a crotchly lie, that's what it is!" And all the time, Mat stood thar lookin' at them trout jist the same as we did tonight.

"So much as I know, Mat was right when he said that no one ever claimed to git any really big trout in here. We didn't. And nor have we this time. In most waters, trout grow slow. I don't see any reason to think that trout grow fast in this little pond. It appears to be fair-to-middlin' trout water an' that's all.

"But if I was to let myself go, I w'ud take my oath that them *big* trout we saw tonight was the same trout that I saw fifty years ago. Yes sir, by crotch, I'll never forget them trout. C'udn't. But yer may watch an' wait until kingdom-come an' ye'll never see them trout in the daylight. They don't even seem to be near-abouts in the daytime. So it figgers out this way: only time ye'll ever see 'em is late in a moonlight night. So I don't know. Sometimes I have wondered if it was a trick the moonlight played, but yer saw the smaller trout before the big ones come in tonight. W'ud yer say that it was a trick of the moonlight on the bottom, Pend?"

Pend replied, "No, it wasn't an illusion."

"Wel'el, maybe it's the Enchanted—eh? Maybe it's like pink, and white, and yellow lady's-slippers. All I know is that I've seen them trout twice. I guess I'm not apt to see them ever ag'in. But maybe you folks will. Yer know, I w'ud have been bad disapp'inted if storm er clouds had hidden the full moon tonight. Wel-el, hope yer sleep sound. So goodnight."

When he had gone to his own camp, Pend and I sat together near the dying fire. And I said, "What do you really think, dear?"

"Think? Why I think that Dud Dean was like an old priest out there tonight. And deep in my heart, I think that the grand old fellow was passing something on to us, something he has loved, and that he wanted to share with us. God bless him."

Fifth Day

Sir Humphrey Davy

(from "Salmonia")

Halieus—Poietes—Ornither—Physicus.

MORNING.

Hal.—Well, is your tackle all ready? It is a fine fresh and cloudy morning, with a gentle breeze—a day made for salmon fishing.

[*They proceed to the river.*]

Hal.—Now, my friends, I give up the two best pools to you till one o'clock; and I shall amuse myself above and below—probably with trout fishing. As there is a promise of a mixed day, with—what is rare in this country—a good deal of sunshine, I will examine your flies a little, and point out those I think likely to be useful; or rather, I will show you my flies, and, as you all have duplicates of them, you can each select the fly which I point out, and place it in a part of the book where it may easily be found. First: when the cloud is on, I advise one of these three golden twisted flies, silk bodies, orange, red and pale blue, with red, orange, and grey hackle, golden pheasant's hackle for tail, and kingfisher's and golden pheasant's brown hackle under the wing; beginning with the brightest fly, and changing to the darker one. Should the clouds disappear, and it become bright, change your flies for darker ones, of which I will point out three:—a fly with a brown body and a red cock's hackle, and one with a dun body and black hackle, with a brown mallard's

wing. All these flies have, you see, silver twist bodies, and all
kingfisher's feather under the wing, and golden pheasant's
feather for the tail. For the size of your flies, I recommend the
medium size, as the water is small this day; but trying all sizes,
from the butterfly size of a hook of half an inch in width, to one
of a quarter. Now, Physicus, cast your orange fly into that rapid
at the top of the pool; I saw a large fish run there this moment.
You fish well, were common trout your object; but, in salmon
fishing, you must alter your manner of moving the fly. It must
not float quietly down the water; you must allow it to sink a
little, and then pull it back by a gentle jerk—not raising it out of
the water,—and then let it sink again, till it has been shown in
motion, a little below the surface, in every part of your cast. That
is right,—he has risen.

Phys.—I hold him. He is a noble fish!

Hal.—He is a large grilse, I see by his play; or a young salmon,
of the earliest born this spring. Hold him tight; he will fight hard.

Phys.—There! he springs out of the water! Once, twice, thrice,
four times! He is a merry one!

Hal.—He runs against the stream, and will soon be tired,—but
do not hurry him. Pull hard now, to prevent him from running
round that stone. He comes in. I will gaff him for you. I have
him! A goodly fish of this tide. But see, Poietes has a larger fish,
at the bottom of the great pool, and is carried down by him
almost to the sea.

Poiet.—I cannot hold him! He has run out all my line. ·

Hal.—I see him: he is hooked foul, and I fear we shall never
recover him, for he is going out to sea. Give me the rod,—I will
try and turn him; and do you run down to the entrance of the
pool, and throw stones, to make him, if possible, run back. Ay!
that stone has done good service; he is now running up into the
pool again. Now call the fisherman, and tell him to bring a long
pole, to keep him if possible from the sea. Now you have a good
assistant, and I will leave you, for tiring this fish will be at least

a work of two hours. He is not much less than 20 lbs. and is hooked under the gills, so that you cannot suffocate him by a straight line. I wish you good fortune; but should he turn sulky, you must not allow him to rest, but make the fisherman move him with the pole again; your chance of killing him depends upon his being kept incessantly in action, so that he may exhaust himself by exercise. I shall go and catch you some river trout, for your dinner;—but I am glad to see, before I take my leave of you, that Ornither has likewise hold of a fish,—and, from his activity, a lusty sea trout.

[He goes, and returns in the afternoon.]

Hal.—Well, Poietes, I hope to see your fish of 20 lbs.

Poiet.—Alas! he broke me,—turned sulky, and went to the bottom; and when he was roused again, my line came back without the fly; so that I conclude he had cut my links by rubbing them against some sharp stone. But, since, I have caught two grilses and a sea trout, and lost two others, salmons or grilses, that fairly got the hooks out of their mouths.

Hal.—And, Ornither, what have you done? Well, I see,—a salmon, a grilse, and a sea trout. And Physicus?

Phys.—I have lost three fish; one of which broke me, at the top of the pool, by running amongst the rocks; and I have only one small sea trout.

Hal.—Your fortune will come another day. Why, you have not a single crimped fish for dinner, and it is now nearly two o'clock; and you have been catching for the picklers, for those fish may all go to the boiling house. I must again be your purveyor. Can you point out to me any part of this pool where you have not fished?

All.—No.

Hal.—Then I have little chance.

Phys.—O yes! you have a charm for catching fish.

Hal.—Let me know what flies you have tried, and I may perhaps tell you if I have a chance. With my small bright humming bird, as you call it, I will make an essay.

Poiet.—But this fishery is really very limited; and two pools for four persons a small allowance.

Hal.—If you could have seen this river twenty years ago, when the cruives were a mile higher up, then you might have enjoyed fishing. There were eight or ten pools, of the finest character possible for angling, where a fisherman of my acquaintance has hooked thirty fish in a morning. The river was then perfect, and it might easily be brought again into the same state; but even as it is now, with this single good pool and this second tolerable one, I know no place where I could, in the summer months, be so secure of sport as here—certainly no where in Great Britain.

Poiet.—I have often heard the Tay and the Tweed vaunted as salmon rivers.

Hal.—They were good salmon rivers, and are still very good, as far as the profit of the proprietor is concerned; but, for angling, they are very much deteriorated. The net fishing, which is constantly going on except on Sundays and in close time, suffers very few fish to escape; and a Sunday's flood offers the sole chance of a good day's sport, and this only in particular parts of these rivers. I remembered the Tweed and the Tay in a far better state. The Tweed, in the late Lord Somerville's time, always contained taking-fish after every flood in the summer: and, between Abbotsford and Melrose, I have known six or seven fish taken by a single rod in the morning. In the Tay, only ten years ago, at Mickleure, I was myself one of two anglers who took eight fine fish,—three of them large salmon,—in a short morning's fishing; but now, except in spring fishing, when the fish are little worth taking, there is no certainty of sport in these rivers; and one, two, or three fish (which last is of rare

occurrence), are all even an experienced angler can hope to take
in a day's skilful and constant angling.

Poiet.—You have fished in most of the salmon rivers of the
north of Europe,—give us some idea of the kind of sport.

Hal.—I have fished in some, but perhaps not in the best; for
this it is necessary to go into barbarous countries—Lapland, or
the extreme north of Norway; and I have generally loved too
much the comforts of life to make any greater sacrifices than
such as are made in this expedition. I have heard the river at
Drontheim boasted of as an excellent salmon river,—and I know
two worthy anglers who have tried it; but I do not think they
took more fish in a day than I have sometimes taken in Scotland
and Ireland. All the Norwegian rivers, that I tried, (and they
were all in the south of Norway,) contained salmon. I fished in
the Glommen, one of the largest rivers in Europe; in the
Mandals, which appeared to me the best fitted for taking
salmon; the Avendal and the Torrisdale;—but, though I saw
salmon rise in all these rivers, I never took any fish larger than
a sea trout; of these I always took many—and even in the *fiords*,
or small inland salt-water bays; but I think never any one more
than a pound. It is true, I was in Norway in the beginning of
July, and in exceedingly bright weather, and when there was no
night; for even at twelve o'clock the sky was so bright, that I read
the smallest print in the columns of a newspaper. I was in
Sweden later—in August: I fished in the magnificent Gotha,
below that grand fall Trolhetta, which to see is worth a voyage
from England; but I never raised there any fish worth taking: yet
a gentleman from Gothenburg told me he had formerly taken
large trout there. I took, in this noble stream, a little trout about
as long as my hand; and the only fish I got to eat at Trolhetta was
bream. The Falkenstein, a darker water, very like a second-rate
Scotch river—say the Don—abounds in salmon; and there I had
a very good day's fishing. I took six fish, which gave me great
sport; they were grilses, under 6 lbs.; but I lost a salmon, which

I think was above 10 lbs. This river I conceive must be, generally, excellent; it is not covered with saw-mills, like the Norwegian rivers in general; its colour is good, and it is not so clear as most of the rivers of the south of Norway.

Phys.—Do you think the saw-mills hurt the fishing?

Hal.—I do not doubt it. The immense quantity of sawdust which floats in the water, and which forms almost hills along the banks, must be poisonous to the fish, by sometimes choaking their gills and interfering with their respiration. I have never fished for salmon in Germany. The Elbe and the Weser, when I have seen them, were too foul for fly fishing; and in the Rhine, in Switzerland, and its tributary streams, I have never seen a salmon rise. I once hooked a fish, under the fall at Schaffausen, which in my youthful ardour I thought was a salmon, but it turned out to be an immense chub—a villanous and provoking substitute. And our islands, as far as I know, may claim the superiority over all other lands for this species of amusement. In England it is, however, a little difficult to get a day's salmon fishing. The best river I know of is the Derwent, that flows from the beautiful Lake of Keswick; and I caught once, in October, a very large salmon there, and raised another; but it is only late in the autumn that there is any chance of sport there, though I have heard the spring salmon fishing boasted of. At Whitwell, in the Hadder, I have heard of salmon and sea trout being taken—but I have never fished in that river. The late Lord Bolinbroke caught many salmon at Christchurch; but a fish a week is as much as can be expected in that beautiful, but scantily stocked, river. Small salmon and sea trout, or *sewens*, as they are called in the country, may be caught, after the autumnal floods, I believe, in most of the considerable Welsh, Devonshire, and Cornish streams; but I have fished in many of them without success. The Conway I may except: this river, in the end of October, will sometimes, after a great flood, furnish a good day's sport,—and if the net fishers could be set aside, several day's sport. I have known two salmon, one above 20 lbs., taken here in a day; and I have taken myself fine sea trout, or *sewens*,—which, in an autumnal flood in Wales, are found in most of the streams near the sea.

Poiet.—I have heard a Northumberland man boast of the rivers of that county, as affording good salmon fishing.

Hal.—I have no doubt that salmon are sometimes caught in the Tyne, the Coquet, and the Till; but, in the present state of these rivers, this is a rare occurrence. I was once, for a week, on a good run of the North Tyne; I fished sometimes, but I never saw a salmon rise; and the only place in this river where, from my own knowledge, I can assert salmon have been caught with the artificial fly, was at Mounsey, very high up the river. There, in 1820, two grilses were caught, in the end of August. I have recorded this as a sort of historical occurrence; and I dare say most of the counties of England in which there are salmon rivers, would, upon a minute inquiry, furnish such instances, if they contained salmon fishers. Yorkshire, Devonshire, and Cornwall, with the sea on both sides, ought to furnish a greater number.

Phys.—Give us some little notice of the Scotch and Irish rivers.

Hal.—I fear I shall tire you by attempting any details on this subject, for they are so many, that I ought to take a map in my hands; but I will say a few words on those in which I have had good sport. First, the Tweed:—of this, as you will understand from what I mentioned before, I fear I must now say *"fuit."* Yet still, for spring salmon fishing, it must be a good river. The last great sport I had in that river was in 1817, in the beginning of April. I caught, in two or three hours, at Merton, above four or five large salmon, and as many in the evening at Kelso—and one of them 25 lbs. But this kind of fishing cannot be compared to the summer fishing: the fish play with much less energy, and in general are in bad season; and the fly used for fishing is almost like a bird—four or five times larger than the summer fly, and the coarsest tackle may be employed. I have heard that Lord Home has sometimes taken thirty fish in a day, in spring fishing. About, and above, Melrose, I have taken, in a morning in July, two or three grilses; and in September the same number: and I have known eighteen taken earlier, by an excellent salmon fisher, at Merton; and the late Lord Somerville often took six or seven fish in a day's angling. The same *"fuit,"* I must apply to most of the Scotch rivers. Of the Tay I have already spoken. The Dee I have never caught salmon in, though I have fished in two parts of it, but in bad seasons. In the Don I have seen salmon rise, and hooked one, but never killed a fish. In the Spey I enjoyed one of the best day's sport (perhaps the very best) I ever had in my life: it was in the beginning of September, in close time; the water was low, and as net fishing had been given over for some days, the lower parts were full of fish. By a privilege, which I owe to the late Duke of Gordon, I fished at this forbidden time, and hooked twelve or thirteen fish in one day. One was above 30 lbs. who broke me by the derangement of my reel. I landed seven or eight,—one above 20 lbs. which gave me great play in the rapids above the bridge. I returned to the same spot in 1813, the year after; the river was in excellent order, and it was the same time of the year, but just after a flood,—I caught nothing; the fish had all run up the river; the pools, where I had had such sport the year before, were empty. I have fished there since, with a like result,—but this was before the 12th of August, the close day. In the Sutherland and Caithness rivers, many salmon, I have no doubt, may still be caught. The Brora, in 1813 and 1814, was an admirable river; I have often rode from the mansion of the princely and hospitable lord and lady of that county, after breakfast, and returned at two or three o'clock, having taken from three to eight salmon—several times eight. There were five pools below the wears of the Brora, which always contained fish; and one pool, which from its size was almost inexhaustible, at the top of which I have taken three or four salmon the same day. Another pool, nearer the sea, was almost equal to it; and at that time I should have placed the Brora above the Ewe for certainty of sport. When I fished there last, in 1817, the case was altered, and I caught only two or three fish in those places where I had six years before been so successful. In the Helmsdale there are some good pools, and I have caught fine fish there when the river has been high. I have fished in the river at Thurso, but without success—it was always foul when I made my essay. I have heard of a good salmon river in Lord Reay's country, the Laxford; its name, of Norwegian origin, would seem to be characteristic.* Along the coast of Scotland, most of the streams, if taken at the right time, afford sport. The Ness, at Inverness, and the Arne and Lochy, I have fished in, but without success. I may say the same of the Ayr, and of the rivers which empty themselves into the Solway Frith. A little preserved stream, at Ardgowan, was formerly excellent, after a flood in September, for sea trout, and later for salmon: I have had good sport there, and some of my friends have had better.

In Ireland there are some excellent rivers; and what you will hardly believe possible, comparing the characters of the two nations, some of them are taken better care of than the Scotch rivers; which arises a good deal from the influence of the Catholic priests, when they are concerned in the interests of the proprietors, or the Catholic peasantry. I should place the Erne, at Ballyshannon, as now the first river, for salmon fishing from the banks with a rod, in the British dominions; and the excellent proprietor of it, Dr. Thiel, is liberal and courteous to all gentlemen fly fishers. The Moy, at Ballina, is likewise an admirable salmon river; and sport, I believe, may almost always be secured there in every state of the waters; but the best fishing can only be commanded by the use of a boat. I have taken in the Erne two

---

*Lax is the Teutonic word for salmon.

or three large salmon in the morning; and in the Moy, three or four grilses, or, as they are called in Ireland, *grauls*; and this was in a very bad season for salmon fishing. The Bann, near Coleraine, abounds in salmon: but except in close time, when it is unlawful to fish there, there are few good casts in this river. In the Bush, a small river about seven miles to the east of the Bann, there is admirable salmon fishing always after great floods; but in fine and dry weather there is little use in trying this river. I have hooked twenty fish in a day, after the first August floods, in this river; and, should sport fail, the celebrated Giant's Causeway is within a mile of its mouth, and offers to the lovers of natural beauty, or of geological research, almost inexhaustible sources of interest. The Blackwater, at Lismore, is a very good salmon river: and the Shannon, above Limerick and at Castle Connel, whenever the water is tolerably high, offers many good casts to the fly fisher; but they can only be commanded by boats. But there is no considerable river along the northern or western coast,— with the exception of the Avoca, which has been spoiled by the copper mines,—that does not afford salmon, and that does not, if taken at the proper time, offer sport to the salmon fisher.—But it is time for us to return to our inn.

THE INN.

Poiet.—Should it be a fine day, to-morrow, I think we shall have good sport: the high tide will bring up fish, and the rain and wind of yesterday will have enlarged the river.

Hal.—To-morrow we must not fish: it is the Lord's day, and a day of rest. It ought likewise to be a day of worship and thanksgiving to the great cause of all the benefits and blessings we enjoy in this life, for which we can never sufficiently express our gratitude.

Poiet.—I cannot see what harm there can be in pursuing an

amusement on a Sunday, which you yourself have called innocent, and which is apostolic: nor do I know a more appropriate way of returning thanks to the Almighty Cause of all being, than in examining and wondering at his works in that great temple of nature, whose canopy is the sky; and where all the beings and elements around us are as it were proclaiming the power and wisdom of Deity.

Hal.—I cannot see how the exercise of fishing can add to your devotional feelings; but independent of this, you employ a servant to carry your net and gaff, and he, at least, has a right to rest on this one day. But even if you could perfectly satisfy yourself as to the abstracted correctness of the practice, the habits of the country in which we now are, form an insurmountable obstacle to the pursuit of the amusement: by indulging in it, you would excite the indignation of the Highland peasants, and might perhaps expiate the offence by a compulsory ablution in the river.

Poiet.—I give up the point: I make it a rule never to shock the prejudices of any person, even when they appear to me ridiculous; and I shall still less do so in a case where your authority is against me; and I have no taste for undergoing persecution, when the cause is a better one. I now remember that I have often heard of the extreme severity with which the sabbath discipline is kept in Scotland. Can you give us the reason of this?

Hal.—I am not sufficiently read in the Church History of Scotland to give the cause historically; but I think it can hardly be doubted that it is connected with the intense feelings of the early Convenanters, and their hatred with respect to all the forms and institutes of the Church of Rome, the ritual of which makes the Sunday more a day of innocent recreation, than severe discipline.

Phys.—Yet the disciples of Calvin, at Geneva, who, I suppose, must have hated the pope as much as their brethren of Scotland, do not so rigidly observe the Sunday; and I remember having been invited by a very religious and respectable Genevese to a shooting party on that day.

Hal.—I think climate and the imitative nature of man modify this cause abroad. Geneva is a little state in a brighter climate than Scotland, almost surrounded by Catholics, and the habits of the French and Savoyards must influence the people. The Scotch with more severity and simplicity of manners, have no such examples of bad neighbours, for the people of the north of England keep the Sunday much in the same way.

Poiet.—Nay, Halieus, call them not bad neighbours; recollect my creed, and respect at least, what, if error, was the error of the Christian world for 1000 years. The rigid observance of the seventh day appears to me rather a part of the Mosaic, than of the Christian dispensation. The Protestants of this country consider the Catholics bigots, because they enjoin to themselves, and perform certain penances for their sins; and surely the Catholics may see a little more like that spirit in the interference of the Scotch in innocent amusements, on a day celebrated as a festive day, that on which our Saviour rose into immortal life, and secured the everlasting hopes of the Christian. I see no reason why this day should not be celebrated with singing, dancing, and triumphal processions, and all innocent signs of gladness and joy. I see no reason why it should be given up to severe and solitary prayers, or to solemn and dull walks; or why, as in Scotland, whistling even should be considered as a crime on Sunday, and humming a tune, however sacred, out of doors, as a reason for violent anger and persecution.

Orn.—I agree with Poietes, in his views of the subject. I have suffered from the peculiar habits of the Scotch Church, and therefore may complain. Once in the north of Ireland, when a very young man, I ventured after the time of Divine Service, to put together my rods, as I had been used to do in the Catholic districts of Ireland, and fish for white trout in the river at Rathmelton, in pure innocence of heart, unconscious of wrong, when I found a crowd collect round me—at first I thought from mere curiosity, but I soon discovered I was mistaken; anger was their motive and vengeance their object. A man soon came up exceedingly drunk, and began to abuse me by various indecent terms: such as a Sabbath breaking papist, &c. It was in vain I assured him I was no papist, and no intentional Sabbath breaker; he seized my rod and carried it off with imprecations; and it was only with great difficulty, and by rousing by my eloquence some women who were present, and who thought I was an ill-used stranger, that I recovered my property. Another time I was walking on Arthur's Seat, with some of the most distinguished professors of Edinburgh attached to the geological opinions of the late Dr. Hutton, a discussion took place upon the phenomena presented by the rocks under our feet, and to exemplify a principle, Professor Playfair broke some stones, in which I assisted the venerable and amiable philosopher. We had hardly examined the fragments, when a man from a crowd, who had been assisting at a field preaching, came up to us and warned us off, saying, "Ye think ye are only stane breakers; but I ken ye are Sabbath breakers, and ye deserve to be staned with your ain stanes!"

Hal.—Zeal of every kind is sometimes troublesome, yet I generally suspect the persons who are very tolerant of scepticism. Those who firmly believe that a particular plan of conduct is essential to the eternal welfare of man, may be pardoned if they show even *anger*, if this conduct is not pursued. The severe observance of the Sabbath is connected with the vital creed of these rigid presbyterians; it is not therefore extraordinary that they should enforce it even with a perseverance that goes beyond the bounds of good manners and courtesy. They may quote the example of our Saviour, who expelled the traders from the temple even by violence.

Phys.—I envy no quality of the mind or intellect in others; not genius, power, wit, or fancy: but if I could choose what would be most delightful, and I believe most useful to me, I should prefer a firm religious belief to every other blessing; for it makes life a discipline of goodness—creates new hopes, when all earthly hopes vanish; and throws over the decay, the destruction of existence, the most gorgeous of all lights; awakens life even in death, and from corruption and decay calls up beauty and divinity: makes an instrument of torture and of shame the ladder of ascent to paradise; and far above all combinations of earthly hopes, calls up the most delightful visions of palms and amaranths, the gardens of the blest, the security of everlasting joys, where the sensualist and the sceptic view only gloom, decay, annihilation and despair!

Hooked Foul

William Senior

(from "Waterside Sketches," 1875)

I T WAS AN unmistakably blank day yonder for the entire company, as somehow it always happens to be when you expect unusual luck, and have every reason for believing it will fall to your lot.

"Come early," the young Squire wrote; "the stream is alive with trout, the c'rect fly is on, and there's something prime in the cellar, to say nothing of duck and green peas at the back of the stables. Further, the wife says you are to come, and that should settle it; I suppose you had better bring B——, though he scarcely knows a fish from a fiddle, and must be handed over to the women-folk."

We accordingly went, and B——, I must say, had the laugh of us. A bitter east wind set in within an hour of our arrival at the Squire's place, and early in the afternoon we gave up angling, nor entertained so much as a forlorn hope of evening chances. We stuck the rods into the lawn, and formed ourselves into a select committee to inquire into the uses of hock and seltzer. The young Squire also told us a little story.

"Some prefer one method and some another," he said to me; "but for real honest sport-yielding pike-fishing, depend upon it there is nothing like a neat spinning-flight.

"Come, come; don't shrug your shoulders!" he observed to the prosaic B——, who had resigned himself to the infliction without concealing his feelings.

"I know too well how terrible a bore an angler is to an unsympathetic town man like you, who have not a soul above a brief-bag, and who would not know a gudgeon from a barbel. Bless you! I should disdain to waste a delicious story of rises, runs, bites, strikes, and gaffings, upon the like of you. *My* pearls are reserved for those who will not turn about and rend me. Still, as you are in my den, and as you have been kind enough to notice my rod-rack, and the rest of my fishing gear yonder—which you may notice is in apple-pie order, ready for immediate use—I will trouble you to listen to one reason of my partiality for the spinning-flight.

"Let me see, it was—Ah! never mind when it happened. It was not this year, nor last, nor the year before that. Enough that I begin with a certain fresh autumn morning. The crunch of the dogcart wheels on the gravel beneath my bed-room window reminded me that I had overslept myself, and that there would be some one outside, cooling his heels, unless he was much altered since I had seen him last, in anything but a Christian frame of mind. My oversleeping was indulged in at the cost of considerable discomfort, inasmuch as when we had sped merrily over a couple of the ten miles before us, I discovered that neither gaff-hook nor landing net had been packed up.

"You call that a trifle do you? A trifle! But, of course, it is useless to argue with *you*. Out of such trifles great what-is-it's spring, if your favourite poet is to be believed.

"Garstanger Park is one of the most beautiful because one of the best timbered in the country. Had that October day on Viscount Garstanger's lake been a blank as to fish, I should have deemed the seventy-mile trip from town, the early rising on a raw morning, and the journey across country more than compensated for by the russet glory of the autumn-tinted woods, the exquisite proportions of the shrubberies, the artistic arrangement of lawn and garden, the wide prospects caught through the beeches on the knolls, the avenues of patriarch trees, the change of landscape at every curve of the path, and the keen clear atmosphere which you gulped rather than breathed.

"This kind of scenery puts you into good humour, and screws up any slack strings of poetry or sentiment there may be in you. It never took me so long before to put my rod together, partly because of the beautiful leaf-tints reflected in the lake, but chiefly because, making ready to enter one of the two punts which belonged to the boat-house, I saw a young lady. She might be handsome or she might not; that I could not determine until she changed her position. It was her compact, flexible figure, and peculiar costume, that first attracted my notice. I was conscious, too, of a freedom of attitude that under any circumstances would have been displeasing. She stood some distance off, her back towards me, with one foot on the stern-board of the punt, and was postured like an athlete, as, turning slightly away from the lake, with rod over her shoulder, she winched up the loosened coils of a fishing-line.

"The boobiest of fellows lay in the bottom of the punt, reading one of Dumas' novels—a shilling edition. He never offered to assist his companion. I would have said 'fair' companion, according to the orthodox method, but I had not, so far, discovered whether she was fair or dark. The foot, so firmly planted on the punt, was the small trim foot which, as a rule, belongs to dark beauties; the hair, though dark, was not black, and it was free from any artificial monstrosity. Dress? I fear you have me there: never was there a worse describer of millinery than your humble servant. To put it roughly, I should say the chief article of that costume was a well-built, shooting-jacket of grey cloth. It was of a perfectly original design, and impressed you as being fitted up with an infinity of pockets and enclosing with sensible tightness a charming, round, lithe figure. I forget the skirts, but they were there.

"It was no use coughing or making a violent noise with the oars strapped to our own punt: she would not look round, or satisfy my curiosity in any degree. The boobiest of fellows lazily looked across, lazily screwed his glass into his eye, and lazily made an observation to his companion, who, to do her justice, appeared not to take the slightest notice of him.

"Who were they? What were they? Which was the angler? I had, in former times, seen ladies fishing for the lively perch, ay, and whipping a dainty little stream with a dainty little fly-rod for dainty little trout, but the boldest of the lady anglers whom it had been my pleasure to know had certainly drawn a line at the 'mighty luce.'

"Doubtless this was a good-natured damsel, encouraging that boobiest of fellows in his abominable idleness, by arranging his tackle for him. He had kindled a cigar by the time she had finished the wenching-up process, but he was in no hurry to move from his lair. He allowed her to deposit the rod in the punt, to step aboard without assistance, and, by all that was unworthy! to cast off the chain.

"A nut-brown maid, she at last proved to be, and a very business-like maid, too, with eyes for nothing but the punt and the fishing materials. Briskly seating himself on the thwart, she took the oars in her gloved hands, and pulled out to the centre of the lake, the strokes regular, strong, and determined. Full well I could appreciate her skill, for a pretty figure my companion cut, in his ignorance of the management of our flat-bottomed craft.

"Staring, and speechlessness, and wonderment did not aid one, as you may suppose. There happened to be no keepers about; the constant breech-loader reports in the distant plantations indicated their whereabouts with sufficient plainness. So, with curiosity unsatisfied, and much more absorbed and reluctant than is my wont with a sheet of well-preserved water, ruffled by a westerly breeze, at my will, I imitated the nut-brown maid, and pushed off, showing how much I was thinking of her by proceeding in a contrary direction to what she had taken, and inwardly resolving to sneak round about her neighbourhood before the day was over.

"Sport was, for a time, indifferent; that is to say, indifferent for Garstanger Park. A few three-pounders were returned to the water, an eight-pounder got away, and as luncheon-time drew nigh, the bag contained only half a dozen fair fish. The fish, you see, so far as I was concerned, were finding an unknown friend in the nut-brown maid.

"The time had arrived when the mystery must be cleared up. My companion paddled me slowly to the upper end of the lake, I making a pretence of spinning the water as we progressed. A sudden bend of the shore gave us sight of the other punt. The boobiest of fellows, still reclined at his ease, and my nut-brown maid stood confessed, a veritable pike-mistress.

"What a figure, too, as she lightly swept the bamboo spinning-rod over her left shoulder, and brought it back again for the cast! It was the freest and most graceful I ever witnessed. The bait fell with a minimum of splash into the water, not an inch less than twenty yards the lee side of the punt, and it was spun home at a speed and depth that bespoke the experienced artist.

"You may laugh, my friend, but do you not speak of a singer, or dancer, or actor as an 'artiste'? Therefore, my signification of the term, your ribald jeer notwithstanding, is quite justifiable. The miserable jester who chuckles over the stale old senseless saying, 'A fool at one end and a worm at the other,' will not, perhaps, understand me, but that large and increasing class of anglers, who are the product of nineteenth century refinement—

yes, I do not withdraw the assertion—these will know how to admire my nymph of the rod. For the space of half an hour she made superb leisurely casts, taking the punt as a centre from which to make the radiations, beginning with a dozen yards, and regularly increasing the distance, until the maximum of twenty yards was reached.

"It was some comfort that she just now caught no fish. I felt so much the less ashamed of myself. A very good angler, according to the estimate of my friends, I confess I here found my master—my lady superior. Never an entanglement, never a false throw, never any trouble with rings or reel, never the faintest appearance of flurry was she guilty of. A toxophilite, of the feminine gender, in the act of discharging an arrow from the bow, a huntress 'lifting' her horse over a stiff fence, a girl bending to the oars on a silver stream, are fit subjects for any painter, but not worthy of comparison with my Angling Divinity of Garstanger Park.

"She answered the purpose, as it were, of a whirlpool to our boat; it began to draw insensibly into the vortex. We approached nearer and nearer. The boobiest of fellows maintained his masterly inactivity; turning over page after page of his buff-covered book, and allowing the nut-brown maid—when, having thoroughly fished her circle, she paddled to new ground—to handle the oars without a scrap of assistance from his long, white, useless fingers.

"Aha! she had him at last—not the supine novel-reader—but a fish! For this I had been waiting. A lady who could spin for pike in this most mistressly style, I had for the first time beheld; but what would she do with it when the critical moment arrived? It was, as I might have known, of a piece with the rest. She handled the fresh-water shark with consummate skill: it ought to have been a pleasure to any well-regulated pike to be so scientifically dealt with. I could tell by the quick jerk of the rod that the deluded fish was a good one, and the sharp, prompt little twist of the lady's wrist was proof positive that the triangles had been well struck into him.

"Sensible woman! Yet it was so like her sex to permit the captive to bolt about wherever he listed, confident that he was secured, and not objecting to enjoy his hopeless struggles before treating him to the *coup de grâce*. The pike seemed particularly uncomfortable, and the lady smiled a smile of calm and virtuous content as he gave evidence of his perturbed state of mind. He kept well down into the deep, describing, as the line indicated, a series of strange mathematical figures.

"The moment the angleress tightened on him, he leaped, shining like gold, a foot out of the water!—bringing another quiet smile into her placid face when he fell back. Her theory was to give her enemy plenty of line—(and let me tell you in an 'aside,' there are worse notions than that for other pursuits than pike-fishing). The line was hauled in and neatly deposited in circles on the floor of the punt; and when, at length, the broad yellow side of the conquered one appeared on the surface at the exact spot necessary for successful bagging, the lady, with a slight flush of cheek and flash of eye, inserted the gaff under his gaping gill, and lifted him deftly over the gunwhale.

"A cheery bell-metal laugh broke the silence. The game— objecting, maybe to the morality of Mons. Dumas—flapped and floundered at the young gentleman in the stern, causing him to splutter, to drop 'Beau Tancrede,' and jump so ludicrously, that the nut-brown maid indulged in several merry peals.

"The fish could not frighten *her*: to be sure, petticoats are a protection to a lady in more ways than one. But she made no effort to get out of his way when he descended against her skirts; on the contrary, she waited her opportunity—thrust her fore-finger and thumb into the eye-sockets, honouring the fish by the act; and, unhooking the gimp to which the hooks were attached from the tracing-swivel, dropped his pikeship, with due regard to decency and preservation, into a large rush basket that, I suspect, had often done similar duty aforetime.

"The lady was uncommonly methodical, I noticed. In precisely the proper place for handiness, there was a tin case, stored with spinning tackle already baited, leaving her nothing to do at each capture but attach the loop to the swivel. This saved her the unpleasant necessity of meddling with the small dead fish employed as bait, and the much more unpleasant necessity of gouging the murderous triangles out of the pike's formidable jaws—labour I fain hoped fell to the share of some male relative at home.

"A complimentary sentence trembled at the tip of my tongue, but her appearance furnished me no encouragement to utter it. Besides, there was no time, since before resuming operations she gave her punt the benefit of half a dozen vigorous strokes of the oars, by which movement the few paces which had separated us were quadrupled; and, as you must confess, it would have been simply ridiculous to make a speaking trumpet of your hand, and bawl at the top of your voice—

" 'Allow me, madam,' or 'dear madam,' as the case might be, 'to congratulate you upon the clever manner in which you killed that fish.'

"Absurd, would it not?

"My amateur boatman furthermore began to taunt me upon my idleness, my non-success, my moon-struck behaviour. To taunt was to rouse. I (metaphorically) girded up my loins, and bade the fish to come on, that I might smite them hip and thigh with great slaughter. I invoked the aid of the late Izaak Walton, Esq., and hummed a bar or two of 'Doughty Deeds.' I so manœuvred the punt that the nut-brown unknown should have me in view, to contrast my manly proportions, if haply she looked our way, with the lanky, flax-headed, insipid dawdler, whose general purpose in the economy of Nature, and particular business in that punt, were unsolved conundrums to me just then.

"Swish! whistle! splash! spin, and at it I went. Heigho! What was this? A tree-trunk submerged? Bravo! It was one of the mighty ones of the lake. Feeling the hooks he went off, pulling like a barge. Twenty, forty, fifty, a hundred yards of line were run straight off the reel, without so much as a 'By your leave.' It was that peculiar run by which a substantial prize is always known, be it salmon, trout, or pike; none of your tug-tugs, dart-darts, here-there-and-everywhere up-and-down trifling, but a steady, heavy, sullen travelling away from the base of assault. The stricken fish headed straight for the bow of the other punt. My companion, taking his commands from me, backed water, and we followed. My lady had paused in her work, and stood, rod in hand, with a dark green belt of firs as a distant background, and the ruddy sun striking slantwise upon her, a model for a statue. She forgot the formal reserve of the lady, in the enthusiasm of the sportswoman.

" 'You have a fine fish there!' she ejaculated, quite as delighted as if it were her luck, and not mine.

" 'Indeed, yes,' I replied, beginning to strain upon the object in question; 'but unfortunately I have no gaff.'

" 'Oh, take mine. Do you think I can help you?' she said.

"The fish was at that moment making a fresh spurt, and it behoved me to be wary; but be the consequences what they might, I was bound to look into her face, and express my thanks with eye as well as lip. Well, never mind. There are obvious reasons why it would be better to say no more upon this part of the proceeding.

"As to the pike, there he is, stuffed and still in the lower case. Judge for yourself the fun we—I advisedly deem it a partnership matter—had before we made his personal acquaintance. We brought the punts close together, and before I knew her intentions, my newly made friend had stepped nimbly into my boat and was at my side, quietly biding the time to strike. I wished to transfer the rod to her, and take the gaffing upon myself; she pleaded hard to have the honour, and I vow that if she had pleaded to gaff me, in lieu of the fish, so charmingly did she plead, I would have interposed no objection.

"Half an hour fully were we privileged to stand side by side waiting for the end. To tell you the whole truth, I delayed the consummation till for very shame I had to present the butt of the rod to the fish; and even that would not have been ventured upon, but for a hint from the lady that the fish's extremity was my opportunity. Thereupon I closed with him, brought him to reaching distance, and enjoyed the felicity of beholding the sharp gaff unerringly employed, and the monster hauled, viciously plunging, out of his native element.

"'Ha! ha! hooked foul!' quoth the nut-brown maid, with a little dance of astonishment. It was even so; the fish was, as anglers put it, 'hooked foul.'

"Then up and spake the being in the other boat, who had been, I am well assured, forgotten by the entire company, while a nobler creature, albeit of the finny order, had engaged our attention. Probably he had been watching us out of the corner of his fishy-looking eye, though now he pretended languidly to put aside his book for the first time.

"'Did I underthtand, Tharah, that you thaid "Hooked foul?"' he drawled.

"She turned a trifle sharply towards him, as if recalled by the question into another and less pleasant state of being; so at least I flattered myself.

"'I don't know what you understood, Frank, but that is what I said. It may not be grammar, but it is a perfectly well-known technical phrase. Yes; I said "hooked foul,"' she boldly answered.

"'And will you tell me, Tharah, what ith "hooked foul?"'

"'Hooked foul, Frank,' she stated, without looking at her questioner, 'means "hooked foul." That is to say you are trying to hook something in one way, fail to do so, but hook it in another not quite so straightforward. You don't get it by hook but by crook.'

"This being not a very lucid explanation, I was emboldened to take up the parable. Said I, with an air of *nonchalant* wisdom—

" 'You see, this fish, if caught in the orthodox way, would have snapped at the baited hooks, and enclosed them with his jaws. He probably went so far as the snap, and missed the bait, but the revolving hooks caught him on the shoulder, as you observe, and here he is. The great point, after all, is that he is hooked somehow.'

" 'It's not a pleasant thing to be hooked foul, Frank,' observed the young lady who had been addressed as Sarah.

" 'P'wapth not, Tharah,' he rejoined, with a greenish tinge in his eye; 'but, ath you thay, the great point ith that your fith ith hooked thomehow.'

"What possessed me, unless the thing called Fate, to take part in a dialogue which had most evidently assumed a meaning personal to the speakers, I know not, but I must needs fix my eye upon the young man, and observe—

" 'Well, that depends on circumstances, you know. A fish hooked foul, you should remember, has a very good chance of shaking itself free.'

"This was but a random shot, but, like many another bow at a venture, it went home. The lisper changed to the colour of tallow, while the nut-brown maid's face was suddenly warmed from within by a crimson flush. However, the mischief was done, and we separated in constraint. The evening drew on apace, and at dusk we found ourselves together again at the lodge, weighing the prize.

"It was sunset. The woods were crowned with the golden glow of the west; the lady stood in the reflection, its queen. The boobiest of fellows sulked at the garden gate, we could afford to dispense with his company.

"It is best to be particular: that fish weighed twenty-nine pounds five ounces and one quarter, by the keeper's steel-yard.

" 'A very fine fish, sir. Good night,' the lady said.

" 'Yes, very fine; good night,' I answered, doffing my deer-stalker, of course; the lout at the gate scowling covertly the while.

"And was that all? What more would you wish? Simply a casual meeting, and an abrupt parting. What more would you have?

"Let me detain you another moment. There was something else. The nut-brown maid was a clergyman's daughter, Miss Graham by name. So much I found out by directly questioning the keeper. I drove out of Garstanger Park, sincerely wishing it had been my fortune to know more of her, debating whether the phase of strong-mindedness I had seen was a desirable symptom for a young lady and a clergyman's daughter, and altogether a little—the smallest bit—in love with her.

"A month or two later came that German episode of mine, and the nut-brown maid, though not absolutely forgotten, was not a frequent or troublesome visitor at Memory's door. She used to knock at it in the quiet hours sometimes, and I would always open it, and admit and keep her there as long as possible. But I can conscientiously aver she was merely as the refrain of a dreamy melody floating from a distance. I was destined to be somewhat rudely reminded of her and hers on my return to England.

"Dozing in the big easy chair of my sitting-room one twilight, the tableau I described at the keeper's lodge came to me in a vision, in which the young man skulking at the gate seemed to change into the pike hanging from the steel-yard. It may seem very like a storyteller's trick to say it, but I was awakened by a knocking at my door, and the young man himself pushed past the servant, and stalked into the room.

" 'Do you thee thith whip?' he said, flourishing a heavy-thonged hunting weapon.

" 'Thit down, young man,' I answered, mockingly, but mighty wrathful, you may be certain, at the outrage, the meaning of which was evident.

" 'Do you thee thith whip?' he shrieked, moving towards me, who had not yet risen from my dozing posture.

"It was an unfortunate occurrence. A week within a day elapsed before he could be removed into the country, and it cost me a lot of money for doctoring him, to say nothing of that possible verdict of 'manslaughter,' which haunted me morning, noon, and night. I must acknowledge, as he did afterwards, that the thrashing did him good; it made him penitent, and during the penitence a fit of communicativeness supervened.

"It appeared (as learned counsel say to juries) that he was a Graham too, a cousin of the young lady with the nut-brown face, and—but you already guess it—engaged to her almost from childhood, in accordance with the fond parents' desires. That they cordially hated each other, both the demands of truth and the requirements of fiction compel me to declare. Only, Harold Graham was not prepared to relinquish the hard cash which was to be his when he married his Cousin Sarah. The day at Garstanger Park was a crisis in their career. Mr. Graham thought fit, after the tableau at the lodge, to remonstrate with his affianced; first, for using the expression 'Hooked foul,' and next, for being what he impertinently characterised unwomanly in her amusements. While my friend and I were rattling through the lanes in happy content, that youthful couple were having, in vulgar parlance, quite a respectable row. Somehow I, the unknown stranger, was introduced into the quarrel, and Mademoiselle indiscreetly made comparisons.

" 'The fact is,' she said, 'I don't forget that that young gentleman so sensibly remarked: "A fish hooked foul *has a very good chance of shaking itself free."* '

"From that moment Sarah Graham devoted herself to the task of shaking herself free: she considered she was 'hooked foul.' From that moment Harold Graham gave himself up to revenge. There was one slight difficulty to be overcome, viz, his ignorance of my name, address, and station. It took him months to get over it. He spent a little fortune, they say, in journeys to London, hoping to meet me by accident. Finally he sought Lord Garstanger, and pretending I had lent him a flask, or winch, or cigar-case, or something which he wished to return, found out my where-abouts. He had, in some inconceivable manner, stumbled upon the notion that I was in communication with his cousin, and that I was supplanting him. She herself rather encouraged the idea to spite him, and by-and-by his hatred of me became a mania.

"Shall I detail you much longer? No. I have placed the ends of the skein in your hands: it is for you to gather them up. Harold Graham was a poor weak creature; he was never known to display energy before the interval between our day at Garstanger Park and the athletic exercise he and I took in my sitting-room, and since then he has subsided into a sort of amateur idiocy.

"And now you ask me whether I do not consider Sarah Graham a very objectionable young woman? In confidence, I assure you I do not. I take your vehement affirmation of a contrary opinion as a sign of profound insight into human character, my young friend. Don't be angry with me, if I suggest we should agree to differ.

"But here's the good wife with the bairns to say 'good even!' Let us ask her to decide between us.

"Does she know the story?

"Pretty well, I believe! Between ourselves, old fellow, she is the nut-brown maid!"

Xiphias Gladius
418 Pounds

Zane Grey

IT TOOK FIVE hours and more of heartbreaking work to catch my 418-pound broadbill swordfish and we did not back up the boat on him when he came threshing to the surface and jab three or four gaffs in him.

I want to tell the exact truth about the taking of this 418-pound broadbill, and see if my readers will not share my idea of the finest and squarest and most thrilling method of catching this magnificent fish.

Much as I have written about old *Xiphias gladius* during the last two years, none of it has gone into print. Broadbill angling is perilously in danger of being ruined, if it is not already ruined. But for the present I must leave such sad truths as that to be told by other anglers.

Nevertheless, as it has long been my ambition and intention to write a narrative and scientific book on *Xiphias gladius*, I want to state that I am doing so, and I mean to tell the truth and to be as accurate as a naturalist-sportsman can be. No book of any kind, fiction or adventure or biology, could make much of a bid for permanence if it did not tell the truth. How can a writer best serve his audience?

Years ago I wrote that to catch fish was not all of fishing. I can say now that the capture of a fish, thrilling and boyhood-recalling as it may be, is the least of the profit which comes to me from roaming the sea. I love the grand old Pacific with its league-long swells, its silver fog banks, its vast sunlit heaving expanse, its mysterious and continuous currents, its life, its beauty and color and movement. There glooms the dark blue sea! The ocean is the mother of life, the maker of rain, the great natural force of the earth.

The beginning of the 1920 season at Avalon found me without a boatman. All the experienced boatmen were engaged for the best months. I made a deal with Captain Sid Boerstler, comparatively a newcomer to the colony. He was an expert engineer, young, strong, willing, but he had not any knowledge of swordfishing. This R. C. and I undertook to teach him. I hope it is not unbecoming to my narrative to mention here that in 1920 and 1921 Captain Sid caught the most swordfish.

He had a boat that he had helped build—a cracker box, some of his facetious rival boatmen called it—and an old automobile engine that gave out the most obnoxious and sickening odor that I ever endured. R. C. and I stood this day after day and week after week, until the ordeal passed into months. Some days it was worse, and on these days we came home sick. We were really suffering from gasoline poisoning, but did not realize that until afterward.

Captain Sid worked over this engine. He lost sleep; he tried out a good many plans; every morning he would beam at us and say: "Got the engine fixed all right. She won't stink any more. You see, the speedometer was refusing to assimilate the gas properly. Then the oil—it was dripping into the carburetor and refused the transmission. This, you see, made the pistons turn round in the cylinders—the wrong way—and so when the spark hit the oil it caught fire and burned. This made the sesquipedalian smell. But it's O.K. now."

R. C. would look skeptically at our genial and intelligent boatman and say: "Sid, you sure know all about engines."

That day the odor would strike us worse than ever. We would come back in a state of coma. Captain Sid would be distracted, and once he really admitted it was a bad smell, and then next morning he would be radiant again.

Moreover, R. C. and I never felt safe in that boat. It was good enough as ordinary motor boats go, but it was far from being invulnerable to a broadbill. We sighted eighty-six broadbills in three months, passed a bait in front of seventy-five of them, got sixteen strikes, had twelve fish hooked, and caught one—my 418 pounder.

R. C. pointed out to me how very easily a gaffed swordfish could make a surge, catch the gaff rope under the propeller, and pull out half the stern of the boat. There are many things a broadbill swordfish can do. Only the anglers who have fished for years for this species have appreciation of the peril.

R. C. and I have had three broadbills threaten to ram us, one of which had thrown the hook. We also had one break the line and circle past our stern so swiftly that we could not believe our eyes. Only the furious boil of the water attested to the speed and proximity of that swordfish. Suppose he had hit us!

Boschen, who introduced fishing for broadbills, told me often of the undoubted danger in the pursuit. Farnsworth, who is the best boatman ever deployed at Catalina, had his boat rammed by a broadbill, and no doubt he would corroborate my statements. Danielson believes the broadbill danger is little understood. Adams, who has caught five broadbills in eight years, will not fight one after dark, which is the time they get thoroughly mad.

I believe most of these heavy fish fought by anglers scarcely know they are hooked. They swim deep and slow, until the line snaps or wears out. But some of them know they are hooked. Mine certainly knew it and he did not let us forget it. To conclude on this point, R. C. and I believe that the 1920 season was not only the hardest ordeal we ever endured, but the most dangerous experience of any kind we ever had. Lassoing mountain lions, hunting the grizzly bear, and stalking the fierce tropical jaguar, former pastimes of ours, are hardly comparable to the pursuit of *Xiphias gladius*. It takes more time, patience, endurance, study, skill, nerve, and strength, not to mention money, of any game known to me through experience or reading. If it ever has been mastered, Boschen and Farnsworth are the only angler and boatman who ever accomplished the feat. Adams with his five swordfish certainly confesses he has not. I have caught two in nine years, and have seen more and hooked more than any angler since Boschen. I have made a special pursuit and study of *Xiphias gladius*, and have had a boat built—the *Gladiator*—just for that purpose. And I have only begun to appreciate the strangeness, intelligence, speed, strength, and endurance of this king of the sea.

In view of these facts, how absurd and unfair for broadbill swordfishing to be falsely represented all over the world! To be sure, most fishing is largely a matter of luck. Anybody can catch almost any kind of a fish in some unheard-of lucky way. Fluke—the anglers say! But there were never any flukes in broadbill swordfishing. The broadbill is caught either fairly or unfairly.

This great and almost unconquerable fish should have a square deal. How is he going to get a square deal when some boatmen are jealous and most anglers keen to excel? I have not the slightest idea. Is sportsmanship and conservation gaining in this country? No! The good old U.S. is going the way of crass materialism. Will there be any fish for our great-grandchildren?

No! Not unless so-called sportsmen band together for conservation.

What is it to catch a broadbill swordfish in a fair battle? To subdue him by dint of your own stalk, skill, strength, and endurance. Boschen's world record 463 pounds was hooked in the heart with two hooks. Boschen was a giant in strength. He managed somehow to hold that fish—to keep him from breaking away—for three strenuous hours, when the fish weakened from loss of blood. That was a fair battle.

Parsons's record swordfish weighed 422. At the end of five hours of terrific and persistent strain Parsons hauled that swordfish close to the boat. Danielson gaffed it. The fish tore a hole in its side and swam away. In another hour of hard work Parsons brought it to the boat again, and they held it. That was a fair battle.

Adams's 377-pound swordfish fought for hours and only gave up when Adams pulled his stomach out. It had swallowed the hook. This was a fair battle.

Danielson and I had a nine-hour battle with a swordfish and lost him. He and R. C. had a eleven-and-one-half-hour fight and lost the fish. My notebooks tell of two seven-hour struggles, three over six hours, two of five, and many under that time—all of which fish were lost. My 260-pound broadbill was hooked in the corner of the mouth and fought six hours exactly. I was sick that night and crippled for days.

There have been innumerable instances of anglers fighting and losing broadbills after long hours. It used to be a joke on the pier. These must all have been fair fights.

But a broadbill gaffed in a few minutes after being hooked— that is not to the credit of the angler. Nor is it a fluke! Nor can it be called good luck! A broadbill that swims to the surface in a half hour or so, to see what is the pesky thing bothering him—to look around—and has a harpoon, or three or four gaffs, jabbed into him is most certainly not caught honestly or fairly.

Every angler is entitled to his own peculiar way of being happy. My way—up to the present—has been to give the fish a square deal, and to try to write that home to less thoughtful anglers. I hope I may be able to stick to my ideal.

On July 19th, of this 1920 season, it chanced that R. C. did not go out with us. There ought always to be three men on a boat, one to hold the rod, the boatmen at the wheel, and the third to stand up high and watch the maneuvers of the swordfish when we circle him with a bait.

The morning was ideal. A high fog hung over the island, letting through a diffused sunlight. The sea was a rippling dark blue, with smooth heaving slicks here and there. When the slight breeze blew the odor from the exhaust into my face I was miserable; when it blew the other way I was happy.

We were roaming the sea in search of the sickle-shaped fins of *Xiphias gladius*. This is the most fascinating of all kinds of stalking game. It has to become experience before it can be appreciated. For an hour or two it is pleasant, exhilarating, beautiful. But the wide expanse, the glare of the sky, the light on the water become hard on the eyes. Darkened glasses are necessary. After three or four hours this constant straining becomes painful. After days and weeks it becomes torture. If you are fortunate in finding swordfish frequently the strain is broken and excitement dominates. Time flies! If you see one swordfish a day you are rewarded. If you miss seeing fins for a stretch of eighteen days, as happened to us once, you are to be congratulated if you stick. I do not believe one angler in a thousand can stand even a few days without seeing fish. They go to hunting tuna or Marlin swordfish, or quit. But that is not what Boschen called broadbill swordfishing.

This day we traveled fifteen miles toward San Pedro before we were out of sight of all boats. Alone on the sea! That to me is one of the allurements of this game. We ran for miles farther toward the California shore, then westward, and then farther inshore, until from my perch on the deck I could see the surf break on the rocks.

The sea changed all the time. Yet it seemed empty. No schools of bait, no splashes of fish, no wheeling shearwater ducks, no wakes of sharks, no life of any kind. But that was only a deceit of the deep. The old ocean was full of fish.

At eleven-thirty I sighted fins far ahead, all of a mile. There are times when I can see a swordfish fully two miles. But I have exceptionally keen sight and have had long experience on desert and sea. There are other times when the smooth opal surface of water deceives, blurs, magnifies. Fog, high or low, is conducive to mystery. This swordfish I saw plainly and the old thrill shot over me. I had come to know why the professional swordfish-ermen of the Atlantic loved this stalk. For it was really stalking big game of the sea.

We ran down to him and found him to be a large-finned fellow, lazily meandering around. My bait was a fresh barracuda nearly three feet long. We kept far away from the fish, and circling him, tried to drag this bait in front of him. After several attempts we succeeded. But the swordfish turned away from it. We tried again, and yet again. He would not show any interest in our barracuda. This is one of the trying circumstances in fishing for swordfish—so few of them will take a bait. One in every ten is my record! I believe they strike better in the fall. It is tantalizing to hunt all day for a swordfish, and find one—only to have him refuse your lure. At last we drove this fellow down.

About noon, some four or five miles off the California shore, Captain Sid sighted another.

I stood up, holding my rod and letting out my line, and really before we were ready or had begun to circle this fish he gave a flirt of his tail and went under in the direction of my bait. And he hit it hard enough to stagger me. That stroke of a swordfish is the most thrilling thing I know of in the angling game. He hit the barracuda with his sword. The blow made my line whip up. I waited, tense and quaking. Never at such moments could I be calm. He hit my bait again. Sid stood beside me, jabbering like a wild man. I did not know what he said. All my sense seemed strained on the wait for the line to begin slipping off my reel. Our quarry struck the bait again, not so hard, and then he swam away with it, slowly and ponderously. Everything was going fine. Then he let go of it. I waited a long time. But he did not take it again.

"There he is," said Sid, tensely, pointing.

And sure enough, our swordfish had come up some distance away.

"We'll let him rest a few moments, then try again," I said, reeling in my bait.

We drifted there, watching him mill on the surface. It occurred to me that he might jump. Broadbills do some strange things. I absolutely believe they will pitch out of the water just to get a look at a boat. I have seen many swordfish do this after we had worked around them for a while. So I got my camera and pointed it in his direction and watched him. Strange to relate, he sank low in the water, and then leaped almost entirely out. It was a spectacle to behold, and I yelled as I clicked my camera on him.

To get a fine photograph of a swordfish was better than killing him. And as his heavy round silver-and-amber body momentarily poised above the surface, my eye caught sight of a huge black remora clinging to him. Then he soused back, and came up again, to show his fins as before.

I was elated. Surely I had snapped my picture just right. Light, time, position could not have been better. And if I had gotten him at all, certainly that remora would show. And if it showed, that would be the finest photograph I had ever taken.

"Sid, did you see that big remora sticking to him?" I asked.

"See nothing! I had buck fever," replied my boatman.

Surely my eyes had not deceived me. Almost positive was I that I had secured a great photograph of this wonderful fish and one of the strange parasites of the deep. The *remora, pilot fish, sucking fish,* and *shipholder* are one and the same. They may differ in size and color, but there is little difference to the unscientific eye. This species has a flat sucker ribbed like a washboard on top of its head and with this it sticks to shark or swordfish, mostly near his gills, from which it sucks blood. I think I have proved that remoras lived inside the gills of Marlin swordfish. I have written elsewhere of this most interesting of parasites, but it will not be amiss to tell of the superstition old-time sailors have for the remora. They call it *shipholder* and claim it attaches itself to the rudder or keel of a ship and retards and sometimes actually stops it. No doubt these ancient mariners still believe this. But it is a fallacy. Powerful as the remora is when he reaches two feet in length, he cannot hold back a ship. The fact that ships have come to a stop at sea is explained by the currentless or dead water in some latitudes. And when at such times sailors have found a remora sticking to their ship they have entertained and spread the strange belief.

Native fishermen in some parts of the world use the remora to catch fish for them—that is to say, they release the remora with line tied to his tail, and let him swim around until he attaches himself to some luckless fish, when they haul him in. The remora does not let go his hold. When the sailors named him *shipholder* there was a good deal of justice, if not strict truth, in its felicitousness.

I recommend the use of the remora to anglers who do not care for the long-drawn and heroic battles with *Xiphias gladius.*

"Let's try him again," suggested Sid. "He took the bait once. Maybe he's hungry."

Assuredly I had the same hope, and meant to try again, but

this particular broadbill had been so obliging that I would have thought well of him if he had taken no more notice of us.

The fact was, however, that on the very first turn, he sailed down and hit my bait so hard I was electrified. I had not even been excited. I had really no hope. The sudden shock then was tremendous. Sid yelled, and I shook all over.

It seemed long until the next move of the swordfish, which was to swim off with the barracuda, not slowly this time! He was suspicious. The line flew off my reel. Suddenly he came out on the surface, threshing with his sword, making the water fly. He had felt the hook. Jamming on my drag, I jerked with all my might. The line straightened, came taut, then strung like a wire, and the swordfish made a tremendous lunge. He smashed the green water white and went down in foam. My tight line slipped off the reel. I had hooked that swordfish. How quickly it had happened! It seemed too good to be true.

He went down, down, down so far that I grew frightened and eased the drag. At perhaps five hundred feet he stopped his sounding and swam off up the channel. I pulled as hard as I could, which labor was absolutely futile as far as recovering line was concerned. But Captain Sid manipulated the boat so that eventually I got back half of what had been off the reel.

For perhaps an hour then the swordfish pulled and I pulled, with all the honors in his favor. When a swordfish stayed down deep the battle was nothing but labor. There was no fun, no excitement—nothing but work. That is why so many anglers have said a broadbill fight is no different from that with a shark. They should keep at the game until they hook a few that stay on long enough to get waked up.

Times does not drag in the early stages of a contest with *Xiphias*. I did not hurt myself, but I worked fairly hard. The second hour I warmed up and began to yield to the aggressiveness this species of fish rouses in an angler. I pumped and reeled steadily, encouraged by a gradual drawing of the swordfish closer to the boat. Sometimes he would make a short hard run, then slow up, enabling us to recover the line. But for the most part he stayed down. Naturally I began to feel that I was tiring him out. Perhaps I was. But not so much as he was tiring me out! The battle was unequal. The odds were in his favor. If he kept up that sort of tactics for long the hope of pulling him up, or angering him into furious exertion, was futile. As it was I began to sweat and burn, to have pains in my back. Hands and arms had long been aching.

Captain Sid had his labors also. A hundred times he had thrown that big clutch in and out. And he was always turning the boat. We worked the earlier stages of this battle without much conversation and without excitement. It was a grueling task.

Somewhere around the end of the third hour the swordfish came to the surface and began to bat around with his sword. The sweep of that long black blade was a frightful sight. He was fighting the leader. And while he was thus occupied we might have run down on him and gaffed him. But I wanted to whip him fair or not at all.

We soon made the discovery that he had caught the leader in his tail. It stuck there and placed him at a disadvantage. The wire must have cut deep into the gristle and wedged tight. For he could not dislodge it. This changed his tactics. He plunged halfway out, wagging his head, a huge bird-shaped marine creature with an enormous bill. The wave he made would have done justice to a ferryboat. Then he plunged under to come clear out, high into the air, a marvelous spectacle of white and silver and bronze, a furious fish with staring black eye, slapping gills, waving sword, and magnificent body instinct with ferocity. He splashed down and began to roll.

Here I worked my hardest. I pulled with all my might. I had him tired, and twisted. He could not get headway, or did not try to. The powerful strain I put on the line would not have amounted to much if it had not been that the leader was caught in his tail. With the hook in his mouth, as I thought then, and the end of the leader fast to his tail, I had him sort of "hog-tied," as the cowboys say. I recognized this fact and I did not spare myself in the least. And I began to drag him closer and closer toward the boat.

That strenuous period might have been long or short, I could not tell, and Captain Sid was beyond remembering anything, but the fact was I pumped and reeled the swordfish close enough to prick him with a gaff. Sid just missed getting the gaff in him. The swordfish made such a sudden and tremendous splash that I was heartily glad Sid had missed him.

Then wild as a wild horse he raced away on the surface, making the water fly like a motor boat. Sid's boat answered the helm quickly and it was fast. He got after him before he had all the line out, and we chased him to get it back. From that time the fight grew thrilling and spectacular.

We chased this swordfish all over the ocean—miles and miles, I was certain. He never sounded once. Most of the time we could see his fins, and always the wake he made. And all the time I kept a heavy strain on him. He did not run straight. He ran off at right angles, and often turned to cross ahead or behind us. It took manipulating of rod and boat to keep a tight line. Somehow, except in a few instances, we accomplished it. The leader was still fouled in his tail and he was plainly wild and bewildered. There did not seem to be the slightest indication that he was tired now.

The time came when he doubled back on his trail, to head straight for us. This was embarrassing by reason of the difficulty in reeling up slack line, and disconcerting because I feared he might ram us. Twice I had Sid run out of his path. The third time, however, when the swordfish sheered toward us, I grew curious or brave or angry, and yelled for Sid to let him come. Meanwhile I wound the reel as fast as I could. Once I actually saw the line come up over his tail, over his body and dorsal fin as he faced us.

That swordfish came to the boat, and swam with us, a little astern and perhaps fifteen feet out. I reeled in until my line was tight. And I stood up. I could not help it; that was an instinctive action. I have been cramped in that fishing chair more than once when a swordfish got too close.

What a fearful and beautiful fish! He seemed tawny in color, short, round, not large at all. Only his naked sword and his black eye looked vicious. He swam with us. I watched him perhaps for ten seconds, and I lost my fear of him. It did not occur to me then that but for the revolving propeller he might have hit us. Why do these swordfish ram ships at sea? It is a common occurrence. The English marine log is full of such recordings. I could see where the leader, clear to the ring, was fast in his tail. But I could not see where it went into his mouth. It was on the other side. Even then I grasped something queer about this.

"Sid, he's a little fish—not over two hundred," I cried as I jammed my rod back in the socket and crowded into the seat. "Let's see."

And I exerted myself to the utmost to haul the swordfish closer. Then I saw he was tired. I rolled him over. But with a fling of his tail that deluged us he plunged away. We followed him, and very soon he did precisely the same thing as before. He came up to us, and when I shut down with all my might on the reel I almost held him.

"We're going to get him," I yelled. What prompted such assumption I could not guess, but I felt it. Captain Sid made wild and whirling use of words.

Before long the swordfish changed his course and eventually came alongside. I had released the strain and did not put it on until he got close. He was certainly growing logy. That renewed my strength and I bent the rod double and cracked my back. Probably I dragged that swordfish a matter of six feet, but I could not have dragged him an inch farther to save my life.

But Sid reached him with a gaff. The ocean seemed to explode. I saw a cloud of spray come aboard. And in it Sid appeared, making frantic movements. He all but went overboard. The gaff rope, after it tore out of his hands, had caught one of his legs. He had a narrow escape.

Our *Xiphias* went roaring away, dragging the gaff and rope. We saw both plainly. My line paid steadily off the reel.

"Say—I got him—high up—near his head!" panted Sid. "What was it—happened?"

"Grab your wheel. He's our fish," I said, grimly.

Then as we set off again after this eagle of the sea we saw a war vessel, a mine sweeper, come bearing down on us, too close for comfort. Sid waved frantically. It soon developed that the officers on that boat saw what we were doing, and they hove to and watched us through their glasses while the swordfish stayed in their vicinity.

He remained on the surface, but did not turn again. I had Sid run up on him until we were within a hundred feet. Then I put all the muscle I had left in the task of stopping him. That muscle, after five hours, was not very much. Nevertheless, it told. He slowed; he rolled; he wearily wagged his great tail. Also he gradually settled in the water, until his fins went under and I could see only his color.

All of a sudden he pitched up, head out, and plunged sullenly, to go down, until he was heading straight. Down, down, down! I watched the line slip off. I knew what that sounding meant. He was a spent fish. But I must stop him or lose him. The fact was I could not stop him. At one thousand feet depth he stopped of his own accord, and there he hung. He never made another move.

I could not budge him an inch, but by holding my reel and having Sid run the boat very gently forward I got him coming. He was a dead weight and every second I looked to see the line snap. But it held. And ever so slowly I reeled it in, inch by inch.

Probably I never worked so hard, in that condition, in my life before. I took half an hour to get him where I could gain any line worth considering. But at last I had him coming up.

Sid nearly fell overboard, looking down to try to find him. When he did see him he let out a stentorian roar.

The swordfish came up tail first, dead. We did not need to gaff him again, but of course we did. I was so exhausted and my hands hurt so that I was of little help to Sid in trying to haul him aboard. We could not lift even his tail out of the water, and we had to tow him back to Avalon. All during that three-hour ride back the swordfish grew larger and larger in my sight.

When he was hauled up on the dock I found the hook fast in his body on the right side. The leader passed between his jaws and down his left side and was embedded in his tail. He had never been hooked in the mouth at all. The ring on my leader must have caught in his tail the very first plunge. If it had loosened I would have lost my swordfish that instant. Four hundred and eighteen pounds!

Parson Blair's Sermon

George Wythe Munford

(from "The Two Parsons," 1884)

OH! FOR SOME place where I can think,—where the mind can revel free,—where the soul, when it feels an inspiration, may breathe forth its outpourings in adoration of the Deity,—where the heart may unloose its loves, its friendships, its pleasures and its woes; where, when reading or dreaming over a pathetic scene, the big tear may start without a cold eye to moderate, or an unbidden laugh to chill and congeal it! Oh! for a private spot, where uninvited footsteps may not intrude, and the very fear of interruption may not prove a *"mare clausum"* to the mind! What can be more trying to an author in the full tide of composition, when the mind is working as smoothly as a well oiled machine, and you see the wheat separated from the chaff, and all ready to be stored, than a visit from one of those good prosy fellows who sits down cosily, and delighted to see you, begins in his dull way, going back to Adam, and a little before Adam, and tells you the minutiae of his affairs through all the succeeding generations; all of which he has narrated before, without a particle of variation, yet oblivious of ever having mentioned the subject to a human being in the whole course of his life! It is a painful thing to fret internally, and still remain apparently polite when all the while you wished to terminate the enjoyment of the intruder by taking him by the collar and leading him gently to the door. After such an interruption you see in your mind's eye the little angels that were unfolding the treasures of your brain, and laying them before you to be read and daguerreotyped with all their beauties of colors and shading, gently closing the doors and folding up the jewels, until all are hid and gone. When these things take place you are ready to go off into *caniptions*, and lament the day you were born.

Thus soliloquized Parson Blair, when he had seated himself in his study (if a room to which every member of the family had free access could be so-called), to compose his sermon for the approaching Sabbath. He took up his Bible reverently, and silently turned over its leaves until he reached the twenty-first chapter of the gospel according to St. John. Then he said, "Here is Jesus after His resurrection, showing Himself for the third time to His disciples, at the sea of Tiberias, where there were seven of them together." Then he stopped at the third verse, " 'Simon Peter saith unto them, I go a fishing.' This shall be my text."

Just as he had reached this point, had removed from his mind its preoccupying thoughts, and had begun to spin the thread for a train of ideas with which to weave the woof and warp of his discourse, an old-fashioned Virginia darkey, who was pretty much mistress over the younger brood of the family, and certainly over all the other servants, both because of her age, respectful demeanor and general good character—in fact was what we, in former days, called "mammy," entered abruptly and said, "Master, missis say, dar aint no sugar in de house, and she sent me to axe you please send for some coffee."

Patience is a great virtue. The good man blandly replied, "I'll attend to it by-and-by." Then, having always had a keen sense of the ridiculous, he soliloquized after this fashion: " 'She sent me!'

Dear, dear, dear. 'To axe you!' As if I was a log of wood to be cut up with an axe. Where did the creature pick up such language? Because there 'ain't no sugar, please send for some coffee'" and then he rummaged in his pockets and said, "A Flemish account of empty boxes." But the sugar and the coffee must be forth-coming. He shut up the Bible, and said aloud, "It is of no use; I am not in the vein." He picked up his pen again and took another tack, in order to remove these last thoughts with something more sprightly; and as we have a copy of the letter he wrote, we will make a few extracts, to show how he relieved his mind when he was otherwise disposed to fret. The letter is directed to Mr. John Rutherfoord, Dublin. Mr. Rutherfoord was the nephew of Mr. Thomas Rutherfoord.

"RICHMOND, 13*th Feb'y,* 1806.

"Dear Sir: I have had a letter ready for you ever since some time in October of the last year, and I mention it to show that I have not been unmindful of you; but I have never known of an opportunity of sending it. Indeed, I never go to your uncle's, or to his worship's, without thinking and hearing of you."

We will simply say, that his worship was no other than our old friend, Parson Buchanan, who occupied so much of his thoughts, and upon whom he took so much pleasure in cracking a sly joke. The good Parson was known to have no taste either for fishing or hunting, and therefore had no skill in either, while Parson Blair, being fond of both recreations, was a first-rate shot and a skilful angler. But we will permit him to proceed in his own way:

"His worship now and then talks about shooting *perdrix* on the ground and catching them in traps; but I tell him, as to you, I certainly saw you shoot one on the wing. Your uncle, who you know deals in tobacco, has seldom failed to tell me of his late advices from your side of the water; such particularly as inform him that *his cargo* proved superior to the choice selection of fifty hogsheads which you made while in this country. Such and so various are the tastes of men!"

He then talks of other matters among the connections of the family.

"Pray have you seen the celebrated river or brook in which the Colonel *killed* so many salmon in a forenoon? I am not certain where it was in Scotland or the West Indies, but should suppose it was in the place farthest distant from America. I think he told us he killed a gross between breakfast and dinner, and from the number one would conclude that the exploit had been achieved at Rhodes, where, you know, the man in the fable made the great jump. If I remember right, our calculations made it about three salmon in four minutes, or two in three minutes, which certainly must have been very expeditious. It must have been fatiguing besides; for supposing, as I think he stated, each fish to have weighed five pounds, they must have been equal in all to about thirteen fifty-sixes. This must have required such exertion of his muscular powers, that I dare say he slept without rocking the night after. I believe, indeed, that you entertained a suspicion that he only dreamt it. Unacquainted as I was with the catching of salmon, I could not judge so well as you; but he told us marvelous things, too, about his shooting grouse on the mountains, and I really did think he shot out of a long gun that time.

"You, my dear sir, may be said to be now entering upon life. Remember that you hold it and all its comforts on a precarious tenure. Then let no company nor temptations of any kind seduce you from the principles of piety and the practice of virtue, which are infinitely the most valuable, and the only lasting portion.

"I am, dear sir, your respectful friend,

"JOHN D. BLAIR."

This was invariably the way in which he endeavored, in the midst of pleasantry and temporal affairs, to lead the mind to think on greater pleasures in store for the righteous in the world to come. The anecdote of fishing was no doubt brought to his mind by the text he had selected.

Having thus come back to the solemn and the serious mood befitting the theme he had chosen, he again took up his note-book and began jotting down the outlines for his discourse. We have had the advantage of running over these notes, and the thoughts for this sermon are mostly taken from them.

" 'Simon Peter saith unto them, I go a fishing. They say unto him, We also go with thee.' We note that the Saviour, after His resurrection, does not chide those whom He had chosen to guide and govern His Church for attending to their secular affairs. These apostles were fishermen. They were partners in ships, in seines, in the business and occupation of fishing, by which they supported themselves and their families. Peter, in particular, we know had a wife; for we are told in the Bible that his wife's mother lay sick of a fever. Early writers testify that she was a most devoted wife, and followed him in all his travels, and clung to him in all his perils, faithfully ministering to him in the blindness of his old age, through all his troubles, to his terrible end. Her name was Perpetua; and it is well for good wives to have their names registered, not only in the hearts of men, but perpetually in that final home suited to their lovely characters.

"Fishing, by individuals, is an occupation which has the advantage of being an amusement, a recreation, an unbending of the mind. It affords time for meditation without the intrusion of others. It furnishes food in moderate supply for an ordinary family. If carried on as a business by co-operative industry, and men devote their labor continually to it, it not only gives employment to large numbers of people, supports them and their families, but gives a scope for extensive operations with large capital. It becomes the nursery for a national marine, aids in building up a navy of hardy and experienced navigators to protect and defend the country, and is the prolific source from whence is drawn the material for carrying on the commerce of the world."

He had just advanced thus far when his little son, Tom, came running into the room, full of glee, in the eagerness of youth, catching him by the sleeve, and saying: "Oh! pa, here is the man with the organ and the monkey. Do, pa, do come and see him. Oh! he is cutting so many capers. Please, pa, give me a four-pence-ha'penny to give to the monkey."

"Dear! dear!" said the patient man. "The monkey! What has become of Peter!"

"Peter," said Tom, "I saw him working in the garden just now."

"Well, well! Peter working in the garden! I thought he had gone a-fishing."

"No, sir; he is rolling out the grass from the asparagus beds. Oh! pa, do come and see the monkey!"

He gave the child the money, and said, "Don't bother me again with organs and monkeys." Tom ran away overjoyed, but the idea of Peter working asparagus beds would not flit away. "I was just thinking," he said, "of St. Peter, who had been crucified in his old age with his head downwards, the position he had begged for himself in humility, as unworthy to occupy, even in death, the position of his blessed Master."

"Oh! Mr. Blair, one of the children has fallen down the steps and hurt his arm," cried Mrs. Blair.

The kind heart drew a long breath, a smothered sigh—first for the interruption, and then for the cause—hustled the papers into the table drawer, and went forth immediately.

There was a terrific scream, and then the holding of the breath, and when nature required an exhalation, another scream. The bystanders had picked up the child and stood him on his feet, and he was bawling lustily. The Parson turned upon his heel and retreated quickly into the house. He was met by his sister, Hannah. "What is the matter, brother?" "Nothing," he said. So it turned out. When a child is severely hurt, it rarely cries loudly. The little scamp, in his hurry to give the fourpence to the monkey, had fallen down the steps and skinned his elbow—that was all. In a few moments he was capering around the monkey, which was dressed in a red uniform, with a cocked hat under its arm and a pair of specs on its nose, and peeping and peering, was catching everything thrown to it with invariable certainty. So much for the monkey and this unfortunate interruption. The man with the monkey, however, was not satisfied. Seeing the Parson going back into the house, he followed him and said, "Parson, don't you wish to see a picture of Shadrach, Meshach and Abednego in the fiery furnace?" This was too much for the Parson's gravity! The man who could compose himself to write anything worthy of the attention of an intelligent audience after such scenes must be more than mortal.

He threw himself back in his chair, put the feathered end of his pen between his teeth, and looked up at the ceiling. Then the association of ideas brought up the thoughts relative to Simon Peter. He mused and said, "I can follow Peter's example—'I go a fishing.' I know I lack the order from the Lord, 'Go thou to the sea and cast a hook, and take up the fish that first cometh up; and when thou hast opened his mouth, thou shalt find a piece of money; take that and give unto them for Me and for thee.' But that was to pay taxes, not to buy sugar and coffee. I can at least compose my mind by the side of a quiet stream, and gather my scattered thoughts. Yet this will probably be the result: notwithstanding all the evidence we have in the Bible of the best of men fishing and hunting, and of the Master of the best of them approving and ordering it, yet some of the good people who are righteous overmuch will think it sacrilege for a parson to go a-fishing. I have already had rebukes whispered at me for doing the self-same thing. I can only reply, 'Ye blind guides, which strain out a gnat and swallow a camel. Woe unto you, scribes and Pharisees, hypocrites; for ye make clean the outside of the cup and the platter, but within they are full of extortion and excess.' But what is that to going deliberately to see a farce?" So the first thing we know, we find the Parson wending his way along the banks of a shady pond (it was Bowles' pond), a few miles from the city, and hear him talking to himself:

> "Worn with the routine of the school
>   And with the mental strain
> Of teaching boys by rote and rule
>   The same thing o'er again,
> I come for recreation and for meditation;
> "I take my fishing rod and lines
>   And seek the limpid streams,
> Where pike and chub near beech and pines
>   Dart swift as lively dreams."

We see him with a few green willow twigs twisted into a hoop, and winding around this hoop the ends of his large silk handkerchief, forming a net, and skimming in the deep holes emptying from the pond. He is catching minnows from the brook, which he carefully drops into a bucket of fresh water, to serve as bait and to keep them alive. Some kind heart will say, "Fishing with live minnows, how cruel!" He seats himself upon an old log, near a clump of brush, then prepares for the sport. He takes his cane, the gift of his old friend, and nicely screws its joints together, forming a beautiful rod. His newest hooks from their case, he inspects one by one; examines the lead, scrutinizes the cork, poises it, unwinds the silken line, adjusts it to the rod, takes out freshest minnow and carefully puts it on the hook, so as not to wound it more than possible. He drops the line gently just outside the clump of brush, and patiently awaits the coming of the finny tribe. In a little while the minnow begins to revive and moves very slowly along, the cork upon the unrippled water showing the weakly motion.

There was a stillness one could almost feel. Not a sound, no one near, all quiet and serene. The good man begins to ruminate. "The Master said, 'Come ye after Me, and I will make you to become fishers of men.' 'And Jesus said unto Simon, Fear not, from henceforth thou shalt catch men.'" He mused here, and thus soliloquized:

"To catch fish there must be time, place and circumstance. The same thing is applicable to the fisher who is endeavoring to catch men for his Master's table. If you neglect this simple rule, you may angle a life-time in vain. You cannot catch fish with a hook and line without suitable bait. Plain bread for some, a worm for others, a buzzing fly and a jumping minnow for the ravenous. Nor can you catch men with the same food. Man, of all animals, is the hardest to please in his appetite. What he eats to-day with a relish disgusts him tomorrow. The oratory which attracts now is stale and insipid then. Some will be satisfied with skimmed milk. Nothing will suit others but the finest flavors, the juciest viands, the richest seasoning, the fattest and freshest solids, served up in silver and gold, and garnished with imagination's raciest, rarest and most tempting appetizers. Some are wearied with the fisherman, worried with his mode of fishing, despise his hooks, turn up their noses at the lightness of his corks and the heaviness of his leads. Some throw their nets on the wrong side, and in the wrong way, and toil all night and catch no fish. Others heeding their Master's command, in full confidence and faith 'cast the net on the right side of the ship,' 'and now they are not able to draw it for the multitude of fishes.'

"Some fish are very shy—dart off if you move; others play around your feet. Some men have wings if you open the Bible in their presence. But they have their feeding times, like fish. There are times when fish will not bite, though you place their favorite bait within reach of their mouths. At other moments they will scarcely wait until the hook touches the water. They snap at it in the twinkling of an eye. It is the part of a good fisherman for men to humor their whims and watch for the appropriate opportunity. They are like cattle in the morning rapidly passing over a field, leaving often the best and richest grass, and seeking the bare and poor spots, but coming back in the evening and delighting to crop what they had before neglected. So," said he, "you must study the habits of fish. You must do more in fishing for men. You must search into the depths of human nature. You have to open up to their view the panorama of heaven and of earth, with their untold riches and all their magnificent surroundings. You must fly on the wings of the wind to keep pace with the rapidity of their aspirations. If you soar with the wings of the morning, with all its freshness, they are still rushing onward and upward. If you come like the Sun of righteousness, with healing in His wings, they will scarcely pause to take the soothing balm. You must study with more than twenty years of lucubration all characters, both sexes, all ages. You must know how they are attracted, by what they are caught, and how they are gathered into the fold. The theme opens upon my view, 'I go a fishing.'"

He looked up; suddenly the cork bobbed up and down twice; then it ran along two or three feet. In a moment he had each muscle strung to its utmost tension. He looked as rigid as a pointer with eyes and head slightly turned towards a flock of partridges. With nerves keenly excited, he held his breath, and gazed at the cork with intense anxiety; then raised the rod with cautious hand, and gently tightened the line. In an instant down went the cork; he gave a rapid twitch, and the line fairly whizzed through the water in the opposite direction, until it was stretched to its full extent. The sudden check whirled the huge fish over. It then ran towards the surface, and flounced its tail out of the water with a splash; and, seeing the parson, darted with the rapidity of light to the bottom; then, changing direction, ran for the shore, bending the rod until every moment it was in danger of being snapped in twain. The experienced angler slipped the rod gradually backward, and catching the line wound it round his hand, saying, "Aha, old fellow, I've got you now; go ahead."

We have heard Parson Buchanan on such occasions cry out, "Play him, brother Blair; play him." But brother Blair was up to all that sort of thing, and knew what he was about. He began forcing the fish to the surface, and when he found it worried and almost exhausted, he gradually curtailed the line, bringing it nearer and nearer, till at last he flounced it on the ground. It was a magnificent chub, weighing six or eight pounds, fluttering, gasping, bouncing, seeming determined never to surrender. He found the hook sticking securely, and as he took it out, said, "That is precisely the way some men act when they feel the workings of the Holy Spirit. They resist with might and main, but by and by they are very still and tractable.

But now the fish began to bite in earnest, rapidly and most excitingly. He could scarcely arrange himself to his work before bite after bite indicated there were many playing around his bait. Sometimes he was a little too quick—didn't give them time enough; they would snap and run, and then let go; then he waited too long, and they would take his bait; but ever and anon he caught large and fine fish, and had all the sport he desired. Pike, silver perch, chub—some of the largest and finest the pond contained. "This silver perch," he said, "is brother Buchanan's; he enjoys its juicy relish." And so he went on, never forgetting brother Buchanan, until, become fatigued, he threw himself upon the grass, and opened a bucket he had brought along, and found wrapped in a clean napkin a nice lunch his good wife had daintily and carefully provided for his comfort, to say nothing of his hunting flask and cup, containing a little something for his stomach's sake. "Simon Peter's wife," he said, "no doubt fixed up many nice things for Peter and his friends when they went a-fishing; but my wife, I think, could beat her making pickle, curing ham, and broiling chickens. I doubt whether Peter's wife would touch a ham, for I dare say she was a Jewess, and a pretty

Jewess too, for they are always pretty. What a blessed thing it is that bacon and greens and jowl and turnip tops are not prohibited now. The only fault of my wife is that she is not Perpetual." And while he lay resting himself, he mused as before upon his theme: "What a pity it is that we should have an enemy among us fishing for men. Ah! the devil is a marvellous tempter. He throws his lines, and takes especial care to hide his hooks. They are covered with the most fascinating baits. He fished for our Saviour. 'And the devil, taking Him up into a high mountain, showed unto Him all the kingdoms of the world in a moment of time.' And he said, 'All this power will I give Thee, and the glory of them; if Thou wilt worship me all shall be Thine.' A most tempting bait; and he assured Him, 'To whomsoever I will, I give it.' How many men and women would have resisted this offer? Suppose I were to say to them, Believe on the Lord Jesus Christ—nothing more—and I will make you president of the United States. Would they bite? Suppose I were to say, not to make it too tempting, Here are from two to five hundred thousand dollars; believe and be baptized, and they shall be for the man and his children who can reach them first. There would be such a rush I should be in danger of being trampled to death.

"When the devil is fishing, he most generally tempts his fish with silver hooks and golden bait. Ah! but he does not limit himself to silver and gold. He offers the bait of vermillion cheeks and cherry lips, diamond eyes and flowing ringlets. Aye, ambition too is an inviting morceau. He dressed it up nicely and tickles the palate with self-deluding flattery, with public applause, crying, 'Hear him, hear him.' They take out the horses from his carriage, and yoke themselves to the traces and draw him through the streets. They tickle his pride with public preferment until the victim is prepared to say and apply it to himself, 'Lift up your heads, O ye gates; and be ye lift up, ye everlasting doors, and the King of glory shall come in.' Forgetting that there is one who asks, 'Who is the King of glory?' And who answers, 'The Lord of hosts, He is the King of glory!' And forgetting that He who weighs him in the balances has the power to say, 'Depart from Me, ye cursed, into everlasting fire, prepared for the devil and his angels.'

"Another thought presents itself. Fish of the same kind swim together, associate together. Different kinds keep asunder. You may sometimes find a shark among them, taking his prey and frightening them to death. But even the shark keeps to his species. You find a large school of shad, an immense school of herring, myriads of salmon, myriads of mackerel, every species and genera, and of all sizes, coming from the same ocean, sometimes one or two different species running in the same stream; but generally each school separate and apart, and each species unerringly true to its instincts and habits, as if guided by one spirit. There is a Master who impressed His law upon them, and they obey it with undeviating aim.

"Do you see no likeness in this to man? I speak of his intercourse in the church. Is there no reason for separate and distinct denominations? The world is the great ocean. Here dwelleth leviathan, and here, the tiniest living thing that hath scales and fins. Thou canst not see even with a microscope the ten thousand myriads of atoms that float through immensity, all of different races and species and genera, governed by laws suited to the purposes for which they were created.

"When a mighty monarch gathers his million army to go forth to battle, they come from every province. Every sub-division, each company, each battalion, each regiment, each brigade, each division, each corps d'armee under separate leaders, are kept together with one great commander—the autocrat, and he saith, 'Go, and he goeth; come and he cometh.' Do the corps of the grand army intermix, the one with another? Military men know better than to make this confusion,—this fruitful source of unmitigated discord. They hurl them in masses, preserving their distinctions, against the enemy; and the result is as God shall decree.

"How are the religious sects formed? Our Saviour proclaims, 'Search the Scriptures, for in them ye think ye have eternal life; and they are they which testify of Me.' They all go to the fountain; but men's minds are various, and the reasons which satisfy you will not satisfy another. The Bible is like other books, susceptible of different constructions. But there is one universal truth which pervades it, and scarcely a sect denies the essentials to salvation. Those who believe that particular passages are construed in one way flock together, because their belief is more congenial to each other, and there is no danger of quarrelling; while those who believe there is another interpretation more in accordance with the tenor and scope of the Divine word, gather themselves together. To keep up their organizations, they require different governments and different rules: bishops, priests, deacons and elders, presbytery, and every other name in accord with their fancy or their interpretation of the Bible, and the traditions of the fathers. Where is the necessity for dissension among them? And yet how bitter and acrimonious some of them are. How many ordinary members can tell what the difference are? They do not even state correctly what their adversaries believe. Why should each set up his opinions as the only true and infallible standard? They are both fallible because they are mortal. The true principle is for each 'to practise Christian forbearance and charity towards the other.' If God hath given unto other sects the like gift as He gave unto us, let us receive them with joy and kindness, and we will fight the common enemy under the same banner of the cross.

"Our Saviour selected His apostles from among fishermen. There was a meaning in this. He intended to make them fishers of men. Some of His most extraordinary miracles were performed with fish, and they had a signification too, to a thoughtful mind.

"Once when He sat down in Simon's ship at the lake of Gennesaret, and taught the people out of the ship, 'when He had left speaking, He said unto Simon, Launch into the deep, and let down your nets for a draught.' 'And when they had this done, they inclosed a great multitude of fishes, and their net brake. And they beckoned to their partners which were in the other ship that they should come and help them. And they came and filled both the ships, so that they began to sink.' And when Peter and all that were with him were alarmed and astonished, 'He said unto Simon, Fear not, for henceforth thou shalt catch men.'

"This miraculous draught of fishes was emblematical, and was designed to show what power they would have after they became fishers of men in drawing great multitudes unto salvation. And when Simon told Him, 'We have toiled all night and have taken nothing,' the immense draught that was taken at the next haul was intended to show that success in catching men would be attended with toil, and many a haul would be made and nothing would be taken; but for all that, perseverance and patience and launching out into the deep—not skimming among the shoals, not clinging close to the shore, but going forth into the deep abyss of the world—into the deep hiding places of iniquity, studying and expounding satisfactorily the deep mysteries of the Scriptures, and then letting down the net, multitudes would be caught, so great as to alarm and astonish those of little faith. And the miracle was intended to show that when the net brake and the ships were about sinking, they must not be discouraged, but beckon to their partners in other ships—men of other denominations—to come and help them. There must be concert and assistance. They must mend and repair their frail endeavors, and make sure of the multitudes they could catch. This miracle was before the resurrection, before the sending of the Holy Ghost, when the nets and the ships were not strengthened by the power that was to come and abide in them.

"The other occasion was after His resurrection, at the sea of

Tiberias, when they had again set their nets at night and caught
nothing. In the morning He saith unto them, 'Children, have ye
any meat?' They answered Him, 'No.' Now they were to go forth
no more in the night, groping in the dark, and taking nothing,
but in the full blaze of day, to throw their nets, made strong and
irresistible, and draw 'the net to the land full of great fishes.' And
for all there were so many, yet the net should not be broken.
They should no more, when asked if they had any meat, answer
'No,' but should have abundance. The Master should say unto
them, 'Come and dine;' and when strengthened for the work
they would become shepherds of the great flock, and go forth
able to obey the commandment, 'Feed My lambs,' and not only
the tender, helpless young, but 'Feed My sheep,' the strong and
mighty of the flock.

"This is a great theme," said he; "We have almost the
indefinite multiplication of fishes by other miracles. 'Do ye not
understand, neither remember the five loaves of the five thousand, and how many baskets ye took up? neither the seven
loaves of the four thousand, and how many baskets ye took up?'
This is designed to show how the bread of life, the inspiration of
holy writ, the outpouring of the Holy Spirit, can be multiplied
until it feeds the world. What mighty events flow from small
causes, when touched by a master hand! There is no end to the
multitudes that may be fed. If there were ten thousand denominations, a few loaves of this bread of life would feed and
strengthen them to mighty works. There is comfort in the
thought that the gospel affords ample food for all, and that it
may be multiplied to suit the number and the condition of all,
without regard to denomination, age or sex, Jew or Gentile.

"There is still another thought. Let down your nets, and drag
them out of the evil net, where they were snared in an evil time,
and give them freedom of life and the joys of salvation. Aye, fish
them from their ignorance, from their bigotry, from their false
gods. Fish them from their conceited wisdom; fish them from

their vanity and their folly. 'Behold, I will send for many fishers, saith the Lord, and they shall fish them; and after will I send for many hunters, and they shall hunt them from every mountain, and from every hill, and out of the holes of the rocks.' And as the Lord will fish up Israel from the land of the north and from all the lands whither He hath driven them, and will bring them again into their land, so shall the fishers sent by the Lord Jesus gather the multitudes from all the corners of the earth. Well might Peter say, 'I go a-fishing;' and well might the other disciples say, 'And we also go with thee.' It was a work worthy of the Lord's disciples.

"Fishing for multitudes of fish implies that after they are caught provision must be made for preserving them for future use. And when you are fishing for multitudes of men, provision must be made for utilizing them for the Lord's service. They must be fed with the bread of life, and with the water 'that shall be in them a well of water springing up into everlasting life.' They must be served with the bread and the wine, the body and the blood of Christ; for He saith, 'He that eateth My flesh and drinketh My blood dwelleth in Me and I in him.' This is the way that men are to be preserved for eternity. Fish are to be salted, that they may be kept for a brief period, but this blood and wine preserveth for ever. But take heed that ye be not offended at this, saith the Lord Jesus. 'It is the Spirit that quickeneth, the flesh profiteth nothing.' I am talking of my flesh and my blood in a spiritual sense. The spirit and the life are the reality to which you must cling. You utilize men by sending them forth to form other swarms, and construct other hives, and gather honey from all herbs and flowers; and when they are dead and gone, their good deeds live on, and the evil that they do is often the warning to be shunned; and the thoughts that they uttered become the food for other generations; and many of those they never uttered are stored in books, to live for ever, and generate other thoughts better and more noble."

He paused, and said, "Many more thoughts crowd upon me; but it is growing late. Our sun may set, but the Sun of righteousness will shine for ever. What inspiration entered the mind of Addison when he wrote that glorious hymn beginning with these words:

> 'The spacious firmament on high,
> With all the blue ethereal sky.'

It opens to the soul the contemplation of all the heavenly host and their great Creator."

He looked at the sun setting, and then repeated:

> " 'Soon as the evening shades prevail,
> The moon takes up the wondrous tale,
> And nightly to the listening earth
> Repeats the story of her birth;
> While all the stars that round her burn,
> And all the planets in their turn,
> Confirm the tidings as they roll,
> And spread the truth from pole to pole.'

"How often have I heard Parson Buchanan repeating these words with the greatest gusto! But I must begone."

We left him gathering up his fish and tackle, well pleased with the results of the day's work.

An Old Salmon-Poaching Story

Gilfrid W. Hartley

(from "Wild Sport and Some Stories," 1912)

ONE MAY MORNING, nearly sixty years ago, a man left his home at the head of Glen Nant, and crossed over the bit of wild moorland which lies between the head of that valley and the Pass of Awe or Brander. He skirted the little wood below his house of Barrachander, where, early though it was, the wood-pigeons were already cooing, passed through a chain of small lochs, and got out on to the heather near the old ruined tower of Balliemore. Long ago this man's ancestors had been people of note in the world: in rough troublesome days their house was a strong one, both in itself and its position. It stands—what is left of it—in a cup or sheltering hollow among the hills, unobtrusive, unnoticeable, and no doubt many an unfriendly traveller has unwittingly passed it by. But at last came the evil day, and it perished, how, or in what period—with what stress of life and shouting and bloodshed—the solemn hills standing around alone know. The burning of Airlie or the siege of such a place as Inverlochy are recorded in history, but she has nothing to say about the end of such a humble mountain fortress as this. On one of the lochs near is an island, with the remains of a building on it; this is called the "Charter-House," the Safety-Place for Balliemore. As it once gave protection to men, so it does now to birds, and the wild ducks and gulls and curlew of Loch Tromlie find in its shelter the quiet and security which it once afforded its old owners.

It has been said that if the last trump had sounded at the end of the great war with France at the beginning of last century, no one but a Macleod would have risen up out of the graveyard of Dunvegan. The MacCorquodales could hardly make the same boast as the great western clan, but their dust must lie thick in the little moorland churchyard of Kilchrenan. It is a good many years since the chief actor in this sketch joined his brethren there. Near his grave is a huge stone erected to the memory of a world-renowned head of a great house, to "Cailean Mor, slain on the Streang of Lorn, A.D. 1294." Next to this is another monument commemorating six Campbells of position, four of whom were killed in some fierce fight in the neighbourhood. So he lies in goodly company, with many members of his clan, and his clan's enemies, side by side with ancient chiefs and warriors, and freebooters, and smugglers, and decent homelike nineteenth-century sheep-farmers and crofters.

It is not likely that Archibald MacCorquodale ever troubled himself very much about his ancestors, or his own humble position. Poor man as he was—earning a precarious living by hard work—he was probably very much better off in most ways than any of them were. He never was obliged to carry off himself and his household goods at a moment's notice to the safety island; he never was awakened at midnight by an ominous flare in the sky, telling him (as it had often told his forebears) that the stacks or cowhouse was aglow; and when he left his home he knew he would find on his return the small wild-looking black-cattle feeding quietly about the croft,—not hear of them being furious driven—a panting, lowing, exhausted herd—to the far-away safe keeping of some lord of the country stronger and bolder than himself. He cut peats and dried them; he made quantities of coarse moorland hay; he worked on his rough, badly-drained fields without being discouraged at the exceeding scantiness of the crops they gave him in return for his labours. He made long journeys twice a-year to Kilmichael, and spent much time and energy—generally in vain—in trying to persuade other people that his two or three beasts were fat instead of thin—well-bred instead of ill-bred—handsome instead of ill-favoured—the pick of the country round instead of its black shots. And for pastime he did a little poaching; as salt to savour his labours, quite as much as for the sake of varying his fare, he killed grouse and hares and salmon whenever he got a chance. Lights were often seen at night in this district at that period, but they were harmless bits of bog-pine roots, used for burning fish-haunted waters instead of substantial byre or rick.

The sun was barely peeping round the shoulder of Ben Bhurich when Archie got on the high bit of tableland where he could look down on the river Awe. The day gave promise of being a very hot one, but as yet a dull white frosty mist lay over the hills, filling up the hollows and corries with its cotton-wool-like masses: every step he took left its trace behind (how often must it have happened in old fighting days that a man has been followed to his death by such trail as this!), and he was soon wet above the knee by the drip from the heather and long grass. In these times, when salmon are scarce and wary, the frosty morning which ushers in a broiling day is not loved by a fisherman, but at that happy period things were different, and better, and he must have been a notice indeed who could not do something almost any time during the season with the fish in the Awe.

When MacCorquodale reached the watershed, he looked down on a district which, save in one respect, sixty years have done little to change. The dark river, flecked with white here and there, made its rapid way to the sea; beyond it stood up the bare grey-green face of Ben Cruachan; and the woods of Inverawe showed, as they show nowadays, against Loch Etive, and the granite face of Bonawe. Far away to the west you can see Morvern, and the higher peaks of Mull. Till quite recently the place must have looked just the same as it has looked for centuries. The railway is the only change—a mighty convenience, but the thin line of iron doubtless takes something from the loneliness of what used to be one of the wildest passes in Scotland.

Archie ran quickly down the hillside till he came to a great rock in the shelter of which lay his rod, with reel and line on it ready for work. Rod and line and fisherman have long been resolved into their component parts, but the reel lies before the writer now—a large wooden one, black painted, worm-eaten, but still in good order; it has a hole in it through which the rod was run. He put on a fly, dark-bodied, with grey heron-wings, very different to the brilliant "Doctors" and "Butchers" which are chiefly in use now, and began to fish his pool. Carefully he fished it—a step and a cast—a step and a cast, the while going through the mental process of anticipation at the start, surprise at the negative result of the first half-dozen throws, disappointment when no boil in the water or pull beneath it awaited him at the first likely place. Before, however, disappointment had time to change into disgust, he felt the pull, raised his rod a little, and found the strain increase; saw the water open enough to let him catch a glimpse of some part of a salmon, and then as rapidly close.

Archie came up the hill a little to have more command over the fish; a thrill of joyful exultation ran through him, and the frown on his face indicated only concentrated attention. With feet well apart, finger ready to check the line, and eyes following anxiously the point where it, slowly moving, cut the water tight as a strained steel wire, he stood on the bank, perhaps at that moment the happiest man in all the far-stretching parish of Glenorchy and Innishail. But near are joys and sorrows in this world; close together, ever watching mankind, sit Fortuna and the Fates.

From behind a grey rock on the opposite side of the river rose up now a grey man—long of leg, tough in sinew, stern of countenance; no greeting gave he to the fisherman, no friendly congratulations or applause. He stalked down to a convenient boulder, which commanded a good view of the pool, and sat down on it; he got out his pipe—his eye the while glued to the point of interest—and soon the gentle wind carried over to Archie's nostrils the fragrant scent of his tobacco.

A Prime Minister, who, thinking he had a certain majority on a critical division, finds the Opposition have it instead, could hardly be more overwhelmed than Archie was at this bodeful appearance. Fishing was fairly free at the time we are writing of, because, as a rule, it was of little value, but on this part of the Awe the owner had lately been asserting his rights and warning off trespassers. Archie had offended, and had been caught; had offended again, with the same result; had offended again—and the patience of the authorities had at length been worn out. So the edict had gone forth that if ever again—only once—he was caught dipping a fly in the river, then would he have to leave his little cottage in Glen Nant, and the tiny well-loved farm,—that never more on all those wide lands would he find a resting-place for his feet, "Not if you lived for a hundred and seventy years!" added the factor, shaking a quill pen at him. But word had come to Archie the previous night that his enemy the keeper had been summoned to see a sick son far away up at Loch Tulla in the Blackmount, a long day's journey for an active man. And lo! regardless of that affection which is felt by all but the basest of men, this unnatural father was lying in wait for him here!

So it came about that Archibald MacCorquodale stood chained to the river by a big salmon within seventy yards of a man whom he looked on as a natural enemy,—from whom he always felt inclined to fly even when merely pursuing his natural lawful occupation. His first thought was to break his line and be off. But what would he gain by that? He would not so shake off his foe. And there was another reason. There is a grim story of a laird of the old school who was busily engaged in playing a very heavy fish when a messenger came to tell him of the sudden and serious illness of his wife. The fisherman reasoning that his wife might recover, but that he was never likely to get hold of such a monstrous specimen of the *Salar* tribe again, could not bring himself to loose his hold, so sent for further tidings. "The mistress is dying," was the answer: but the laird now found that he was engaged in a struggle with such a creature as Tweedside in all its history had never seen the like of, and again he hardened his heart; and it was only when he heard that all was over that he reluctantly broke, and went up to the house. "She was a good wife to you, laird!" cried a weeping and sympathising retainer. "Ay, she was that, Jeanie, she was a' that!" said the disconsolate widower; "but eh, woman! yon was the varra mucklest fish that eyes of man ever yet saw on Tweed!"

The crofter felt something like the old laird: he had not seen the fish, beyond the merest glimpse of it as it slowly edged away out into the stream after being hooked, but he judged from the weight put on his hand and arm, and from the strain on the rod, that if it were only once on the bank, good kipper to eat with his porridge would be plentiful in his house for many a day to come. Always provided—and this was indeed a very large "if"—no one prevented him carrying it off when it *was* landed. So in a swither of discomfiture and uncertainty Archie played his fish for five or ten minutes, and then, unable to bear the silence any longer, cried out to the man on the other shore—

"It's a fine day this!"

"It'll be a day you'll be wishing it was night, before I've done wi' ye!" was the grim answer that came back, and Archie almost fell into the river at the response.

"It'll be a bad day's work for me this!" he cried out almost in a whine.

"It'll be all that, my man!" replied the keeper cheerfully.

The fish, so passive hitherto, had behaved as large fish often do behave,—he had shown no hurry or undignified alarm. The disagreeable thing he had got into his mouth would soon be swallowed or spat out. So he sailed up and down the pool, unwilling to allow that there was any force guiding or compelling him from above. Then all of a sudden he got irritated, and made a furious rush across and down the stream without breaking water. The stiff unoiled reel screeched as it had never done before, and a red streak showed on the man's thumb as the coarse horse-hair line cut it almost to the bone. The salmon nearly ran aground in the shoaling water on the keeper's side, and then turned and went up-stream again, and the latter saw the great white belly flash under the thin water as the mighty rudder of a tail twisted it round as on a pivot. Something like five feet of blue-brown back came shooting up the pool close to the bank, and then disappeared like a ghost in the deep stream above. Archie thought he had hold of a prize, but the other knew it, and his experienced eye told him that he had just seen the heaviest salmon which had ever come into his ken either in or out of the Awe. "By——, he is a fish!" he cried to himself, as with straining eyes he followed the wake in the water.

Great, indeed, was this keeper's wrath and indignation. It was bad enough that this poaching crofter should be at the river at all, but that he should fall on such a piece of luck as this was almost more than mortal man could bear. It made matters still worse for the spectator to think that he had been sitting for half an hour within twenty yards of the fish, and might have been playing him himself—if only he had known. The thought flashed through his brain that perhaps this was the way in which he was to be punished for the elaborate manœuvre by which MacCorquodale had been decoyed to the river.

If Rory MacGilp was miserable, Archibald was in a much more parlous state. He would have felt very diffident at working a salmon before this keeper's critical eye under the most favourable and lawful circumstances, and to do justice to himself he would require the ever-ready help of a thoroughly sympathetic friend. Indeed it would be incorrect to speak at this period of the fish as a captive. Archie was the captive: the creature did what it liked with him; moved up and down the slack water just as it chose; stopped and sank, and dug its nose down into the bottom when it wanted without asking any leave from the man on the bank. If such things were to be done in the green tree, what might be expected in the dry? If the salmon was all-powerful in the smooth, quiet pool, what would be his proceedings when he went seawards—into the wild rapids, and among the dangerous sunken rocks down the stream? Archie felt he *would* go down sooner or later—it was merely a question of time; and the perspiration poured from his forehead, his legs shook, and his hands trembled as he moved to and fro along the grassy bank. Whether he landed it, or whether it broke him, the end would be the same; certainly this time the offence would not be overlooked: he might say farewell to Barrachander, and bonnie Loch Tromlie, and green primrose-haunted Glen Nant.

The fish moved down to the tail of the pool, and sunk himself there; he got his nose upstream, and began to "jig" at the line, each jig taking him a little farther down, and each vibration communicating a dreadful shock to the heart of the man above. "In five minutes," thought Archie, "I'll be likely a mile down, with my rod broken, and that old heathen grinning at me! Oh, for a friend now!"

"Rory!" he cried out softly to his enemy—"Rory!" But no answer came back across the water. Rory sat like a carved statue on his rock.

"Mr. MacGilp!—my fingers is cut to the quick! Will ye no pitch a stone in below him and turn him up!" Still there was no answer. "My back's fairly broken!" cried Archie piteously.

"I'm right glad to hear it," roared back the keeper—"of that same back!"

"He's forty pounds weight!" cried Archie, appealingly.

"HE'S SIXTY!" screamed Rory, jumping off his rock, and dancing about on the bank. "You poaching deevil! I hope he'll break your neck and drown you afterwards!"

"Oh—what'll I do if he goes down?" howled the other man; "he's off—he's off—what'll I do if he goes down?"

The fish lay now on the top of the rapid stream furiously flapping his tail.

"Give him line!" shouted Rory, "you great——!" "But what am I doing?" he cried to himself. "Let him break—I hope he will!"

Archie lowered the point of his rod, and the fish—as they so often will—stopped at the strain being taken off. But he was too far down to get back,—foot by foot he walloped down; he was fairly out of the pool, he got into the stream, he struggled against it for a moment, and the next he was raging away down the river: now deep down in it, now showing his huge breadth of tail at the top, turning over and over like a porpoise, careless where he went so long as he got clear.

Archie stood in the old place on the bank with his mouth open and most of his hundred yards of line run out, as incapable of checking its movements as if it had been a hundredweight of iron.

"Rin! rin! after him!" roared Rory, forgetting himself again. "Keep him in—But let him alone, you fool!" was again his second thought; "let him be! he'll never get by the point!"

The keeper ran down the bank, hopping highly over the boulders, and never taking his eye off the bit of foaming water where he judged the runaway to be; and Archie, his first stupefaction over, did the same, and got a slight pull on the salmon some two hundred yards farther down.

Rory, when coming up in the morning, had left his rod here, and now got possession of it, and of his gaff, which latter he slung over his back. A little lower the river turned, and the two men and the fish followed the curve, and got—the last at any rate—into a bad bit of rock-protected stream, dangerous enough now, though much worse in low water. Whatever knowledge the fisherman had of the place was clean driven out of him by the agitation he was in, and it would have been purely by luck, and not by any sort of guidance, that he would have found a safe passage through. But every inch of the passage was known to the other: every rock and shoal was as clearly photographed on his mind as if it lay before him in bodily shape; the information which for fifty years had slowly percolated to his brain was complete; his hands twitched and his heart leapt when he saw the salmon make for a bad bit of water, and he was quite unable to stop himself from shouting out directions, though all the time he was heartily hoping that the fish would break his hold. The advice, which was plentifully accompanied with abuse of Archie, was always immediately followed by denunciation of himself—the giver of it.

"Keep your rod west and bring him in!" roared the keeper; "are ye no' seeing the muckle rock there?"—the said rock being at the time six feet under water. Then to himself, "Whisht, you old fool, and let him cut!" "Let him come in my side, you black thief!" he thundered again, "or he'll be round yon stob!"—"and I hope he will, and be damned to him! If it isn't enough to sicken a fox to see him wi' such a fish as that!"

By that time Archie had got three-quarters of a mile down the river, and was much more exhausted than the salmon. What with keeping a tight hold on it when sulking, and hopping among slippery smooth rocks and stones when it was lively, listening to the threatening advice from the other side—the penalty, moreover, which he would have to pay for his sport ever being present in his mind—he thought he had never had such a time of it since he was born, and felt that the hardest day's work he had ever done was child's play to what he was going through.

"If I was only quit of this cursed fish for good and all!" he now thought to himself, "ay, if I was lying on my back wi' lumbago like Johnnie Ross, as I was pityin' sae much!"

The playing of a salmon is not often monotonous, and is sometimes exciting in the very highest degree, but, alas! how hopeless a task it is to attempt to communicate the exhilaration by written words! The reel "screeches" or "whirrs," according as it is well-oiled, or a rusty implement like our poacher's. The line "cuts the water," the gaff "went with a soft plunge" into the thick back. "Fresh up from the sea with the lice on him." All these words are appropriate and expressive, and they have been used over and over again hundreds and hundreds of times; scarce an account of a day's salmon-fishing is complete without them. The horrid vibration of the line as a big fish "jigs" at it, and every thrill runs like an electric shock right into the very heart of the rod-holder, has been referred to in almost every account of a tussle with a heavy salmon. How stale the words are! how difficult to put in fresher or better ones! and yet how very freshly every individual shock comes home in practice! Each jig you think will be the last—will find out the weak place in the hold, or the gear, and he will be off. I was once playing a big salmon in a very heavy rough pool: he was nearly done, and was being slowly wound up to the kneeling gaffsman, when he gave two or three wriggles and slipped off the hook. The heavy stream kept the line pretty tight, and the other man never noticed what had happened, or that the rod-top was straight. Then I suddenly jerked the fly out of the water, right in front of him, as if preparing to make a new cast, and shall never forget his face as he turned round and stared at me. And I would not like to put down here what he said.

What a cold-blooded animal must that acquaintance of Mr. Stoddart's have been who considered the hooking of a fish to be the only thing worth accomplishing, and who was accustomed then to "hand the rod to an attendant," to spare himself what he was pleased to call the "drudgery" of playing it! How easily might a master of the English language utterly fail to convey to his audience almost any part of the effect produced on him at times when playing a great salmon in a wide, rough, rock-sprinkled river! He has him well on—the fish of the season—the fish of many seasons—perhaps of his life. The next hour will see him the happiest or the most miserable of men. Think of the feelings of the late Mr. Dennison—not a novice but a fine fisherman—when, after eight hours' work on the Ness, the handle of his reel caught in his watch-chain, and the salmon broke him—the salmon of his life escaped! Grilse must get off at times, and ten, and twenty, and even thirty pounders, but surely monsters ought not to be allowed to escape and make a man's life a howling desolation for a week, with a mournful reminiscence attached to it ever afterwards. The very magnitude of such calamities sometimes makes people preternaturally calm: we have seen a friend, not remarkable for extreme moderation in his language, reel up the late tightly held and now merely dancing fly, after a long fruitlessly ending battle, without saying a word. Like the man who, pulling up at the top of a long hill, looked back and saw the flour which ought to have been in his cart whitening it for a mile—he was not equal to it. Often fish escape through no fault of the fisherman, often through his want of skill, but what when the loss is to be put down to pure carelessness? Think of the feelings of those hapless beings—we heard of another of them the other day—who, when putting the line on the reel, omit to fasten the one to the other, and see their salmon go off with the eighteenth part of a mile of cord trailing behind him! The last victim of this sort we know of was standing on a bridge and couldn't follow. John Bright is said to have taken a header after a line so disappearing.

On a big river a man will have 120 yards of line on his reel: seldom, indeed, will he require the whole of this. But if even sixty yards are run out the fish is a long way from you, and with a strong wind blowing down the stream it is very difficult to know what strain you are putting on the tackle. What a moment is that when—at such a distance—a salmon suddenly turns and comes back at you, with every chance in his favour of shaking out a light-holding hook, or getting round a rock or tree! What a dreadful sight is a big salmon jumping just opposite you, when your line lies in a huge drowned bag far below you both! worse than jigging or anything else that! There is a good illustration of what we mean in a plate in Scrope's 'Days and Nights of Salmon-Fishing,' but the angler looks singularly calm for such an emergency.

At six o'clock Archie rose his fish; at half-past seven he was more than a mile down the river, pretty well beaten. He had passed through all the mental phases we have spoken of—apprehension, hope, and deadly fear; and now, after all this manœuvring, it seemed as if the end had come, and he would be able to reel up—what he had left—and go home to make arrangements for his "flitting." The fish made a wild rush up the river, turned above a big upstanding stone, and then swam slowly down again. The line touched the stone, and Archie could not clear it; the surface was smooth, and it still ran a little, but the end was near: unless the salmon at once retraced his path, he was a free salmon soon.

A good spring landed Rory out on a green-topped slippery boulder with twelve inches of water running over it. He heard the reel opposite give out its contents in sudden uncertain jerks; he caught sight of a huge bar of yellowish-white coming wobbling down towards him—lost it—saw it again, and delivered his stroke. Up came the great wriggling, curling mass—bright silver now—out of the river: with both hands close to the gaff-head, he half lifted half dragged the fish to shore, struggling, and all but losing his footing in the passage; then up the bank with it till he was able to lie down on it and get his hand into its gills.

Twenty minutes later Archie, with a sinking heart, had crossed the bridge of Awe and travelled up the north bank. The keeper was sitting on a stone, quietly smoking, with no trace of anger on his face, and before him, on a bit of smooth thymy turf, lay a salmon such as many a man has dreamt about, but few, indeed, seen with mortal eyes. Then for the first time that day the poor crofter forgot his troubles: for half a minute his only feeling was one of intense pride—at such a victory.

"Well—he's safe now," Rory said at length.

"Ay!" replied Archie, still gaping at him.

"Erchibald," went on the keeper, "oh, man! you worked him just deevilish!" The other shook his head deprecatingly. "Just deevilish!—frae start tae finish!"

"That was no' a bad bit o' work for a man o' my years," the keeper continued. "Gin I hadna' been waiting for him there when he came by, it's little you'd have ever seen of your fish!"

"I ken that fine," said Archie.

"Gin I had no' been quick enough to slip it into him there—it would be at Bonawe he would be by this time."

"I'm believing that," replied the crofter.

"It was no' an easy job neither. Stand you on yon stane and see what footing you'll have."

"There was few could do it, indeed, Mr. MacGilp."

"He was far more like a stirk to lift out of the water than a decent saumon!"

"He was, Mr. MacGilp—far more, indeed, like a very heavy stirk!"

"If it hadna been my knowledge of all they sunken rocks, and shouting myself hoarse to guide you, where would you have been, my man, by this time?"

"It was your inteemate acquaintance with the stanes which saved me, indeed," once more agreed the crofter.

"There's no anither man in the whole wide world could have steered you down yon places as I did!"

"There is certainly not one in many hundred score would have taken such a vast o' trouble about it."

"I gaffed him—an' I told you the road to take him—an' saved him many a time—"

"You did all that an' more, Mr. MacGilp. It's much obligeed—"

"I doubt I made the varra fly that rose him?"

"You did that, indeed," said poor Archie, hopelessly. (He had made it himself the night before.)

"Dod!" cried the keeper, "I believe I got yon muckle fish *mysell!*"

The other stared at him.

"Erchie, lad," said the keeper,—and the voice of the man was changed now, and he spoke so softly and low it was difficult to recognise the same organ which a few moments before had been hurling denunciations across the river,—"I've been fishing here all my life; man and boy I've been fishing here for nearly fifty years, an' I never yet had the luck to get the grip of such a fish as that!"

MacCorquodale looked at him curiously, and he was never able to say positively—he was never quite sure in his own mind—whether it was a tear which rolled down over the rough cheek or not. Then there was long silence.

"An' where will it be ye'll be flitting too?" the old man asked, in quite another tone, and so suddenly that it made the crofter—deep in a reverie—jump.

"Where'll I be—where—oh!—Mr. MacGilp!"

"I believe I got yon muckle fish MYSELL!" with great emphasis on the last word.

Archie looked north and east and west, and then at the salmon.

"MYSELL!" as if finally and for the last time.

"I believe—that—too," said Archie, with a groan. The last three words came out with a gulp.

"Well—he'll be an ugly burden to bear away doun. But a man canna pick an' choose as he would in this world! Good day to you then, Erchibald. And you might be going on wi' that new bit o' garden you're sae proud of; I'll gie you a wheen grand potatoes—next year—for seed for't."

So MacCorquodale set out under the hot sun homewards. Once more he had a reprieve, and he wondered how it was he did not feel happier. During the exciting fight he had many times pictured to himself the little house from which he would be banished at Whitsunday, its rough meadow in front, and the peat-stacks, and the sunny untidy bit of garden, half-filled with currant bushes and ribes and southernwood, over which the bees came in the gloaming, slow flying after their afternoon labour on the moor. Now he thought only of the battle he had won, which was not to bring him in any honour now, or happy reminiscences afterwards.

"'Deed, I'll never have the chance of doing the like of yon again," muttered the poor crofter to himself.

Shorty:
A Native Fisherman Who Takes 'Em on a Fly

Thad S. Up de Graff

(from "Bodines, or Camping on the Lycoming," 1879)

E VERY NEIGHBORHOOD POSSESSES its "character,"—a chap who from some peculiarity, some oddity in dress, manner, habits, or style of speech, renders himself conspicuous among his fellowmen, so that he stands out in bold relief, a target for the ridicule of all with whom he comes in contact.

Such a man is Shorty,—additionally styled the "Shark of the Stream." So ostensible are Shorty's traits of character, that he is perhaps as well known, by name at least, as any denizen of the Lycoming valley. Where he originally came from the Lord only knows, for his own version of his life is so conflicting and crammed so full of startling incidents, blood-curdling situations and hair-raising adventures, as to more than occupy the full measure of time allotted by any half-dozen of the long-lived backwoodsmen of this epoch. Had he never existed at all, much less in the lively manner we are forced to acknowledge he does disport himself, the streams of the Lycoming region would be far more populous with trout, and afford a correspondingly in-

creased amount of pleasure to the true sportsmen who seek
these waters for recreation.

We had heard of Shorty and his depredations upon Pleasant
Stream, with nets, set poles, out-lines, and other abominable
contrivances for slaughtering the fish of this delightful of all
trout streams; but it was years before we encountered him face
to face in our excursions thither.

One day in early June, Hamlin and I were casting the fly upon
its banks, being bountifully rewarded, not only in the large
number of trout taken, and in their gamy quality, but also by our
picturesque surroundings. The stream is broad, clear of brush,
and comes tumbling down between two lofty mountains, whose
moss- and fern-covered rocks, and immense hemlock, pine, and
beech trees, are a sight to behold, while its cool, crystal waters
sparkle and ripple over many little cascades in a manner that
would at once delight the eye of any lover of nature and make
him bless the day that brought him to the spot. Hamlin and I
were casting our flies over the same pool, and my rod being
rewarded with a fine, large fish, we were both devoting our
energies to land him. My companion was in the pool, waist-
deep, seeking to thrust the landing-net under the fish that was
calmly floating on the surface of the water, an indication that he
had abandoned the struggle and was ready to be lifted into the
creel. But, just as the net touched his silver sides, a spark of
electric energy seemed to be imparted to him, when away he
dived again, this time making toward Hamlin's legs for a harbor
of safety, causing that individual to make sundry comical
plunges to escape from the entanglement. The fish was soon
reeled in again and quieted down, the net once more placed
under him, only to stir him up to renewed exertions of spright-
liness. This time he got the best of Hamlin, tangling him up in
net, leader, and trout in such an indescribable manner as to tax
our ingenuity to the utmost to unravel him.

The trout was darting hither and thither, between Hamlin's

legs, then my own, while both of us were diving for him with our landing-nets in the most frantic manner, when with one last, desperate effort, in which he seemed to bring the force of all his previous jumps into one, he made a leap clear over my net, and landed safe and free in the pool beyond. Hamlin looked at me, I looked at him; and before either of us could make an exclamation, the bushes suddenly parted on the bank, and a voice, followed by a man, greeted us, saying,—

"I know you'd lose 'im. I caught one bigger'n him, over on Pine Creek, once and he mixed three on us up just at this 'un did you fellers, and jumped clean over my head and knocked my boy down. That 'un there" (pointing to his young hopeful of about thirteen years of age, who sat shivering and grinning from the bank on the other side).

As the fish had departed, we turned our attention to the newcomer, who presented himself so mysteriously and unannounced in our presence. He was a man of about fifty years of age, short of stature, with a small, round head, densely covered with long, shaggy, unkempt hair,—an equal mixture of auburn and gray,—while whiskers of the same bountiful supply and of like hue, almost concealed a pale and plump face. His eyes were blue and bright, mouth large, and well filled with tobacco-stained teeth that were exposed by the broad grin wrinkling his cheeks. He wore a black coat, threadbare, and abundantly patched, while his trousers (what was left of them) exposed a once white shirt, from front and rear, and a well-bronzed skin at the knees. This uniform was topped out with a black slouch hat, profusely ornamented with artificial flies, which seemed to have been collected from the back leaves of the fly-books of all the fishermen who had visited this stream for the past two years. On his shoulder rested a pole that evidently had been cut in the woods, while in his hand was an old, six-quart tin pail, covered with a dirty rag, a hole cut in the centre, through which to thrust his trout, when captured in the mysterious manner known only to himself and the boy on the other bank; and this was "Shorty." We knew him from the description given of him, from his introductory story, from his tin pail, and boy with the plethoric black bag, which he said contained lunch, but which we suspected was the receptacle for his most taking fly,—*a net.*

The wind was blowing from the north somewhat cold, and, it being about time to take our nooning, we concluded to build a fire, cook our trout, and in the interval interview Shorty. He watched our preparations, divined what we were about, and, catching up his pail in one hand and pole in the other, exclaimed,—

"Oh, if you'r'n want of a fire, one that'll cook yer fish and toast yer shins too, jest cum this way, and I'll show you 'en. Ye see, I allers start *my* fires jest off ov the stream a ways, so I won't be bothered with nobody that happens along."

Following him through the dense underbrush for a few rods, we came to a bright, glowing fire, built under an old hemlock stump, that was fanned into a glowing coal in the brisk wind that was just then blowing. While preparing our fish for the roast, Shorty watched the proceedings, and, with mouth watering at the prospect of so luscious a meal as seemed to be in prospect, observed,—

"I reckon them trout'll be mighty good cooked that there way. I never seen it done so afore. That buttered paper is to keep 'em from burnin', I s'pose. Now I calkerlate that's a heap sight better way than to cook 'em on a stick, and burnin' ov 'em."

"Yes; trout are very delicious when prepared in this manner, Shorty. Do you fish upon this stream much?"

"Do I? Why, Lor' bless yer soul, I've fished this yer stream from top to bottom for nigh onto twenty years now, and I known every rock on its bottom, and every stump and root on its shore."

"You catch many fine fish, no doubt; take them all on a fly, I suppose?"

"Indeed I does. Nobody on this 'ere stream has no bisness with me a-fishin' with flies. Why, ye only jest oughter a-bin up here this mornin', afore the wind got to blowin'; why, I ketched— well, ye kin see"—(uncovering the six-quart pail for our inspection, revealing it more than two-thirds full of trout, from one inch to twelve in length)—"I ketched every blessed one on 'em in less'n a hour. I never seed 'em jump so; why, I took 'em four and five at a time."

"Four and five at a time!" exclaimed Hamlin, who had just lighted his pipe, and was holding a burning ember aloft, to catch the direction of the wind. "Why, man, how many flies do you usually attach to a leader?"

"Oh, sometimes ten and sometimes twelve, accordin' as to how they're a bitin'!"

"Ten and twelve flies at a cast! Hail Columbia! Why, you must throw a whole out-line," observes Hamlin, with a sly wink and a characteristic spit over his left shoulder.

"How many fish can you take here in a day?" I inquired, while carefully covering the roll of prepared trout with the burning embers.

"Well, the biggest hull I ever made was three years ago, out o' that ere hole ye see yonder. I jist looked into it off ov that rock that hangs over it, and counted one hundred and twenty-two busters, every one on 'em weighing mor'n a pound. Now, thinks I, them there trout are mine, every one on 'em; so what does I do but jest throws the hole full of brush, so as no other feller could see 'em or ketch 'em out, and then went to feedin' ov 'em."

"Feeding them? What for, pray?"

"Why, ye see, I wanted to git 'em all; so I feeds 'em to make 'em kinder wanted to the place, ye see. Well, I fed 'em every night and mornin' fur—"

"What on?"

"On-on-let's see; what *did* I give 'em?" (scratching his head and looking into the fire, as though in search of something to feed those trout upon.) "Oh, I fed 'em on chicken innards, and mighty fond of 'em they wus, too. Ye would o' laughed yersels nigh unto death to see one big feller tackle one ov them long innards and start to runnin', with about fifty more a-pullin' at the t'other eend of it to get it away from him, jist like I hev seed a parcel ov pigs a-doin' manys the time."

"But it seems to me you must have slaughtered a good many chickens to have fed your trout twice a day in that manner."

"Yes, I did; but ye see we live purty much on chickens in the summer, does the old 'oman and me and the six childrens, and then we raised 'em on purpose."

"Oh, I see."

"Well, as I was a-sayin', I fed 'em twice a day, and arter they got so they knowed me, I would feed 'em up stream a little higher, every day, until I let 'em 'round into that little run ye see a-comin' in jest 'round yender pint. I built a brush dam acrost the mouth ov it, and put in a board to shet the water off when I wanted to. After I got 'em in there, don't yer see? I had 'em tight. I jest shet down that board, and picked out every blessed one on 'em with my bare hands!"

"But I cannot see any fun in that sort of fishing, Shorty. Why did you not catch them on a fly, and so enjoy it?"

"That's all werry well for you fellers what's got lots o' money and nuthin' to do to talk about. But when a poor feller like me, with a big family a-dependin' on 'im for sumthin' to eat, why, he's got to—"

"You don't mean to tell me you ate them?"

"No; ye didn't let me finish. I sold every one on 'em, alive, to Mister Drake what's got a pond down the road, and he give me a hundred and fifty dollars for 'em in cash!"

"Pretty good price that, Shorty."

"Well, I dunno; one on 'em what weighed nigh onto four pounds had only one eye, and that 'un was right in the middle of his forrid,—jest as true as I'm a-sittin' here,—and it did make him look mighty comikel, I can tell ye."

"A regular Cyclops," we interposed.

"Yes, he was a sly chops, for a fact; why, his mouth was bigger'n that," placing the palms of his two hands together, and separating them as far as the wrists.

"Shorty, what fly are they taking to-day?" inquired Hamlin, who seemed inclined to divert him from the stories that were becoming somewhat of an infliction.

"Well, I dunno, but 'pears to me the great dun is as good as enny," at the same time removing his hat and passing every fly, with which the band was covered, between his fingers.

"Of whom do you purchase your flies? I see you have quite a collection," was the next query.

"Oh, my 'oman makes all *my* flies."

"Indeed; let us look at them," we both replied in chorus.

He passed over the hat, and, taking a seat nearer, commenced expatiating upon their relative value, as he pointed out each fly with a long, bony finger.

"That 'un there," he said, pointing to one of McBride's grizzly kings, "that 'un she made yesterday, and I reckon on its bein' first-class, cause I took a whopper with it this mornin' already."

"Where did you procure the feathers?" we ventured to inquire.

"Them speckled ones?"

"Yes; and the hackle, too."

Reaching down into his dirty pocket, his face assuming a somewhat puzzled expression, he took out a quarter of a yard of the most villainous-looking plug-tobacco, placed one corner of it between his strong teeth, yanked it back and forth, much as a dog would a wood-chuck, until the desired quantity was secured within his mouth. Then, after working his jaws vigorously for a few moments, expectorated a quantity of black-looking fluid over Hamlin's leg into the stream beyond; and, slapping the plug upon his thigh, replied,—

"Them purty little speckled 'uns I got offna woodpecker, and that what you calls a hackle offna woodcock."

"Good gracious, doctor, do let him alone! he'll try to make us believe this stream will reverse its current by to-morrow, and that we must stand on our heads to fish it; come, let up," observed Hamlin, while he rose and scratched among the coals for the package of trout placed there twenty minutes before.

"Come," he further added, "the trout are done by this time, the tea cool enough to drink, and I'm as hungry as need be for the occasion."

So we spread our luncheon upon a log that lay conveniently near, using clean, flat stones for plates, and fell to eating. Shorty watched the proceedings, as did his boy, who deposited his black bag on the bank across the creek and drew nearer, wiping his mouth with his hat and looking wistfully in the direction of the edibles. I could not resist his imploring gaze, but took a slice of bread, bountifully covered with butter, and garnished with a steaming trout, and held it toward him, saying,—

"Come here, you young scalawag, and have a bite."

He approached shyly, bending his body forward and, reaching as far as his ragged-clad arm would permit, grabbed the morsel, much as a trout would have taken a fly, and disappeared into the brush.

"Hev ye forgot yer manners?" Shorty observed, looking after him; but it was too late, the boy had gone out of hearing, and was doubtless satisfying his hunger unseen. Hamlin supplied Shorty with a like piece, which he devoured ravenously, grunting his satisfaction between each mouthful.

"Shorty, where do you live?" I asked, after an interval of quiet.

"Jest down here aways; ye see them pine-trees down there about a mile?" using his pants and sleeve for a napkin, as he rose, pointing in the direction indicated. "Well, right there's a bridge that goes acrost the creek; my shanty's there, in the clearin'."

"What do you do for a living?"

"In summer I raises pertaters and corn; fishes, and sells my fish to city chaps what comes here a-fishin' and ketches nothing', and shoemakes in the winter."

"You make enough to support yourself and family, do you?"

"Oh, yes; easy. Why, I make as high as twelve dollars a day sum days, a-fishin'. I keeps all the fish me and the boys ketches, and when I can't sell 'em to the city fellers, I jest runs down to Williamsport, and gets fifty cents a pound for 'em."

"What, such little ones as you have there in your bucket?"

"Yis, sir; they all counts in a pound."

"It's a shame, Shorty, to take those little fish from the stream; you will soon ruin the fishing."

"Yes, you city fellers all says, that; but I allers notices that you never throws 'em in yourselves. They all says them little 'uns is so sweet to eat, you know."

"But no *true* sportsman will do that, Shorty."

"Well, I dunno: it 'pears to me what you calls yer true 'uns never comes this way, then."

"I'm sorry our city sportsmen set you so bad an example, Shorty; but tell me, do you never fish with anything but a hook and line? for, you see, I'm a little skeptical about your being able to catch a hundred of those little trout—less than two inches in length—upon a hook. I have always found them the hardest to capture with flies the size of those you wear on your hat."

"That may all be; but me and my boys ketches 'em easy enough." Then, twisting off another chew from his enormous plug, he stowed it away under his cheek, giving his face the appearance of a person suffering from *ranula*, and prepared his mouth for another squirt; at which symptoms Hamlin shifted his seat, fearing, doubtless, that the aim might miss and the shot be-spatter his legs. He then added: "Oh, sometimes we puts out a few set-lines at night, and ketches some nice ones that way."

"Indeed! How do you set them?"

"Why, I takes a line about *so* long," indicating three feet between his extended hands, "and ties it to a branch of some tree that hangs over a deep hole, and puts a live minney on the hook. His wiggling is too much for a big trout: he just goes for it, and swallers 'im hull. Then I has 'im; 'cause the limb bends just like a pole, and he can't tear hisself loose, ye see."

"How large a trout did you ever catch in that manner?"

"It is nigh onto five years now, I reckon since I ketched a reg'lar walloper that way. He weighed three pounds fifteen ounces, and three-quarters! By golly! I *did* want to make him weigh even four pounds, but Squire Bodine weighed him and shaved him clost. It was a dark night, and the eels were a-runnin' powerful strong. I set a hook on a riff near my house, and along came a eel, just thirty inches long, and swallered the hook, and a while afterward that big trout tackled Mr. eel and swallered him; so next mornin' I had 'em both."

"Was the eel alive?" I innocently inquired.

"Alive! In *course* he was; and the way he must o' stirred up that trout's innards was a caution! I reckon he was awful sick to his stummick."

"Well, I should say so. You do catch eels here, then?"

"Oh, yes; frequent. I ketched one last fall that weighed four pounds, and I swar to goodness if a big trout didn't try to swaller him, and got ketched at it hisself. He took Mr. eel tail on, and the minnit the eel felt sumthin' a-ticklin' of his tail he just curled it around so"—indicating the bend by a crook of his finger—"and ketched him through the gills, and held him there till mornin', when I got the two of 'em!"

"If I were you I'd keep a lot of eels on hand, Shorty, and set them every night; they beat the 'eagle's-claw trap' all to pieces," Hamlin observed.

"Well, I was a-thinkin' o' that there myself, but the're so

blessed slippery a feller can't do much in the way of a-trainin' of 'em."

At this, Hamlin looked at his watch, remarked that it was three o'clock, that the wind had gone down, and if we desired to catch any fish that day we had better be at it. So, I rinsed out our tea-pot, hung it to my creel-strap, lighted my pipe, and was ready for a march down the stream. At this demonstration Shorty also rose, looked up and down stream for his boy, and, not seeing him, gave a peculiar whistle through his fingers. Presently the lad, with the black knapsack on his back, broke covert, but seeing us, retreated into the bushes again.

Hamlin and I entered the stream, unreeled our lines, and, with a good-bye salutation to Shorty, passed on, leaving him watching us from the bank. After turning the first bend in the creek, we were surprised to see Shorty there, and when we came within hailing distance he shouted at the top of his voice, so that he might be heard above the roar of the cascade,—

"Say, you 'uns, I forgot to ax ye, doesn't ye wanter buy my trout?"

"Buy your trout! You whimpering, shivering scoundrel, what do you take us for?" Hamlin cried, with supreme disgust depicted upon every line of his face. "We are not pot-hunters, you miserable shark; get out!"

"Well, ye needn't git mad about it; I didn't know but what ye *might* buy 'em; but I didn't see no flask a-hangin' over yer shoulder, I must say, but thought, maybe, ye carried it in yer basket."

"Flask! flask! What's that got to do with it?" Hamlin inquired.

"Oh, a heap. I allers notices that them fellers whot carries their basket under one arm and a flask a-hangin' under t'other have more luck a-drinkin' than they do a-ketchin' ov fish, so I allers sell 'em my trout, and gets a good price for 'em, too."

"That's all right, Shorty; but we have no use for your fish; we are out for sport only, not to see how many trout we can destroy. By-bye."

"Good-bye, surs. When ye cum this way agin ye will most allers find me here on this stream, sumwheres about, a-ready to build fires or do any other work ye may stand in want of." Then, with an awkward flourish of his gayly-trimmed hat and an attempt at what resembled a bow, he quitted us; and as the willows closed behind him we heard his voice above the roar of the rapid—"Y-o-u John-*nee*!" to which a ghostly response came from somewhere up the stream—"Hal-*loo*!" We passed on down the cascade and left father and son to the contemplation of nature—and the defenceless fish.

Fourth Day

Izaak Walton

(from "The Compleat Angler," 1653)

Pisc. Good morrow, good hostess; I see my brother Peter is still in bed: come, give my scholar and me a morning drink, and a bit of meat to breakfast; and be sure to get a good dish of meat or two against supper, for we shall come home as hungry as hawks. Come, scholar, let's be going.

Ven. Well now, good master, as we walk towards the river give me direction, according to your promise, how I shall fish for a trout.

Pisc. My honest scholar, I will take this very convenient opportunity to do it.

The trout is usually caught with a worm or a minnow (which some call a penk) or with a fly, viz., either a natural or an artificial fly: concerning which three I will give you some observations and directions.

And, first, for worms: of these there be very many sorts: some breed only in the earth, as the earth-worm; others of or amongst plants, as the dung-worm; and others breed either out of excrements, or in the bodies of living creatures, as in the horns of sheep or deer; or some of dead flesh, as the maggot or gentle, and others.

Now these be most of them particularly good for particular fishes: but for the trout, the dew-worm (which some also call the lob-worm) and the brandling are the chief; and especially the first for a great trout, and the latter for a less. There be also of lob-worms some called squirrel-tails (a worm that has a red head, a streak down the back, and a broad tail) which are noted to be the best, because they are the toughest and most lively, and live longest in the water: for you are to know that a dead worm is but a dead bait, and like to catch nothing, compared to a lively, quick, stirring worm: and for a brandling, he is usually found in an old dunghill, or some very rotten place near to it: but most usually in cow-dung, or hog's dung, rather than horse-dung, which is somewhat too hot and dry for that worm. But the best of them are to be found in the bark of the tanners, which they cast up in heaps after they have used it about their leather.

There are also divers other kinds of worms, which for colour and shape alter even as the ground out of which they are got; as the marsh-worm, the tag-tail, the flag-worm, the dock-worm, the oak-worm, the gilt-tail, the twachel, or lob-worm, which of all others is the most excellent bait for a salmon; and too many to name, even as many sorts as some think there be of several herbs or shrubs, or of several kinds of birds in the air; of which I shall say no more, but tell you that what worms soever you fish with are the better for being well scoured, that is, long kept before they be used: and in case you have not been so provident, then the way to cleanse and scour them quickly is to put them all night in water, if they be lob-worms, and then put them into your bag with fennel. But you must not put your brandlings above an hour in water, and then put them into fennel, for sudden use: but if you have time, and purpose to keep them long, then they be best preserved in an earthen pot, with good store of moss, which is to be fresh every three or four days in summer, and every week or eight days in winter; or, at least, the moss taken from them and clean washed, and wrung betwixt your hands till it be dry, and then put it to them again. And when your worms, especially the brandling, begins to be sick and lose of his bigness, then you may recover him by putting a little milk or cream (about a spoonful in a day) into them, by drops on the moss; and if there be added to the cream an egg beaten and boiled in it, then it will both fatten and preserve them long. And note, that when the knot, which is near to the middle of the brandling, begins to swell, then he is sick; and, if he be not well looked to, is near dying. And for moss, you are to note, that there be divers kinds of it, which I could name to you, but I will only tell you that that which is likest a buck's-horn is the best, except it be soft white moss, which grows on some heaths, and is hard to be found. And note, that in a very dry time, when you are put to an extremity for worms, walnut-tree leaves squeezed into water, or salt in water, to make it bitter or salt, and then that water poured on the ground, where you shall see worms are used to rise in the night, will make them to appear above ground presently. And you may take notice, some say that camphor, put into your bag with your moss and worms, gives them a strong and so tempting a smell, that the fish fare the worse and you the better for it.

And now I shall show you how to bait your hook with a worm, so as shall prevent you from much trouble, and the loss of many a hook too, when you fish for a trout with a running-line, that is to say, when you fish for him by hand at the ground: I will direct you in this as plainly as I can, that you may not mistake.

Suppose it be a big lob-worm, put your hook into him somewhat above the middle, and out again a little below the middle; having so done, draw your worm above the arming of your hook: but note that at the entering of your hook it must not be at the head-end of the worm, but at the tail-end of him, that the point of your hook may come out toward the head-end, and having drawn him above the arming of your hook, then put the point of your hook again into the very head of the worm, till it come near to the place where the point of the hook first came out: and then draw back that part of the worm that was above the shank or arming of your hook, and so fish with it. And if you mean to fish with two worms, then put the second on before you turn back the hook's-head of the first worm: you cannot lose above two or three worms before you attain to what I direct you; and having attained it, you will find it very useful, and thank me for it, for you will run on the ground without tangling.

Now for the Minnow or Penk: he is not easily found and caught till March, or in April, for then he appears first in the river; nature having taught him to shelter and hide himself, in the winter, in ditches that be near to the river; and there both to hide, and keep himself warm, in the mud, or in the weeds, which rot not so soon as in a running river, in which place if he were in winter, the distempered floods that are usually in that season would suffer him to take no rest, but carry him headlong to mills and weirs, to his confusion. And of these minnows; first you are to know that the biggest size is not the best; and next, that the middle size and the whitest are the best; and then you are to know, that your minnow must be so put on your hook, that it must turn round when 'tis drawn against the stream; and, that it may turn nimbly, you must put it on a big-sized hook, as I shall now direct you, which is thus: put your hook in at his mouth, and out at his gill; then, having drawn your hook two or three inches beyond or through his gill, put it again into his mouth, and the point and beard out at his tail; and then tie the hook and his tail about, very neatly, with a white thread, which will make it the apter to turn quick in the water: that done, pull back that part of your line which was slack when you did put your hook into the minnow the second time; I say, pull that part of your line back, so that it shall fasten the head, so that the body of the minnow shall be almost straight on your hook: this done, try how it will turn, by drawing it across the water or against the stream; and if it do not turn nimbly, then turn the tail a little to the right or left hand, and try again, till it turn quick; for if not, you are in danger to catch nothing: for know, that it is impossible that it should turn too quick; and you are yet to know, that in case you want a minnow, then a small loach or a stickle-bag, or any other small fish that will turn quick, will serve as well: and you are to know, that you may salt them, and by that means keep them ready and fit for use three or four days or longer; and that of salt, bay-salt is the best.

And here let me tell you, what many old anglers know right well, that at some times, and in some waters, a minnow is not to be got; and therefore let me tell you, I have (which I will show you) an artificial minnow, that will catch a trout as well as an artificial fly, and it was made by a handsome woman that had a fine hand, and a live minnow lying by her: the mould or body of the minnow was cloth, and wrought upon or over it thus with a needle: the back of it with very sad French green silk, the paler green silk towards the belly, shadowed as perfectly as you can imagine, just as you see a minnow; the belly was wrought also with a needle, and it was a part of it white silk, and another part of it with silver thread; the tail and fins were of a quill which was shaven thin; the eyes were of two little black beads, and the head was so shadowed, and all of it so curiously wrought, and so exactly dissembled that it would beguile any sharp-sighted trout in a swift stream. And this minnow I will now show you; look, here it is, and, if you like it, lend it you, to have two or three made by it; for they be easily carried about an angler, and be of excellent use; for note, that a large trout will come as fiercely at a minnow as the highest mettled hawk doth seize on a partridge, or a greyhound on a hare. I have been told that a hundred and sixty minnows have been found in a trout's belly; either the trout had devoured so many, or the miller that gave it to a friend of mine had forced them down his throat after he had taken him.

Now for flies, which is the third bait wherewith trouts are usually taken. You are to know that there are so many sorts of flies as there be of fruits: I will name you but some of them; as the dun-fly, the stone-fly, the red-fly, the moor-fly, the tawny-fly, the shell-fly, the cloudy or blackish-fly, the flag-fly, the vine-fly; there be of flies, caterpillars, and canker-flies, and bear-flies; and indeed too many either for me to name, or for you to remember: and their breeding is so various and wonderful, that I might easily amaze myself, and tire you in a relation of them.

And, yet, I will exercise your promised patience by saying a little of the caterpillar, or the palmer-fly or worm; that by them you may guess what a work it were, in a discourse, but to run over those very many flies, worms, and little living creatures with which the sun and summer adorn and beautify the river-banks and meadows, both for the recreation and contemplation of us anglers; pleasures which, I think, I myself enjoy more than any other man that is not of my profession.

Pliny holds an opinion that many have their birth or being from a dew that in the spring falls from the leaves of trees; and that some kinds of them are from a dew left upon herbs or flowers; and others, from a dew left upon coleworts or cabbages: all which kinds of dews being thickened and condensed, are by the sun's generative heat most of them hatched, and in three days made living creatures; and these of several shapes and colours; some being hard and tough, some smooth and soft; some are horned in their head, some in their tail, some have none; some have hair, some none; some have sixteen feet, some less, and some have none; but (as our Topsel hath with great diligence observed) those which have none move upon the earth, or upon broad leaves, their motion being not unlike to the waves of the sea. Some of them, he also observes, to be bred of the eggs of other caterpillars, and that those in their time turn to be butterflies; and again, that their eggs turn the following year to be caterpillars. And some affirm that every plant has his particular fly or caterpillar, which it breeds and feeds. I have seen, and may therefore affirm it, a green caterpillar or worm, as big as a small peascod, which had fourteen legs, eight on the belly, four under the neck, and two near the tail. It was found on a hedge of privet, and was taken thence and put into a large box, and a little branch or two of privet put to it, on which I saw it feed as sharply as a dog gnaws a bone; it lived thus five or six days, and thrived and changed the colour two or three times; but by some neglect in the keeper of it, it then died, and did not turn to a fly: but if it had lived, it had doubtless turned to one of those flies that some call flies of prey, which those that walk by the rivers may, in summer, see fasten on smaller flies, and, I think, make them their food. And 'tis observable, that as there be these flies of prey, which be very large, so there be others, very little, created, I think, only to feed them, and breed out of I know not what; whose life, they say, nature intended not to exceed an hour: and yet that life is thus made shorter by other flies, or by accident.

It is needless to tell you what the curious searchers into nature's productions have observed of these worms and flies: but yet I shall tell you what Aldrovandus, our Topsel, and others say of the palmer-worm, or caterpillar, that whereas others content themselves to feed on particular herbs or leaves (for most think those very leaves that gave them life and shape give them a particular feeding and nourishment, and that upon them they usually abide) yet he observes that this is called a pilgrim, or palmer-worm, for his very wandering life and various food: not contenting himself, as others do, with any one certain place for his abode, nor any certain kind of herb or flower for his feeding, but will boldly and disorderly wander up and down, and not endure to be kept to a diet, or fixed to a particular place.

Nay, the very colours of caterpillars are, as one has observed, very elegant and beautiful. I shall (for a taste of the rest) describe one of them; which I will, some time the next month, show you feeding on a willow-tree; and you shall find him punctually to answer this very description: his lips and mouth somewhat yellow; his eyes black as jet; his forehead purple; his feet and hinder parts green; his tail two-forked and black; the whole body stained with a kind of red spots, which run along the neck and shoulder-blade, not unlike the form of St Andrew's cross, or the letter X, made thus cross-wise, and a white line drawn down his back to his tail; all which add much beauty to his whole body. And it is to me observable, that at a fixed age this caterpillar gives over to eat, and towards winter comes to be covered over with a strange shell or crust, called an aurelia: and so lives a kind of dead life, without eating, all the winter; and, as others of several kinds turn to be several kinds of flies and vermin the spring following, so this caterpillar then turns to be a painted butterfly.

Come, come, my scholar, you see the river stops our morning walk, and I will also here stop my discourse; only as we sit down under this honeysuckle hedge, whilst I look a line to fit the rod that our brother Peter hath lent you, I shall for a little confirmation of what I have said, repeat the observation of Du Bartas.

> God, not contented to each kind to give,
> And to infuse the virtue generative,
> By His wise power made many creatures breed
> Of lifeless bodies, without Venus' deed.
>
> So the cold humour breeds the salamander,
> Who, in effect like to her birth's commander,
> With child with hundred winters, with her touch
> Quencheth the fire, though glowing ne'er so much.

So in the fire, in burning furnace springs
The fly Perausta, with the flaming wings;
Without the fire it dies, in it it joys,
Living in that which all things else destroys.

So slow Boötes underneath him sees,
In th' icy islands, goslings hatch'd of trees,
Whose fruitful leaves, falling into the water,
Are turn'd ('tis known) to living fowls soon after.

So rotten planks of broken ships do change
To barnacles. O transformation strange!
'Twas first a green tree, then a broken hull,
Lately a mushroom, now a flying gull.

Ven. O my good master, this morning-walk has been spent to my great pleasure and wonder: but I pray, when shall I have your direction how to make artificial flies, like to those that the trout loves best, and also how to use them?

Pisc. My honest scholar, it is now past five of the clock, we will fish till nine, and then go to breakfast. Go you to yon sycamore-tree and hide your bottle of drink under the hollow root of it; for about that time, and in that place, we will make a brave breakfast with a piece of powdered beef, and a radish or two that I have in my fish-bag; we shall, I warrant you, make a good, honest, wholesome, hungry breakfast, and I will then give you direction for the making and using of your flies; and in the meantime there is your rod, and line, and my advice is, that you fish as you see me do, and let's try which can catch the first fish.

Ven. I thank you, master, I will observe and practise your direction as far as I am able.

Pisc. Look you, scholar, you see I have hold of a good fish: I now see it is a trout, I pray put that net under him, and touch not my line, for if you do, then we break all. Well done, scholar, I thank you.

Now for another. Trust me, I have another bite: come, scholar, come lay down your rod, and help me to land this as you did the other. So now we shall be sure to have a good dish of fish for supper.

Ven. I am glad of that; but I have no fortune: sure, master, yours is a better rod and better tackling.

Pisc. Nay, then, take mine, and I will fish with yours. Look you, scholar, I have another. Come, do as you did before. And now I have a bite at another. Oh me! he has broke all: there's half a line and a good hook lost.

Ven. Ay, and a good trout too.

Pisc. Nay, the trout is not lost; for pray take notice, no man can lose what he never had.

Ven. Master, I can neither catch with the first nor second angle: I have no fortune.

Pisc. Look you, scholar, I have yet another. And now, having caught three brace of trouts, I will tell you a short tale as we walk towards our breakfast. A scholar (a preacher I should say) that was to preach to procure the approbation of a parish, that he might be their lecturer, had got from his fellow pupil the copy of a sermon that was first preached with great commendation by him that composed it: and though the borrower of it preached it, word for word, as it was at first, yet it was utterly disliked as it was preached by the second to his congregation: which the sermon-borrower complained of to the lender of it; and thus was answered: "I lent you, indeed, my fiddle, but not my fiddlestick; for you are to know that every one cannot make music with my words, which are fitted to my own mouth." And so, my scholar, you are to know, that as the ill pronunciation or ill accenting of words in a sermon spoils it, so the ill carriage of your line, or not fishing even to a foot in a right place, makes you lose your labour: and you are to know, that though you have my fiddle, that is, my very rod and tacklings with which you see I catch fish, yet you have not my fiddlestick, that is, you yet have not skill to know how to carry your hand and line, or how to guide it to a right place: and this must be taught you (for you are to remember, I told you angling is an art) either by practice or a long observation, or both. But take this for a rule, when you fish for a trout with a worm, let your line have so much, and not more lead than will fit the stream in which you fish; that is to say, more in a great troublesome stream than in a smaller that is quieter; as near as may be, so much as will sink the bait to the bottom, and keep it still in motion, and not more.

But now let's say grace and fall to breakfast: what say you, scholar, to the providence of an old angler? Does not this meat taste well? and was not this place well chosen to eat it? for this sycamore-tree will shade us from the sun's heat.

Ven. All excellent good, and my stomach excellent good too. And now I remember and find that true which devout Lessius says: "That poor men, and those that fast often, have much more pleasure in eating than rich men and gluttons, that always feed before their stomachs are empty of their last meat, and call for more: for by that means they rob themselves of that pleasure that hunger brings to poor men." And I do seriously approve of that saying of yours, "that you would rather be a civil, well-governed, well-grounded, temperate, poor angler than a drunken lord." But I hope there is none such; however, I am certain of this, that I have been at very many costly dinners that have not afforded me half the content that this has done, for which I thank God and you.

And now, good master, proceed to your promised direction for making and ordering my artificial fly.

Pisc. My honest scholar, I will do it; for it is a debt due unto you by my promise: and because you shall not think yourself more engaged to me than indeed you really are, I will freely give you such directions as were lately given to me by an ingenious brother of the angle, an honest man and a most excellent fly-fisher.

You are to note, that there are twelve kinds of artificially made flies to angle with on the top of the water. Note, by the way, that the fittest season of using these is in a blustering windy day, when the waters are so troubled that the natural fly cannot be seen, or rest upon them. The first is the dun-fly, in March: the body is made of dun wool; the wings, of the partridge's feathers. The second is another dun-fly: the body of black wool; and the wings made of the black drake's feathers, and of the feathers under his tail. The third is the stone-fly, in April: the body is made of black wool; made yellow under the wings and under the tail, and so made with the wings of the drake. The fourth is the ruddy-fly, in the beginning of May: the body made of red wool, wrapt about with black silk; and the feathers are the wings of the drake, with the feathers of a red capon also, which hang dangling on his sides next to the tail. The fifth is the yellow or greenish fly (in May likewise): the body made of yellow wool: and the wings made of the red cock's hackle or tail. The sixth is the black-fly, in May also: the body made of black wool, and lapped about with the herle of a peacock's tail; the wings are made of the wings of a brown capon, with his blue feathers in his head. The seventh is the sad yellow-fly, in June: the body is made of black wool, with a yellow list on either side; and the wings taken off the wings of a buzzard, bound with black braked hemp. The eighth is the moorish-fly: made with the body of duskish wool; and the wings made of the blackish mail of the drake. The ninth is the tawny-fly, good until the middle of June: the body made of tawny wool, the wings made contrary, one against the other, made of the whitish mail of the wild drake. The tenth is the wasp-fly, in July: the body made of black wool, lapped about with yellow silk; the wings made of the feathers of the drake, or of the buzzard. The eleventh is the shell-fly, good in mid-July: the body made of greenish wool, lapped about with the herle of a peacock's tail, and the wings made of the wings of the buzzard. The twelfth is the dark drake-fly, good in August:

the body made with black wool, lapped about with black silk; his wings are made with the mail of the black drake, with a black head. Thus have you a jury of flies, likely to betray and condemn all the trouts in the river.

I shall next give you some other directions for fly-fishing, such as are given by Mr Thomas Barker, a gentleman that hath spent much time in fishing; but I shall do it with a little variation.

First, let your rod be light, and very gentle; I take the best to be of two pieces: and let not your line exceed (especially for three or four links next to the hook), I say, not exceed three or four hairs at the most, though you may fish a little stronger above, in the upper part of your line; but if you can attain to angle with one hair, you shall have more rises, and catch more fish. Now you must be sure not to cumber yourself with too long a line, as most do. And before you begin to angle, cast to have the wind on your back; and the sun, if it shines, to be before you; and to fish down the stream; and carry the point or top of your rod downward, by which means, the shadow of yourself and rod too will be least offensive to the fish; for the sight of any shade amazes the fish, and spoils your sport—of which you must take a great care.

In the middle of March (till which time a man should not, in honesty, catch a trout) or in April, if the weather be dark, or a little windy or cloudy, the best fishing is with the palmer-worm, of which I last spoke to you; but of these there be divers kinds, or at least of divers colours; these and the May-fly are the ground of all fly-angling, which are to be thus made:

First, you must arm your hook with the line in the inside of it, then take your scissors, and cut so much of a brown mallard's feather, as in your own reason will make the wings of it, you having withal regard to the bigness or littleness of your hook; then lay the outmost part of your feather next to your hook, then the point of your feather next the shank of your hook; and having done so, whip it three or four times about the hook with the same silk with which your hook was armed; and, having made the silk fast, take the hackle of a cock or capon's neck, or a plover's top, which is usually better; take off the one side of the feather, and then take the hackle, silk, or crewel, gold or silver thread, make these fast at the bent of the hook, that is to say, below your arming; then you must take the hackle, the silver or gold thread, and work it up to the wings, shifting or still removing your finger, as you turn the silk about the hook; and still looking at every stop or turn, that your gold, or what materials soever you make your fly of, do lie right and neatly; and if you find they do so, then, when you have made the head, make all fast and then work your hackle up to the head, and make that fast: and then with a needle or pin divide the wing into two, and then with the arming silk whip it about crossways betwixt the wings, and then with your thumb you must turn the point of the feather towards the bent of the hook, and then work three or four times about the shank of the hook, and then view the proportion, and if all be neat and to your liking, fasten.

I confess, no direction can be given to make a man of a dull capacity able to make a fly well: and yet I know this, with a little practice, will help an ingenious angler in a good degree; but to see a fly made by an artist in that kind is the best teaching to make it. And then an ingenious angler may walk by the river and mark what flies fall on the water that day, and catch one of them, if he sees the trouts leap at a fly of that kind; and then having always hooks ready hung with him, and having a bag always with him, with bear's hair, or the hair of a brown or sad-coloured heifer, hackles of a cock or capon, several coloured silk and crewel to make the body of the fly, the feathers of a drake's head, black or brown sheep's wool, or hog's wool or hair, thread of gold and of silver; silk of several colours (especially sad-coloured, to make the fly's head) and there be also other coloured feathers, both of little birds and of speckled fowl—I say, having those with him in a bag, and trying to make a fly, though he miss at first, yet shall he at last hit it better, even to such a perfection as none can well teach him; and if he hit to make his fly right, and have the luck to hit also where there is store of trouts, a dark day, and a right wind, he will catch such store of them, as will encourage him to grow more and more in love with the art of fly-making.

Ven. But, my loving master, if any wind will not serve, then I wish I were in Lapland, to buy a good wind of one of the honest witches, that sell so many winds there, and so cheap.

Pisc. Marry, scholar, but I would not be there, nor indeed from under this tree: for look how it begins to rain; and by the clouds, if I mistake not, we shall presently have a smoking shower; and therefore sit close; this sycamore-tree will shelter us: and I will tell you, as they shall come into my mind, more observations of fly-fishing for a trout.

But first, for the wind; you are to take notice, that of the winds, the south wind is said to be the best. One observes that

> . . . when the wind is south,
> It blows your bait into a fish's mouth.

Next to that, the west wind is believed to be the best; and having told you that the east wind is the worst I need not tell you which wind is the best in the third degree: and yet (as Solomon observes), that "he that considers the wind shall never sow," so he that busies his head too much about them (if the weather be not made extreme cold by an east wind) shall be a little superstitious: for as it is observed by some that "there is no good horse of a bad colour," so I have observed, that if it be a cloudy day, and not extreme cold, let the wind set in what corner it will and do its worst, I heed it not. And yet take this for a rule, that I would willingly fish standing on the lee-shore: and you are to take notice, that the fish lies or swims nearer the bottom, and in deeper water, in winter than in summer; and also nearer the bottom in any cold day, and then gets nearest the lee-side of the water.

But I promised to tell you more of the fly-fishing for a trout, which I may have time enough to do, for you see it rains May-butter. First, for a May-fly, you may make his body with greenish-coloured crewel or willowish colour, darkening it in most places with waxed silk, or ribbed with black hair, or some of them ribbed with silver thread; and such wings for the colour as you see the fly to have at that season, nay, at that very day on the water. Or you may make the oak-fly with an orange tawny and black ground, and the brown of a mallard's feather for the wings; and you are to know, that these two are most excellent flies, that is, the May-fly and the oak-fly. And let me again tell you that you keep as far from the water as you can possibly, whether you fish with a fly or worm, and fish down the stream: and when you fish with a fly, if it be possible, let no part of your line touch the water, but your fly only; and be still moving your fly upon the water, or casting it into the water, you yourself being also always moving down the stream. Mr Barker commends several sorts of the palmer-flies, not only those ribbed with silver and gold, but others that have their bodies all made of black, or some with red, and a red hackle; you may also make the hawthorn-fly, which is all black, and not big, but very small, the smaller the better; or the oak-fly, the body of which is orange colour and black crewel, with a brown wing; or a fly made with a peacock's feather is excellent in a bright day. You must be sure you want not in your magazine-bag the peacock's feather, and grounds of such wool and crewel as will make the grasshopper; and note, that usually the smallest flies are the best; and note also, that the light fly does usually make most sport in a dark day, and the darkest and least fly in a bright or clear day; and lastly, note that you are to repair upon any occasion to your magazine-bag, and upon any occasion vary and make them lighter or sadder, according to your fancy, or the day.

And now I shall tell you that the fishing with a natural fly is excellent, and affords much pleasure. They may be found thus: the May-fly, usually in and about that month, near to the riverside, especially against rain: the oak-fly, on the butt or body of an oak or ash, from the beginning of May to the end of August; it is a brownish fly and easy to be so found, and stands usually with his head downward, that is to say, towards the root of the tree: the small black-fly, or hawthorn-fly, is to be had on any hawthorn bush after the leaves be come forth. With these and a short line (as I showed, to angle for a chub), you may drape or dop, and also with a grasshopper, behind a tree, or in any deep hole; still making it to move on the top of the water, as if it were alive, and still keeping yourself out of sight, you shall certainly have sport if there be trouts; yea, in a hot day, but especially in the evening of a hot day, you will have sport.

And now, scholar, my direction for fly-fishing is ended with this shower, for it has done raining; and now look about you, and see how pleasantly that meadow looks; nay, and the earth smells as sweetly too. Come, let me tell you what holy Mr Herbert says of such days and flowers as these; and then we will thank God that we enjoy them, and walk to the river and sit down quietly, and try to catch the other brace of trouts.

> Sweet day, so cool, so calm, so bright,
> The bridal of the earth and sky,
> Sweet dews shall weep thy fall to-night—
> For thou must die.

> Sweet rose, whose hue, angry, and brave,
> Bids the rash gazer wipe his eye,
> Thy root is ever in its grave—
> And thou must die.

Sweet spring, full of sweet days and roses,
A box where sweets conpacted lie;
My music shows you have your closes—
      And all must die.

Only a sweet and virtuous soul,
Like season'd timber, never gives;
But when the whole world turns to coal,
      Then chiefly lives.

Ven. I thank you, good master, for your good direction for fly-fishing, and for the sweet enjoyment of the pleasant day, which is so far spent without offence to God or man: and I thank you for the sweet close of your discourse with Mr Herbert's verses, who, I have heard, loved angling; and I do the rather believe it, because he had a spirit suitable to anglers, and to those primitive Christians that you love, and have so much commended.

Pisc. Well, my loving scholar, and I am pleased to know that you are so well pleased with my direction and discourse.

And since you like these verses of Mr Herbert's so well, let me tell you what a reverend and learned divine that professes to imitate him (and has indeed done so most excellently) hath writ of our *Book of Common Prayer*; which I know you will like the better, because he is a friend of mine, and I am sure no enemy to angling.

What! Prayer by the Book? and Common? Yes! why not?
      The spirit of grace
      And supplication
      Is not left free alone
      For time and place,
But manner too: to read, or speak, by rote,
      Is all alike to him that prays
      In's heart, what with his mouth he says.

They that in private, by themselves alone,
Do pray, may take
What liberty they please,
In choosing of the ways
Wherein to make
Their soul's most intimate affections known
To him that sees in secret, when
They're most conceal'd from other men.

But he that unto others leads the way
In public prayer,
Should do it so
As all that hear may know
They need not fear
To turn their hearts unto his tongue, and say,
Amen; not doubt they were betrayed
To blaspheme, when they meant to have pray'd.

Devotion will add life unto the letter:
And why should not
That which authority
Prescribes, esteemed be
Advantage got?
If the prayer be good, the commoner the better;
Prayer in the Church's words as well
As sense, of all prayers bears the bell.

CH. HARVIE

And now, scholar, I think it will be time to repair to our
angle-rods, which we left in the water to fish for themselves; and
you shall choose which shall be yours; and it is an even lay, one
of them catches.

And, let me tell you, this kind of fishing with a dead rod, and
laying night-hooks, are like putting money to use; for they both
work for the owners, when they do nothing but sleep, or eat, or
rejoice; as you know we have done this last hour, and sat as
quietly and as free from cares under this sycamore as Virgil's

Tityrus and his Melibœus did under their broad beech-tree. No life, my honest scholar, no life so happy and so pleasant as the life of a well-governed angler, for when the lawyer is swallowed up with business, and the statesman is preventing or contriving plots, then we sit on cowslip banks, hear the birds sing, and possess ourselves in as much quietness as these silent silver streams, which we now see glide so quietly by us. Indeed, my good scholar, we may say of angling, as Dr Boteler said of strawberries, "Doubtless God could have made a better berry, but doubtless God never did"; and so (if I might be judge) "God never did make a more calm, quiet, innocent recreation than angling."

I'll tell you, scholar, when I sat last on this primrose bank, and looked down these meadows, I thought of them, as Charles the emperor did of the city of Florence, "That they were too pleasant to be looked on, but only on holidays." As I then sat on this very grass, I turned my present thoughts into verse: 'twas a wish, which I'll repeat to you.

THE ANGLER'S SONG

I in these flowery meads would be:
These crystal streams should solace me;
To whose harmonious bubbling noise
I with my angle would rejoice,
    Sit here, and see the turtle dove
    Court his chaste mate to acts of love:

Or, on that bank, feel the west wind
Breathe health and plenty: please my mind,
To see sweet dewdrops kiss these flowers,
And then wash'd off by April showers,
    Hear, hear my Kenna sing a song[1];
    There, see a blackbird feed her young,

---

[1] Like *Hermit Poor*.

Or a leverock build her nest:
Here, give my weary spirits rest,
And raise my low-pitch'd thoughts above
Earth, or what poor mortals love:
    Thus, free from lawsuits and the noise
    Of princes' courts, I would rejoice;

Or, with my Bryan and a book,
Loiter long days near Shawford brook;
There sit by him, and eat my meat;
There see the sun both rise and set;
There bid good morning to next day;
There meditate my time away;
    And angle on, and beg to have
    A quiet passage to a welcome grave.

When I had ended this composure, I left this place, and saw a
brother of the angle sit under that honeysuckle hedge (one that
will prove worth your acquaintance): I sat down by him, and
presently we met with an accidental piece of merriment, which
I will relate to you; for it rains still.

On the other side of this very hedge sat a gang of gipsies, and
near to them sat a gang of beggars. The gipsies were then to
divide all the money that had been got that week, either by
stealing linen or poultry, or by fortune-telling, or legerdemain,
or indeed by any other sleights and secrets belonging to their
mysterious government. And the sum that was got that week
proved to be but twenty and some odd shillings. The odd money
was agreed to be distributed amongst the poor of their own
corporation; and for the remaining twenty shillings, that was to
be divided unto four gentlemen gipsies, according to their
several degrees in their commonwealth.

And the first or chiefest gipsy was, by consent, to have a third
part of the 20s., which all men know is 6s. 8d.

The second was to have a fourth part of the 20s., which all
men know to be 5s.

The third was to have a fifth part of the 20s., which all men know to be 4s.

The fourth and last gipsy was to have a sixth part of the 20s., which all men know to be 3s. 4d.

As for example,

$$
\begin{array}{lll}
\text{3 times } 6s.\ 8d.\ \text{is} & . & . & 20s. \\
\text{And so is 4 times } 5s. & . & . & 20s. \\
\text{And so is 5 times } 4s. & . & . & 20s. \\
\text{And so is 6 times } 3s.\ 4d. & . & . & 20s.
\end{array}
$$

And yet he that divided the money was so very a gipsy, that though he gave to every one these said sums, yet he kept 1s. of it for himself.

As for example,

	s.	d.
	6	8
	5	0
	4	0
	3	4
make but .	19	0

But now you shall know, that when the four gipsies saw that he had got 1s. by dividing the money, though not one of them knew any reason to demand more, yet, like lords and courtiers, every gipsy envied him that was the gainer, and wrangled with him, and every one said the remaining shilling belonged to him: and so they fell to so high a contest about it, as none that knows the faithfulness of one gipsy to another will easily believe; and only we that have lived these last twenty years are certain that money has been able to do much mischief. However, the gipsies were too wise to go to law, and did therefore choose their choice friends Rook and Shark, and our late English Gusman, to be their arbitrators and umpires; and so they left this honeysuckle hedge, and went to tell fortunes, and cheat, and get more money and lodging in the next village.

When these were gone, we heard a high contention amongst the beggars, whether it was easiest to rip a cloak or to unrip a cloak. One beggar affirmed it was all one. But that was denied by asking her if doing and undoing were all one. Then another said 'twas easiest to unrip a cloak, for that was to let it alone. But she was answered by asking her how she unripped it, if she let it alone: and she confessed herself mistaken. These and twenty suchlike questions were proposed, and answered with as much beggarly logic and earnestness as was ever heard to proceed from the mouth of the most pertinacious schismatic: and sometimes all the beggars (whose number was neither more nor less than the poet's nine muses) talked all together about this ripping and unripping, and so loud that not one heard what the other said: but at last one beggar craved audience, and told them that old father Clause, whom Ben Jonson in his *Beggar's Bush* created king of their corporation, was to lodge at an alehouse called "Catch-her-by-the-way," not far from Waltham Cross, and in the high road towards London; and he therefore desired them to spend no more time about that and suchlike questions, but refer all to father Clause at night, for he was an upright judge, and in the meantime draw cuts what song should be next sung, and who should sing it. They all agreed to the motion; and the lot fell to her that was the youngest and veriest virgin of the company; and she sung Frank Davison's song, which he made forty years ago; and all the others of the company joined to sing the burthen with her. The ditty was this: but first the burthen:

> Bright shines the sun: play, beggars, play!
> Here's scraps enough to serve to-day.

What noise of viols is so sweet
　　As when our merry clappers ring?
What mirth doth want when beggars meet?
　　A beggar's life is for a king,
Eat, drink, and play, sleep when we list,
Go where we will—so stocks be miss'd.
　　Bright shines the sun; play, beggars, play!
　　Here's scraps enough to serve to-day.

The world is ours, and ours alone;
　　For we alone have world at will.
We purchase not—all is our own;
　　Both fields and streets we beggars fill.
Nor care to get, nor fear to keep.
Did ever break a beggar's sleep.
　　Bright shines the sun; play, beggars, play!
　　Here's scraps enough to serve to-day.

A hundred herds of black and white
　　Upon our gowns securely feed;
And yet if any dare us bite,
　　He dies, therefore, as sure as creed.
Thus beggars lord it as they please,
And only beggars live at ease.
　　Bright shines the sun; play, beggars, play!
　　Here's scraps enough to serve to-day.

Ven. I thank you, good master, for this piece of merriment, and
this song, which was well humoured by the maker, and well
remembered by you.

Pisc. But, I pray, forget not the catch which you promised to
make against night; for our countryman, honest Coridon, will
expect your catch, and my song, which I must be forced to patch
up, for it is so long since I learnt it, that I have forgotten a part
of it. But come, now it hath done raining, let's stretch our legs a
little in a gentle walk to the river, and try what interest our
angles will pay us for lending them so long to be used by the

trouts; lent them, indeed, like usurers, for our profit and their destruction.

Ven. Oh me! look you, master, a fish! a fish! Oh, alas, master, I have lost her!

Pisc. Ay, marry, sir, that was a good fish indeed: if I had had the luck to have taken up that rod, then 'tis twenty to one he should not have broke my line by running to the rod's end, as you suffered him. I would have held him within the bent of my rod (unless he had been fellow to the great trout that is near an ell long, which was of such a length and depth that he had his picture drawn, and now is to be seen at mine host Rickabie's, at the George, in Ware), and it may be by giving that very great trout the rod, that is, by casting it to him into the water, I might have caught him at the long run; for so I use always to do when I meet with an overgrown fish; and you will learn to do so too hereafter: for I tell you, scholar, fishing is an art; or at least, it is an art to catch fish.

Ven. But, master, I have heard that the great trout you speak of is a salmon.

Pisc. Trust me, scholar, I know not what to say to it. There are many country people that believe hares change sexes every year: and there be very many learned men think so too, for in their dissecting them they find many reasons to incline them to that belief. And to make the wonder seem yet less, that hares change sexes, note, that Doctor Mer. Casaubon affirms in his book of credible and incredible things, that Gaspar Peucerus, a learned physician, tells us of a people that once a year turn wolves, partly in shape and partly in conditions. And so, whether this were a salmon when he came into the fresh water, and his not returning into the sea hath altered him to another colour or kind, I am not able to say; but I am certain he hath all the signs of being a trout both for his shape, colour, and spots; and yet many think he is not.

Ven. But, master, will this trout which I had hold of die? for it is like he hath the hook in his belly.

Pisc. I will tell you, scholar, that unless the hook be fast in his very gorge, 'tis more than probable he will live; and a little time, with the help of the water, will rust the hook, and it will in time wear away; as the gravel doth in the horse-hoof, which only leaves a false quarter.

And now, scholar, let's go to my rod. Look you, scholar, I have a fish too, but it proves a logger-headed chub; and this is not much amiss, for this will pleasure some poor body, as we go to our lodging to meet our brother Peter and honest Coridon. Come, now bait your hook again, and lay it into the water, for it rains again: and we will even retire to the sycamore-tree, and there I will give you more directions concerning fishing; for I would fain make you an artist.

Ven. Yes, good master, I pray let it be so.

Pisc. Well, scholar, now we are sat down and are at ease, I shall tell you a little more of trout-fishing, before I speak of salmon (which I purpose shall be next) and then of the pike or luce. You are to know there is night as well as day-fishing for a trout, and that in the night the best trouts come out of their holes: and the manner of taking them is on the top of the water, with a great lob or garden-worm, or rather two, which you are to fish within a place where the waters run somewhat quietly, for in a stream the bait will not be so well discerned. I say, in a quiet or dead place, near to some swift: there draw your bait over the top of the water, to and fro; and if there be a good trout in the hole he will take it, especially if the night be dark; for then he is bold, and lies near the top of the water, watching the motion of any frog, or water-rat, or mouse that swims between him and the sky: these he hunts after if he sees the water but wrinkle or move in one of these dead holes, where these great old trouts usually lie near to their holds; for you are to note, that the great old trout is both subtle and fearful, and lies close all day, and does not usually stir out of his hold but lies in it as close in the day as the timorous hare does in her form, for the chief feeding of either is seldom in the day, but usually in the night, and then the great trout feeds very boldly.

And you must fish for him with a strong line, and not a little hook; and let him have time to gorge your hook, for he does not usually forsake it, as he oft will in the day-fishing. And if the night be not dark, then fish so with an artificial fly of a light colour, and at the snap: nay, he will sometimes rise at a dead mouse, or a piece of cloth, or anything that seems to swim across the water, or to be in motion. That is a choice way, but I have not often used it, because it is void of the pleasures that such days as these, that we two now enjoy, afford an angler.

And you are to know that in Hampshire, which I think exceeds all England for swift, shallow, clear, pleasant brooks, and store of trouts, they use to catch trouts in the night, by the light of a torch or straw, which, when they have discovered, they strike with a trout-spear, or other ways. This kind of way they catch very many; but I would not believe it till I was an eye-witness of it, nor do I like it now I have seen it.

Ven. But, master, do not trouts see us in the night?

Pisc. Yes, and hear and smell too, both then and in the daytime; for Gesner observes, the otter smells a fish forty furlongs off him in the water: and that it may be true, seems to be affirmed by Sir Francis Bacon, in the eighth century of his *Natural History*, who there proves that water may be the medium of sounds, by demonstrating it thus: "that if you knock two stones together very deep under the water, those that stand on a bank near to that place may hear the noise without any diminution of it by the water." He also offers the like experiment concerning the letting an anchor fall, by a very long cable or rope, on a rock, or the sand within the sea. And this being so well observed and demonstrated as it is by that learned man, has made me to believe that eels unbed themselves and stir at the noise of thunder; and not only, as some think, by the motion or stirring of the earth, which is occasioned by that thunder.

And this reason of Sir Francis Bacon (Exper. 792) has made me crave pardon of one that I laughed at, for affirming that he knew carps come to a certain place in a pond, to be fed, at the ringing of a bell, or the beating of a drum; and however, it shall be a rule for me to make as little noise as I can when I am fishing, until Sir Francis Bacon be confuted, which I shall give any man leave to do.

And, lest you may think him singular in his opinion, I will tell you, this seems to be believed by our learned Dr. Hakewill, who (in his *Apology of God's Power and Providence*, fol. 360) quotes Pliny to report that one of the emperors had particular fish-ponds, and in them several fish that appeared and came when they were called by their particular names; and St. James tells us (Chap. 3. 7) that all things in the sea have been tamed by mankind. And Pliny tells us (lib. 9, 35) that Antonia, the wife of Drusus, had a lamprey, at whose gills she hung jewels or ear-rings; and that others have been so tender-hearted as to shed tears at the death of fishes which they have kept and loved. And these observations, which will to most hearers seem wonderful, seem to have a further confirmation from Martial (lib. 4, Epigr. 30), who writes thus:

PISCATOR, FUGE; NE NOCENS, ETC.
Angler! wouldst thou be guiltless? then forbear;
For these are sacred fishes that swim here,
Who know their sovereign, and will lick his hand;
Than which none's greater in the world's command:
Nay more, they've names, and when they called are,
Do to their several owners' call repair.

All the further use that I shall make of this shall be, to advise anglers to be patient and forbear swearing, lest they be heard, and catch no fish.

And so I shall proceed next to tell you, it is certain, that certain fields near Leominster, a town in Herefordshire, are observed to make the sheep that graze upon them more fat than the next, and also to bear finer wool; that is to say that that year in which they feed in such a particular pasture, they shall yield finer wool than they did that year before they came to feed in it, and coarser again if they shall return to their former pasture; and again return to a finer wool, being fed in the fine-wool ground. Which I tell you, that you may the better believe that I am certain, if I catch a trout in one meadow he shall be white and faint, and very like to be lousy; and as certainly, if I catch a trout in the next meadow, he shall be strong, and red, and lusty, and much better meat. Trust me, scholar, I have caught many a trout in a particular meadow, that the very shape and the enamelled colour of him hath been such as have joyed me to look on him; and I have then with much pleasure concluded with Solomon, "Everything is beautiful in season."

I should by promise speak next of the salmon; but I will by your favour say a little of the umber or grayling, which is so like a trout for his shape and feeding, that I desire I may exercise your patience with a short discourse of him, and then the next shall be of the salmon.

Observations of the Umber or Grayling; and Directions how to Fish for him

Pisc. The umber and grayling are thought by some to differ, as the herring and pilchard do. But though they may do so in other nations, I think those in England differ in nothing but their names. Aldrovandus says they be of a trout kind; and Gesner says, that in his country (which is in Switzerland) he is accounted the choicest of all fish. And in Italy, he is in the month of May so highly valued, that he is sold at a much higher rate than any other fish. The French (which call the club *un vilain*) call the umber of the lake Leman *un umble chevalier*; and they value the umber or grayling so highly, that they say he feeds on gold, and say that many have been caught out of their famous river Loire, and of whose bellies grains of gold have been often taken. And some think that he feeds on water-thyme, and smells of it at his first taking out of the water; and they may think so with as good reason as we do that our smelts smell like violets at their first being caught, which I think is a truth. Aldrovandus says, the salmon, the grayling, and trout, and all fish that live in clear and sharp streams, are made by their mother nature of such exact shape and pleasant colours purposely to invite us to a joy and contentedness in feasting with her. Whether this is a truth or not is not my purpose to dispute; but 'tis certain, all that write of the umber declare him to be very medicinable. And Gesner says, that the fat of an umber or grayling, being set, with a little honey, a day or two in the sun, in a little glass, is very excellent against redness, or swarthiness, or anything that breeds in the eyes. Salvian takes him to be called umber from his swift swimming, or gliding out of sight, more like a shadow or a ghost than a fish. Much more might be said both of his smell and taste; but I shall only tell you, that St. Ambrose, the glorious bishop of Milan (who lived when the church kept fasting days) calls him the flower-fish, or flower of fishes: and that he was so far in love with him that he would not let him pass without the honour of a long discourse; but I must, and pass on to tell you how to take this dainty fish.

First, note, that he grows not to the bigness of a trout; for the biggest of them do not usually exceed eighteen inches. He lives in such rivers as the trout does, and is usually taken with the same baits as the trout is, and after the same manner; for he will bite both at the minnow, or worm, or fly; though he bites not often at the minnow, and is very gamesome at the fly, and much simpler, and therefore bolder than a trout; for he will rise twenty

times at a fly, if you miss him, and yet rise again. He has been
taken with a fly made of the red feathers of a parakita, a strange
outlandish bird; and he will rise at a fly not unlike a gnat or a
small moth, or indeed at most flies that are not too big. He is a
fish that lurks close all winter, but is very pleasant and jolly after
mid-April, and in May, and in the hot months: he is of a very
fine shape, his flesh is white; his teeth, those little ones that he
has, are in his throat, yet he has so tender a mouth, that he is
oftener lost after an angler has hooked him, than any other fish.
Though there be many of these fishes in the delicate river Dove
and in Trent, and some other small rivers, as that which runs by
Salisbury, yet he is not so general a fish as the trout, nor to me
so good to eat or to angle for. And so I shall take my leave of him;
and now come to some observations of the salmon, and how to
catch him.

Observations of the Salmon; with Directions how to Fish for him

Pisc. The salmon is accounted the king of fresh-water fish; and is
ever bred in rivers relating to the sea, yet so high or far from it
as admits of no tincture of salt or brackishness. He is said to
breed, or cast his spawn, in most rivers, in the month of August:
some say that then they dig a hole or grave in a safe place in the
gravel, and there place their eggs or spawn (after the melter has
done his natural office), and then hide it most cunningly, and
cover it over with gravel and stones, and then leave it to their
Creator's protection, who, by a gentle heat which He infuses into
that cold element, makes it brood and beget life in the spawn,
and to become samlets early in the spring next following.

The salmons having spent their appointed time, and done this
natural duty in the fresh waters, they then haste to the sea
before winter, both the melter and spawner; but if they be

stopped by flood-gates or weirs or lost in the fresh waters, then those so left behind by degrees grow sick, and lean, and unreasonable, and kipper; that is to say, have bony gristles grow out of their lower chaps (not unlike a hawk's beak) which hinders their feeding; and in time such fish, so left behind, pine away and die. 'Tis observed that he may live thus one year from the sea; but he then grows insipid and tasteless, and loses both his blood and strength, and pines and dies the second year. And 'tis noted that those little salmons called skeggers, which abound in many rivers relating to the sea, are bred by such sick salmons that might not go to the sea; and that though they abound, yet they never thrive to any considerable bigness.

But if the old salmon gets to the sea, then that gristle, which shows him to be kipper, wears away, or is cast off (as the eagle is said to cast his bill) and he recovers his strength, and comes next summer to the same river, if it be possible, to enjoy the former pleasures that there possessed him; for (as one has wittily observed) he has, like some persons of honour and riches, which have both their winter and summer houses, the fresh rivers for summer, and the salt water for winter, to spend his life in; which is not (as Sir Francis Bacon hath observed in his *History of Life and Death*) above ten years. And it is to be observed that though the salmon does grow big in the sea, yet he grows not fat but in fresh rivers; and it is observed that the farther they get from the sea, they be both the fatter and better.

Next I shall tell you, that though they make very hard shift to get out of the fresh rivers into the sea, yet they will make a harder shift to get out of the salt into the fresh rivers, to spawn, or possess the pleasures that they have formerly found in them: to which end they will force themselves through flood-gates, or over weirs or hedges, or stops in the water, even to a height beyond common belief. Gesner speaks of such places as are known to be above eight feet high above water. And our Camden mentions (in his *Britannia*) the like wonder to be in

Pembrokeshire, where the river Tivy falls into the sea; and that the fall is so downright, and so high, that the people stand and wonder at the strength and sleight by which they see the salmon use to get out of the sea into the said river; and the manner and height of the place is so notable, that it is known, far, by the name of the "Salmon-leap." Concerning which, take this also out of Michael Drayton, my honest old friend, as he tells it you in his *Polyolbion*:

> And when the salmon seeks a fresher stream to find,
> Which hither from the sea comes yearly by his kind;
> As he tow'rds season grows, and stems the wat'ry tract
> Where Tivy falling down makes a high cataract,
> Forced by the rising rocks that there her course oppose,
> As though within her bounds they meant her to inclose;
> Here, when the labouring fish does at the foot arrive,
> And finds that by his strength he does but vainly strive,
> His tail takes in his mouth, and, bending, like a bow,
> That's to full compass drawn, aloft himself doth throw;
> Then springing at his height, as doth a little wand
> That, bended end to end, and started from man's hand,
> Far oft itself doth cast; so does the salmon vault:
> And if at first he fail, his second summersault
> He instantly essays; and from his nimble ring,
> Still yerking, never leaves until himself he fling
> Above the opposing stream——

This Michael Drayton tells you of this leap or summersault of the salmon.

And next I shall tell you, that it is observed by Gesner and others, that there is no better salmon than in England; and that though some of our northern counties have as fat and as large as the river Thames, yet none are of so excellent a taste.

And as I have told you that Sir Francis Bacon observes, the age of a salmon exceeds not ten years; so let me next tell you, that his growth is very sudden; it is said, that after he is got into the sea, he becomes from a samlet not so big as a gudgeon, to be a salmon, in as short a time as a gosling becomes to be a goose. Much of this has been observed by tying a ribbon, or some known tape or thread, in the tail of some young salmons, which have been taken in weirs as they have swimmed towards the salt water, and then by taking a part of them again with the known mark at the same place at their return from the sea, which is usually about six months after; and the like experiment hath been tried upon young swallows, who have, after six months' absence, been observed to return to the same chimney, there to make their nests and habitations for the summer following: which has inclined many to think, that every salmon usually returns to the same river in which it was bred, as young pigeons taken out of the same dovecote have also been observed to do.

And you are yet to observe farther, that the he-salmon is usually bigger than the spawner; and that he is more kipper, and less able to endure a winter in the fresh water than she is: yet she is, at that time of looking less kipper and better, as watery, and as bad meat.

And yet you are to observe that as there is no general rule without an exception, so there are some few rivers in this nation that have trouts and salmons in season in winter, as it is certain there be in the river Wye, in Monmouthshire, where they be in season (as Camden observes) from September till April. But, my scholar, the observation of this and many other things, I must in manners omit, because they will prove too large for our narrow compass of time, and therefore I shall next fall upon my directions how to fish for this salmon.

And for that, first you shall observe, that usually he stays not long in a place (as trouts will), but (as I said) covets still to go nearer the spring head; and that he does not (as the trout and many other fish) lie near the water-side, or bank, or roots of trees, but swims in the deep and broad parts of the water, and usually in the middle, and near the ground; and that there you are to fish for him, and that he is to be caught as the trout is, with a worm, a minnow (which some call a penk), or with a fly.

And you are to observe that he is very seldom observed to bite at a minnow (yet sometimes he will) and not usually at a fly; but more usually at a worm, and then most usually at a lob or garden-worm, which should be well scoured, that is to say, kept seven or eight days in moss before you fish with them: and if you double your time of eight into sixteen, twenty, or more days, it is still the better; for the worms will still be clearer, tougher, and more lively, and continue so longer upon your hook; and they may be kept longer by keeping them cool and in fresh moss, and some advise to put camphor into it.

Note also, that many used to fish for a salmon with a ring of wire on the top of their rod, through which the line may run to as great a length as is needful when he is hooked. And to that end, some use a wheel about the middle of their rod, or near their hand; which is to be observed better by seeing one of them, than by a large demonstration of words.

And now I shall tell you that which may be called a secret: I have been a-fishing with old Oliver Henley (now with God), a noted fisher both for trout and salmon, and have observed that he would usually take three or four worms out of his bag, and put them into a little box in his pocket, where he would usually let them continue half-an-hour or more before he would bait his hook with them. I have asked him his reason, and he has replied: "He did but pick the best out to be in readiness against he baited his hook the next time"; but he has been observed, both by others and myself, to catch more fish than I or any other body that has ever gone a-fishing with him could do, and especially salmons; and I have been told lately by one of his most intimate and secret friends, that the box in which he put those worms was anointed with a drop, or two or three, of the oil of ivy-berries, made by expression or infusion; and told, that by the worms remaining in that box an hour, or a like time, they had incorporated a kind of smell that was irresistibly attractive, enough to force any fish within the smell of them to bite. This I heard not long since from a friend, but have not tried it; yet I grant it probable, and refer my reader to Sir Francis Bacon's *Natural History*, where he proves fishes may hear, and doubtless can more probably smell; and I am certain Gesner says the otter can smell in the water, and I know not but that fish may do so too; 'tis left for a lover of angling, or any that desires to improve that art, to try this conclusion.

I shall also impart two other experiments (but not tried by myself), which I will deliver in the same words that they were given me, by an excellent angler, and a very friend, in writing: he told me the latter was too good to be told but in a learned language, lest it should be made common.

"Take the stinking oil drawn out of the polybody of the oak by a retort, mixed with turpentine and hive-honey, and anoint your bait therewith, and it will doubtless draw the fish to it."

The other is this: "*Vulnera hederæ grandissimæ inflicta sudant balsamum oleo gelato, albicantique persimile, odoris vero longe suavissimi.*"

'Tis supremely sweet to any fish, and yet asafœtida may do the like.

But in these things I have no great faith, yet grant it probable, and have had from some chemical men (namely, from Sir George Hastings and others) an affirmation of them to be very advantageous: but no more of these, especially not in this place.

I might here, before I take my leave of the salmon, tell you that there is more than one sort of them; as, namely, a tecon, and another called in some places a samlet, or by some a skegger; but these and others, which I forbear to name, may be fish of another kind, and differ as we know a herring and pilchard do, which, I think, are as different as the rivers in which they breed, and must by me be left to the disquisitions of men of more leisure, and of greater abilities, than I profess myself to have.

And lastly, I am to borrow much of your promised patience as to tell you that the trout or salmon, being in season, have, at their first taking out of the water (which continues during life) their bodies adorned, the one with such red spots, and the other with such black or blackish spots, as give them such an addition of natural beauty, as I think was never given to any woman by the artificial paint or patches in which they so much pride themselves in this age. And so I shall leave them both, and proceed to some observations on pike.

Observations of the Luce, or Pike; with Directions how to Fish for him

Pisc. The mighty Luce, or Pike, is taken to be the tyrant (as the salmon is the king) of the fresh waters. 'Tis not to be doubted but that they are bred, some by generation, and some not, as namely, of a weed called pickerel weed, unless learned Gesner be much mistaken, for he says this weed and other glutinous matter, with the help of the sun's heat, in some particular months, and some ponds apted for it by nature, do become pikes. But, doubtless, divers pikes are bred after this manner, or are brought into some ponds some such other ways as is past man's finding out, of which we have daily testimonies.

Sir Francis Bacon, in his *History of Life and Death*, observes the pike to be the longest lived of any fresh-water fish; and yet he computes it to be not usually above forty years; and others think it to be not above ten years; and yet Gesner mentions a pike taken in Swedeland, in the year 1449, with a ring about his neck, declaring he was put into that pond by Frederick the Second more than two hundred years before he was last taken, as by the inscription in that ring (being Greek) was interpreted by the then Bishop of Worms. But of this no more but that it is observed that the old or very great pikes have in them more of state than goodness; the smaller or middle-sized pikes being, by the most and choicest palates, observed to be the best meat; and, contrary, the eel is observed to be the better for age and bigness.

All pikes that live long prove chargeable to their keepers, because their life is maintained by the death of so many other fish, even those of their own kind; which has made him by some writers to be called the tyrant of the rivers, or the fresh-water wolf, by reason of his bold, greedy, devouring disposition; which is so keen, as Gesner relates a man going to a pond (where it seems a pike had devoured all the fish) to water his mule, had a pike bit his mule by the lips; to which the pike hung so fast that the mule drew him out of the water, and by that accident the owner of the mule angled out the pike. And the same Gesner observes, that a maid in Poland had a pike bit her by the foot, as she was washing clothes in a pond. And I have heard the like of a woman in Killingworth pond, not far from Coventry. But I have been assured by my friend Mr. Seagrave (of whom I spake to you formerly) that keeps tame otters, that he hath known a pike in extreme hunger fight with one of his otters for a carp that the otter had caught, and was then bringing out of the water. I have told you who relate these things, and tell you they are persons of credit; and shall conclude this observation, by telling you what a wise man has observed, "It is a hard thing to persuade the belly, because it has no ears."

But if these relations be disbelieved, it is too evident to be doubted, that a pike will devour a fish of his own kind that shall be bigger than his belly or throat will receive, and swallow a part of him, and let the other part remain in his mouth till the swallowed part be digested, and then swallow that other part that was in his mouth, and so put it over by degrees; which is not unlike the ox and some other beasts, taking their meat, not out of their mouth immediately into their belly, but first into some place betwixt, and then chew it, or digest it by degrees after, which is called chewing the cud. And, doubtless, pikes will bite when they are not hungry; but, as some think, even for very anger, when a tempting bait comes near to them.

And it is observed that the pike will eat venomous things (as some kind of frogs are) and yet live without being harmed by them; for, as some say, he has in him a natural balsam, or antidote against all poison: and he has a strange heat, that though it appears to us to be cold, can yet digest or put over any fish-flesh, by degrees, without being sick. And others observe that he never eats the venomous frog till he have first killed her, and then (as ducks are observed to do to frogs in spawning time, at which time some frogs are observed to be venomous) so thoroughly washed her, by tumbling her up and down in the water, that he may devour her without danger. And Gesner affirms that a Polonian gentleman did faithfully assure him, he had seen two young geese at one time in the belly of a pike. And doubtless a pike, in his height of hunger, will bite at and devour a dog that swims in a pond; and there have been examples of it, or the like; for, as I told you, "The belly has no ears when hunger comes upon it."

The pike is also observed to be a solitary, melancholy, and a bold fish: melancholy because he always swims or rests himself alone, and never swims in shoals or with company, as roach and dace and most other fish do: and bold, because he fears not a shadow, or to see or be seen of anybody, as the trout and chub and all other fish do.

And it is observed by Gesner, that the jaw-bones, and hearts and galls of pikes are very medicinable for several diseases; or to stop blood, to abate fevers, to cure agues, to oppose or expel the infection of the plague, and to be many ways medicinable and useful for the good of mankind; but he observes that the biting of a pike is venomous, and hard to be cured.

And it is observed that the pike is a fish that breeds but once a year, and that other fish (as namely loaches) do breed oftener, as we are certain tame pigeons do almost every month; and yet the hawk (a bird of prey, as the pike is of fish) breeds but once in twelve months. And you are to note, that his time of breeding, or spawning, is usually about the end of February, or somewhat later, in March, as the weather proves colder or warmer; and to note, that his manner of breeding is thus: a he and a she pike will usually go together out of a river into some ditch or creek, and that there the spawner casts her eggs, and the melter hovers over her all that time that she is casting her spawn, but touches her not.

I might say more of this, but it might be thought curiosity or worse, and shall therefore forbear it; and take up so much of your attention as to tell you, that the best of pikes are noted to be in rivers; next, those in great ponds or meres; and the worst, in small ponds.

But before I proceed further, I am to tell you, that there is a great antipathy betwixt the pike and some frogs; and this may appear to the reader of Dubravius (a bishop in Bohemia) who, in his book *Of Fish and Fish-ponds*, relates what, he says, he saw with his own eyes, and could not forbear to tell the reader, which was:

"As he and the Bishop Thurzo were walking by a large pond in Bohemia they saw a frog, when the pike lay very sleepily and quiet by the shore side, leap upon his head; and the frog having expressed malice or anger by his swollen cheeks and staring eyes, did stretch out his legs and embraced the pike's head, and presently reached them to his eyes, tearing with them and his teeth those tender parts: the pike, moved with anguish, moves up and down the water, and rubs himself against weeds and whatever he thought might quit him of his enemy; but all in vain, for the frog did continue to ride triumphantly, and to bite and torment the pike till his strength failed, and then the frog sunk with the pike to the bottom of the water; then presently the frog appeared again at the top and croaked, and seemed to rejoice like a conqueror; after which he presently retired to his secret hole. The bishop that had beheld the battle called his fisherman to fetch his nets, and by all means to get the pike that they might declare what had happened; and the pike was drawn forth, and both his eyes eaten out; at which when they began to wonder, the fisherman wished them to forbear, and assured them he was certain that pikes were often so served."

I told this, which is to be read in the sixth chapter of the first book of Dubravius, unto a friend, who replied, "It was as improbable as to have the mouse scratch out the cat's eyes." But he did not consider that there be fishing frogs (which the Dalmatians call the water-devil) of which I might tell you as wonderful a story; but I shall tell you, that 'tis not to be doubted, but that there be some frogs so fearful of the water-snake, that, when they swim in a place in which they fear to meet with him, they then get a reed across into their mouths, which, if they two meet by accident, secures the frog from the strength and malice of the snake; and note, that the frog usually swims the fastest of the two.

And let me tell you, that as there be water and land-frogs, so there be land and water-snakes. Concerning which, take this observation, that the land-snake breeds and hatches her eggs, which become young snakes, in some old dunghill, or a like hot place; but the water-snake, which is not venomous (and, as I have been assured by a great observer of such secrets), does not hatch, but breed her young alive, which she does not then forsake, but bides with them, and in case of danger will take them into her mouth and swim away from any apprehended danger, and then let them out again when she thinks all danger to be passed; these be accidents that we anglers sometimes see, and often talk of.

But whither am I going? I had almost lost myself, by remembering the discourse of Dubravius. I will therefore stop here, and tell you, according to my promise, how to catch the pike.

His feeding is usually of fish and frogs, and sometimes a weed of his own called pickerel-weed, of which I told you some think

pikes are bred; for they have observed that where none have
been put into ponds, yet they have there found many, and that
there has been plenty of that weed in those ponds, and that that
weed both breeds and feeds them; but whether those pikes so
bred will ever breed by generation as the others do, I shall leave
to the disquisitions of men of more curiosity and leisure than I
profess myself to have; and shall proceed to tell you that you
may fish for a pike either with a ledger or a walking-bait; and
you are to note, that I call that a ledger-bait which is fixed or
made to rest in one certain place when you shall be absent from
it; and I call that a walking-bait which you take with you, and
have ever in motion. Concerning which two, I shall give you this
direction, that your ledger-bait is best to be a living bait, though
a dead one may catch, whether it be a fish or a frog; and that you
may make them live the longer, you may, or indeed you must,
take this course:

First, for your live-bait of fish, a roach or dace is, I think, best
and most tempting, and a perch is the longest lived on a hook;
and having cut off his fin on his back, which may be done
without hurting him, you must take your knife (which cannot
be too sharp) and betwixt the head and the fin on the back, cut
or make an incision, or such a scar, as you may put the
arming-wire of your hook into it, with as little bruising or
hurting the fish as art and diligence will enable you to do; and so
carrying your arming-wire along his back, unto or near the tail
of your fish, betwixt the skin and the body of it, draw out that
wire or arming of your hook at another scar near to his tail: then
tie him about with thread, but no harder than of necessity to
prevent hurting the fish; and the better to avoid hurting the fish,
some have a kind of probe to open the way, for the more easy
entrance and passage of your wire or arming; but as for these,
time and a little experience will teach you better than I can by
words; therefore I will for the present say no more of this, but
come next to give you some directions how to bait your hook
with a frog.

Ven. But, good master, did you not say even now that some frogs are venomous, and is it not dangerous to touch them?

Pisc. Yes; but I will give you some rules or cautions concerning them. And first, you are to note, that there are two kinds of frogs; that is to say (if I may so express myself) a flesh and a fish-frog: by flesh-frogs, I mean frogs that breed and live on the land; and of these there be several sorts also, and of several colours, some being speckled, some greenish, some blackish or brown: the green frog, which is a small one, is by Topsel taken to be venomous, and so is the paddock or frog paddock, which usually keeps or breeds on the land, and is very large and bony and big, especially the she-frog of that kind; yet these will sometimes come into the water, but it is not often; and the land-frogs are some of them observed by him to breed by laying eggs, and others to breed of the slime and dust of the earth, and that in winter they turn to slime again, and that the next summer that very slime returns to be a living creature; this is the opinion of Pliny, and Cardanus (in his tenth book *De Subtilitate*) undertakes to give a reason for the raining of frogs: but if it were in my power, it should rain none but water-frogs, for those I think are not venomous, especially the right water-frog, which about February or March breeds in ditches by slime, and blackish eggs in that slime: about which time of breeding the he and she-frogs are observed to use divers summersaults, and to croak and make a noise, which the land-frog, or paddock-frog, never does. Now of these water-frogs, if you intend to fish with a frog for a pike, you are to choose the yellowest that you can get, for that the pike ever likes best. And thus use your frog, that he may continue long alive:

Put your hook into his mouth, which you may easily do from the middle of April till August, and then the frog's mouth grows up, and he continues so for at least six months without eating, but is sustained none but He whose name is Wonderful knows how: I say, put your hook, I mean the arming-wire, through his

mouth and out at his gills; and then with a fine needle and silk
sew the upper part of his leg, with only one stitch, to the
arming-wire of your hook; or tie the frog's leg, above the upper
joint, to the arming-wire; and, in so doing, use him as though
you loved him, that is, harm him as little as you may possibly,
that he may live the longer.

And now, having given you this direction for the baiting your
ledger-hook with a live fish or frog, my next must be to tell you
how your hook thus baited must or may be used, and it is thus:
Having fastened your hook to a line, which, if it be not fourteen
yards long, should not be less than twelve, you are to fasten that
line to any bough near to a hole where a pike is, or is likely to
lie, or to have a haunt, and then wind your line on any forked
stick, all your line, except half a yard of it, or rather more, and
split that forked stick with such a nick or notch at one end of it
as may keep the line from any more of it ravelling from about
the stick than so much of it as you intend; and choose your
forked stick to be of that bigness as may keep the fish or frog
from pulling the forked stick under the water till the pike bites;
and then the pike having pulled the line forth of the cleft or nick
of that stick in which it was gently fastened, he will have line
enough to go to his hold and pouch the bait; and if you would
have this ledger-bait to keep at a fixed place, undisturbed by
wind or other accidents which may drive it to the shore side (for
you are to note, that it is likeliest to catch a pike in the midst of
the water), then hang a small plummet of lead, a stone, or piece
of tile, or a turf in a string, and cast it into the water with the
forked stick, to hang upon the ground, to be a kind of anchor to
keep the forked stick from moving out of your intended place till
the pike come. This I take to be a very good way, to use so many
ledger-baits as you intend to make trial of.

Or if you bait your hooks thus with live fish or frogs, and in a
windy day, fasten them thus to a bough or bundle of straw, and
by the help of that wind can get them to move across a pond or

mere, you are like to stand still on the shore and see sport presently if there be any store of pikes; or these live baits may make sport, being tied about the body or wings of a goose or duck, and she chased over a pond; and the like may be done with turning three or four live baits thus fastened to bladders, or boughs, or bottles of hay or flags, to swim down a river, whilst you walk quietly alone on the shore, and are still in expectation of sport. The rest must be taught you by practice, for time will not allow me to say more of this kind of fishing with live baits.

And for your dead bait for a pike, for that you may be taught by one day's going a-fishing with me, or any other body that fishes for him, for the baiting your hook with a dead gudgeon or a roach, and moving it up and down the water, is too easy a thing to take up any time to direct you to do it; and yet, because I cut you short in that, I will commute for it by telling you that that was told me for a secret: it is this:

"Dissolve gum of ivy in oil of spike, and therewith anoint your dead bait for a pike, and then cast it into a likely place, and when it has lain a short time at the bottom, draw it towards the top of the water, and so up the stream, and it is more than likely that you have a pike follow with more than common eagerness."

And some affirm, that any bait anointed with the marrow of the thigh-bone of an hern is a great temptation to any fish.

These have not been tried by me, but told me by a friend of note, that pretended to do me a courtesy; but if this direction to catch a pike thus do you no good, yet I am certain this direction how to roast him when he is caught is choicely good, for I have tried it, and it is somewhat the better for not being common; but with my direction you must take this caution, that your pike must not be a small one, that is, it must be more than half a yard, and should be bigger.

First, open your pike at the gills, and if need be, cut also a little slit towards the belly; out of these take his guts and keep his liver, which you are to shred very small with thyme, sweet marjoram, and a little winter-savory; to these put some pickled oysters, and some anchovies, two or three, both these last whole (for the anchovies will melt, and the oysters should not); to these you must add also a pound of sweet butter, which you are to mix with the herbs that are shred, and let them all be well salted (if the pike be more than a yard long, then you may put into these herbs more than a pound, or if he be less, then less butter will suffice): these being thus mixed with a blade or two of mace, must be put into the pike's belly, and then his belly so sewed up as to keep all the butter in his belly, if it be possible, if not, then as much of it as you possibly can; but take not off the scales: then you are to thrust the spit through his mouth out at his tail; and then take four, or five, or six split sticks or very thin laths, and a convenient quantity of tape or filleting: these laths are to be tied round about the pike's body from his head to his tail, and the tape tied somewhat thick to prevent his breaking or falling off from the spit: let him be roasted very leisurely, and often basted with claret wine and anchovies and butter mixed together, and also with what moisture falls from him into the pan: when you have roasted him sufficiently, you are to hold under him (when you unwind or cut the tape that ties him) such a dish as you purpose to eat him out of; and let him fall into it with the sauce that is roasted in his belly; and by this means the pike will be kept unbroken and complete: then, to the sauce which was within, and also that sauce in the pan, you are to add a fit quantity of the best butter, and to squeeze the juice of three or four oranges: lastly, you may either put into the pike with the oysters two cloves of garlick, and take it whole out, when the pike is cut off the spit; or to give the sauce a *haut-gout* let the dish (into which you let the pike fall) be rubbed with it: the using or not using of this garlick is left to your discretion.—M. B.

This dish of meat is too good for any but anglers, or very honest men; and I trust you will prove both, and therefore I have trusted you with this secret.

Let me next tell you that Gesner tells us there are no pikes in Spain; and that the largest are in the lake Thrasymene in Italy; and the next, if not equal to them, are the pikes of England; and that in England, Lincolnshire boasteth to have the biggest. Just so doth Sussex boast of four sorts of fish; namely, an Arundel Mullet, a Chichester Lobster, a Shelsey Cockle, and an Amerly Trout.

But I will take up no more of your time with this relation, but proceed to give you some observations of the Carp, and how to angle for him, and to dress him, but not till he is caught.

Observations of the Carp; with Directions how to Fish for him

Pisc. The Carp is the queen of rivers; a stately, a good, and a very subtle fish; that was not at first bred, nor hath been long in England, but is now naturalised. It is said they were brought hither by one Mr. Mascal, a gentleman that then lived at Plumstead, in Sussex, a county that abounds more with fish than any in this nation.

You may remember that I told you Gesner says there are no pikes in Spain; and doubtless there was a time, about a hundred or a few more years ago, when there were no carps in England, as may seem to be affirmed by Sir Richard Baker, in whose *Chronicle* you may find these verses:

> Hops and turkeys, carps and beer,
> Came into England all in a year.

And doubtless, as of sea-fish the herring dies soonest out of the water, and of fresh-water fish, the trout, so (except the eel) the carp endures most hardness, and lives longest out of his own proper element. And, therefore, the report of the carp's being brought out of a foreign country into this nation is the more probable.

Carps and loaches are observed to breed several months in one year, which pikes and most other fish do not. And this is partly proved by tame and wild rabbits; and also by some ducks, which will lay eggs nine out of the twelve months; and yet there be other ducks that lay not longer than about one month. And it is the rather to be believed, because you shall scarce or never take a male carp without a melt, or a female without a roe or spawn, and for the most part, very much, and especially all the summer season. And it is observed that they breed more naturally in ponds than in running waters (if they breed there at all); and that those that live in rivers are taken by men of the best palates to be much the better meat.

And it is observed that in some ponds carps will not breed, especially in cold ponds; but where they will breed they breed innumerably: Aristotle and Pliny say six times in a year, if there be no pikes or perch to devour their spawn, when it is cast upon grass, or flags, or weeds, where it lies ten or twelve days before it is enlivened.

The carp, if he have water room and good feed, will grow to a very great bigness and length; I have heard, to be much above a yard long. 'Tis said (by Jovius, who hath writ of fishes) that in the lake Lurian in Italy carps have thriven to be more than fifty pounds weight; which is the more probable, for as the bear is conceived and born suddenly, and being born, is but short-lived, so, on the contrary, the elephant is said to be two years in his dam's belly (some think he is ten years in it), and being born, grows in bigness twenty years; and 'tis observed, too, that he lives to the age of a hundred years. And 'tis also observed that the crocodile is very long-lived, and more than that, that all that long life he thrives in bigness; and so I think some carps do, especially in some places; though I never saw one above twenty-three inches, which was a great and a goodly fish; but have been assured they are of a far greater size, and in England too.

Now, as the increase of carps is wonderful for their number, so there is not a reason found out, I think, by any, why they should breed in some ponds, and not in others of the same nature for soil and all other circumstances. And as their breeding, so are their decays also very mysterious: I have both read it, and been told by a gentleman of tried honesty, that he has known sixty or more large carps put into several ponds near to a house, where, by reason of the stakes in the ponds, and the owner's constant being near to them, it was impossible they should be stole away from him; and that when he has, after three or four years, emptied the pond, and expected an increase from them by breeding young ones (for that they might do so, he had, as the rule is, put in three melters for one spawner), he has, I say, after three or four years, found neither a young nor old carp remaining. And the like I have known of one that had almost watched the pond, and at a like distance of time, at the fishing of the pond, found, of seventy or eighty large carps, not above five or six; and that he had foreborne longer to fish the said pond, but that he saw, in a hot day in summer, a large carp swim near the top of the water with a frog upon his head; and that he, upon that occasion, caused his pond to be let dry: and I say, of seventy or eighty carps, only found five or six in the said pond, and those very sick and lean, and with every one a frog sticking so fast on the head of the said carps, that the frog would not be got off without extreme force or killing. And the gentleman that did affirm this to me, told me he saw it; and did declare his belief to be (and I also believe the same) that he thought the other carps, that were so strangely lost, were so killed by the frogs, and then devoured.

And a person of honour, now living in Worcestershire, assured me he had seen a necklace or collar of tadpoles, hang like a chain or necklace of beads about a pike's neck, and to kill him; whether it be for meat or malice must be to me a question.

But I am fallen into this discourse by accident, of which I

might say more, but it has proved longer than I intended, and possibly may not to you be considerable; I shall therefore give you three or four more short observations of the carp, and then fall upon some directions how you shall fish for him.

The age of carps is by Sir Francis Bacon, in his *History of Life and Death*, observed to be but ten years; yet others think they live longer. Gesner says a carp has been known to live in the Palatinate above a hundred years; but most conclude, that (contrary to the pike or luce) all carps are the better for age and bigness. The tongues of carps are noted to be choice and costly meat, especially to them that buy them: but Gesner says carps have no tongue like other fish, but a piece of flesh-like fish in their mouth like to a tongue, and should be called a palate: but it is certain it is choicely good; and that the carp is to be reckoned amongst those leather-mouthed fish, which I told you have their teeth in their throat, and for that reason he is very seldom lost by breaking his hold, if your hook be once stuck into his chaps.

I told you that Sir Francis Bacon thinks that the carp lives but ten years; but Janus Dubravius has writ a book, *Of Fish and Fish-ponds*, in which he says, that carps begin to spawn at the age of three years, and continue to do so till thirty: he says also, that in the time of their breeding, which is in summer, when the sun hath warmed both the earth and water, and so apted them also for generation, that then three or four male carps will follow a female; and that then, she putting on a seeming coyness, they force her through weeds and flags, where she lets fall her eggs or spawn, which sticks fast to the weeds; and then they let fall their melt upon it, and so it becomes in a short time to be a living fish: and, as I told you, it is thought that the carp does this several months in the year. And most believe that most fish breed after this manner except the eel. And it has been observed, that when the spawner has weakened herself by doing that natural office, that two or three melters have helped her from off the weeds, by bearing her up on both sides, and guarding her into the deep. And you may note, that though this may seem a curiosity not worth observing, yet *others* have judged it worth their time and cost to make glass hives, and order them in such a manner as to see how bees have bred and make their honeycombs, and how they have obeyed their king, and governed their commonwealth. But it is thought that all carps are not bred by generation; but that some breed other ways, as some pikes do.

The physicians make the galls and stones in the heads of carps to be very medicinable. But 'tis not to be doubted but that in Italy they made great profit of the spawn of carps, by selling it to the Jews, who make it into red caviare; the Jews not being by their law admitted to eat of caviare made of the sturgeon, that being a fish that wants scales, and (as may appear in Lev. 11) by them reputed to be unclean.

Much more might be said out of him, and out of Aristotle, which Dubravius often quotes in his Discourse of Fishes; but it might rather perplex than satisfy you; and therefore I shall rather choose to direct you how to catch, than spend more time in discoursing either of the nature or the breeding of this carp, or of any more circumstances concerning him; but yet I shall remember you of what I told you before, that he is a very subtle fish, and hard to be caught.

And my first direction is, that if you will fish for a carp, you must put on a very large measure of patience; especially to fish for a river carp: I have known a very good fisher angle diligently four or six hours in a day, for three or four days together, for a river carp, and not have a bite: and you are to note that in some ponds it is as hard to catch a carp as in a river; that is to say, where they have store of feed, and the water is of a clayish colour; but you are to remember that I have told you there is no rule without an exception; and therefore being possessed with that hope and patience which I wish to all fishers, especially to the carp-angler, I shall tell you with what bait to fish for him. But first, you are to know that it must be either early or late; and let me tell you that in hot weather (for he will seldom bite in cold) you cannot be too early or too late at it. And some have been so curious as to say the tenth of April is a fatal day for carps.

The carp bites either at worms or at paste; and of worms I think the bluish marsh or meadow worm is best; but possibly another worm not too big may do as well, and so may a green gentle: and as for pastes, there are almost as many sorts as there are medicines for the toothache; but doubtless sweet pastes are the best; I mean pastes made with honey or with sugar; which, that you may the better beguile this crafty fish, should be thrown in the pond or place in which you fish for him some hours, or longer, before you undertake your trial of skill with the angle-rod; and doubtless if it be thrown into the water a day or two before, at several times, and in small pellets, you are the likelier, when you fish for the carp, to obtain your desired sport. Or, in a large pond, to draw them to a certain place, that they may the better and with more hope be fished for, you are to throw into it, in some certain place, either grains or blood mixed with cow-dung, or with bran; or any garbage, as chickens' guts or the like; and then some of your small sweet pellets with which you purpose to angle: and these small pellets being a few of them also thrown in as you are angling, will be the better.

And your paste must be thus made: take the flesh of a rabbit or cat cut small; and bean flour; and if that may not be easily got, get other flour; and then mix these together, and put to them either sugar, or honey, which I think better; and then beat these together in a mortar, or sometimes work them in your hands (your hands being very clean); and then make it into a ball, or two, or three, as you like best, for your use; but you must work or pound it so long in the mortar as to make it so tough as to hang upon your hook, without washing from it, yet not too hard; or, that you may the better keep it on your hook, you may knead with your paste a little (and not much) white or yellowish wool.

And if you would have this paste keep all the year, for any other fish, then mix with it virgin wax, and clarified honey, and work them together with your hands before the fire; then make these into balls, and they will keep all the year.

And if you fish for a carp with gentles, then put upon your hook a little piece of scarlet about this bigness ☐, it being soaked in or anointed with oil of peter, called by some oil of the rock; and if your gentles be put two or three days before into a box or horn anointed with honey, and so put upon your hook as to preserve them to be living, you are as like to kill this crafty fish this way as any other; but still, as you are fishing, chew a little white or brown bread in your mouth, and cast it into the pond about the place where your float swims. Other baits there be; but these, with diligence and patient watchfulness, will do it better than any that I ever practised, or heard of: and yet I shall tell you that the crumb of white bread and honey, made into a paste, is a good bait for a carp; and you know it is more easily made. And having said thus much of a carp, my next discourse shall be of the bream; which shall not prove so tedious, and therefore I desire the continuance of your attention.

But, first, I will tell you how to make this carp, that is so curious to be caught, so curious a dish of meat, as shall make him worth all your labour and patience; and though it is not without some trouble and charges, yet it will recompense both.

Take a carp (alive if possible), scour him, and rub him clean with water and salt, but scale him not; then open him, and put him, with his blood, and his liver (which you must save when you open him) into a small pot or kettle; then take sweet marjoram, thyme, and parsley, of each half a handful, a sprig of rosemary, and another of savory, bind them into two or three small bundles, and put them to your carp, with four or five whole onions, twenty pickled oysters, and three anchovies. Then pour upon your carp as much claret wine as will only cover him, and season your claret well with salt, cloves, and mace, and the rinds of oranges and lemons; that done, cover your pot and set it on a quick fire till it be sufficiently boiled; then take out the carp and lay it with the broth into the dish, and pour upon it a quarter of a pound of the best fresh butter, melted and beaten with half-a-dozen spoonfuls of the broth, the yolks of two or three eggs, and some of the herbs shred; garnish your dish with lemons, and so serve it up, and much good do you.

Observations of the Bream; and Directions to Catch him

Pisc. The Bream, being at a full growth, is a large and stately fish: he will breed both in rivers and ponds; but loves best to live in ponds, and where, if he likes the water and air, he will grow not only to be very large, but as fat as a hog: he is by Gesner taken to be more pleasant or sweet than wholesome: this fish is long in growing, but breeds exceedingly in a water that pleases him: yea, in many ponds so fast as to overstore them, and starve the other fish.

He is very broad, with a forked tail, and his scales set in excellent order; he hath large eyes, and a narrow sucking mouth; he hath two sets of teeth, and a lozenge-like bone, a bone to help his grinding. The melter is observed to have two large melts; and the female two large bags of eggs or spawn.

Gesner reports, that in Poland a certain and a great number of large breams were put into a pond, which in the next following winter were frozen up into one entire ice, and not one drop of water remaining, nor one of these fish to be found, though they were diligently searched for; and yet the next spring, when the ice was thawed, and the weather warm, and fresh water got into the pond, he affirms they all appeared again. This Gesner affirms, and I quote my author because it seems almost as incredible as the resurrection to an atheist: but it may win something, in point of believing it, to him that considers the breeding or renovation of the silk-worm, and of many insects. And that is considerable, which Sir Francis Bacon observes in his *History of Life and Death* (fol. 20), that there be some herbs that die and spring every year, and some endure longer.

But though some do not, yet the French esteem this fish highly, and to that end have this proverb, "He that hath breams in his pond is able to bid his friend welcome." And it is noted that the best part of a bream is his belly and head.

Some say that breams and roaches will mix their eggs and melt together, and so there is in many places a bastard breed of breams, that never come to be either large or good, but very numerous.

The baits good to catch this Bream are many. First, paste made of brown bread and honey, gentles, or the brood of wasps that be young (and then not unlike gentles), and should be hardened in an oven, or dried on a tile before the fire, to make them tough; or there is at the root of docks or flags, or rushes in watery places, a worm not unlike a maggot, at which tench will bite freely. Or he will bite at a grasshopper with his legs nipped off, in June or July, or at several flies under water, which may be found on flags that grow near to the water-side. I doubt not but that there be many other baits that are good; but I will turn them all into this excellent one, either for a carp or bream, in any river or mere: it was given to me by a most honest and excellent angler; and hoping you will prove both, I will impart it to you.

1. Let your bait be as big a red worm as you can find, without a knot; get a pint or quart of them in an evening in garden walks, or chalky common, after a shower of rain, and put them with clean moss well washed and picked, and the water squeezed out of the moss as dry as you can, into an earthen pot or pipkin set dry, and change the moss fresh every three or four days, for three weeks or a month together; then your bait will be at the best, for it will be clear and lively.

2. Having thus prepared your baits, get your tackling ready

and fitted for this sport. Take three long angling rods, and as many and more silk, or silk and hair lines, and as many large swan or goose-quill floats. Then take a piece of lead, made after this manner, and fasten them to the low ends of your lines; then fasten your link-hook also to the lead, and let there be about a foot or ten inches between the lead and the hook; but be sure the lead be heavy enough to sink the float or quill a little under the water, and not the quill to bear up the lead, for the lead must lie on the ground. Note, that your link next the hook may be smaller than the rest of your line, if you dare adventure, for fear of taking the pike or perch, who will assuredly visit your hooks, till they be taken out (as I will show you afterwards), before either carp or bream will come near to bite. Note also, that when the worm is well baited, it will crawl up and down as far as the lead will give leave, which much enticeth the fish to bite without suspicion.

3. Having thus prepared your baits, and fitted your tackling, repair to the river, where you have seen them swim in skulls or shoals, in the summer time, in a hot afternoon, about three or four of the clock, and watch their going forth of their deep holes and returning (which you may well discern), for they return about four of the clock, most of them seeking food at the bottom, yet one or two will lie on the top of the water, rolling and tumbling themselves whilst the rest are under him at the bottom, and so you shall perceive him to keep sentinel; then mark where he plays most, and stays longest (which commonly is in the broadest and deepest place of the river), and there, or near thereabouts, at a clear bottom and a convenient landing-place, take one of your angles ready fitted as aforesaid, and sound the bottom, which should be about eight or ten feet deep (two yards from the bank is the best). Then consider with yourself whether that water will rise or fall by the next morning, by reason of any water-mills near, and according to your discretion take the depth of the place, where you mean after to

cast your ground-bait, and to fish, to half an inch, that the lead lying on or near the ground-bait, the top of the float may only appear upright half an inch above the water.

Thus you having found and fitted for the place and depth thereof, then go home and prepare your ground-bait, which is, next to the fruit of your labours, to be regarded.

THE GROUND-BAIT

You shall take a peck, or a peck and a half (according to the greatness of the stream and deepness of the water where you mean to angle) of sweet gross-ground barley malt, and boil it in a kettle (one or two warms is enough), then strain it through a bag into a tub (the liquor whereof hath often done my horse much good), and when the bag and malt is near cold, take it down to the water-side about eight or nine of the clock in the evening, and not before; cast in two parts of your ground-bait, squeezed hard between both your hands; it will sink presently to the bottom, and be sure it may rest in the very place where you mean to angle; if the stream run hard or move a little, cast your malt in handfuls a little the higher, upwards the stream. You may, between your hands, close the malt so fast in handfuls, that the water will hardly part it with the fall.

Your ground thus baited and tackling fitted, leave your bag with the rest of your tackling and ground-bait near the sporting-place all night, and in the morning about three or four of the clock visit the water-side, but not too near, for they have a cunning watchman, and are watchful themselves too.

Then gently take one of your three rods, and bait your hook, casting it over your ground-bait; and gently and secretly draw it to you, till the lead rests about the middle of the ground-bait.

Then take a second rod, and cast in about a yard above, and your third a yard below the first rod: and stay the rods in the ground; but go yourself so far from the water-side, that you perceive nothing but the top of the floats, which you must watch most diligently. Then when you have a bite, you shall perceive the top of your float to sink suddenly into the water; yet, nevertheless, be not too hasty to run to your rods, until you see that the line goes clear away, then creep to the water-side, and give as much line as you possibly can: if it be a good carp or bream, they will go to the farther side of the river: then strike gently, and hold your rod at a bent a little while; but if you both pull together, you are sure to lose your game, for either your line, or hook, or hold will break; and after you have overcome them, they will make noble sport, and are very shy to be landed. The carp is far stronger and more mettlesome than the bream.

Much more is to be observed in this kind of fish and fishing, but it is far better for experience and discourse than paper. Only, thus much is necessary for you to know, and to be mindful and careful of, that if the pike or perch do breed in that river, they will be sure to bite first, and must first be taken. And for the most part they are very large; and will repair to your ground-bait, not that they will eat of it, but will feed and sport themselves amongst the young fry that gather about and hover over the bait.

The way to discern the pike and to take him, if you mistrust your bream-hook (for I have taken a pike a yard long several times at my bream-hooks, and sometimes he hath had the luck to share my line), may be thus:

Take a small bleak, or roach, or gudgeon, and bait it, and set it alive among your rods, two feet deep from the cork, with a little red worm on the point of the hook; then take a few crumbs of white bread, or some of the ground-bait, and sprinkle it gently amongst your rods. If Mr Pike be there, then the little fish will skip out of the water at his appearance, but the live-set bait is sure to be taken.

Thus continue your sport from four in the morning till eight, and if it be a gloomy, windy day, they will bite all day long. But this is too long to stand to your rods at one place, and it will spoil your evening sport that day, which is this:

About four of the clock in the afternoon repair to your baited place; and as soon as you come to the water-side, cast in one half of the rest of your ground-bait, and stand off: then whilst the fish are gathering together (for there they will most certainly come for their supper) you may take a pipe of tobacco; and then in with your three rods, as in the morning: you will find excellent sport that evening till eight of the clock; then cast in the residue of your ground-bait, and next morning by four of the clock visit them again for four hours, which is the best sport of all; and after that, let them rest till you and your friends have a mind to more sport.

From St James's-tide until Bartholomew-tide is the best; when they have had all the summer's food, they are the fattest.

Observe lastly, that after three or four days' fishing together, your game will be very shy and wary, and you shall hardly get above a bite or two at a baiting; then your only way is to desist from your sport about two or three days; and in the meantime (on the place you late baited, and again intend to bait) you shall take a tuft of green, but short grass, as big or bigger than a round trencher; to the top of this turf, on the green side, you shall with a needle and green thread, fasten one by one as many little red worms as will near cover all the turf; then take a round board or trencher, make a hole in the middle thereof, and through the turf, placed on the board or trencher, with a string or cord as long as is fitting, tied to a pole, let it down to the bottom of the water, for the fish to feed upon without disturbance about two or three days; and after that you have drawn it away, you may fall to and enjoy your former recreation.

Observations of the Tench; and Advice how to Angle for him

Pisc. The Tench, the physician of fishes, is observed to love ponds better than rivers, and to love pits better than either; yet Camden observes, there is a river in Dorsetshire that abounds with tenches, but doubtless they retire to the most deep and quiet places in it.

This fish hath very large fins, very small and smooth scales, a red circle about his eyes, which are big and of a gold colour, and from either angle of his mouth there hangs down a little barb. In every tench's head there are two little stones, which foreign physicians make great use of, but he is not commended for wholesome meat, though there be very much use made of them for outward applications. Rondeletius says, that at his being at Rome, he saw a great cure done by applying a tench to the feet of a very sick man. This, he says, was done after an unusual manner, by certain Jews. And it is observed, that many of those people have many secrets yet unknown to Christians; secrets that have never yet been written, but have been since the days of their Solomon (who knew the nature of all things, even from the cedar to the shrub) delivered by tradition, from the father to the son, and so from generation to generation, without writing, or (unless it were casually) without the least communicating them to any other nation or tribe; for to do that they account a profanation, And yet it is thought that they, or some spirit worse than they, first told us that lice swallowed alive were a certain cure for the yellow-jaundice. This, and many other medicines, were discovered by them, or by revelation; for, doubtless, we attained them not by study.

Well, this fish, besides his eating, is very useful both dead and alive for the good of mankind. But I will meddle no more with that; my honest humble art teaches no such boldness; there are too many foolish meddlers in physic and divinity, that think themselves fit to meddle with hidden secrets, and so bring destruction to their followers. But I'll not meddle with them any further than to wish them wiser; and shall tell you next (for I hope I may be so bold) that the tench is the physician of fishes, for the pike especially; and that the pike, being either sick or hurt, is cured by the touch of the TENCH. And it is observed that the tyrant pike will not be a wolf to his physician, but forbears to devour him though he be never so hungry.

This fish, that carries a natural balsam in him to cure himself and others, loves yet to feed in very foul water, and amongst weeds. And yet I am sure he eats pleasantly, and doubtless you will think so too, if you taste him. And I shall therefore proceed to give you some few, and but a few, directions how to catch this Tench, of which I have given you these observations.

He will bite a paste made of brown bread and honey, or at a marsh-worm, or a lob-worm; he inclines very much to any paste with which tar is mixed; and he will bite also at a smaller worm, with his head nipped off, and a cod-worm put on the hook before that worm; and I doubt not but that he will also in the three hot months (for in the nine colder he stirs not much) bite at a flag-worm, or at a green gentle; but I can positively say no more of the tench, he being a fish I have not often angled for; but I wish my honest scholar may, and be ever fortunate when he fishes.

Observations of the Perch; and Directions how to Fish for him

Pisc. The Perch is a very good and a very bold-biting fish. He is one of the fishes of prey that, like the pike and trout, carries his teeth in his mouth, which is very large; and he dare venture to kill and devour several other kinds of fish. He has a hooked or hog back, which is armed with sharp and stiff bristles, and all his skin armed or covered over with thick dry hard scales, and hath (which few other fish have) two fins on his back. He is so bold that he will invade one of his own kind, which the pike will not do willingly, and you may therefore easily believe him to be a bold biter.

The perch is of great esteem in Italy, saith Aldrovandus, and especially the least are there esteemed a dainty dish. And Gesner prefers the perch and pike above the trout, or any fresh-water fish: he says the Germans have this proverb, "More wholesome than a perch of Rhine"; and he says the river perch is so wholesome that physicians allow him to be eaten by wounded men, or by men in fevers, or by women in child-bed.

He spawns but once a year, and is, by physicians, held very nutritive; yet, by many, to be hard of digestion. They abound more in the river Po, and in England (says Rondeletius) than other parts, and have in their brain a stone which is in foreign parts sold by apothecaries, being there noted to be very medicinable against the stone in the reins. These be a part of the commendations which some philosophical brains have bestowed upon the fresh-water perch; yet they commend the sea-perch, which is known by having but one fin on his back (of which, they say, we English see but a few) to be a much better fish.

The perch grows slowly, yet will grow, as I have been credibly informed, to be almost two feet long; for an honest informer told me such a one was not long since taken by Sir Abraham Williams, a gentleman of worth, and a brother of the angle (that yet lives, and I wish he may): this was a deep bodied fish, and doubtless durst have devoured a pike of half his own length; for I have told you he is a bold fish, such a one as, but for extreme hunger, the pike will not devour; for to affright the pike, and save himself, the perch will set up his fins, much like as a turkey-cock will sometimes set up his tail.

But, my scholar, the perch is not only valiant to defend

himself, but he is (as I said) a bold-biting fish, yet he will not bite at all seasons of the year; he is very abstemious in winter, yet will bite then in the midst of the day, if it be warm: and note, that all fish bite best about the midst of a warm day in winter, and he hath been observed by some not usually to bite till the mulberry-tree buds, that is to say, till extreme frosts be past the spring, for when the mulberry-tree blossoms, many gardeners observe their forward fruit to be past the danger of frosts, and some have made the like observation on the perch's biting.

But bite the perch will, and that very boldly: and as one has wittily observed, if there be twenty or forty in a hole, they may be at one standing all catched one after another, they being, as he says, like the wicked of the world, not afraid, though their fellows and companions perish in their sight. And you may observe, that they are not like the solitary pike, but love to accompany one another, and march together in troops.

And the baits for this bold fish are not many: I mean, he will bite as well at some or at any of these three, as at any or all others whatsoever: a worm, a minnow, or a little frog (of which you may find many in hay-time); and of worms, the dunghill-worm, called a brandling, I take to be best, being well scoured in moss or fennel; or he will bite at a worm that lies under cow-dung, with a bluish head. And if you rove for a perch with a minnow, then it is best to be alive, you sticking your hook through his back fin, or a minnow with the hook in his upper lip, and letting him swim up and down about mid-water, or a little lower, and you still keeping him to about that depth by a cork, which ought not to be a very little one; and the like way you are to fish for the perch, with a small frog, your hook being fastened through the skin of his leg, towards the upper part of it; and lastly, I will give you but this advice, that you give the perch time enough when he bites, for there was scarce ever any angler that has given him too much. And now I think best to rest myself, for I have almost spent my spirits with talking so long.

Ven. Nay, good master, one fish more, for you see it rains still, and you know our angles are like money put to usury, they may thrive, though we sit still and do nothing but talk and enjoy one another. Come, come, the other fish, good master.

Pisc. But, scholar, have you nothing to mix with this discourse, which now grows both tedious and tiresome? Shall I have nothing from you, that seem to have both a good memory and a cheerful spirit?

Ven. Yes, master, I will speak you a copy of verses that were made by Doctor Donne, and made to show the world that he could make soft and smooth verses when he thought smoothness worth his labour; and I love them the better because they allude to rivers, and fish and fishing. They be these:

> Come live with me, and be my love,
> And we will some new pleasures prove,
> Of golden sands and crystal brooks,
> With silken lines and silver hooks.
>
> There will the river whisp'ring run,
> Warm'd by thy eyes more than the sun,
> And there th' enamell'd fish will stay,
> Begging themselves they may betray.
>
> When thou wilt swim in that live bath,
> Each fish, which every channel hath,
> Most amorously to thee will swim,
> Gladder to catch thee, than thou him.
>
> If thou to be so seen be'st loath,
> By sun or moon, thou darkenest both;
> And if mine eyes have leave to see,
> I need not their light, having thee.
>
> Let others freeze with angling-reeds,
> And cut their legs with shells and weeds,

> Or treacherously poor fish beset,
> With strangling snares, or windowy net:
>
> Let coarse bold bands, from slimy nest,
> The bedded fish in banks outwrest;
> Let curious traitors sleave silk flies,
> To witch poor wandering fishes' eyes:
>
> For thee thou need'st no such deceit,
> For thou thyself art thine own bait:
> That fish that is not catch'd thereby
> Is wiser far, alas! than I.

Pisc. Well remembered, honest scholar; I thank thee for these choice verses, which I have heard formerly, but had quite forgot till they were recovered by your happy memory. Well, being I have now rested myself a little, I will make you some requital, by telling you some observations of the eel, for it rains still, and because (as you say) our angles are as money put to use, that thrives when we play, therefore we'll sit still and enjoy ourselves a little longer under this honeysuckle hedge.

Observations of the Eel, and other Fish that want Scales; and how to Fish for them

Pisc. It is agreed by most men, that the eel is a most dainty fish; the Romans have esteemed her the Helena of their feasts, and some the queen of palate-pleasure. But most men differ about their breeding: some say they breed by generation as other fish do, and others, that they breed (as some worms do) of mud; as rats and mice, and many other living creatures are bred in Egypt, by the sun's heat, when it shines upon the overflowing of the river Nilus; or out of the putrefaction of the earth, and divers other ways. Those that deny them to breed by generation as other fish do, ask, if any man ever saw an eel to have a spawn or melt? and they are answered, that they may be as certain of their breeding as if they had seen spawn: for they say, that they are certain that eels have all parts, fit for generation, like other fish, but so small as not to be easily discerned, by reason of their fatness; but that discerned they may be; and that the he and the she-eel may be distinguished by their fins. And Rondeletius says he has seen eels cling together like dew-worms.

And others say that eels, growing old, breed other eels out of the corruption of their own age; which, Sir Francis Bacon says, exceeds not ten years. And others say, that as pearls are made of glutinous dew-drops, which are condensed by the sun's heat in those countries, so eels are bred of a particular dew, falling in the months of May or June on the banks of some particular ponds or rivers (apted by nature for that end), which in a few days are, by the sun's heat, turned into eels; and some of the ancients have called the eels that are thus bred the offspring of Jove. I have seen, in the beginning of July, in a river not far from Canterbury, some parts of it covered over with young eels, about the thickness of a straw; and these eels did lie on the top of that water, as thick as motes are said to be in the sun; and I have heard the like of other rivers, as namely, in Severn (where they are called yelvers), and in a pond, or mere, near unto Stafford-shire, where, about a set time in summer, such small eels abound so much that many of the poorer sort of people that inhabit near to it, take such eels out of this mere with sieves or sheets; and make a kind of eel-cake of them, and eat it like as bread. And Gesner quotes venerable Bede, to say, that in England there is an island called Ely, by reason of the innumer-able number of eels that breed in it. But that eels may be bred as some worms, and some kind of bees and wasps are, either of dew, or out of the corruption of the earth, seems to be made probable by the barnacles and young goslings bred by the sun's heat and the rotten planks of an old ship, and hatched of trees; both which are related for truths by Du Bartas and Lobel, and also by our learned Camden, and laborious Gerard, in his *Herbal*.

It is said by Rondeletius, that those eels that are bred in rivers that relate to or be nearer to the sea, never return to the fresh waters (as the salmon does always desire to do), when they have once tasted the salt water; and I do the more easily believe this, because I am certain that powdered beef is a most excellent bait to catch an eel. And though Sir Francis Bacon will allow the eel's life to be but ten years, yet he, in his *History of Life and Death*, mentions a lamprey belonging to the Roman emperor, to be made tame, and so kept for almost threescore years; and that such useful and pleasant observations were made of this lamprey, that Crassus the orator (who kept her) lamented her death. And we read (in Dr Hakewill) that Hortensius was seen to weep at the death of a lamprey that he had kept long and loved exceedingly.

It is granted by all, or most men, that eels, for about six months (that is to say, the six cold months of the year) stir not up and down, neither in the rivers, nor in the pools in which they usually are, but get into the soft earth or mud; and there many of them together bed themselves, and live without feeding upon anything (as I have told you some swallows have been observed to do in hollow trees, for those six cold months) ; and this the eel and swallow do, as not being able to endure winter weather: for Gesner quotes Albertus to say, that in the year 1125 (that year's winter being more cold than usually) eels did by nature's instinct get out of the water into a stack of hay in a meadow upon dry ground, and there bedded themselves, but yet at last a frost killed them. And our Camden relates, that in Lancashire fishes were digged out of the earth with spades, where no water was near to the place. I shall say little more of the eel, but that, as it is observed, he is impatient of cold; so it hath been observed, that in warm weather an eel has been known to live five days out of the water.

And lastly, let me tell you that some curious searchers into the natures of fish observe, that there be several sorts or kinds of eels, as the silver eel, and green or greenish eel (with which the river of Thames abounds, and those are called grigs); and a blackish eel, whose head is more flat and bigger than ordinary eels; and also an eel whose fins are reddish, and but seldom taken in this nation, and yet taken sometimes: these several kinds of eels are (say some) diversely bred; as namely, out of the corruption of the earth, and some by dew, and others ways (as I have said to you): and yet it is affirmed by some for certain, that the silver eel is bred by generation, but not by spawning as other fish do, but that her brood come alive from her, being then little live eels, no bigger nor longer than a pin; and I have had too many testimonies of this to doubt the truth of it myself; and if I thought it needful I might prove it, but I think it is needless.

And this eel, of which I have said so much to you, may be caught with divers kinds of baits; as namely, with powdered beef, with a lob or garden-worm, with a minnow, or gut of a hen, chicken, or the guts of any fish, or with almost anything, for he is a greedy fish; but the eel may be caught especially with a little, a very little lamprey, which some call a pride, and may in the hot months be found many of them in the river Thames, and in many mud-heaps in other rivers, yea, almost as usually as one finds worms in a dunghill.

Next note, that the eel seldom stirs in the day, but then hides himself; and therefore he is usually caught by night, with one of these baits of which I have spoken; and may be then caught by laying hooks, which you are to fasten to the bank, or twigs of a tree; or by throwing a string across the stream with many hooks at it, and those baited with the aforesaid baits, and a clod, or plummet, or stone, thrown into the river with this line, that so you may in the morning find it near to some fixed place; and then take it up with a draghook, or otherwise: but these things are, indeed, too common to be spoken of; and an hour's fishing with an angler will teach you better, both for these and many

other common things, in the practical part of angling, than a
week's discourse. I shall therefore conclude this direction for
taking the eel by telling you, that in a warm day in summer I
have taken many a good eel by sniggling, and have been much
pleased with that sport.

And because you, that are but a young angler, know not what
sniggling is, I will now teach it to you. You remember I told you
that eels do not usually stir in the daytime; for then they hide
themselves under some covert; or under boards or planks about
flood-gates, or weirs, or mills; or in holes on the river banks: so
that you, observing your time in a warm day, when the water is
lowest, may take a strong small hook, tied to a strong line, or to
a string about a yard long; and then into one of these holes, or
between any boards about a mill, or under any great stone or
plank or any place where you think an eel may hide or shelter
herself, you may, with the help of a short stick, put in your bait,
but leisurely, and as far as you may conveniently; and it is scarce
to be doubted, but if there be an eel, within the sight of it, the eel
will bite instantly, and as certainly gorge it; and you need not
doubt to have him if you pull him not out of the hole too
quickly, but pull him out by degrees; for he, laying folded double
in his hole, will, with the help of his tail, break all, unless you
give him time to be wearied with pulling; and so get him out by
degrees, not pulling too hard.

And to commute for your patient hearing this long discourse,
I shall next tell you how to make this eel a most excellent dish
of meat.

First, wash him in water and salt, then pull off his skin below
his vent or navel, and not much further: having done that, take
out his guts as clean as you can, but wash him not; then give him
three or four scotches with a knife, and then put into his belly
and those scotches, sweet herbs, an anchovy, and a little nutmeg
grated, or cut very small; and your herbs and anchovies must
also be cut very small, and mixed with good butter and salt:

having done this, then pull his skin over him all but his head, which you are to cut off, to the end you may tie his skin about that part where his head grew; and it must be so tied as to keep all his moisture within his skin: and having done this, tie him with tape or packthread to a spit, and roast him leisurely, and baste him with water and salt till his skin breaks, and then with butter; and having roasted him enough, let what was put into his belly and what he drips be his sauce.—S.F.

When I go to dress an eel thus, I wish he were as long and big as that which was caught in Peterborough river in the year 1667, which was a yard and three-quarters long. If you will not believe me, then go and see at one of the coffee-houses in King Street, in Westminster.

But now let me tell you, that though the eel thus dressed be not only excellent good, but more harmless than any other way; yet it is certain, that physicians account the eel dangerous meat: I will advise you, therefore, as Solomon says of honey, Prov. 25, "Hast thou found it, eat no more than is sufficient, lest thou surfeit; for it is not good to eat much honey." And let me add this, that the uncharitable Italian bids us "give eels and no wine to our enemies."

And I will beg a little more of your attention to tell you Aldrovandus, and divers physicians, commend the eel very much for medicine, though not for meat. But let me tell you one observation, that the eel is never out of season, as trouts, and most other fish are at set times: at least most eels are not.

I might here speak of many other fish, whose shape and nature are much like the eel, and frequent both the sea and fresh rivers; as namely, the lamprel, the lamprey, and the lamperne: as also of the mighty conger, taken often in Severn, about Glouces-ter; and might also tell in what high esteem many of them are for the curiosity of their taste; but these are not so proper to be talked of by me, because they make us anglers no sport; therefore I will let them alone, as the Jews do, to whom they are forbidden by their law.

And, scholar, there is also a flounder, a sea-fish, which will wander very far into fresh rivers, and there lose himself and dwell; and thrive to a hand's breadth, and almost twice so long: a fish without scales, and most excellent meat; and a fish that affords much sport to the angler, with any small worm, but especially a little bluish worm gotten out of marsh-ground or meadows, which should be well scoured: but this, though it be most excellent meat, yet it wants scales, and is, as I told you, therefore an abomination to the Jews.

But, scholar, there is a fish that they in Lancashire boast very much of, called a char; taken there (and I think there only), in a mere called Winander Mere: a mere, says Camden, that is the largest in this nation, being ten miles in length, and some say as smooth in the bottom as if it were paved with polished marble. This fish never exceeds fifteen or sixteen inches in length; and 'tis spotted like a trout; and has scarce a bone but on the back. But this, though I do not know whether it make the angler sport, yet I would have you take notice of it, because it is a rarity, and of so high esteem with persons of great note.

Nor would I have you ignorant of a rare fish called a guiniad; of which I shall tell you of what Camden and others speak. The river Dee (which runs by Chester) springs in Merionethshire; and, as it runs towards Chester, it runs through Pemble-Mere, which is a large water: and it is observed, that though the river Dee abounds with salmon, and Pemble-Mere with the guiniad, yet there is never any salmon caught in the mere, nor a guiniad in the river. And now my next observation shall be of the Barbel.

Observations of the Barbel; and Directions how to Fish for him

Pisc. The Barbel is so called (says Gesner) by reason of his barb or wattles at his mouth, which are under his nose or chaps. He is one of those leather-mouthed fishes, that I told you of, that does very seldom break his hold if he be once hooked: but he is so strong that he will often break both rod and line, if he proves to be a big one.

But the barbel, though he be of a fine shape, and looks big, yet he is not accounted the best fish to eat, neither for his wholesomeness nor his taste: but the male is reputed much better than the female, whose spawn is very hurtful, as I will presently declare to you.

They flock together, like sheep, and are at the worst in April, about which time they spawn, but quickly grow to be in season. He is able to live in the strongest swifts of the water, and in summer they love the shallowest and sharpest streams; and love to lurk under weeds, and to feed on gravel against a rising ground, and will root and dig in the sands with his nose like a hog, and there nest himself: yet sometimes he retires to deep and swift bridges, or floodgates, or weirs, where he will nest himself amongst piles, or in hollow places, and take such hold of moss or weeds, that be the water never so swift, it is not able to force him from the place that he contends for. This is his constant custom in summer, when he and most living creatures sport themselves in the sun; but at the approach of winter, then he forsakes the swift streams and shallow waters, and by degrees retires to those parts of the river that are quieter and deeper; in which places (and I think about that time) he spawns, and, as I have formerly told you, with the help of the melter, hides his spawn or eggs in holes, which they both dig in the gravel, and then they mutually labour to cover it with the same sand, to prevent it from being devoured by other fish.

There be such store of this fish in the river Danube, that Rondeletius says, they may in some places of it, and in some months of the year, be taken by those that dwell near to the river, with their hands, eight or ten load at a time: he says, they begin to be good in May, and that they cease to be so in August; but it is found to be otherwise in this nation: but thus far we agree with him, that the spawn of a barbel, if it be not poison, as he says, yet that it is dangerous meat, and especially in the month of May; which is so certain, that Gesner and Gasius declare it had an ill effect upon them, even to the endangering of their lives.

This fish is of a fine cast and handsome shape, with small scales, which are placed after a most exact and curious manner, and, as I told you, may be rather said not to be ill, than to be good meat: the chub and he have (I think) both lost part of their credit by ill cookery, they being reputed the worst or coarsest of fresh-water fish. But the barbel affords an angler choice sport, being a lusty and a cunning fish; so lusty and cunning as to endanger the breaking of the angler's line, by running his head forcibly towards any covert, or hole, or bank, and then striking at the line, to break it off with his tail (as is observed by Plutarch in his book, *De Industria Animalium*); and also so cunning to nibble and suck off your worm close to the hook, and yet avoid the letting the hook come into his mouth.

The barbel is also curious for his baits; that is to say, that they be clean and sweet; that is to say, to have your worms well scoured, and not kept in sour and musty moss, for he is a curious feeder; but at a well-scoured lob-worm he will bite as boldly as at any bait, and especially if, the night or two before you fish for him, you shall bait the places where you intend to fish for him with big worms cut into pieces; and note, that none did ever overbait the place, nor fish too early or too late for a barbel. And the barbel will bite also at gentles, which (not being too much scoured, but green) are a choice bait for him; and so is cheese, which is not to be too hard, but kept a day or two in a wet linen cloth to make it tough: with this you may also bait the water a day or two before you fish for the barbel, and be much the likelier to catch store; and if the cheese were laid in clarified honey a short time before (as namely, an hour or two) you are still the likelier to catch fish; some have directed to cut the cheese into thin pieces, and toast it, and then tie it on the hook with fine silk: and some advise to fish for the barbel with sheep's tallow and soft cheese beaten or worked into a paste, and that it is choicely good in August, and I believe it; but doubtless the lob-worm well scoured, and the gentle not too much scoured, and cheese ordered as I have directed, are baits enough, and I think will serve in any month, though I shall commend any angler that tries conclusions, and is industrious to improve the art. And now, my honest scholar, the long shower and my tedious discourse are both ended together; and I shall give you but this observation, that when you fish for barbel, your rod and line be both long and of good strength, for (as I told you) you will find him a heavy and a dogged fish to be deal withal, yet he seldom or never breaks his hold if he be once strucken. And if you would know more of fishing for the umber or barbel, get into favour with Dr Sheldon, whose skill is above others; and of that the poor that dwell about him have a comfortable experience.

And now let us go and see what interest the trouts will pay us for letting our angle-rods lie so long, and so quietly in the water, for their use. Come, scholar, which will you take up?

Ven. Which you think fit, master.

Pisc. Why, you shall take up that, for I am certain, by viewing the line, it has a fish at it. Look you, scholar! well done! Come, now take up the other too: well! now you may tell my brother Peter, at night, that you have caught a leash of trouts this day. And now let's move towards our lodging, and drink a draught of red cow's milk as we go; and give pretty Maudlin and her honest mother a brace of trouts for their supper.

Ven. Master, I like your motion very well; and I think it is now about milking-time; and yonder they be at it.

Pisc. God speed you, good woman! I thank you both for our songs last night: I and my companion have had such fortune a-fishing this day, that we resolve to give you and Maudlin a brace of trouts for supper; and we will now taste a draught of your red cow's milk.

Milk-W. Marry, and that you shall with all my heart; and I will still be your debtor when you come this way. If you will but speak the word, I will make you a good syllabub of new verjuice; and then you may sit down in a haycock and eat it; and Maudlin shall sit by and sing you the good old song of the *Hunting in Chevy Chase*, or some other good ballad, for she hath store of them; Maudlin, my honest Maudlin, hath a notable memory, and she thinks nothing too good for you, because you be such honest men.

Ven. We thank you; and intend once in a month to call upon you again, and give you a little warning; and so, good-night; good-night, Maudlin. And now, good master, let's lose no time; but tell me somewhat more of fishing; and, if you please, first, something of fishing for a gudgeon.

Pisc. I will, honest scholar.

Observations of the Gudgeon, the Ruffe, and the Bleak; and how to Fish for them

Pisc. The Gudgeon is reputed a fish of excellent taste, and to be very wholesome: he is of a fine shape, of a silver colour, and beautified with black spots both on his body and tail. He breeds two or three times in the year, and always in summer. He is commended for a fish of excellent nourishment: the Germans call him groundling, by reason of his feeding on the ground; and he there feasts himself in sharp streams, and on the gravel. He and the barbel both feed so, and do not hunt for flies at any time, as most other fishes do: he is a most excellent fish to enter a young angler, being easy to be taken with a small red worm, on or near to the ground. He is one of those leather-mouthed fish that has his teeth in his throat, and will hardly be lost off from the hook if he be once strucken. They be usually scattered up and down every river in the shallows, in the heat of summer; but in autumn, when the weeds begin to grow sour and rot, and the weather colder, then they gather together, and get into the deep parts of the water, and are to be fished for there, with your hook always touching the ground, if you fish for him with a float, or with a cork; but many will fish for the gudgeon by hand, with a running line upon the ground, without a cork, as a trout is fished for; and it is an excellent way, if you have a gentle rod and as gentle a hand.

There is also another fish called a pope, and by some a ruffe, a fish that is not known to be in some rivers: he is much like the perch for his shape, and taken to be better than the perch, but will not grow to be bigger than a gudgeon. He is an excellent fish, no fish that swims is of a pleasanter taste, and he is also excellent to enter a young angler, for he is a greedy biter; and they will usually lie abundance of them together, in one reserved place, where the water is deep, and runs quietly; and an easy angler, if he has found where they lie, may catch forty or fifty, or sometimes twice as many, at a standing.

You must fish for him with a small red worm; and if you bait the ground with earth, it is excellent.

There is also a bleak, or fresh-water sprat, a fish that is ever in motion, and therefore called by some the river swallow; for just as you shall observe the swallow to be most evenings in summer ever in motion, making short and quick turns when he flies to catch flies in the air (by which he lives) so does the bleak at the top of the water. Ausonius would have him called bleak from his whitish colour: his back is of a pleasant sad or sea-water green, his belly white and shining as the mountain snow; and doubtless, though he have the fortune (which virtue has in poor people) to be neglected, yet the bleak ought to be much valued, though we want Allamot salt, and the skill that the Italians have to turn them into anchovies. This fish may be caught with a Paternoster line; that is, six or eight very small hooks tied along the line, one half a foot above the other: I have seen five caught thus at one time, and the bait has been gentles, than which none is better.

Or this fish may be caught with a fine small artificial fly, which is to be of a very sad brown colour, and very small, and the hook answerable. There is no better sport than whipping for bleaks in a boat, or on a bank, in the swift water, in a summer's evening, with a hazel top about five or six foot long, and a line twice the length of the rod. I have heard Sir Henry Wotton say, that there be many that in Italy will catch swallows so, or especially martins (this bird-angler standing on the top of a steeple to do it, and with a line twice so long as I have spoken of). And let me tell you, scholar, that both martins and bleaks be most excellent meat.

And let me tell you, that I have known a hern, that did constantly frequent one place, caught with a hook baited with a big minnow or small gudgeon. The line and hook must be strong, and tied to some loose staff, so big as she cannot fly away with it, line not exceeding two yards.

Is of Nothing, or that which is Nothing Worth

Pisc. My purpose was to give you some directions concerning roach and dace, and some other inferior fish, which make the angler excellent sport, for you know there is more pleasure in hunting the hare than in eating her; but I will forbear at this time to say any more, because you see yonder come our brother Peter and honest Coridon: but I will promise you, that as you and I fish, and walk to-morrow towards London, if I have now forgotten anything that I can then remember, I will not keep it from you.

Well met, gentlemen: this is lucky that we meet so just together at this very door. Come, hostess, where are you? Is supper ready? Come, first give us drink, and be as quick as you can, for I believe we are all very hungry. Well, brother Peter, and Coridon, to you both; come drink, and then tell me what luck of fish: we two have caught but ten trouts, of which my scholar caught three: look, here's eight, and a brace we gave away: we have had a most pleasant day for fishing and talking, and are returned home both weary and hungry, and now meat and rest will be pleasant.

Pet. And Coridon and I have had not an unpleasant day, and yet I have caught but five trouts: for indeed we went to a good honest ale-house, and there we played at shovel-board half the day; all the time that it rained we were there, and as merry as they that fished; and I am glad we are now with a dry house over our heads, for hark how it rains and blows. Come, hostess, give us more ale, and our supper with what haste you may; and when we have supped, let us have your song, Piscator, and the catch that your scholar promised us; or else Coridon will be dogged.

Pisc. Nay, I will not be worse than my word; you shall not want my song, and I hope I shall be perfect in it.

Ven. And I hope the like for my catch, which I have ready too; and therefore let's go merrily to supper, and then have a gentle touch at singing and drinking; but the last with moderation.

Cor. Come, now for your song; for we have fed heartily. Come, hostess, lay a few more sticks on the fire. And now sing when you will.

Pisc. Well, then, here's to you, Coridon; and now for my song.

> O the gallant fisher's life,
> It is the best of any!
> 'Tis full of pleasure, void of strife,
> And 'tis beloved by many:
>   Other joys
>   Are but toys;

Only this
Lawful is;
For our skill
Breeds no ill,
But content and pleasure.

In a morning up we rise
Ere Aurora's peeping;
Drink a cup to wash our eyes;
Leave the sluggard sleeping.
Then we go
To and fro
With our knacks
At our backs
To such streams
As the Thames,
If we have the leisure.

When we please to walk abroad
For our recreation,
In the fields is our abode,
Full of delectation:
Where in a brook,
With a hook,
Or a lake,
Fish we take;
There we sit
For a bit,
Till we fish entangle.

We have gentles in a horn,
We have paste and worms too;
We can watch both night and morn,
Suffer rain and storms too.
None do here
Use to swear;
Oaths do fray
Fish away:
We sit still

And watch our quill;
Fishers must not wrangle.

If the sun's excessive heat
   Make our bodies swelter,
To an osier-hedge we get
   For a friendly shelter;
      Where in a dike,
      Perch or pike,
      Roach or dace,
      We do chase;
      Bleak or gudgeon,
      Without grudging:
   We are still contented.

Or we sometimes pass an hour
   Under a green willow,
That defends us from a shower—
   Making earth our pillow:
      Where we may
      Think and pray,
      Before death
      Stops our breath:
      Other joys
      Are but toys,
   And to be lamented.

                              JO. CHALKHILL

Ven. Well sung, master: this day's fortune and pleasure, and
this night's company and song, do all make me more and more
in love with angling. Gentlemen, my master left me alone for an
hour this day; and I verily believe he retired himself from talking
with me, that he might be so perfect in this song: was it not,
master?

Pisc. Yes, indeed; for it is many years since I learned it, and
having forgotten a part of it, I was forced to patch it up by the
help of mine own invention, who am not excellent at poetry, as

my part of the song may testify: but of that I will say no more, lest you should think I mean by discommending it to beg your commendations of it. And therefore, without replications, let us hear your catch, scholar, which I hope will be a good one; for you are both musical, and have a good fancy to boot.

Ven. Marry, and that you shall; and as freely as I would have my honest master tell me some more secrets of fish and fishing as we walk and fish towards London to-morrow. But, master, first let me tell you, that, that very hour which you were absent from me, I sat down under a willow-tree by the water-side, and considered what you had told me of the owner of that pleasant meadow in which you had then left me; that he had a plentiful estate, and not a heart to think so; that he had at this time many law-suits depending, and that they both damped his mirth and took up so much of his time and thoughts, that he himself had not leisure to take the sweet content that I (who pretended no title to them) took in his fields: for I could sit there quietly, and looking on the water, see some fishes sport themselves in the silver streams, others leaping at flies of several shapes and colours; looking on the hills, I could behold them spotted with woods and groves; looking down the meadows, could see, here a boy gathering lilies and lady-smocks, and there a girl cropping culverkeys and cowslips, all to make garlands suitable to this present month of May: these, and many other field-flowers, so perfumed the air, that I thought that very meadow like that field in Sicily (of which Diodorus speaks) where the perfumes arising from the place make all dogs that hunt in it to fall off, and to lose their hottest scent. I say, as I thus sat, joying in my own happy condition, and pitying this poor rich man that owned this and many other pleasant groves and meadows about me, I did thankfully remember what my Saviour said, that the meek possess the earth; or rather, they enjoy what the others possess and enjoy not; for anglers and meek quiet-spirited men are free from those high, those restless thoughts which corrode the sweets of life; and they, and they only, can say, as the poet has happily expressed it:

> Hail blest estate of lowliness!
>   Happy enjoyments of such minds
> As, rich in self-contentedness,
>   Can, like the reeds in roughest winds,
> By yielding make that blow but small,
> At which proud oaks and cedars fall.

There came also into my mind, at that time, certain verses in praise of a mean estate and an humble mind; they were written by Phineas Fletcher, an excellent divine, and an excellent angler, and the author of excellent piscatory eclogues, in which you shall see the picture of this good man's mind, and I wish mine to be like it.

> No empty hopes, no courtly fears him fright;
> No begging wants his middle fortune bite;
> But sweet content exiles both misery and spite.

> His certain life, that never can deceive him,
>   Is full of thousand sweets and rich content;
> The smooth-leaved beeches in the field receive him,
>   With coolest shade till noontide's heat be spent.

> His life is neither toss'd in boisterous seas
> Or the vexatious world, or lost in slothful ease;
> Pleased and full bless'd he lives, when he his God can
>   please.

> His bed, more safe than soft, yields quiet sleeps,
>   While by his side his faithful spouse hath place;
> His little son into his bosom creeps,
>   The lively picture of his father's face;
> His humble house or poor state ne'er torment him—

Less he could like, if less his God had lent him;
And when he dies, green turfs do for a tomb content him.

Gentlemen, these were a part of the thoughts that then possessed me. And I there made a conversion of a piece of an old catch, and added more to it, fitting them to be sung by anglers. Come, master, you can sing well; you must sing a part of it as it is in this paper.

> Man's life is but vain, for 'tis subject to pain
> And sorrow, and short as a bubble;
> 'Tis a hodgepodge of business, and money, and care,
> And care, and money, and trouble.
> But we'll take no care when the weather proves fair;
> Nor will we vex now, though it rain;
> We'll banish all sorrow and sing till to-morrow
> And angle, and angle again.

Pet. Ay, marry, sir, this is music indeed: this has cheered my heart, and made me to remember six verses in praise of music, which I will speak to you instantly.

> Music! miraculous rhetoric, that speakest sense
> Without a tongue, excelling eloquence;
> With what ease might thy errors be excused,
> Wert thou as truly loved as thou'rt abused!
> But though dull souls neglect, and some reprove thee,
> I cannot hate thee 'cause the angels love thee.

Ven. And the repetition of these last verses of music has called to my memory what Mr Ed. Waller (a lover of the angle) says of love and music.

> Whilst I listen to thy voice,
> Chloris, I feel my heart decay:
> That powerful voice

Calls my fleeting soul away:
O suppress that magic sound,
Which destroys without a wound!

Peace, Chloris, peace, or singing die,
That together you and I
To heaven may go;
For all we know
Of what the blessed do above
Is—that they sing, and that they love.

Pisc. Well remembered, brother Peter: these verses came
seasonably, and we thank you heartily. Come, we will all join
together, my host and all, and sing my scholar's catch over again,
and then each man drink the other cup, and to bed, and thank
God we have a dry house over our heads.

Pisc. Well now, good-night to everybody.

Pet. And so say I.

Ven. And so say I.

Cor. Good-night to you all, and I thank you.

The Fishing Hole

Guy de Maupassant

INFLICTING BLOWS AND wounds causing death. Such was the charge on which M. Léopold Renard, upholsterer, appeared before the assizes.

In court were the chief witnesses, Mme Flamèche, widow of the victim; Louis Ladureau, cabinetmaker; and Jean Durdent, plumber: while close to the accused was his wife, in black—small, ugly, like a monkey dressed up as a woman.

And here is Renard (Léopold)'s account of the drama.

"As God is my witness, this is a catastrophe where, far from being the cause, I was all along the chief victim. The facts speak for themselves, My Lord. I am a decent man, a hard-working man, upholsterer these sixteen years in the same street, known, liked, respected, well thought of by all, as you've heard the neighbors say, even the house-porter, who speaks a sane word now and then. I'm fond of work, I'm fond of thrift, I'm fond of honest folk and of harmless pleasures. That's been my undoing, worse luck. Still, as I did nothing of intent, I feel no shame.

"Well, every Sunday for five years my wife here and I have

spent the day at Poissy. That takes us into the open air—to say nothing of our love of fishing. Why, we're as keen on that as on spring onions! Mélie's the one that gave me the craze, the wretch, and that she's madder on it than I am, the sinner, you can see from all this trouble having come about through her, as assuredly it did, as you'll learn.

"As for me, I'm no soft one, yet I'm easy-going, without a penny-worth of wickedness. But as for her, well, well! You'd think her quite harmless, she's so small and skinny. Let me tell you, though, she's more spiteful than a cat. I'm not denying that she has her points; indeed she has, and important ones for one like me in business. But her disposition! Just you ask the neighbors, and even the house-porter, who put in a word for me a moment ago—she can tell you things.

"Day in day out she kept harping on about my softness. 'I wouldn't put up with this. I wouldn't put up with that.' Had I listened to her, My Lord, I'd have been in three scraps a month at least."

Mme Renard cut in: "Keep on. He laughs best who laughs last."

He turned towards her, not mincing his words: "Oh well, I can say what I like about you, seeing it's not you that's on trial, you."

Then turning to the judge again, he said:

"I proceed. We always went, then, to Poissy on Saturday evenings to be able to start our fishing next morning at day-break. That custom became a kind of second nature, as the saying goes. Three years past this summer I discovered a swim—and such a swim! Shaded, eight feet of water at the least, perhaps ten. What a spot it was with its hollows under the bank—a regular lair of fishes! Talk about an angler's heaven! This hole, My Lord, I could look on as my own, seeing I was its Christopher Columbus. Everyone in the district knew it for mine, everyone—not a soul to dispute it. 'That, oh, that's Renard's spot,' they'd say, and nobody dreamt of going there, not even M. Plumeau, who is notorious, and no offence meant in saying it, for pinching the places of others.

"Well, certain always of my place, I went back and back to it just like an owner. The moment I arrived on Saturdays I boarded *Dalila* with my wife. *Dalila*, I should explain, is a Norwegian boat I had made for me by Fournaise—light yet strong. I was saying, then, that we boarded *Dalila*, and we would set about baiting the swim. As for baiting, there's no one to touch me, and well my pals all know it. You want to hear what I bait with? Well, I can't tell you. It has nothing to do with the case, I just can't tell you. It's my secret. Hundreds have asked me for it. I've been offered drinks and dainties no end to make me part with it. But just go and see if the chub come! Oh yes, they've tried to pet my patent out through my tummy. But not another soul knows it apart from my wife, and she won't tell it any more than I shall. Isn't that so, Mélie?"

The judge interrupted: "Just get to the point as soon as you can."

Whereupon the accused went on: "I'm getting to it, I'm getting to it. Well, on Saturday, the 8th of July, we left by the 5:25 train, and, as we always did on Saturdays, went before dinner to bait the swim. The weather promised to be fine. I said to Mélie: 'Great work tomorrow, great work.' And she answered: 'Looks like it.' We never talk more than that to each other.

"Then we came back to dinner. I was feeling good, and I was dry. That's where the whole trouble began, My Lord. I said to Mélie: 'Look here, Mélie, I think it would be an idea if I had a bottle of "nightcap."' That's a light white wine we've christened so, because, if you drink too much of it, it keeps you awake and is just the opposite of a nightcap. You get the idea?

"She replied: 'Have your way, but you'll be upset again and won't be able to get up tomorrow.' There for you was truth, wisdom, prudence, discernment—I own it. Still I couldn't resist, and back I knock the bottle. Whence the whole trouble.

"Well, I couldn't sleep. Good Lord! that grape-juice nightcap kept me awake till two in the morning. Then in a twinkling, over I go, and so soundly that I'd have been deaf to the last trump itself.

"To be brief, my wife woke me at six. Out of bed I spring. On in a jiffy with my trousers and jersey, a dash of water on my mug, and into *Dalila* we jump. Too late. When I get to the swim it is already taken. Never had that happened before, My Lord, never in three years. Why, I was being robbed before my very eyes! 'Well, I'm damned, I'm damned, I'm damned,' I cried. And then my wife began to rail at me: 'That's your nightcap for you. Get out, you soaker. Are you satisfied now, you stupid fool?'

"I answered nothing. Everything she said was true.

"I went ashore, however, near the spot, by way of making the best of a bad job. Perhaps the fellow wouldn't catch anything after all, and would clear out.

"He was a little skinny chap, in white drill and with a large straw hat. His wife was with him, a fat woman, who was sitting behind, sewing.

"When she saw us taking up our position near the spot, what do you think she muttered?

" 'Is this, then, the only place on the river?'

"And my wife, fuming, replied:

" 'People of ordinary decency usually make a point of finding out local ways. It keeps them off others' preserves.'

"As I didn't want a row, I said to her:

" 'Hold your tongue, Mélie. Don't answer back, don't answer back. We'll see about this all right.'

"Well, we had tied up *Dalila* under the willows and had got out and were fishing side by side, Mélie and I, right beside the other two.

"Here, My Lord, I must go into detail.

"We hadn't been there five minutes, when down went my neighbor's line twice, thrice, and lo and behold, he hauled out a chub, big as my thigh, a bit less perhaps, but not much! My heart gave a jump, my brow broke into a sweat, and Mélie cried: 'Hi, you toper, did you see that?"

"Just then, M. Bru, the grocer of Poissy, a dab with the gudgeon, passed by in his boat and shouted:

"'So somebody's taken your place, M. Renard?' 'Yes, M. Bru,' I replied, 'there are some toughs in this world who don't know how to behave.'

"The little fellow in drill at my side pretended not to hear. His fat lump of a wife likewise, the cow."

The judge interrupted a second time: "Careful of your language. You insult the widow, Mme Flamèche, here."

Renard made excuse: "Pardon me, pardon me, my feelings ran away with me."

"Well, a quarter of an hour had hardly gone, when what should the little devil in drill do but yank out another fish, a chub, and then another on top of it, and still another five minutes later.

"I tell you I was on the verge of tears, and I could sense Mme Renard bursting with rage. She kept on rating me without pausing for breath: 'You miserable fool, don't you see you're being robbed of your fish? Don't you see it? You'll catch nothing, you, nothing, nothing, not even a frog. Don't my hands itch merely to think of it?'

"All I said, and to myself, was: 'Just wait till noon. He'll go to lunch then, this poaching fellow, and you'll get back your place.' You see, My Lord, we lunch every Sunday on the spot. We bring food with us in *Dalila*.

"Bah! Twelve struck. The wretch had a chicken wrapped up in a newspaper, and, would you believe it, while he ate he actually caught another chub!

"Mélie and I had a crumb, hardly anything. As things were, we didn't feel like it.

"Then to aid digestion I took up my newspaper. Every Sunday I read *Gil Blas* like that in the shade by the waterside. Sunday is Columbine's day, Columbine, you know, who writes articles in *Gil Blas*. I've a way of infuriating Mme Renard by pretending to know this Columbine. It's all a yarn. I don't know her at all, have never even seen her. Still she writes well, hits out and to the point, for a woman. She suits me down to the ground. After all, there're not so many of her kind.

"Well, then, I began ragging my wife, but at once she got angry, furiously angry, and then angrier still. So I said no more.

"Just at this moment our two witnesses here, M. Ladureau and M. Durdent, appeared on the other bank. We know each other by sight.

"The little fellow had begun fishing again and to such tune that I shook from sheer vexation. Then his wife said: 'This is a thundering good spot, we'll keep on coming here, Désiré.'

"A cold shiver ran down my spine, and Mme Renard kept on saying: 'Call yourself a man, call yourself a man! You chicken heart!'

"'Look here,' I said quickly, 'I'd rather clear out. I shall only do something I'll regret.'

"She hissed as if she'd scald me: 'Call yourself a man! Now you're running away, giving up your place! Run away then, you Bazaine!'

"That went home. Still I did not wince.

"Then what does the other fellow do but drag out a bream! Never had I seen such a thumper before. Never.

"And now my wife began to talk out loud—pretending to be merely thinking. You see what a she-devil she is. 'That is what one might call stolen fish,' she said, 'seeing it was we who baited the swim. They ought at least to pay us for the bait.'

"Whereupon the little drill-clad bloke's fat wife chipped in: 'Is it us you're getting at madam?'

" 'I'm getting at fish thieves, those who profit by what's been spent by others.'

" 'Are you calling us fish thieves then?'

"Then they began explaining—then slanging. Good Lord! they knew the words all right—real stingers. They bawled so, that our two witnesses, who were on the other bank, called out by way of a joke: 'Hi, you, over there, less row, you'll spoil your husbands' sport!'

"The fact is that the little fellow in drill and myself remained stock still. We stuck where we were, our noses glued to the water, as if we'd never heard.

"But Lord help me, we heard all right!

" 'You're nothing but a liar.'—'And you a strumpet.'—'And you a trollop.'—'And you a trull.' And so on and so on. A sailor couldn't have beat them.

"Suddenly I heard a noise behind me and turned round. There was the other woman, the great fat thing, belaboring my wife with her parasol. Whack! whack! Mélie took a couple. But now she was fairly roused, and when Mélie's roused she lams about, I tell you. She seized the fat dame by the hair and then smack! smack! smack! the blows fell like a shower of ripe plums.

"I'd have left them to it—the women to themselves, the men to themselves. Why mix the thing? But up like a devil comes the little drill-suit chap making to spring at my wife. 'No, no, hardly that, my hearty,' says I, and I received the old cock-sparrow flush on the end of my fist. Biff! biff! One on the nose, the other in the guts. Up go his arms, up go his legs, and he falls on his back clean in the river, right in the middle of the swim.

"Most certainly I would have fished him out, My Lord, if I'd had the time just then. But now, to crown all, the fat woman gained the upper hand and was making mincemeat of Mélie. I know well I shouldn't have rescued her while the other was drinking his fill. Still I didn't think he would be drowned. I said to myself: 'Ugh! that'll cool him down.'

"I ran, then, to separate the women. I was pommelled, scratched, bitten. Good Lord, what vixen!

"The long and the short of it was that it took me a good five minutes, nearer ten, perhaps, to part this pair of clingers.

"I turned round. There was nothing to be seen. The water was as smooth as a lake. And the fellows on the other bank kept shouting: 'Fish him out, fish him out.'

"That was all very well, but I can't swim, much less dive, believe me.

"At last, after more than a quarter of an hour it would be, the lockkeeper came along and two men with boat-hooks. They found him at the bottom of the pool, under eight feet of water, as I have said, but there he was, the little fellow in his drill suit.

"These are the facts as I swear to them. On my word of honor I am innocent."

The witnesses having testified in the same sense, the accused was acquitted.

The Strangest
Trout Stream on Earth

Ernest Schwiebert

STEAM RISES HIGH on cold September mornings, drifting across the river. Skeletal trees lie in bleached jackstraw tangles besides the smoking wasteland of geysers and hot springs downstream. The steam lingers over the river like fog, smelling of sulfur deep in the seams of the earth. It lingers in the pale windless mornings like an encampment of cookfires. The river eddies over its ancient ledges, flowing cold and swimming-pool green into a reach of trailing weeds.

Chutes of boiling water spill into the river across a richly colored outcropping of lava, hissing steam when they reach the river. Fish rise softly to the daily hatch of tiny *Baetis* and *Paraleptophlebia* flies, rolling and porpoising only inches from the scalding currents.

The Firehole River in Yellowstone Park is unique among the famous trout streams of the world. Its smooth weed-trailing currents are like those of the famous Hampshire chalkstreams in England, where dry-fly fishing was born a century ago, slow and rich with insect life and fat surface-feeding trout. These fish rise freely on most days, dimpling for minute insects beside weed beds and undercut meadow banks, but unlike the cold British chalkstreams, the Firehole is warmed by thousands of boiling springs and geysers like Old Faithful.

Sulfurous fumes and steam blossom high above its buffalo-grass meadows in a weirdly smoking landscape. The trout sometimes rise inches away from steaming currents that could literally cook them alive. Geysers rumble ominously beside inviting trout-filled runs, causing the fisherman to watch their smoking vents with a worried frown while he tries his luck. Other bankside geysers sometimes erupt, showering the river-banks with lethal torrents of boiling water. Black volcanic sand bottoms the difficult stillwater bends of Biscuit Basin, and the swifter reaches are broken with strange lava ledges. Such fast-water runs sometimes produce rainbows, but the Firehole is primarily a brown-trout river.

Its warm currents spawn almost continually year-round hatches of the many-brooded *Baetis* mayflies, and its meadows are alive with terrestrials like ants and leafhoppers. Firehole trout take such minuscule insects with soft little rises that often hide surprisingly large fish; unlike the chalkstream browns of En-gland, these Firehole fish seldom see insects larger than size sixteen flies. Most Firehole hatches are smaller, and such minute insects emerging on mirror-smooth currents cause some of the most difficult trout fishing in the world. The cold mornings of September and October sometimes find trout rising to such minutae in clouds of geyser steam that obscure the river. The wind carries strange fumes long imprisoned in the molten viscera of the earth, and on such mornings the Firehole seems like a river of the netherworld, the strangest trout stream this side of the River Styx.

John Colter discovered the Yellowstone country in 1807, after participating in the earlier Lewis and Clark expedition, but Jim Bridger first explored the Firehole Basin. His outlandish catalogue of exaggerations about Colter's Hell gave the Yellowstone its own Bunyanlike mythology as much as fifty years before President Ulysses Grant signed the law making it into a national park.

Bridger delighted in spinning his Yellowstone tales, and one yarn described a river that was glacier-cold at its source and flowed downhill so fast that friction heated the water and cooked its trout. The Firehole was that mythical river. Bridger exaggerated about its currents, but there are places where its bottom is actually hot. The lava crust which forms the river bottom is so thin in places that it is heated by the boiling springs and geysers underneath. Downstream from Ojo Caliente spring, which spews frightening torrents of scalding water into the Firehole, there are places where the rhyolite bedrock is so thin that the bottom feels hot through the soles of English wading brogues.

Although the Firehole is heavily populated with good trout that rise freely to almost daily hatches, fishing over them can be extremely frustrating. Minute insect forms and quiet currents can pose problems for anglers unfamiliar with such fishing, and trout fished over by thousands of eager Yellowstone visitors are unbelievably sophisticated.

The average fisherman finds them almost impossible, and the experienced fly fisherman who is unprepared to match fly hatches smaller than size sixteen will end most Firehole sessions talking to himself. Selective feeding, which finds the trout refusing anything that does not resemble their natural food, is the rule rather than the exception.

Through some forty-odd years of experience with these Firehole trout, I have found them relatively easy only during a few June mayfly hatches and the late-summer grasshopper fishing. Other times are frustrating.

My first session on the Firehole occurred in the Nez Percé meadows, which border the highway. These meadows have beautiful open water that quickens the pulse of the most knowledgeable angler, although its trout are perhaps too accessible to the tourist hordes. Hundreds of free-rising trout dimple there every day, readily visible from the highway, and this stretch of the river attracts a lot of pressure. Its brown trout are tourist-shy and difficult. The first morning I fished the Nez Percé water was cloudless and bright. Trout were rising everywhere to some minute Blue-winged Olive mayflies, but catching them was another matter. None of my flies was small enough, and the best fish seemed frightened witless by my 4X leaders. There were some sixteen Blue Quills in my fly boxes, but they looked like battleships beside the naturals, and the fish mostly refused them.

The second morning was easier. The hatching mayflies were larger, and the current was riddled with wind and drizzling rain. The looping meadow bends of Biscuit Basin surrendered fifty-odd trout under these less difficult conditions, and I felt my Firehole problems had been solved.

The third morning I returned to the Nez Percé meadows, determined to vindicate my earlier failures. Good trout were rising everywhere in the bright September sunlight. Minute mayflies rode and fluttered down the deep channels between the ledges and undulating weeds. For several hours my 4X leaders and sixteen flies proved worthless. Two days later I left the Firehole, frustrated and fishless and talking to myself, and resolved to return the following year with a lighter rod and smaller flies and finer leader tippets.

That was twenty years ago. Since then our tackle has witnessed a minor revolution: lighter fly rods are commonplace and size twenty-eight flies have become available in the best tackle shops and modern nylons have produced practical 8X leaders. The Firehole has since yielded many of its secrets during subsequent visits, and careful studies of its character and its fly hatches have paid off over the years. Those studies reveal the unique qualities that make the Firehole one of the strangest and best trout streams on earth.

The river rises in Madison Lake above Old Faithful and flows northward through a plateau of rhyolite, looping its placid currents through clustered pines and straw-colored meadows and steaming geyser basins. Since the Firehole drains the principal geyser region in the Yellowstone, considerable temperature and ecological changes occur where the river receives its hydrothermal discharges. Other changes occur below its small cold-water tributaries. These changes and their remarkable effect on both the fish and the fly hatches have been ferreted out in some fifteen years of Firehole observations.

The river is closed to fishing above Old Faithful campground to protect both its qualities as drinking water and the best nursery areas in its headwaters. Such natural spawning is important to the management of the entire watershed. These headwaters are cold from the springs and snowmelt on the Continental Divide, seldom rising above fifty-six degrees in midsummer. Their chemical properties are average for good western trout waters, and both the hatches and the growth rate of the trout are typical. Below the tourist area at Old Faithful, with the influx of its strange pools and geysers and boiling springs, the Firehole changes radically. Even more changes occur below Riverside Geyser, where the winter river temperatures are typical, but the summer temperatures hover at eighty-odd degrees and alkalinity is almost doubled. Such increased alkalinity improves both the fly hatches and the potential trout population. These changes increase progressively until the Firehole reaches Biscuit Basin. The intense hydrothermal flowages there are partly balanced by the waters of the Little Firehole, which enters the main river not far above the Biscuit Basin footbridge. The Firehole is shallow here, flowing over broken strangely patterned ledges, and the average size of its trout has increased. Fly hatches are more numerous, and some big browns are found both in the lava pockets and under the undercut banks of Iron Spring and the Little Firehole itself.

Below this Biscuit Basin water, the alkaline richness of the river is greatly increased and its river temperatures seldom drop below fifty degrees, making for excellent fly hatches and greater growth rate of the trout and better wintering. This stretch is scenic water, with serpentine bends in meadows bordered with spruce and lodgepole pine. There are some swift-flowing side channels and black-lava bottoms, where wise old browns savor minute mayflies along their grassy banks. The river is friendly and shallow here, and its trout are easily frightened by bad casting and a careless approach and heavy leaders.

The experienced Firehole fisherman fishes only to specific rises and spends much time on hands and knees, creeping and crawling to get within casting range without spooking his quarry. The stretch from the mouth of the Little Firehole to the bottom of the Biscuit Basin meadows, where a short loop-road provides parking near the river, is a mile of first-rate water.

The next two miles, between the loop-road and the Iron Bridge just off the highway, is varied water that offers both good browns and an occasional fat rainbow in the faster places. Ledges and deadfalls shelter some selective lunkers. Park rangers warn that grizzlies frequently cross the river in this stretch, and the angler should be watchful there. There are several convenient places for parking. The water above the Iron Bridge is excellent, and was described by Ray Bergman in his familiar classic *Trout*, in the passages about the Firehole and its exceptional dry-fly fishing fifty years ago. Both cold and hot springs add their seepage in this mileage of river, raising its median temperatures while decreasing its alkalinity. The stretch is especially good for caddis hatches and the fishing is excellent.

Between the Iron Bridge and the Midway Geyser Basin, where the river again parallels the highway, is a mile of broken water with both browns and rainbows. Here the Firehole is a series of fast runs and shallow lava-pocket pools, with occasional hot springs and comical geysers, like the miniature volcano with a *putt-putt* rhythm like a tiny one-lung engine. Temperatures remain relatively warm, although several hot springs raise the alkalinity somewhat. Hatches are good, and there is an occasional lunker brown among the potholes that scar the bottom at Mule Shoe.

The water that lies between the highway and the steep geyser-covered shoreline is often obscured by clouds of sulfurous steam. The geyser waters stain these banks with varicolored deposits where they reach the river. There are several first-rate pools beside the highway, but their trout are hard-fished and shy. Above the Midway footbridge, where torrents of steaming water tumble into the river, the Firehole trout rise steadily to the hatching flies, only inches away from temperatures that could cook them alive. The exaggerations of Jim Bridger about the river were partly true.

Below the Midway footbridge, there is an excellent four-mile stretch of river, accessible from two places off the Fountain Freight Road. About a mile below the Iron Bridge, there is a twin-rut trail that forks down to the river. Temperatures on this water seldom sink below fifty-eight degrees in winter, providing hatches and optimum feeding conditions throughout the year. Its trout grow deep-bellied like Florida bass. The alkalinity is high, creating rich weedy water and heavy fly hatches.

Another half-mile on the Fountain Freight Road is the turnoff to the Goose and Feather Lake picnic grounds. Anglers leave their cars there and hike down to the river bottoms below the trees. There are side channels and undercut banks here, where some really large trout lie hidden, and several excellent pools. One side-channel pocket above the picnic area was the setting for an important Firehole lesson on a September evening long ago. The river looked shallow over an open gravel bottom, and a fish was rising tight against the grass. The rises seemed insignificant. Since the Firehole brown had treated me shabbily that afternoon, even a small fish was a prize, and I worked stealthily into casting position. Kneeling in the shallow current, I watched the rises and selected a tiny Adams to imitate the minute brownish caddisflies on the water. The cast settled right and the float looked good. The little dry fly flirted with the bankside grasses and disappeared in a sipping dimple. Suddenly the hooked fish exploded from beneath the grass, porpoising and wallowing wildly in the gravel shallows. The leader sheared like a cobweb when the mammoth brown tunneled into the upstream weeds. The lesson was important, and I have never attempted to judge the size of a Firehole brown by its rises again.

Above the Foundation Freight Bridge, there are clearings and meadows where buffalo and elk are often found grazing. The water above the bridge is fast and broken, tumbling over terraced lava ledges and outcroppings. There are good trout in the pockets. Rainbows are often found in these swift well-aerated places.

Below the bridge, violent Ojo Caliente spring spills its steaming waters into the river, raising temperatures and alkalinity to the highest levels in its fifteen-odd miles. Downstream the currents are slow and choked with undulating beds of weeds, over a bottom that varies from rhyolite bedrock to insect-rich layers of marl. Fly hatches here are excellent. Two cold-water tributaries, meandering Fairy and Sentinel creeks, add their flowage to the Firehole below Ojo Caliente.

This reach of the river provides optimal wintering conditions for its trout. When the midsummer temperatures rise too high, which has happened sometimes since the earthquake of 1959 changed the underground hot springs, the fish congregate in the cooler current-tongues below the two feeder creeks. Gene Anderegg and I spent a week on this water once, taking some heavy browns that were selectively feeding in the mouths of these tributaries and the cold runs below them.

The Firehole returns to the highway in the Nez Percé meadows another mile downstream. This is one of the best dry-fly
stretches on the river. Large browns populate its deep pools and
main weed channels, but it is almost too popular and easily
accessible from the highway. The deep stillwater pool just above
the mouth of Nez Percé Creek produced an eleven-pound brown
in grasshopper season a few years back. The trout free-rise in
this mile of water on most days, and because they are so
hard-fished through the tourist season, their tippet-shy selectiv-
ity is a challenge.

Nez Percé Creek adds its cooling currents and alkalinity to the
Firehole near the highway, stabilizing the temperatures and
alkaline riches of the six miles below. About a mile below the
mouth of the Nez Percé is the famous Rainbow Riffle, which has
given up some slab-sided trout with carmine flanks and gill-
covers. There are also some heavy browns in this stretch, but
with the highway beside the river, they are hard-fished and
easily spooked. These educated Firehole lunkers usually lie in
the weed channels and runs along the opposite bank, beyond
the range of the average fisherman and the rock-throwing
children of the tourists. There is some big water here and
felt-soled chest waders are needed. Two miles farther downstream, there are some first-rate pools and pockets above the
Cascades of the Firehole, but they are adjacent to scenic turnouts
and parking areas, and are heavily fished. However, after
September there are few visitors in the Yellowstone, and the
skilled angler can find them productive.

Two miles below the Cascades, there is a reach of relatively
unproductive water above the Firehole Falls. Downstream is
some better fishing in the half mile of side channels and pocket
water that lies between the falls and the campground at Madison
Junction. This stretch is seldom fished, because most anglers
become preoccupied with the more accessible meadows of the
Madison and Gibbon rivers below the camping area, but in late

autumn, when the spawning browns and rainbows from Hebgen Lake are stopped by the Firehole Falls, this bottom half mile of river will regularly produce trophy-size fish.

The river ends in its meadow confluence with the Gibbon, which drains the Norris Geyser Basin to the northeast, and the two rivers join to form the Upper Madison. Some thirteen miles downstream on the Madison is the town of West Yellowstone, and the western entrance to Yellowstone Park. Regular air service to West Yellowstone is welcome news for Firehole devotees from Los Angeles to Boston, since it is possible to leave either coast in the morning and cover the Biscuit Basin stretch before nightfall.

With few exceptions, the fly patterns needed to fool these ultraselective Firehole browns are small. There is some variation in the distribution of the natural hatches with the fluctuations of alkalinity and temperature. For example, the best hatches of the larger *Ephemerella* mayflies occur in the upper reaches of the river, between Lone Star Geyser and Ojo Caliente. The brief early-season hatches of big drakes are concentrated in the weedy silt-bottomed water that provides the proper environment for the burrowing *Ephemera* nymphs. Caddis hatches are heavily distributed on the entire river, especially below Biscuit Basin. The large *Acroneuria* and dark-colored *Pteronarcys* stonefly nymphs, known erroneously as hellgrammites on western rivers, are numerous in the fast-water stretches, with particularly dense concentrations in the Rainbow Riffle and above Riverside Geyser, and the Iron Bridge. Minute mayflies like the *Paraleptophlebia* and *Baetis* groups are thick, especially in the quiet weedy stretches, and are numerous enough to form a staple diet for the Firehole surface feeders.

Since most fly hatches on the Firehole are small, the typical flies in the boxes of its regulars are tied on hooks between #14 and #24. Typical patterns are traditionals like the Dark Hendrickson, Light Hendrickson, Red Quill, Blue Quill, Light Cahill,

Blue-winged Olive, Iron Blue Dun, Pale Watery Dun, and the Adams. Terrestrial imitations like ants, Jassids, beetles, and grasshoppers are also effective, along with standby wets like the Partridge and Olive, Grouse and Green, Partridge and Brown, and the Gold-ribbed Hare's Ear. Regional patterns like the Muskrat Nymph, Montana Nymph, Whitcraft, and Muddler are also useful, and during the big *Ephemera* hatches, the Dark Donnelly Variant in sizes ten and twelve is needed.

Perhaps the most unusual quality of the Firehole lies in its management regulations. Millions of visitors pass through its valley every season, and the Firehole is possibly the hardest fished trout stream anywhere. Public water everywhere else has degenerated to put-and-take stocking under fishing pressure, with the result that we have trout streams without trout, except on scheduled fish-truck days. Even big western rivers like the Snake and the Yellowstone and the Big Hole, while far from being fished-out, are declining noticeably each year because of excessive kill-limits and thoughtless irrigation methods and rapidly increasing numbers of fishermen. The Firehole lies within a few hours of all these bigger rivers, and although it is fished even harder than the remaining public mileage of eastern streams like the Beaverkill and the Brodheads in the shadow of New York, its fishing has remained pretty much the same in my fifteen years' experience.

Local experts like Bud Lilly and Pat Barnes, who operate famous shops in West Yellowstone and fish the Firehole regularly, point out that the river has not been stocked in the past twenty-odd years.

How can the Firehole remain the same without stocking? asks a typical first-timer.

The answer is surprisingly simple: the river has been restricted to fly fishing for almost thirty years, and its kill-limit is only five trout per day. The result is a watershed in natural balance between its spawning potential and the wild trout harvested each season, even with the extremely heavy fishing pressure.

There has been a slight decline in the number of big trout and the average size in recent years, although a heavy population of fish to sixteen inches is still present. Perhaps the unique qualities of the Firehole should be recognized and its kill-limits even more restricted. Regulations making it a fish-for-fun river with no killing whatsoever, or a trophy-fishing river where one or two trout above fifteen inches are permitted, would probably make its fishing even better. The sulfur content of its water makes most Firehole fish ordinary table fare anyway.

Similar regulations will probably be necessary on all wadable, easily fished streams in the future, if Americans want to enjoy decent trout fishing on their public waters under population pressures, and the Firehole is a graphic example of future management techniques.

The last time I fished above Biscuit Basin, there was a twenty-inch brown rising regularly in a shallow lava pocket. It was a difficult place to approach without frightening the trout, and I spent almost fifteen minutes circling around below his position and working stealthily up the ledgerock riffles on hands and knees. Finally I was in position for a delicate presentation and dragless float, and started false casting when some tourists from Nebraska came down the path to the river. The man was wearing a white shirt and his wife had a bright yellow dress.

Catching anything? they asked innocently.

The big brown had spooked long before they reached me. Their children began running up and down the bank, throwing rocks into the water and splashing in the shallows with sticks. The smaller trout stopped rising in terror. There was no point in fishing after such bedlam, and I reeled-in unhappily to look for a quieter reach of water.

Riverside Geyser erupted as I reached the car, putting on the sporadic show that dwarfs Old Faithful. Tourist cars began stopping everywhere, until crowds of people were milling around me. Cameras were clicking furiously as I put my rod away. The geyser reached its peak and began to subside and torrents of scalding water cascaded down the banks. The morning was filled with the acrid choking odors of sulfur. Clouds of steam towered into the crisp September air and billowed across the landscape until it was impossible to drive or see the river. Such experiences are typical and make the Firehole the strangest trout stream on earth.

The Angler

~~~~~~~~~~

Washington Irving

I T   I S   S A I D that many an unlucky urchin is induced to run
away from his family, and betake himself to a seafaring life, from
reading the history of Robinson Crusoe; and I suspect that, in
like manner, many of those worthy gentlemen who are given to
haunt the sides of pastoral streams with angle rods in hand, may
trace the origin of their passion to the seductive pages of honest
Izaak Walton. I recollect studying his *Compleat Angler* several
years since, in company with a knot of friends in America, and
moreover that we were all completely bitten with the angling
mania. It was early in the year; but as soon as the weather was
auspicious, and that the spring began to melt into the verge of
summer, we took rod in hand and sallied into the country, as
stark mad as was ever Don Quixote from reading books of
chivalry.

One of our party had equalled the Don in the fullness of his
equipments; being attired *ca-à-pie* for the enterprise. He wore a
broad-skirted fustian coat, perplexed with half a hundred pockets; a pair of stout shoes and leathern gaiters; a basket slung on

one side for fish; a patent rod, a landing-net, and a score of other inconveniences, only to be found in the true angler's armory. Thus harnessed for the field, he was as great a matter of stare and wonderment among the country folk, who had never seen a regular angler, as was the steel-clad hero of La Mancha among the goatherds of the Sierra Morena.

Our first essay was along a mountain brook, among the highlands of the Hudson; a most unfortunate place for the execution of those piscatory tactics which had been invented along the velvet margins of quiet English rivulets. It was one of those wild streams that lavish, among our romantic solitudes, unheeded beauties, enough to fill the sketch book of a hunter of the picturesque. Sometimes it would leap down rocky shelves, making small cascades, over which the trees threw their broad balancing sprays, and long nameless weeds hung in fringes from the impending banks, dripping with diamond drops. Sometimes it would brawl and fret along a ravine in the matted shade of a forest, filling it with murmurs; and, after this termagant career, would steal forth into open day with the most placid demure face imaginable; as I have seen some pestilent shrew of a housewife, after filling her home with uproar and ill-humor, come dimpling out of doors, swimming and courtseying, and smiling upon all the world.

How smoothly would this vagrant brook glide, at such times, through some bosom of green meadow-land among the mountains; where the quiet was only interrupted by the occasional tinkling of a bell from the lazy cattle among the clover, or the sound of a woodcutter's axe from the neighboring forest.

For my part, I was always a bungler at all kinds of sport that required either patience or adroitness, and had not angled above half an hour before I had completely "satisfied the sentiment," and convinced myself of the truth of Izaak Walton's opinion, that angling is something like poetry—a man must be born to it. I hooked myself instead of the fish; tangled my line in every tree;

lost my bait; broke my rod; until I gave up the attempt in despair, and passed the day under the trees, reading old Izaak; satisfied that it was his fascinating vein of honest simplicity and rural feeling that had bewitched me, and not the passion for angling. My companions, however, were more persevering in their delusion. I have them at this moment before my eyes, stealing along the border of the brook, where it lay open to the day, or was merely fringed by shrubs and bushes. I see the bittern rising with hollow scream as they break in upon his rarely invaded haunt; the kingfisher watching him suspiciously from his dry tree that overhangs the deep black millpond, in the gorge of the hills; the tortoise letting himself slip sideways from off the stone or log on which he is sunning himself; and the panic-struck frog plumping in headlong as they approach, and spreading an alarm throughout the watery world around.

I recollect also, that, after toiling and watching and creeping about for the greater part of a day, with scarcely any success, in spite of all our admirable apparatus, a lubberly country urchin came down from the hills with a rod made from a branch of a tree, a few yards of twine, and, as Heaven shall help me! I believe a crooked pin for a hook, baited with a vile earthworm—and in half an hour caught more fish than we had nibbles throughout the day!

But, above all, I recollect the "good, honest, wholesome, hungry" repast, which we made under a beech-tree, just by a spring of pure sweet water that stole out of the side of a hill; and how, when it was over, one of the party read old Izaak Walton's scene with the milkmaid, while I lay on the grass and built castles in a bright pile of clouds, until I fell asleep. All this may appear like mere egotism; yet I cannot refrain from uttering these recollections, which are passing like a strain of music over my mind, and have been called up by an agreeable scene which I witnessed not long since.

In a morning stroll along the banks of Alun, a beautiful little stream which flows down from the Welsh hills, and throws itself into the Dee, my attention was attracted to a group seated on the margin. On approaching, I found it to consist of a veteran angler and two rustic disciples. The former was an old fellow with a wooden leg, with clothes very much but very carefully patched, betokening poverty, honestly come by, and decently maintained. His face bore the marks of former storms, but present fair weather; its furrows had been worn into a habitual smile; his iron-gray locks hung about his ears, and he had altogether the good-humored air of a constitutional philosopher who was disposed to take the world as it went. One of his companions was a ragged wight, with the skulking look of an arrant poacher, and I'll warrant could find his way to any gentleman's fish-pond in the neighborhood in the darkest night. The other was a tall, awkward, country lad, with a lounging gait, and apparently somewhat of a rustic beau. The old man was busy in examining the maw of a trout which he had just killed, to discover by its contents what insects were seasonable for bait; and was lecturing on the subject to his companions, who appeared to listen with infinite deference. I have a kind feeling towards all "brothers of the angle," ever since I read Izaak Walton. They are men, he affirms, of a "mild, sweet, and peaceable spirit"; and my esteem for them has been increased since I met with an old *Tretyse of fishing with the Angle*, in which are set forth many of the maxims of their inoffensive fraternity. "Take good hede," sayeth this honest little tretyse, "that in going about your disportes ye open no man's gates, but that ye shet them again. Also ye shall not use this forsayd crafti disport for no covetousness to the encreasing and sparing of your money only, but principally for your solace, and to cause the helth of your body and specyally of your soule."

I thought that I could perceive in the veteran angler before me an exemplification of what I had read; and there was a cheerful contentedness in his looks that quite drew me towards him. I could not but remark the gallant manner in which he stumped from one part of the brook to another; waving his rod in the air, to keep the line from dragging on the ground, or catching among the bushes; and the adroitness with which he would throw his fly to any particular place; sometimes skimming it lightly along a little rapid; sometimes casting it into one of those dark holes made by a twisted root or overhanging bank, in which the large trout are apt to lurk. In the meanwhile he was giving instructions to his two disciples; showing them the manner in which they should handle their rods, fix their flies, and play them along the surface of the stream. The scene brought to my mind the instructions of the sage Piscator to his scholar. The country around was of that pastoral kind which Walton is fond of describing. It was a part of the great plain of Cheshire, close by the beautiful vale of Gessford, and just where the inferior Welsh hills begin to swell up from among fresh-smelling meadows. The day, too, like that recorded in his work, was mild and sunshiny, with now and then a soft-dropping shower, that sowed the whole earth with diamonds.

I soon fell into conversation with the old angler, and was so much entertained, that, under pretext of receiving instructions in his art, I kept company with him almost the whole day; wandering along the banks of the stream, and listening to his talk. He was very communicative, having all the easy garrulity of cheerful old age; and I fancy was a little flattered by having an opportunity of displaying his piscatory lore; for who does not like now and then to play the sage?

He had been much of a rambler in his day, and had passed some years of his youth in America, particularly in Savannah, where he had entered into trade and had been ruined by the indiscretion of a partner. He had afterwards experienced many ups and downs in life, until he got into the navy, where his leg was carried away by a cannon-ball, at the battle of Camper-down. This was the only stroke of real good fortune he had ever experienced, for it got him a pension, which, together with some small paternal property brought him in a revenue of nearly forty pounds. On this he retired to his native village where he lived quietly and independently; and devoted the remainder of his life to the "noble art of angling."

I found that he had read Izaak Walton attentively, and he seemed to have imbibed all his simple frankness and prevalent good humor. Though he had been sorely buffeted about the world, he was satisfied that the world, in itself, was good and beautiful. Though he had been as roughly used in different countries as a poor sheep that is fleeced by every hedge and thicket, yet he spoke of every nation with candor and kindness, appearing to look only on the good side of things; and, above all, he was almost the only man I had ever met with who had been an unfortunate adventurer in America and had honesty and magnanimity enough to take the fault to his own door, and not to curse the country. The lad that was receiving his instructions, I learnt, was the son and heir apparent of a fat old widow who kept the village inn, and of course a youth of some expectation, and much courted by the idle gentleman-like personages of the place. In taking him under his care, therefore, the old man had probably an eye to a privileged corner in the taproom, and an occasional cup of cheerful ale free of expense.

There is certainly something in angling, if we could forget, which anglers are apt to do, the cruelties and tortures inflicted on worms and insects, that tends to produce a gentleness of spirit, and a pure serenity of mind. As the English are methodical, even in their recreation, and are the most scientific of sportsmen, it has been reduced among them to perfect rule and system. Indeed, it is an amusement peculiarly adapted to the mild and highly cultivated scenery of England, where every roughness has been softened away from the landscape. It is delightful to saunter along those limpid streams which wander, like veins of silver, through the bosom of this beautiful country; leading one through a diversity of small home scenery; sometimes winding through ornamented grounds; sometimes brimming along through rich pasturage, where the fresh green is mingled with sweet-smelling flowers; sometimes venturing in sight of villages and hamlets, and then running capriciously away into shady retirements. The sweetness and serenity of nature, and the quiet watchfulness of the sport, gradually bring on pleasant fits of musing, which are now and then agreeably interrupted by the song of a bird, the distant whistle of the peasant, or perhaps the vagary of some fish, leaping out of the still water, and skimming transiently about its glassy surface. "When I would beget content," says Izaak Walton, "and increase confidence in the power and wisdom and providence of Almighty God, I will walk the meadows by some gliding stream, and there contemplate the lilies that take no care, and those very many other little living creatures that are not only created, but feed (man knows not how) by the goodness of the God of nature, and therefore trust in him."

I cannot forbear to give another quotation from one of those ancient champions of angling, which breathes the same innocent and happy spirit:

> Let me live harmlessly, and near the brink
> Of Trent or Avon have a dwelling-place,
> Where I may see my quill, or cork, down sink,
> With eager bite of pike, or bleak, or dace;
> And on the world and my Creator think:
> Whilst some men strive ill-gotten goods t' embrace;
> And others spend their time in base excess
> Of wine, or worse, in war, or wantonness.
> Let them that will, these pastimes still pursue,
> And on such pleasing fancies feed their fill;
> So I the fields and meadows green may view;
> And daily by fresh rivers walk at will,
> Among the daisies and the violets blue,
> Red hyacinth and yellow daffodil.

On parting with the old angler, I inquired after his place of abode, and happening to be in the neighborhood of the village a few evenings afterwards, I had the curiosity to seek him out. I found him living in a small cottage, containing only one room, but a perfect curiosity in its method and arrangement. It was on the skirts of the village, on a green bank, a little back from the road, with a small garden in front, stocked with kitchen herbs, and adorned with a few flowers. The whole front of the cottage was overrun with a honeysuckle. On the top was a ship for a weathercock. The interior was fitted up in a truly nautical style, his ideas of comfort and convenience having been acquired on the berth-deck of a man-of-war. A hammock was slung from the ceiling, which, in the daytime, was lashed up so as to take but little room. From the center of the chamber hung a model of a ship, of his own workmanship. Two or three chairs, a table, and a large seachest, formed the principal moveables. About the wall were stuck up naval ballads, such as "Admiral Hosier's Ghost," "All in the Downs," and "Tom Bowling," intermingled with pictures of sea-fights, among which the battle of Camperdown held a distinguished place. The mantlepiece was decorated with sea-shells, over which hung a quadrant, flanked by two wood-cuts of most bitter-looking naval commanders. His implements for angling were carefully disposed on nails and hooks about the room. On a shelf was arranged his library, containing a work on angling, much worn, a Bible covered with canvas, an odd volume or two of voyages, a nautical almanack, and a book of songs.

His family consisted of a large black cat with one eye, and a parrot which he had caught and tamed, and educated himself, in the course of one of his voyages; and which uttered a variety of sea phrases with the hoarse brattling tone of a veteran boat-swain. The establishment reminded me of that of the renowned Robinson Crusoe; it was kept in neat order, everything being "stowed away" with the regularity of a ship of war; and he informed me that he "scoured the deck every morning, and swept it between meals."

I found him seated on a bench before the door, smoking his pipe in the soft evening sunshine. His cat was purring soberly on the threshold, and his parrot describing some strange evolutions in an iron ring that swung in the center of his cage. He had been angling all day, and gave me a history of his sport with as much minuteness as a general would talk over a campaign; being particularly animated in relating the manner in which he had taken a large trout, which had completely tasked all his skill and wariness, and which he had sent as a trophy to mine hostess of the inn.

How comforting it is to see a cheerful and contented old age; and to behold a poor fellow, like this, after being tempest-tost through life, safely moored in a snug and quiet harbor in the evening of his days! His happiness, however, sprung from within himself, and was independent of external circumstances; for he had that inexhaustible good nature, which is the most precious gift of Heaven; spreading itself like oil over the troubled sea of thought, and keeping the mind smooth and equable in the roughest weather.

On inquiring further about him, I learnt that he was a universal favorite in the village, and the oracle of the tap-room; where he delighted the rustics with his songs, and, like Sinbad, astonished them with his stories of strange lands, and ship-wrecks, and sea-fights. He was much noticed, too, by gentlemen sportsmen of the neighborhood; had taught several of them the art of angling; and was a privileged visitor of their kitchens. The whole tenor of his life was quiet and inoffensive, being princi-pally passed about the neighboring streams, when the weather and season were favorable; and at other times he employed himself at home, preparing his fishing tackle for the next campaign, or manufacturing rods, nets, and flies, for his patrons and pupils among the gentry.

He was a regular attendant at church on Sundays, though he generally fell asleep during the sermon. He had made it his particular request that when he died he should be buried on a green spot, which he could see from his seat in church, and which he had marked out ever since he was a boy, and had thought of when far from home on the raging sea, in danger of being food for the fishes—it was the spot where his father and mother had been buried.

I have done, for I fear that my reader is growing weary; but I could not refrain from drawing the picture of this worthy "brother of the angle"; who has made me more than ever in love with the theory, though I fear I shall never be adroit in the practice, of his art; and I will conclude this rambling sketch in the words of honest Izaak Walton, by craving the blessing of St. Peter's master upon my reader, "and upon all that are the true lovers of virtue; and dare trust in his providence: and be quiet; and go a angling."

Jack
the Giant Killer

A. J. McClane

SHORTLY AFTER MOVING to Florida I met a man who knew all the snook hot spots for miles around. Until that time I had never caught a snook, so the first day we went fishing together, I watched how Sammy Sharp worked his plug, and generally tried to absorb those nuances of technique that were strange to me. I used a silly little spinning rod that was vastly under-calibered for the job, but since I had no idea of what I was supposed to catch, it really didn't matter.

I'd walked a long distance down the beach, looking for a hole or a channel, when I saw something pushing water. I cast my surface plug in front of the wake and began to retrieve. The lure swam about one foot before it was taken in a tremendous swirl. The fish charged across the flat, leaving a muddy trail, and I turned the brake tighter to slow him down. Nothing happened. For almost fifteen minutes I cranked and pumped, increased and decreased the drag. Eventually the fish showed signs of tiring and I led him back toward the beach. When I saw the cause of all the rumpus, I couldn't believe my eyes. The fish didn't weigh more than 2½ or 3 pounds—it was without a doubt the strongest little fish I'd ever caught up to that time.

Five minutes later I hooked another fish and my line snapped. From then on my luck was bad. Monofilaments were unreliable in those days, and before long I had lost four plugs. Sammy finally came down the beach and waved me out of the water. "Nothing but jacks," he said. "Let's go."

"What's the matter with jacks?" I asked.

"Are you kiddin'?"

I have probably heard and been guilty of the same sin a thousand times, but now I make expiation because the cold truth is that jack is a giant killer—yet nobody wants to admit it. Pound for pound the crevalle is one of the toughest fish in the sea. For sheer brawling power, old *Caranx hippos* is a heller, and probably one of the most underrated gamefish in U.S. waters.

If all this seems implausible, then you have never tangled with a jack. The crevalle is a blunt-headed, beady-eyed barroom fighter who humiliates tourists by busting their tackle. Jacks don't jump when they're hooked; they just pull your arm out of its socket, and when you finally whup one he grunts piglike. And they're not much good to eat; you can cut off the tail and bleed them, which helps some, and they can be made tolerable on charcoal with a lot of barbecue sauce, but nobody really fishes for crevalle as food. In short, the jack doesn't give you much reason to pursue him. But his swift, slashing strike at a surface plug is electrifying. At that moment he has the style of a champ.

When we talk about jacks we're splitting a large and diverse family of fish. In fact, the crevalle has twenty close relatives around North American shores, such as the green jack, yellow jack, socorro jack, blue runner, Atlantic horse-eye jack, bar jack, Mazatlán jack, cottonmouth jack, and many others. This doesn't even include seven other family groups with forty-eight more species that are also carangids.

These jacks have more aliases than the Cosa Nostra. Some of them, like the permit, the roosterfish, the greater amberjack, and the California yellowtail, are by now legend. What the jacks have in common is their strong, fast swimming. I think the bar jack, for instance, is about as tough a little gamefish (they seldom go over 4 pounds) as you'll ever see.

Nobody really knows how many jacks exist throughout the world. I have caught huge bluish-colored ones near the mouth of the Congo (they were tentatively identified as lyre-fish) and small brown ones off Brazil (which were probably black jacks). One important reason why science has not learned too much about the carangids is that many species undergo drastic changes in body shape and fin structure, not to mention coloration, as they grow older. The jack is a puzzle to everybody.

The crevalle—or jack crevalle, cavally, horse crevalle, and toro—is believed to occur almost around the world in tropical and subtropical waters. In the Atlantic it ranges from Uruguay to Nova Scotia, with the chief center of abundance in the Gulf of Mexico, around Florida and north to Georgia. In the eastern Pacific the crevalle is found from Peru into the northern Gulf of California and around the outer coast of Baja California. One of its many look-alike relatives is the spotted jack of Hawaii. In the islands there are about a dozen species called ulua, and fishing ulua is the most important form of inshore angling. A big Hawaiian jack in a running surf is plenty of *pilikia*, but trouble is the jack's middle name in any language.

The crevalle is usually bluish green on the back, fading to a golden or silvery underside. There is a prominent black spot on the gill cover and a more obscure one on his long, scimitar-shaped pectorals. The Atlantic form has twenty-six to thirty-five scutes at the tail end of its arched lateral line; the Pacific form grows a few more. A crevalle's body is as rigid as a steel bar. When you grab one to pull a plug loose, you think that rigor mortis has already set in.

Not much is known about the crevalle's life history. The clan is believed to spawn in offshore water sometime from spring to fall. This jack does have a tolerance for brackish water, however, and is occasionally caught far inland in rivers of very low salinity. Probably more crevalle are taken in shallow bays, creek mouths, and inlets than anywhere else, but they appear in the surf quite often with tarpon, bluefish, and snook.

It's the jack's proclivity for getting mixed up with larger or perhaps more desirable gamefish that bugs the veteran angler. Common is the lad who zeroes in on a lunker snook and hits a big jack instead. You might have to play tug-of-war for an hour. In the meantime the snook has romped out of sight. I have seen people cut their line and lose a good plug rather than go the limit with a heavyweight.

Guide Willie McKoosh calls the jack his "money fish." When we get an unseasonable blow in winter, and the more delicate species are lying around on the creek bottom in their fur-lined underwear, the crevalle are almost as busy as the tourists. Jacks are not bothered by cold weather. If anything, it stirs their appetites. Willie, like a lot of other people in town, knows a hole where the fish congregate when the mercury dips. We ordinarily avoid it because the touted fishing is for snook farther upriver. But in cold weather Willie makes a beeline for Jacks Pool, and after easing the boat into position he tells his sport to cast. If the man is a real greenhorn, McKoosh gets a pained expression on his face the instant the plug hits the water.

"Stop!" says Willie. "It's a school of jack!" Then he shivers like a bird dog, and if the sport looks bewildered he gives him the fast one-two.

"You don't want to hook a jack on *that* rod," warns McKoosh. Of course, no man will ignore such a challenge, and before he can properly turn the spool his rod is bent in a quivering hoop. The fish won't weigh more than 4 or 5 pounds, but by the time the poor snowbird gets back to the dock he feels as if he'd shot a herd of elephants with a BB gun. The McKoosh charade invariably works.

Willie is doing anglers a favor. After all, what makes a gamefish? Must it jump? The bonefish doesn't. Must it be edible? The tarpon isn't. Must it win a beauty prize? Most fish are homely. The definition of gamefish is "an unyielding spirit," and that fits the jack like his scales. But even the International Game Fish Association, which lists such unlikely subjects as the codfish, flounder, and sea bass, ignores the jack. A crevalle could eat all three, including the lead sinkers, without a burp.

The fact of the matter is that the jack never has been fashionable, and McKoosh in his own way is setting the matter straight. One of several things in the crevalle's favor is the fact that he's a first-class light-tackle fish that can be caught on fly, plug, or spinning. He'll even wallop a bass bug around the mangrove knees just for laughs.

Small crevalle up to 6 or 7 pounds travel in schools. As they get older the big jacks occur in pods, and sometimes you'll see a single or a pair belling along at top speed. Crevalle seldom linger in one spot. When food, such as mullet, is abundant, several schools apparently join forces to execute some of the fanciest maneuvers since the Fourth Armored Division hit the beach. Jacks run the mullet right up on the sand, against seawalls, or into a boat. In open water they herd the baitfish into a compact mass, then plow through it from all sides.

The individual crevalle takes his dining seriously. Here and there a mullet will rise above the surface, doing front and back flips, then leaping madly in all directions, with a telltale swirl countering each shift. If the hapless baitfish is lucky, it may elude the jack for two or three jumps, but sooner or later it'll land in the crevalle's jaws. You can drift through acres of frantic mullet and actually observe this single-minded pursuit. They'll chase a lure into the tip-top of a rod.

Ordinarily we catch jacks where we find them, and with whatever tackle we're using at the time. Plugging is probably the ideal method for most people, but live bait, such as mullet or pinfish, is deadly for the noncaster. Streamer flies tied on #2/0 and #3/0 hooks are the usual fly-rod fodder. Incidentally, I always bring along a casting outfit because there are days when fish don't visibly show, and after I have located them with a plug I can use my fly tackle. This is a generally sensible procedure for most types of saltwater fishing except, of course, on tailing fish. The characteristics feathering slash of a jack at baitfish can be seen for a long distance, so there's usually ample time to decide whether or not you want to fight him with the fly rod.

The thing to remember about jack fishing is that whatever lure you use should be retrieved progressively faster. A crevalle may slam a plug, for instance, the instant it hits the water, or take it within the first few feet. But if a fish merely boils under it, then speed the plug along. A lure that tops or just doodles along is invariably refused. The faster you pull the bait through the water, the more strikes you'll earn. Besides, you'll miss a lot more fish on a slow retrieve, perhaps because of the jack's relatively tough mouth or the speed with which he raps the lure.

When a school is excited and feeding wildly, the rule is even more inviolable. A whip retrieve is ideal. When fly fishing, you are bound to get into trouble because it's difficult to keep the feathers moving fast enough to get a strike, a situation you find with many other dynamite-charged saltwater gamefish, such as the dolphin, king mackerel, and the cero, to name a few. With a little practice, however, it's possible (because you have a visible target) to put the fly in front of a jack, then strip line in hard pulls, though the strike nearly wrenches the rod out of your hand.

One of the silliest performances ever put on by fishermen occurred the day that Johnny Dieckman and I ran back and forth along a seawall, trying to hook a crevalle on streamed flies. The jacks had the mullet in a cul-de-sac against a one-hundred-yard stretch of cement. Although we were four or five feet above the water, we both got soaked every time the fish drove the mullet into the wall. It was impossible to cast to them, simply because the fish were boiling directly below our feet. Dangling the fly did no good because it wasn't moving. Then I discovered that by running along the narrow ledge and dragging the streamer across the surface the jacks would hit it.

Of course, in our excitement it was inevitable that we should run into each other, as we had to sprint while looking to the rear. At least a hundred 10- to 12-pound crevalle churned the water to a froth. The jacks would make a wide circle at the edge of the channel, then chase the mullet straight into the wall with a wet *thwack*. Between running, jumping off the end of the wall to play a fish, climbing back, and doing a *pas de deux*, we were exhausted. Finally we both hooked a lunker jack that emptied our reels of backing. The lines just went out and out without a pause, and the fish hadn't slowed down one bit when the leaders parted.

I once played a jack for a little over two hours in the Palm Beach inlet. I'd hooked him while casting with 8-pound-test spinning gear. I guessed that the fish weighed between 30 and 40 pounds. If we hadn't been able to follow him with the skiff, he'd have busted off on the very first run. In common with the permit, large jacks always seem to have an extra ounce of energy in reserve. Their tactics are dogged and unrelenting. It's not uncommon to play a 20-pounder for an hour or more on light tackle.

The maximum size of the crevalle isn't really known. Since he has only recently gained recognition in the new Saltwater Division of the Field & Stream Fishing Contest, no authoritative records have been available on the species. The maximum weight has been given as 36 pounds by some authorities, but this is misleading. The six top crevalle taken by members of our local fishing club in the past six months are a 45-pounder caught by Bryant Hilliard; a 42½-pounder by Jimmy Branch, Jr.; a 40-

pounder by Fred Mewbown; a 40-pounder by John E. Leg; a 38-pounder by Edward Kelly; and a 36-pounder by Carlton Smith.

One of the all-time greats was a 55-pound jack caught by Lake "Pud" Lytal, Jr., in 1959. In a gesture reminiscent of the mighty Bobby Jones, who penalized himself one stroke and thereby almost lost the National Open, Pud proved his manhood. Though he stood to win a $1,000 prize, young Lytal disqualified himself after realizing that his catch involved a minor violation of the contest rules. In the excitement, a well-meaning friend had reached over and grabbed his line to halt the wild rush of the crevalle. Lytal, today a law student at the University of Florida, withdrew his entry when he learned that nobody may touch the tackle except the angler—inadvertently or not. This purely voluntary gesture cost the lad a lot of dough, but the funny thing is that while we can't remember who *did* win the contest, everybody remembers Pud. In our eyes, Mr. Lytal is already qualified for the Supreme Court.

Among the smaller jacks, the Atlantic horse-eye, the Pacific horse-eye, and the bar jack are topflight gamefish. Generally speaking, this trio runs from 1 to 2 pounds, but occasionally a school of larger fish appears in channels and around the edges of bonefish flats. The bar jack doesn't have the real blunt profile of a crevalle, and its gray-blue body has a dark-blue or black stripe along the back. Both horse-eyes are distinguished by their comparatively large eyes, and their generally dark coloration rapidly fades when the fish moves over a sandy or light-colored bottom.

Horse-eyes have a characteristic black-tipped dorsal fin that, during the period when their sale was banned in West Indian markets because of suspected poisoning (ciguatera), the commercials would cut off to conceal their identity. But the bar jack is one of few carangids that is an excellent food fish. I built a smokehouse at Deep Water Cay several years ago and experimented with a number of possible gourmet items, such as the houndfish, needlefish, bonefish, porgy, yellowtail snapper, and bar jack. The latter was by far the most delicious; unlike the red-meated crevalle, the bar jack has firm white flesh and can be pan-fried, broiled, or smoked.

Admittedly, there is a tendency to play favorites in angling, so the tarpon, bonefish, permit, and a few others will be the monarchs of the flats. The crevalle isn't likely to be fitted for one of their crowns, but come a day when the TV antenna moans in the wind and all the glamour-pusses shamelessly snooze in their aquatic playpens, you'll find brother jack cutting capers with the tourists.

That's what I call a real gamefish.